14th International Workshop on Finite State Methods and Natural Language Processing (FSMNLP 2019)

Dresden, Germany
23-25 September 2019

ISBN: 978-1-5108-9440-2

FSMNLP 2019

The 14th International Conference on Finite-State Methods and Natural Language Processing

Proceedings of the Conference

September 23 - 25, 2019
Dresden, Germany

Introduction

These are the proceedings of the 14th International Conference on Finite-State Methods and Natural Language Processing (FSMNLP 2019), which was held September 23-25, 2019 in Dresden, Germany.

The conference series FSMNLP is the premier forum of the ACL Special Interest Group on Finite-State Methods (SIGFSM). It serves researchers and practitioners working on natural language processing (NLP) applications or language resources, theoretical and implementational aspects, or their combinations, that make use of finite-state methods.

FSMNLP 2019 received 20 submissions, each of which was carefully reviewed by at least three experts in the field. On the basis of these reviews the program committee selected 12 papers to be accepted for presentation at the conference.

In addition to the regular papers, one tutorial and two invited talks were presented:

Tutorial:

Aarne Ranta (University of Gothenburg, Sweden)
Grammatical Framework: an Interlingual Grammar Formalism

Invited talks:

Frank Drewes (Umeå University, Sweden)
A Survey of Recent Advances in Efficient Parsing for Graph Grammars

Kilian Gebhardt (Technische Universität Dresden, Germany)
Latent Variable Grammars for Discontinuous Parsing

We would like to express our gratitude to all authors for submitting their papers to FSMNLP 2019, to the members of the program committee and the four subreviewers for their excellent work in selecting the best papers, and to the members of the research group Foundations of Programmming Languages, TU Dresden for their help with the local arrangements.

Andreas Maletti and Heiko Vogler
co-chairs

Program Co-Chairs

Andreas Maletti and Heiko Vogler

Tutorial Speaker

Aarne Ranta, University of Gothenburg, Sweden

Invited Speakers

Frank Drewes, Umeå University, Sweden

Kilian Gebhardt, Technische Universität Dresden, Germany

Program Committee

Johanna Björklund (Umeå Universitet, Sweden)

Mathieu Constant (Université de Lorraine, France)

Jan Daciuk (Gdańsk University of Technology, Poland)

Frank Drewes (Umeå Universitet, Sweden)

Tim Fernando (Trinity College Dublin, Ireland)

Mike Hammond (University of Arizona, USA)

Thomas Hanneforth (Universität Potsdam, Germany)

Colin de la Higuera (Université de Nantes, France)

Mans Hulden (University of Colorado Boulder, USA)

András Kornai (Budapest Institute of Technology, Hungary)

Marco Kuhlmann (Linköpings Universitet, Sweden)

Andreas Maletti (Universität Leipzig, Germany, co-chair)

Mark-Jan Nederhof (University of St Andrews, UK)

Jakub Piskorski (Polish Academy of Sciences, Poland)

Anoop Sarkar (Simon Fraser University, Canada)

Richard Sproat (Google, USA)

Heiko Vogler (Technische Universität Dresden, Germany, co-chair)

Bruce William Watson (Stellenbosch University, South Africa)

Anssi Yli-Jyrä (University of Helsinki, Finland)

Menno van Zaanen (Universiteit van Tilburg, Netherlands)

Subreviewers

Henning Fernau, Universität Trier, Germany

Zoltan Fülöp, University of Szeged, Hungary

Kilian Gebhardt, Technische Universität Dresden, Germany

Luisa Herrmann, Technische Universität Dresden, Germany

Local Organization

Kerstin Achtruth

Kilian Gebhardt

Richard Mörbitz

Thomas Ruprecht

Heiko Vogler

Grammatical Framework: an Interlingual Grammar Formalism
Aarne Ranta 1

A Survey of Recent Advances in Efficient Parsing for Graph Grammars
Frank Drewes 3

Latent Variable Grammars for Discontinuous Parsing
Kilian Gebhardt 4

Bottom-Up Unranked Tree-to-Graph Transducers for Translation into Semantic Graphs
Johanna Björklund, Shay B. Cohen, Frank Drewes and Giorgio Satta 7

On the Compression of Lexicon Transducers
Marco Cognetta, Cyril Allauzen and Michael Riley 18

MSO with tests and reducts
Tim Fernando, David Woods and Carl Vogel 27

Finite State Transducer Calculus for Whole Word Morphology
Maciej Janicki 37

Weighted parsing for grammar-based language models
Richard Mörbitz and Heiko Vogler 46

Regular transductions with MCFG input syntax
Mark-Jan Nederhof and Heiko Vogler 56

A Syntactically Expressive Morphological Analyzer for Turkish
Adnan Ozturel, Tolga Kayadelen and Isin Demirsahin 65

Using Meta-Morph Rules to develop Morphological Analysers: A case study concerning Tamil
Kengatharaiyer Sarveswaran, Gihan Dias and Miriam Butt 76

Distilling weighted finite automata from arbitrary probabilistic models
Ananda Theertha Suresh, Brian Roark, Michael Riley and Vlad Schogol 87

Silent HMMs: Generalized Representation of Hidden Semi-Markov Models and Hierarchical HMMs
Kei Wakabayashi 98

Latin script keyboards for South Asian languages with finite-state normalization
Lawrence Wolf-Sonkin, Vlad Schogol, Brian Roark and Michael Riley 108

Transition-Based Coding and Formal Language Theory for Ordered Digraphs
Anssi Yli-Jyrä 118

Conference Program

Sunday, September 22nd	
19:00	welcome reception (restaurant at Weberplatz 3, Dresden)

Monday, September 23rd	
08:00–08:50	registration
08:50–09:00	opening
09:00–09:45	Tutorial (part 1) Aarne Ranta (University of Gothenburg, Sweden) *Grammatical Framework: an Interlingual Grammar Formalism*
09:45–10:15	coffee break
10:15–11:00	Tutorial (part 2) Aarne Ranta (University of Gothenburg, Sweden) *Grammatical Framework: an Interlingual Grammar Formalism*
11:00–11:30	Tutorial (part 3) Aarne Ranta (University of Gothenburg, Sweden) *Grammatical Framework: an Interlingual Grammar Formalism*
12:00–13:30	lunch break
13:30–14:00	Anssi Yli-Jyrä. *Transition-Based Coding and Formal Language Theory for Ordered Digraphs*
14:00–14:30	Marco Cognetta, Cyril Allauzen, and Michael Riley. *On the Compression of Lexicon Transducers*
14:30–15:00	coffee break
15:00–15.30	Ananda Theertha Suresh, Brian Roark, Michael Riley, and Vlad Schogol. *Distilling weighted finite automata from arbitrary probabilistic models*
15:30–16:00	Kei Wakabayashi. *Silent HMMs: Generalized Representation of Hidden Semi-Markov Models and Hierarchical HMMs*

Tuesday, September 24th

09:00–10:00	Invited lecture: Frank Drewes (Umeå University, Sweden) *A Survey of Recent Advances in Efficient Parsing for Graph Grammars*
10:00–10:30	coffee break
10:30–11:00	Adnan Ozturel, Tolga Kayadelen, and Isin Demirsahin. *A Syntactically Expressive Morphological Analyzer for Turkish*
11:00–11:30	Kengatharaiyer Sarveswaran, Gihan Dias, and Mirriam Butt. *Using Meta-Morph Rules to develop Morphological Analysers:* *A case study concerning Tamil*
11:30–12:00	Maciej Janicki. *Finite State Transducer Calculus for Whole Word Morphology*
12:00–13:30	lunch break
13:30–14:00	Lawrence Wolf-Sonkin, Vlad Schogol, Brian Roark, and Michael Riley. *Latin script keyboards for South Asian languages with finite-state* *normalization*
14:00–14:30	Johanna Björklund, Shay B. Cohen, Frank Drewes, and Giorgio Satta. *Bottom-Up Unranked Tree-to-Graph Transducers for Translation into* *Semantic Graphs*
14:30–15:00	coffee break
15:00–16:30	SIGFSM business meeting
18:00–18:45 19:00	excursion (guided tour through Dresden) conference dinner

Wednesday, September 25th

09:00–10:00	Invited lecture: Kilian Gebhardt (Technische Universität Dresden, Germany) *Latent Variable Grammars for Discontinuous Parsing*
10:00–10:30	coffee break
10:30–11:00	Mark-Jan Nederhof and Heiko Vogler. *Regular transductions with MCFG input syntax*
11:00–11:30	Tim Fernando, David Woods, and Carl Vogel. *MSO with tests and reducts*
11:30–12:00	Richard Mörbitz and Heiko Vogler. *Weighted parsing for grammar-based language models*
12:00	closing of FSMNLP 2019

Grammatical Framework:
an Interlingual Grammar Formalism
Tutorial

Aarne Ranta

Department of Computer Science and Engineering
Chalmers University of Technology and University of Gothenburg
Sweden

Abstract Grammatical Framework (GF) was born at Xerox Research Centre Europe in 1998. Its purpose was to provide a declarative grammar formalism for interlingual translation systems. The core of GF is Constructive Type Theory (CTT), also known as Logical Framework, which is used for building interlingual representations. On top of these representations, GF provides a functional programming language for defining reversible mappings from interlinguas to concrete languages, equivalent to Parallel Multiple Context-Free Grammars (PMCFG).

Open-source since 1999, GF has a world-wide community that has built comprehensive grammars for over 40 languages. GF is also used in several companies to build applications for translation, natural language generation, semantic analysis, chatbots, and dialogue systems. The focus has been on Controlled Natural Languages (CNL), but recent research has also combined GF with statistical and machine learning techniques, such as neural dependency parsing. In this way, GF can scale up to robust and wide-coverage language processing, without sacrificing explainability.

The tutorial is meant for an audience that has some experience with formal language theory and its use in practical implementations. However, it is self contained and does not assume specific knowledge such as CTT or PMCFG. The structure is the following:

1. Hands-on introduction (45 min). Interactive coding in the GF Cloud to get an idea of how GF works.

2. Theoretical background (45 min). GF as a formalism and programming language, with references to its main inspirations (constructive type theory, Montague grammar, categorial grammars, XFST)

3. The GF Ecosystem (30 min). Software tools, on-going academic research, commercial applications, and open-source community activities.

Proceedings of the 14th International Conference on Finite-State Methods and Natural Language Processing, pages 1–2
Dresden, Germany, September 23-25, 2019. ©2019 Association for Computational Linguistics

References

Krasimir Angelov, *The Mechanics of the Grammatical Framework*, PhD Thesis, Chalmers University of Technology, 2011. *Standard reference on the internals of GF, from both implementation and formal language theory point of view.*

Peter Ljunglöf, *Expressivity and Complexity of the Grammatical Framework*, PhD Thesis, University of Gothenburg, 2004. *Detailed study of the language-theoretic properties of GF, placing it among mildly context-sensitive formalisms.*

Aarne Ranta, *Grammatical Framework: Programming with Multilingual Grammars*, CSLI, Stanford, 2011. *Standard reference on the GF programming language, with a tutorial and reference manual.*

Aarne Ranta, "What are Grammars Good for? Reflections on Twenty Years of Grammatical Framework", in Cleo Condoravdi and Tracy Holloway King (eds), *Tokens of Meaning. Papers in Honor of Lauri Karttunen*, CSLI, Stanford, 2019, pp. 545–568. *Follow-up of recent research themes, with some parallels to Xerox Finite State Tool, which was an important inspiration for GF.*

GF homepage: `http://www.grammaticalframework.org/`
Speaker's homepage: `http://www.cse.chalmers.se/~aarne/`

A Survey of Recent Advances in Efficient Parsing for Graph Grammars

Invited Talk

Frank Drewes

Umeå University, Sweden

Abstract Context-free graph grammars, in particular hyperedge replacement graph grammars, look back on over 30 years of history. They share many of the good properties of context-free string languages. Unfortunately, the complexity of parsing is the big exception: early results in the field showed that even for fixed grammars, the membership problem can be NP-complete. Moreover, the known results about polynomial parsing that were obtained afterwards, while constituting nice theoretical work, seemed to be of limited practical value. This is because they were either based on very "impractical" restrictions, or the degree of the polynomial running time depended on the grammar and could thus become large.

In the current decade, the question received renewed interest because hyperedge replacement is one of the candidate formalisms for specifying semantic graphs in natural language processing. Using graph grammars in this area requires parsing algorithms that are not only polynomial in theory, but efficient in practice. Preferably, the degree of the polynomial bounding their running time should be a (small) constant independent of the grammar, or else it should depend on parameters not likely to be large. The talk will present an overview of results towards this goal, discussing their requirements, advantages, and disadvantages as well as a few possible directions for future work.

Speaker's homepage: `https://www.umu.se/en/staff/frank-drewes/`

Proceedings of the 14th International Conference on Finite-State Methods and Natural Language Processing, page 3
Dresden, Germany, September 23-25, 2019. ©2019 Association for Computational Linguistics

Latent Variable Grammars for Discontinuous Parsing

Invited Talk

Kilian Gebhardt

Technische Universität Dresden, Germany

Abstract Latent variable context-free grammars are powerful models for predicting the syntactic structure of sentences (Matsuzaki, Miyao, and Tsujii 2005; Petrov, Barrett, et al. 2006; Petrov and Klein 2007). When trained on annotated corpora, the resulting latent variables can be shown to capture different distributions for, e.g., NPs in subject and object position. Several languages (and in consequence also syntactic treebanks for these languages) such as Dutch (Lassy van Noord 2009), German (NeGra, Skut et al. 1997; TiGer Brants et al. 2004), but also English (Penn Treebank, Marcus, Santorini, and Marcinkiewicz 1993, Evang and Kallmeyer 2011) contain structures that cannot be adequately modelled by context-free grammars. In consequence, a class of more power grammar formalisms called mildly context-sensitive has been studied (cf. Kallmeyer 2010). Although parsing with these models is polynomial in the length of the input sentence (Seki et al. 1991), it has for a long time been regarded prohibitively slow. However, in recent years it was shown that the application of mildly-context sensitive grammars is feasible in coarse-to-fine parsing approaches (van Cranenburgh 2012; Ruprecht and Denkinger 2019).

In this talk I consider how both the latent variable approach and mildly context-sensitive grammars can be joined and applied to discontinuous treebanks:

1. A large class of latent variable grammars can be captured as a probabilistic regular tree grammar combined with an algebra. I show how the training methodology of latent variable PCFG can be generalized for this class.

2. I recall two mildly context-sensitive grammar formalisms: linear context-free rewriting systems (LCFRS, Vijay-Shanker, Weir, and Joshi 1987) and hybrid grammars (Nederhof and Vogler 2014; Gebhardt, Nederhof, and Vogler 2017). In particular, I consider the induction of hybrid grammars, which can be parametrized such that the polynomial complexity of parsing is of bounded degree. This way also hybrid grammars that are structurally equivalent to finite state automata can be obtained.

3. I analyse different trends when training latent variable LCFRS and hybrid grammars on different discontinuous treebanks and applying them for parsing.

Proceedings of the 14th International Conference on Finite-State Methods and Natural Language Processing, pages 4–6
Dresden, Germany, September 23-25, 2019. ©2019 Association for Computational Linguistics

References

Brants, Sabine, Stefanie Dipper, Peter Eisenberg, Silvia Hansen-Schirra, Esther König, Wolfgang Lezius, Christian Rohrer, George Smith, and Hans Uszkoreit (2004). "TIGER: Linguistic Interpretation of a German Corpus". In: *Research on Language and Computation* 2 (4), pp. 597–620. DOI: 10.1007/s11168-004-7431-3.

van Cranenburgh, Andreas (2012). "Efficient parsing with Linear Context-Free Rewriting Systems". In: *Proceedings of the 13th Conference of the European Chapter of the Association for Computational Linguistics*. Avignon, France: Association for Computational Linguistics, pp. 460–470. URL: https://www.aclweb.org/anthology/E12-1047.

Evang, Kilian and Laura Kallmeyer (2011). "PLCFRS Parsing of English Discontinuous Constituents". In: *Proceedings of the 12th International Conference on Parsing Technologies*. Dublin, Ireland, pp. 104–116. ISBN: 978-1-932432-04-6. URL: https://www.aclweb.org/anthology/W11-2913.

Gebhardt, Kilian, Mark-Jan Nederhof, and Heiko Vogler (2017). "Hybrid Grammars for Parsing of Discontinuous Phrase Structures and Non-Projective Dependency Structures". In: *Computational Linguistics* 43 (3), pp. 465–520. DOI: 10.1162/COLI_a_00291.

Kallmeyer, Laura (2010). *Parsing Beyond Context-Free Grammars*. 1st. Springer Publishing Company, Incorporated. ISBN: 364214845X, 9783642148453.

Marcus, M. P., B. Santorini, and M. A. Marcinkiewicz (1993). "Building a Large Annotated Corpus of English: The Penn Treebank". In: *Computational Linguistics* 19 (2), pp. 313–330. URL: http://aclweb.org/anthology/J93-2004.

Matsuzaki, Takuya, Yusuke Miyao, and Jun'ichi Tsujii (2005). "Probabilistic CFG with Latent Annotations". In: *Proceedings of the 43rd Annual Meeting on Association for Computational Linguistics*. Ann Arbor, Michigan, pp. 75–82. DOI: 10.3115/1219840.1219850.

Nederhof, Mark-Jan and Heiko Vogler (2014). "Hybrid Grammars for Discontinuous Parsing". In: *Proceedings of COLING 2014, the 25th International Conference on Computational Linguistics: Technical Papers*. Dublin, Ireland, pp. 1370–1381. URL: https://www.aclweb.org/anthology/C14-1130.

van Noord, Gertjan (2009). "Huge Parsed Corpora in LASSY". In: *Proceedings of the Seventh International Workshop on Treebanks and Linguistic Theories (TLT 7)*. Groningen, The Netherlands.

Petrov, Slav, Leon Barrett, Romain Thibaux, and Dan Klein (2006). "Learning Accurate, Compact, and Interpretable Tree Annotation". In: *Proceedings of the 21st International Conference on Computational Linguistics and the 44th Annual Meeting of the Association for Computational Linguistics*. Sydney, Australia, pp. 433–440. DOI: 10.3115/1220175.1220230.

Petrov, Slav and Dan Klein (2007). "Improved Inference for Unlexicalized Parsing". In: *Human Language Technologies 2007: The Conference of the North American Chapter of the Association for Computational Linguistics; Proceedings of the Main Conference*. Rochester, New York, pp. 404–411. URL: https://www.aclweb.org/anthology/N07-1051.

Ruprecht, Thomas and Tobias Denkinger (2019). "Implementation of a Chomsky-Schützenberger n-best parser for weighted multiple context-free grammars". In: *Proceedings of the 2019 Conference of the North American Chapter of the Association for Computational Linguistics*. Minneapolis, Minnesota: Association for Computational Linguistics, pp. 178–191. DOI: 10.18653/v1/N19-1016.

Seki, Hiroyuki, Takashi Matsumura, Mamoru Fujii, and Tadao Kasami (1991). "On multiple context-free grammars". In: *Theoretical Computer Science* 88 (2), pp. 191–229. ISSN: 0304-3975. DOI: 10.1016/0304-3975(91)90374-B.

Skut, Wojciech, Brigitte Krenn, Thorsten Brants, and Hans Uszkoreit (1997). "An Annotation Scheme for Free Word Order Languages". In: *Fifth Conference on Applied Natural Language Processing*. Washington, DC, USA: Association for Computational Linguistics, pp. 88–95. DOI: 10.3115/974557.974571.

Vijay-Shanker, Krishnamurti, David J. Weir, and Aravind K. Joshi (1987). "Characterizing Structural Descriptions Produced by Various Grammatical Formalisms". In: *Proceedings of the 25th Annual Meeting of the Association for Computational Linguistics*. Stanford, California, USA, pp. 104–111. DOI: 10.3115/981175.981190.

Speaker's homepage: https://wwwtcs.inf.tu-dresden.de/~kilian/

Bottom-Up Unranked Tree-to-Graph Transducers
for Translation into Semantic Graphs

Johanna Björklund
Umeå University
Umeå, Sweden
johanna@cs.umu.se

Shay B. Cohen
University of Edinburgh
Edinburgh, UK
scohen@inf.ed.ac.uk

Frank Drewes
Umeå University
Umeå, Sweden
drewes@cs.umu.se

Giorgio Satta
University of Padova
Padova, Italy
satta@dei.unipd.it

Abstract

We propose a formal model for translating
unranked syntactic trees, such as dependency
trees, into semantic graphs. These tree-to-
graph transducers can serve as a formal basis of transition systems for semantic parsing
which recently have been shown to perform
very well, yet hitherto lack formalization. Our
model features "extended" rules and an arc-
factored normal form, comes with an efficient
translation algorithm, and can be equipped
with weights in a straightforward manner.

1 Introduction

In dependency semantic parsing, one is given a
natural language sentence and has to output a
directed graph representing an associated, most-
likely semantic analysis. Semantic parsing in-
tegrates tasks that have usually been addressed
separately in statistical natural language processing, such as named entity recognition, word sense
disambiguation, semantic role labeling, and co-
reference resolution. Semantic parsing is currently
receiving considerable attention, as attested by the
number of approaches being proposed for its solution (Oepen et al., 2014, 2015) and by the variety
of existing semantic representations and available
datasets (Kuhlmann and Oepen, 2016).

A successful approach to dependency semantic
parsing by Wang et al. (2015b,a) first parses the
input sentence into a dependency tree t, and then
applies a transition-based algorithm that translates
t into a dependency graph in Abstract Meaning
Representation (AMR), a popular semantic representation developed by Banarescu et al. (2013). In
this work, we present a finite-state transducer for
tree-to-graph translation that can serve as a mathematical model for transition-based systems such as
the one by Wang et al. (2015b) and, more in general, for work on the syntax-semantics interface.

Bottom-up tree transducers (Thatcher, 1973)
have gained significant attention in the field of machine translation, where they are used to map syntactic phrase structure trees from source to target
languages. This holds in particular for their "extended" version, which may process, in a single
step, sections of the input consisting of several
symbols; see (Maletti et al., 2009) and references
therein. We propose a similar formalism for dependency semantic parsing, mapping syntactic dependency trees into directed graphs that represent
the associated semantic interpretation.

When translating dependency trees into graphs
in a bottom-up fashion, we face two problems.
Firstly, bottom-up tree transducers process *ranked*
trees, i.e., the number of children at each node is
bounded by some constant. Thus, typically, these
tree transducers use a single rule to process in one
shot a node along with all of its (previously processed) children in the source tree. In contrast,
in the case of dependency trees there is no global
constant that limits the number of children a node
may have, and processing all of the children by
means of a single rule is problematic.

Secondly, in an output tree of a bottom-up tree
transducer, nodes that are located near one another
are translations of nodes in a source tree that are in
close proximity as well. This condition is often referred to as *locality*. Locality does no longer hold
true when translating trees into graphs. In fact,
so-called reentrancy nodes in a graph have several parents, which are translations of nodes in the
source tree whose distance from one another may
not be bounded by a constant. Reentrancies thus
require some form of nonlocal processing, generally not found in tree transducers.

The main contribution of this work is a finite-
state tree-to-graph transducer that processes dependency trees in a bottom-up, left-to-right fashion. Our solution to the two problems mentioned
above is rather simple. Each node is processed together with its children in several translation steps
which consume the children left to right. Furthermore, in order to implement reentrancy, each
translated subtree produces a graph annotated with
a record of selected vertices, to be made accessible
later in the translation process.

7

Proceedings of the 14th International Conference on Finite-State Methods and Natural Language Processing, pages 7–17
Dresden, Germany, September 23-25, 2019. ©2019 Association for Computational Linguistics

While our transducers use extended translation rules in the sense of Maletti et al. (2009), they can be cast in a simple normal form, facilitating algorithmic processing. We provide a polynomial time algorithm for translating an input dependency tree into a packed graph forest, from which each translation graph can efficiently be recovered.

Related work. Bottom-up tree-to-graph transducers were introduced by Engelfriet and Vogler (1994, 1998) who based their work on hyperedge replacement. Since the graph construction mechanism we use is equivalent to hyperedge replacement, our notion of tree-to-graph transducers is essentially an unranked and extended generalization of theirs, except for the fact that ours cannot create multiple copies of unbounded material in the input. This ability seems inappropriate for modeling natural language semantics.

The system by Wang et al. (2015b) has inspired our work. A technical comparison between their formalism and ours is made in Remark 1. An alternative approach to the syntax-semantics interface exploits multi-component synchronous tree-adjoining grammars; see Nesson and Shieber (2006) and references therein. However, these formal models yield tree-like semantic representations, as opposed to general graphs.

A common approach in semantic parsing is to extend existing syntactic dependency parsers to produce graphs, realizing translation models from strings to graphs, as opposed to the tree-to-graph model investigated here. On this line, transition-based, greedy parsers have been adapted by Ballesteros and Al-Onaizan (2017), Damonte et al. (2017), Hershcovich et al. (2017), Peng et al. (2018) and Vilares and Gómez-Rodríguez (2018). Despite the fact that the input is a bare string, these systems exploit features obtained from a precomputed run of a dependency parser, thus committing to some best parse tree, similarly to the pipeline model of Wang et al. (2015b). Dynamic programming parsers have also been adapted to produce graphs by Kuhlmann and Jonsson (2015) and Schluter (2015). Semantic translation from strings to graphs is further investigated by Jones et al. (2012) and Peng et al. (2015) using synchronous hyperedge replacement grammars, who provide unsupervised learning algorithms for grammar extraction. Finally, Groschwitz et al. (2018) use a neural supertag parser to map a string into a dependency-style tree representation of the com-

positional structure of the corresponding AMR graph. More precisely, this tree is a term in a special algebra: its constants denote lexicalized AMR graph fragments, which are combined into larger and larger AMR graphs by two binary algebraic operations for graph combination. These operations supply a partial AMR graph either with an argument or with a modifier. The evaluation of the term then yields the output AMR for the input sentence. The tree-to-graph mapping is entirely deterministic, in contrast to our approach. Groschwitz et al. (2018) also provide an unsupervised alignment algorithm that extracts rules from semantic graph banks.

2 Preliminaries

In this section we introduce the notation and terminology that is used throughout this paper.

General Notation. The set of natural numbers (including zero) is denoted by $\mathbb{N}$, and $\mathbb{N}_+ = \mathbb{N} \setminus \{0\}$. For $n \in \mathbb{N}$ the set $\{1, \ldots, n\}$ is abbreviated to $[n]$. In particular, $[0] = \emptyset$. The set of all finite sequences of elements of a set S is written S^*, ε is the empty sequence, $S^+ = S^* \setminus \{\varepsilon\}$, and 2^S is the powerset of S. Given a sequence w, we write $[w]$ for the set of its elements. Concatenation of sequences s, s' is denoted by juxtaposition or, if preferred for notational clarity, as $s \cdot s'$.

Trees. Let Σ be an alphabet. The set T_Σ of (unranked) trees over Σ is the smallest set such that, for all $f \in \Sigma$ and $t_1, \ldots, t_n \in T_\Sigma$ ($n \in \mathbb{N}$), we have $f(t_1, \ldots, t_n) \in T_\Sigma$. In particular $f()$, which we abbreviate by f, is in T_Σ.

The nodes of a tree are identified by their Gorn addresses, which are sequences in $\mathbb{N}_+^*$: the root has the address ε, and if α is the address of a node in t_i then $i\alpha$ is the address of that node in $f(t_1, \ldots, t_n)$. The set of all nodes of t is $N(t)$ and the size of t is $|t| = |N(t)|$.

The label of node α in t is $t(\alpha)$, and the subtree rooted at node α is t/α. For $\Sigma' \subseteq \Sigma$, the set of all nodes $\alpha \in N(t)$ with $t(\alpha) \in \Sigma'$ is denoted by $N_{\Sigma'}(t)$. Throughout the paper, a subset $\{\alpha_1, \ldots, \alpha_k\}$ of the set of nodes of a tree t is denoted as $(\alpha_1, \ldots, \alpha_k)$ to express that its nodes are listed in lexicographic order.

The following notion will play a crucial role in the definition of the translation step for our transducers in Section 3. Let $\square \notin \Sigma$ be a special symbol. A **context** is a tree $c \in T_{\Sigma \cup \{\square\}}$ that contains exactly one occurrence of $\square$, and this occurrence is a leaf. Given such a context and a tree t, we let $c[t]$ denote the tree obtained from c by replacing $\square$ with t. Thus, $c[t] = t$ if $c = \square$, and otherwise $c[t] = f(s_1, \ldots, s_{i-1}, s_i[t], s_{i+1}, \ldots, s_n)$, where $c = f(s_1, \ldots, s_n)$ and $s_i \in T_{\Sigma \cup \{\square\}}$ is the context among $s_1, \ldots, s_n$. For contexts $c \neq \square$, the notation $c[t]$ is straightforwardly extended to $c[t_1, \ldots, t_k]$ for trees $t_1, \ldots, t_k$ ($k \in \mathbb{N}$). It yields the tree obtained by inserting the sequence of subtrees $t_1, \ldots, t_k$ at the position marked by $\square$. (This yields a tree since we only use it if $c \neq \square$.) To be precise, if $c = f(s_1, \ldots, s_n)$ and $i \in [n]$ is the index such that $\square$ occurs in s_i, then $c[t_1, \ldots, t_k]$ is equal to $f(s_1, \ldots, s_{i-1}, t_1, \ldots, t_k, s_{i+1}, \ldots, s_n)$ if we have $s_i = \square$; otherwise, it is $f(s_1, \ldots, s_{i-1}, s_i[t_1, \ldots, t_n], s_{i+1}, \ldots, s_n)$.

Graphs. The translation process we propose assembles the output graph by combining smaller graphs into larger ones in a stepwise fashion. For this, every graph has a designated group of vertices, called ports. In the assembly step, ports from the graphs to be combined can be merged.

For a given alphabet Δ, the set $\mathcal{G}_\Delta$ of graphs with labels in Δ consists of all quintuples $G = (V, E, lab, port)$ such that

1. V is a finite set of **vertices**,
2. $E \subseteq V \times \Delta \times V$ is the set of labeled **edges**,
3. $lab \colon V \to \Delta$ is a function labeling each vertex, and
4. $port \in V^*$ is a sequence of pairwise distinct vertices called **ports**.

The **size** of G is $|G| = |V| + |E|$. If $port = v_1 \cdots v_n$, then the p-th port v_p of G, $p \in [n]$, is denoted by $port(p)$ and $type(G) = |port|$ is the **type** of G. If the components of G are not explicitly named, they are denoted by V_G, E_G, lab_G, and $port_G$, respectively. To keep the notation simple, we do not use separate sets for the labels of vertices and edges. Such a distinction may of course be added by partitioning Δ into two sets, but for the present paper this is unnecessary.

3 Bottom-Up Unranked Tree-to-Graph Transducers

Informally, our transducers process the input tree in a locally bottom-up, left-to-right manner. To apply a translation rule with a left-hand side s at a given node α, s must cover α together with $k \geq 0$ of its leftmost subtrees. Hence, these subtrees must have been processed earlier, to the ex-

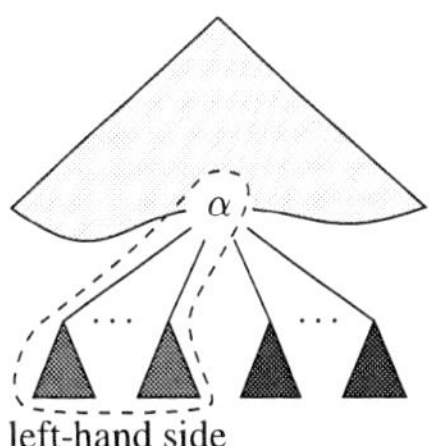

Figure 1: Rule application at node α is locally leftmost (any number, including zero, of the leftmost children of α are consumed) and bottom-up (the left-hand side covers those subtrees all the way down to the leaves). The result of applying a rule at α deletes the subtrees covered by the left-hand side and turns the label of α (a state or input symbol) into a state q.

tent necessary to make the part to be processed identical to s. Applying the rule then removes the subtrees and turns α into a state (or turns it from one state into another, if it already was a state due to an earlier step). Disregarding for the moment the partial output graphs involved, this is depicted schematically in Figure 1.

Note that, in particular, the number k of processed children can be zero, which means that single nodes can initially be turned into states by translation rules whose left-hand sides consist of just one node. More generally, rules in which the root of the left-hand side is an input symbol (with or without children) can be viewed as initializing the processing of the remaining children of that node by turning their parent into an "initial" state.

An (unranked, linear, nondeleting) **bottom-up tree-to-graph transducer** (briefly t2g transducer) is a tuple $\Theta = (\Sigma, \Lambda, Q, R, \mu, F)$ consisting of

1. finite input and output alphabets Σ and Δ;
2. a finite set Q of **states** disjoint with Σ, where every state $q \in Q$ has a type $type(q) \in \mathbb{N}$;
3. a finite set R of translation rules defined below;
4. a merging function $\mu \colon 2^\Delta \setminus \{\emptyset\} \to \Delta$; and
5. a set $F \subseteq Q$ of **final states**.

Note that the merging function is finite (because Δ is). It allows us to determine the label of a vertex obtained by merging vertices with different labels. We do not place any restrictions on μ, but consider it as an unknown function that is to be learnt from data. However, it is reasonable to assume that in linguistic settings, μ will be generated by a binary function in the sense that $\mu(\{\delta\}) = \delta$ and $\mu(\Delta' \cup \{\delta\}) = \mu(\{\mu(\Delta'), \delta\})$ for all $\delta \in \Delta$

and $\Delta' \in 2^\Delta \setminus \{\emptyset\}$. Thus, in this case μ can be efficiently represented by a table of size $|\Delta|^2$.

As already mentioned, a translation rule reads a tree fragment of the input, say ϕ, replaces it with a single node labeled by a state, and produces as output some graph fragment ϕ'. The tree ϕ cannot be a single node labeled by a state: see Section 7 for discussion of this restriction. Some nodes α within ϕ may be labeled by a state. This means that the input tree has already undergone some partial processing, at the position corresponding to α, resulting in an output graph fragment which is "associated" with α. Finally, the graph fragment ϕ' produced by the translation rule is obtained by combining the graph fragments associated with the nodes within ϕ labeled by a state, in some way which is specified by the right-hand side of the rule itself. Formally, a **translation rule** $s \to \langle q, G \rangle$ consists of a left-hand side $s \in T_{\Sigma \cup Q} \setminus Q$ and a right-hand side $\langle q, G \rangle$, where $q \in Q$ and G is a graph with $type(G) = type(q)$. Further, G must fulfill the following condition: if $P = \{\alpha{:}p \mid \alpha \in N_Q(s), p \in [type(s(\alpha))]\}$ then $G \in \mathcal{G}_{\Delta \cup (2^P \setminus \{\emptyset\})}$ and every $\alpha{:}p \in P$ occurs at most once in the labels of vertices in G. A vertex v carrying a label in $2^P \setminus \{\emptyset\}$ is called a **docking vertex**. Intuitively, each $\alpha{:}p \in lab_G(v)$ is a syntactic name (or formal parameter) referring to the p-th port of the graph G_α associated with the node matched by α. During the application of the rule, the p-th port of G_α will be merged with v. This is formalized next.

A **configuration** of Θ is a pair $\langle t, \Gamma \rangle$ with $t \in T_{\Sigma \cup Q}$ such that $\Gamma \colon N_Q(t) \to \mathcal{G}_\Delta$, where $type(\Gamma(\alpha)) = type(t(\alpha))$ for every $\alpha \in N_Q(t)$. Given an input tree $t_0 \in T_\Sigma$, the computation of a transducer starts with $\langle t_0, \Gamma_0 \rangle$ where Γ_0 is the function with the domain $N_Q(t_0) = \emptyset$. Suppose inductively that, after some computation steps, a configuration $\langle t, \Gamma \rangle$ has been reached. A translation rule $s \to \langle q, G \rangle$ can be applied to this configuration if t can be written as $t = c[f(t_1, \ldots, t_n)]$, such that $s = f(t_1, \ldots, t_k)$ for some $k \leq n$. If so, let α be the node in c such that $c(\alpha) = \square$. Then there is a computation step $\langle t, \Gamma \rangle \to_\Theta \langle \overline{t}, \overline{\Gamma} \rangle$ with $\overline{t} = c[q(t_{k+1}, \ldots, t_n)]$, where $\overline{\Gamma}$ is as follows:

1. For every node $\overline{\beta} \in N_Q(\overline{t}) \setminus \{\alpha\}$, if β is the corresponding node in t, then $\overline{\Gamma}(\overline{\beta}) = \Gamma(\beta)$.[1]

---

[1] Here, the node corresponding to $\overline{\beta}$ is defined in the obvious way, to take care of the change of Gorn addresses that results from the deletion of $t_1, \ldots, t_k$: if $\overline{\beta} = \alpha i \gamma$ ($i \in \mathbb{N}_+$), then its corresponding node in t is $\alpha(k+i)\gamma$. If α is not a proper prefix of $\overline{\beta}$, then the corresponding node is $\overline{\beta}$ itself.

2. $\overline{\Gamma}(\alpha)$ is obtained as follows:

First, take the disjoint union of G and all graphs $\Gamma(\alpha\beta)$, $\beta \in N_Q(s)$, the ports of the resulting graph being those of G.

Second, for every docking vertex $v \in V_G$, if $lab_G(v) = \{\beta_1{:}p_1, \ldots, \beta_m{:}p_m\}$, then merge v with all $v_i = port_{\Gamma(\alpha \cdot \beta_i)}(p_i)$ for $i \in [m]$ and label the merged vertex by $\mu(\{lab_{\Gamma(\alpha \cdot \beta_1)}(v_1), \ldots, lab_{\Gamma(\alpha \cdot \beta_m)}(v_m)\})$.

Example 1 Consider the sentence "The emperor loves, respects, and fears himself." A simplified Universal Dependencies parse tree of the sentence is shown leftmost in Figure 2. Here, we have removed the "and" node as well as the additional root node above the "loves" node. Further, the edge labels in the tree should be considered as intermediate nodes (since our trees, for simplicity, and in contrast to graphs, do not have edge labels). The figure shows how a t2g transducer may turn the tree into a semantic graph akin to AMR.

In Step 1 we assume for the sake of illustration that the learning algorithm has seen the leftmost path of the tree ("The emperor loves") often enough to construct an individual ("extended") translation rule for it, and that it has also learned that the emperor referred to is usually Julius. Thus, the translation rule

$$\text{loves}(\texttt{nsubj}(\text{emperor}(\texttt{det}(\text{The})))) \to \langle q_0, G_0 \rangle$$

turns node "loves" into the state q_0 and its first dependent vanishes. The pair $\langle q_0, \Gamma(\varepsilon) \rangle = \langle q_0, G_0 \rangle$ is illustrated by a dashed box with $\Gamma(\varepsilon)$ shown inside. The numbers next to the vertices indicate the ports. Thus, all three vertices are ports. Note that the rule, for illustration purposes, anticipates the existence of a direct object (or patient) of "love", but labels the corresponding node with a question mark because the processed part of the tree does not determine the argument.

In Step 2, we apply a translation rule of the form $q_0(\texttt{conj}(\text{respects})) \to \langle q_{\text{conj}}, G \rangle$ to add two vertices and four edges to the graph. The graph G in the right-hand side is shown in Figure 3. The ports of G become the ports of $\Gamma(\varepsilon)$, and each of the vertices labeled $\varepsilon{:}p$ is merged with the p-th port of G_0 (i.e., of the $\Gamma(\varepsilon)$ of the previous step).

Step 3 processes $\text{fears}(\texttt{dobj}(\text{himself}))$, turning this subtree into a graph with two ports, with a

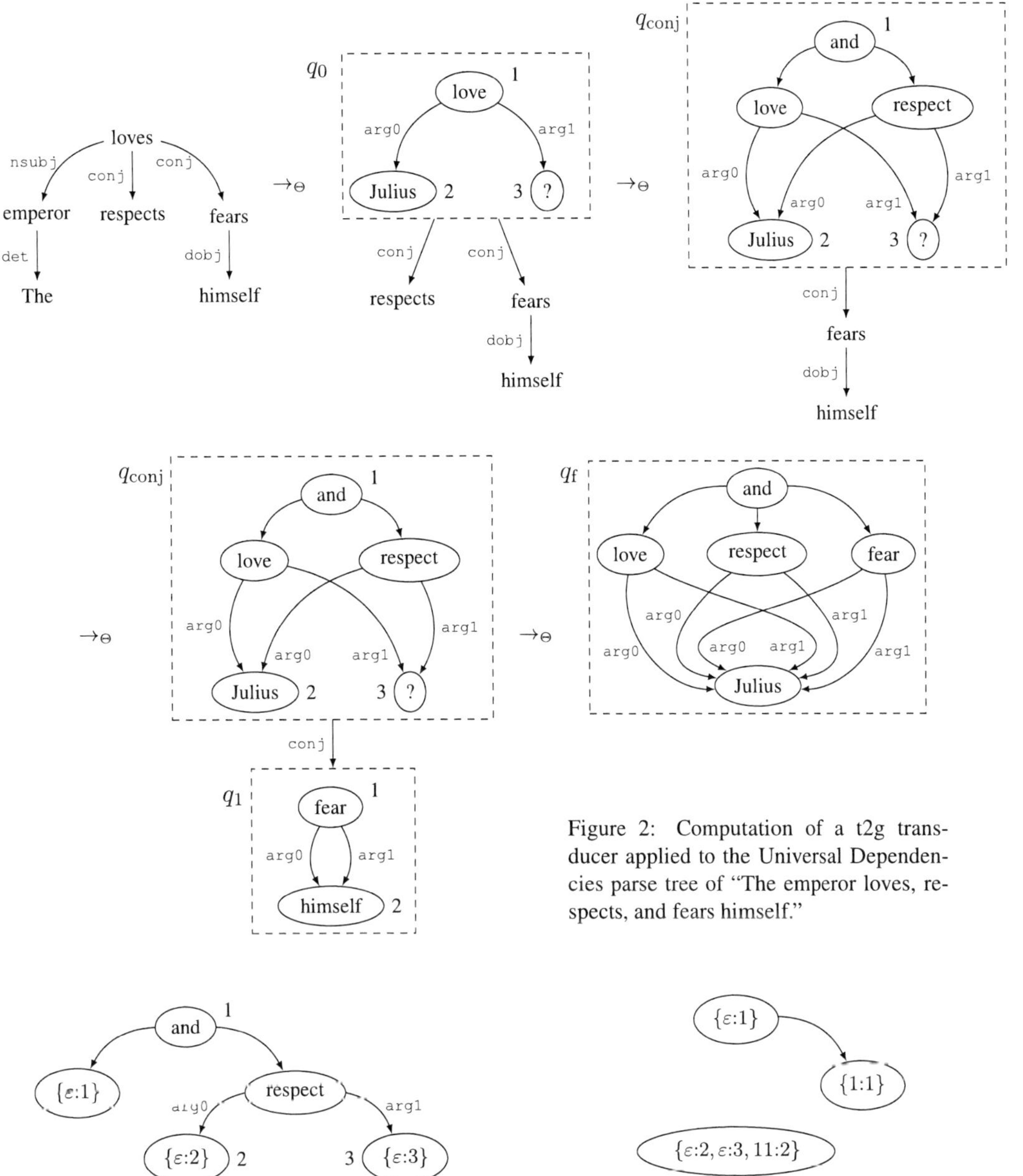

Figure 2: Computation of a t2g transducer applied to the Universal Dependencies parse tree of "The emperor loves, respects, and fears himself."

Figure 3: The graph G used in the translation rule $q_0(\mathtt{conj}(\text{respects})) \to \langle q_{\mathrm{conj}}, G \rangle$ of Step 2.

Figure 4: The graph H used in the translation rule $q_{\mathrm{conj}}(\mathtt{conj}(q_1)) \to \langle q_{\mathrm{f}}, H \rangle$ of Step 4.

reentrancy caused by the semantics of "himself". Note that, similarly to Step 1, it is still unclear at this stage which entity "himself" refers to, so we assume that the rule just keeps it. It may be instructive to note that Step 3 is independent of Steps 1 and 2, hence it could just as well have been executed at the very beginning or in between these two.

Finally, Step 4 combines the two graphs by applying a rule of the form $q_{\mathrm{conj}}(\mathtt{conj}(q_1)) \to \langle q_{\mathrm{f}}, H \rangle$. The graph H (shown in Figure 4) contains a vertex with label $\{\varepsilon{:}2, \varepsilon{:}3, 11{:}2\}$, causing the vertices labeled "Julius", "?", and "himself" to be merged. The function μ determines the label of the merged node. Here, we assume that μ gives proper names precedence over pronouns, which in turn take precedence over "?".

11

Remark 1 The transition-based system of Wang et al. (2015b) and subsequent versions translate dependency trees to AMR by visiting nodes and dependency arcs of the input tree bottom-up and left-to-right. At each node or arc, it greedily applies one out of eight alternative actions, turning the tree into a graph. Six actions are local, meaning that they involve nodes at a close distance in the input tree. These include node or arc relabelling, reversing arc directions, deleting a node, and deleting an arc by merging its two nodes. Each of these actions can easily be captured by some individual translation rule of a t2g transducer.

Two remaining actions are nonlocal: one reattaches a node and the other creates a new arc to form a reentrancy. These actions are restricted to local actions for efficiency reasons (Wang et al., 2015b, Section 3.2), so reattachment attaches to the grandparent or great grandparent, and reentrancy involves sibling nodes only. While t2g transducers can simulate reattachment, a major difference between the two models lies in the creation of reentrancies, as discussed below.

Wang's system can repeatedly apply the reentrancy action, turning for instance n sibling nodes into a clique, for any n. This is not possible in our model, since translation rules can create reentrancies only by accessing a fixed number of vertices "remembered" as ports. We believe this restriction to be linguistically adequate: while the repeated use of conjunctions and modifiers can yield AMR nodes with unbounded node degree, structures resembling cliques of unbounded size would correspond to an unbounded number of concepts, arguments or modifiers, pairwise dependent on each other. This does not appear to be a reasonable linguistic pattern.

However, note that t2g transducers *can* implement a weak form of nonlocality by percolating port nodes across any distance in the underlying derivation tree, though not in any number. This makes it possible to create reentrancies that extend further than to sibling nodes. In terms of translation power, the two formalisms seem close to each other in practice, but we conjecture that they are formally incomparable.

Readers who are familiar with the concept of hyperedge replacement may have noticed that, except for the role of the merging function, the process described in item 3 in the definition of $\rightarrow_\Theta$ is just hyperedge replacement (where the replaced hyperedges are kept implicit).

A configuration $\langle t, \Gamma \rangle$ is **final** if $t \in F$, i.e., if the first component has been reduced to a single state, which is final. For an input tree t_0, the set of all output graphs computed by Θ is denoted by $\Theta(t_0)$. It is the set of all graphs $\Gamma(\varepsilon)$ such that $\langle t_0, \Gamma_0 \rangle \rightarrow_\Theta^* \langle t, \Gamma \rangle$ for some final configuration $\langle t, \Gamma \rangle$. The **transduction** computed by Θ is the set $\{(t, g) \in T_\Sigma \times \mathcal{G}_\Delta \mid g \in \Theta(t)\}$. The **domain language** of Θ is $\{t \in T_\Sigma \mid \Theta(t) \neq \emptyset\}$.

We define the **size** of Θ to be the sum of the sizes of its rules. The size of a rule is the size of the tree in the left-hand side plus the size of the graph in the right-hand side. This notion will be used in the next sections for the computational analysis of the algorithms we present.

4 Derivation Trees

In this section, we describe how a computation of a t2g transducer Θ can be represented by means of a tree over the alphabet R, the set of translation rules of Θ. We call these trees **derivation trees** of Θ. Derivation trees will be used in Section 6 to design efficient translation algorithms. We also show that the derivation trees of Θ form a regular tree language (and, in fact, even a local one).

Consider a computation γ of Θ that has the form $\langle t_0, \Gamma_0 \rangle \rightarrow_\Theta^+ \langle q, \Gamma \rangle$ with $t_0 \in T_\Sigma$ and $q \in Q$. If γ consists of a single step, then a translation rule of the form $r_0 : t_0 \rightarrow \langle q, G \rangle$ has been used. In this case the derivation tree associated with γ, written $d(\gamma)$, is simply r_0.

If γ consists of more than one step, assume that at the last step of γ we have used a translation rule r_0 of the form $s \rightarrow \langle q, G \rangle$. We can then write γ as $\langle t_0, \Gamma_0 \rangle \rightarrow_\Theta^+ \langle s, \Gamma' \rangle \rightarrow_{r_0} \langle q, \Gamma \rangle$. Let γ' denote the first part $\langle t_0, \Gamma_0 \rangle \rightarrow_\Theta^+ \langle s, \Gamma' \rangle$ of the computation.[2] We define $rk(r_0) = |N_Q(s)|$ to be the **rank** of r_0. In the derivation tree $d(\gamma)$, r_0 has $rk(r_0)$ direct subtrees. If $N_Q(s) = (\alpha_1, \ldots, \alpha_{rk(r_0)})$, then the i-th subtree of r_0 corresponds to the sub-derivation that ended in the state at α_i. Accordingly, we proceed to split the input tree t_0 into smaller pieces on the basis of the node addresses α_i.

In order to describe this thoroughly, we need to determine a correspondence between nodes in s and nodes in t_0. Intuitively, s is a segment at the top of t_0 that extends to the right. To see this, ob-

---

[2] Recall that $N_Q(s)$ is the set of all nodes in s labeled by states in Q, and that we write $N_Q(s) = (\alpha_1, \ldots, \alpha_{rk(r_0)})$ to indicate that $\alpha_1, \ldots, \alpha_{rk(r_0)}$ are listed in lexicographic order.

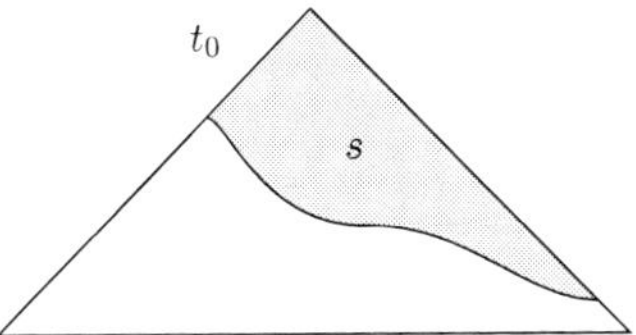

Figure 5: Schematic illustration of the part s of an input tree t_0 which is left after some computation steps. (Note that this is only a structural illustration; some of the node labels in s are not the same as in t_0 anymore, but have been replaced with states.)

serve that the root ε of s corresponds to the root of t_0. Some of the children of ε in t_0 may have been consumed by γ' and thus are no longer present in s. However, this happens strictly from left to right. Therefore, if a child of ε in t_0 is still present in s, then all of its siblings to the right are still present, too. The same pattern continues recursively at the children of these nodes in s. The situation is illustrated schematically in Figure 5.

Formally, for a node $\alpha \in N(s)$ we define the pre-image $\overline{\alpha} \in N(t_0)$ of α inductively over the structure of s, as follows:

1. $\overline{\varepsilon} = \varepsilon$.
2. Assume that $\alpha \cdot 1, \ldots, \alpha \cdot k \in N(s)$ are the children of a node α in s. Then it should be clear that the children of $\overline{\alpha}$ in t_0 are $\overline{\alpha} \cdot 1, \ldots, \overline{\alpha} \cdot n$ for some $n \geq k$. We would like to identify the k-th last children of the preimage with the k children of the postimage, and so we let $\overline{\alpha \cdot i} = \overline{\alpha} \cdot (i + n - k)$ for all $i \in [k]$.

For a set $N \subseteq N(s)$ of node addresses, we let $\overline{N} = \{\overline{\alpha} \mid \alpha \in N\}$.

We are now ready to split t_0 into the subtrees that, via the computation γ', gave rise to the states at $\alpha_1, \ldots, \alpha_{rk(r_0)}$. We do this by defining the sets $N_i \subseteq N(t_0)$ of their nodes, $i \in [rk(r_0)]$. For each $i \in [rk(r_0)]$, N_i is the set of all nodes $\beta \in N(t_0)$ such that $\overline{\alpha_i}$ is the first node in $\overline{N(s)}$ that appears on the path from β to the root of t_0.

Thus, N_i consists of $\overline{\alpha_i}$ and those of its descendants which are not in s anymore, i.e., which have already been "consumed" by the computation γ' in the process of producing node α_i in s. For each $i \in [rk(r_0)]$, define tree t_i as the portion of tree t_0 that is induced by the nodes in N_i.

For each $i \in [rk(r_0)]$, consider the translation rules of γ' that are applied to nodes in N_i. Clearly, the restriction of γ' to them yields a computation γ_i of the form $\langle t_i, \Gamma_0 \rangle \to_{\Theta}^+ \langle s(\alpha_i), \Gamma_i \rangle$ whose

length is at most the length of γ' and thus less than the length of γ. Let $d(\gamma_i)$ be the derivation tree associated with γ_i. Then we define the derivation tree $d(\gamma)$ to be $r_0(d(\gamma_1), \ldots, d(\gamma_{rk(r_0)}))$.

The inductive procedure above associates a unique derivation tree $d(\gamma)$ with each computation γ of Θ. Observe that each node of $d(\gamma)$ has a label $r \in R$ and a number of children $rk(r)$. This means that the set of derivation trees of Θ, written $D(\Theta)$, is defined over a finite, ranked alphabet. The set $D(\Theta)$ can be recognized by a bottom-up finite-state tree automaton M, as follows.[3] The set of states of M is Q, with F being the subset of accepting states. Its set of rules consists of all $r(q_1, \ldots, q_k) \to q$ such that:

1. $r : t \to \langle q, G \rangle$ is a translation rule of Θ,
2. $N_Q(t) = (\alpha_1, \ldots, \alpha_k)$, and
3. $t(\alpha_i) = q_i$ for all $i \in [k]$.

Recall from Section 3 that the size of Θ is the sum of the sizes of its translation rules. We can easily construct rule $r(q_1, \ldots, q_k) \to q$ of M in time linear in the size of r. Hence, M can be constructed in time (and space) linear in the size of Θ.

Given a derivation tree $dt \in D(\Theta)$, such that $dt = r(dt_1, \ldots, dt_k)$, we can compute its input tree $in(dt)$ and its output graph $out(dt)$ recursively, as follows. Suppose the root r of dt is the translation rule $r : t \to \langle q, G \rangle$ with $N_Q(t) = (\alpha_1, \ldots, \alpha_{rk(r)})$.

1. If $t_i = in(dt_i)$ for all $i \in [k]$, then $in(dt)$ is obtained from t and $t_1, \ldots, t_k$ by fusing each node α_i with the root of t_i and making $t_i(\varepsilon)$ the label of the fused node. The subtrees of t_i are added to the left of the leftmost subtree of α_i in t. (If α_i is a leaf, t_i just replaces α_i.)
2. If $G_i = out(dt_i)$ for all $i \in [k]$, then the graph $out(dt)$ is obtained from the disjoint union of G and $G_1, \ldots, G_k$ by merging each docking vertex $v \in V_G$ with ports in $G_1, \ldots, G_k$, as follows: if $lab_G(v) = \{\alpha_{i_1} : p_1, \ldots, \alpha_{i_m} : p_m\}$, then v is merged with all $v_j = port_{G_{i_j}}(p_j)$, $j \in [m]$, and the resulting vertex is labeled by $\mu(\{lab_{G_{i_1}}(v_1), \ldots, lab_{G_{i_m}}(v_m)\})$.

Note that the definition of $out(dt)$ simply reiterates the way in which computations are defined to construct output graphs. As a consequence, it is a straightforward task to show that $dt = d(\gamma)$ for a computation γ that consumes $in(dt)$ and yields the output graph $out(dt)$.

---

[3] For bottom-up tree automata, see e.g. (Comon et al., 2002, Chapter 1).

13

Finally, let ρ be the size of the largest translation rule used in dt. It is not difficult to see that, following the recursive procedure above, both $in(dt)$ and $out(dt)$ can be constructed in time $\mathcal{O}(\rho \cdot |dt|)$.

5 Arc-Factored Normal Form

Extended left-hand sides are convenient for specifying transducers, but in order to prove formal properties about transducers or implement algorithms based on them, it is useful to express the transition rules in a more restricted normal form. The normal form introduced in this section processes a tree by first turning every node into a state, and then by visiting the individual arcs of the tree one at each step. A translation rule is in **arc-factored normal form** if its left-hand side is in Σ or has the form $q(q')$ where $q, q' \in Q$. A t2g transducer is in arc-factored normal form if each of its translation rules is in arc-factored normal form.

We now show that every t2g transducer Θ can effectively be transformed into a t2g transducer in arc-factored normal form which computes the same transduction. First, introduce a new state q_f of type 0 for every $f \in \Sigma$ that occurs in the left-hand side of some translation rule, add the rule $f \rightarrow \langle q_f, \emptyset \rangle$ (where $\emptyset$ denotes the empty graph), and replace f by q_f in the left-hand sides of all original rules. Clearly, the computed transduction remains the same and all rules which violate the condition of the arc-factored normal form have left-hand sides in T_Q.

Now, we split rules with large left-hand sides into smaller ones. As long as the transducer is not in arc-factored normal form, select any translation rule $s \rightarrow \langle q, G \rangle$ such that $|s| > 2$. Then s has the form $c[q_1(q_2, t_1, \ldots, t_n)]$ for some context c, states q_1, q_2, and trees $t_1, \ldots, t_n$ $(n \geq 0)$. If $k = type(q_1)$ and $\ell = type(q_2)$, we decompose the translation rule into two rules, namely $q_1(q_2) \rightarrow \langle q_{1;2}, H \rangle$ and $c[q_{1;2}(t_1, \ldots, t_n)] \rightarrow \langle q, G' \rangle$, where $q_{1;2}$ is a fresh state with $type(q_{1;2}) = k + \ell$.

The intermediate graph H consists of $k + \ell$ isolated vertices $u_1, \ldots, u_k, v_1, \ldots, v_\ell$ with $port_H = u_1 \cdots u_k v_1 \cdots v_\ell$ and, for all $i \in [k]$ and $j \in [\ell]$, $lab_H(u_i) = \varepsilon{:}i$ and $lab_H(v_j) = 1{:}j$. The effect of this translation rule is to take the disjoint union of the graphs associated with the two nodes, concatenating the port sequences.

The graph G' is obtained from G by appropriately renaming the references of the form $\alpha{\cdot}1{:}p$ where α is the address of $\square$ in c: for every $p \in [\ell]$, if $\alpha{\cdot}1{:}p$ occurs in a label of a vertex in G, then it is replaced by $\alpha{:}(\ell + p)$. Moreover, in every label each port reference of the form $\alpha{\cdot}i{:}p$ for $i > 1$ is replaced by $\alpha{\cdot}(i - 1){:}p$.

It should be clear that the two translation rules, executed one after the other, have precisely the same effect as the original one. This completes the proof of the arc-factored normal form.

Note that the size increase implied by the preceding construction is modest. More precisely, each rule will be decomposed into as many rules as there are arcs in the original left-hand side, and the size of graphs in the right-hand sides of intermediate translation rules is at most twice the largest type τ of states in Q. Hence, the total size of the new rules replacing $s \rightarrow \langle q, G \rangle$ is $\mathcal{O}(|s| \cdot \tau + |G|)$. More sophisticated constructions can result in a smaller transducer. A rather simple optimization is to drop all ports from the discrete graph H which do not occur in G, and to identify those referenced in the label of the same docking vertex. We do not further pursue this here.

6 Translation into a Packed Forest

Given a transducer $\Theta = (\Sigma, \Delta, Q, R, \mu, F)$ and an unranked tree t, we construct a suitable representation for the set of all graphs that are translations of t under Θ. We solve the problem in two steps, specified below. To simplify the presentation, we assume Θ is in arc-factored normal form.

6.1 Grounding

The first step annotates every occurrence of a symbol in t with its address, yielding $\hat{t}$, and constructs a new t2g transducer $\Theta_t = (\Sigma', \Delta, Q', R', \mu, F')$ with domain language $\{\hat{t}\}$ and output graphs that are the translations of t by Θ. Let $N(\hat{t}) = N(t)$ and $\hat{t}(\alpha) = t(\alpha)^\alpha$ for all $\alpha \in N(t)$. We restrict the domain language of Θ to the set $\{\hat{t}\}$, in such a way that the translation process of Θ is "preserved". We call this construction the **grounding** of Θ to t. For this, let $k_\alpha = \min\{i \in \mathbb{N}_+ \mid \alpha i \notin N(t)\}$ for every $\alpha \in N(t)$, i.e., k_α is the number of children of α plus one.

1. The input alphabet Σ' consists of all symbols appearing in $\hat{t}$.

2. The set Q' consists of all $\langle q, \alpha, i \rangle$ such that $q \in Q$, $\alpha \in N(t)$, and $i \in [k_\alpha]$. Intuitively, α records the position in the tree and i is the number of the next child to be consumed.

3. The set F' is $\{\langle q, \varepsilon, k_\varepsilon \rangle \mid q \in F\}$.

4. For every translation rule $f \to \langle q, G \rangle$ of Θ and every $\alpha \in N(t)$ with $t(\alpha) = f$, we include $f^\alpha \to \langle \langle q, \alpha, 1 \rangle, G \rangle$ in R'.

5. For every translation rule $q_1(q_2) \to \langle q, G \rangle$ of Θ and every $\alpha i \in N(t)$ $(i \in \mathbb{N}_+)$, we let $\langle q_1, \alpha, i \rangle (\langle q_2, \alpha i, k_{\alpha i} \rangle) \to \langle \langle q, \alpha, i+1 \rangle, G \rangle$ be a translation rule in R'.

Note that the grounding algorithm above bears close similarity with the notion of parsing by intersection, which makes use of the construction proposed by Bar-Hillel et al. (1964) for producing a context-free grammar that generates the intersection of the languages of a context-free grammar and a finite-state (string) automaton. It should thus be clear that $\Theta_t(\hat{s}) = \emptyset$ for all $s \in T_\Sigma \setminus \{t\}$, and $\Theta_t(\hat{t}) = \Theta(t)$.

The construction of Θ_t can be carried out in time proportional to the product of the sizes of Θ and t. In practice, many of the translation rules of Θ_t may be useless. It is possible to avoid this by interleaving the construction of the translation rules of Θ_t with a simulation of the process of parsing by Θ on input t. This has the advantage of pruning the construction, so that useless translation rules are filtered out.

6.2 Graph Forest

In the second step of our translation algorithm, we construct a suitable representation of all the graphs that are obtained in any translation of t based on Θ. Using the t2g transducer Θ_t from the previous step, we can apply the construction outlined in Section 4 and produce a bottom-up finite-state tree automaton M_t whose language is the set $D(\Theta_t)$ of all derivation trees of Θ_t. Together with the interpretation of generated derivation trees dt as $out(dt)$ this yields the desired compact representation of the set $\Theta(t)$ of graphs t translates into. We therefore call M_t a **graph forest** for the translation of t under Θ.

One can now use standard algorithms to, e.g., generate the graphs of the form $out(dt)$. Further, if the rules of Θ are equipped with weights from some weight structure, these weights carry over to the rules of M_t in the obvious way. If we now turn every such weighted rule $r(q_1, \ldots, q_k) \to^w q$ of M_t into the weighted context-free string production $q \to^w r(q_1, \ldots, q_k)$, where states become nonterminal symbols, and rule names, parentheses and commas are viewed as terminal symbols, we get an equivalent weighted context-free gram-mar generating $D(\Theta_t)$ (where trees are viewed as strings over the mentioned alphabet). One can now apply Knuth's generalization of Dijkstra's shortest paths algorithm (Knuth, 1977) to find the best-scoring derivation tree in $D(\Theta_t)$, and thus the "best" translation of t. As Knuth's algorithm runs in time $O(n \log n)$ in the size of the grammar, the total time required by this process is $O(m \log m)$, where m is the product of the sizes of Θ and t.

7 Discussion

We have developed a novel finite-state transducer that implements nonlocal processing to translate unranked dependency trees into general graphs for semantic representation of natural language.

Our formalism is essentially a finite-state device processing unranked trees in a bottom-up fashion, following a well-assessed tradition in natural language processing. We remark that tree preprocessing to convert unranked trees into binary trees, in the style of the stepwise tree automata of Martens and Niehren (2005), is not attractive from a linguistic standpoint since it might destroy the linguistic intuition underlying translation rules. Therefore, our solution to the problem of processing unranked trees uses on-the-fly binarization at each node. This solution was previously adopted by the Z-automata of Björklund et al. (2019), recognizing dependency trees. In fact, if we remove the graph component from the right-hand side of translation rules in t2g transucers, we obtain Z-automata.

Our definition of translation rules forbids the rewriting of single nodes labeled by a state. This is done to avoid cycling on the same input node for an unbounded number of steps. This ability would make it possible to turn a single input tree into infinitely many semantic graphs that can be arbitrarily larger than the input syntactic tree. Such a model would not be linguistically adequate.

As already remarked, there is a deep similarity between the definition of computation step in t2g transducers and hyperedge replacement. In fact a synchronous hyperedge replacement grammar could easily simulate a t2g transducer.

The next step in this project is the development of algorithms for unsupervised extraction of t2g translation rules from semantic graph corpora.

References

Miguel Ballesteros and Yaser Al-Onaizan. 2017. AMR parsing using stack-LSTMs. In *Proceedings of the 2017 Conference on Empirical Methods in Natural Language Processing*, pages 1269–1275. Association for Computational Linguistics.

Laura Banarescu, Claire Bonial, Shu Cai, Madalina Georgescu, Kira Griffitt, Ulf Hermjakob, Kevin Knight, Philipp Koehn, Martha Palmer, and Nathan Schneider. 2013. Abstract meaning representation for sembanking. In *Proc. 7th Linguistic Annotation Workshop and Interoperability with Discourse*, pages 178–186.

Yehoshua Bar-Hillel, Micha Perles, and Eliyahu Shamir. 1964. On formal properties of simple phrase structure grammars. In Y. Bar-Hillel, editor, *Language and Information: Selected Essays on their Theory and Application*, chapter 9, pages 116–150. Addison-Wesley.

Johanna Björklund, Frank Drewes, and Giorgio Satta. 2019. Z-automata for compact and direct representation of unranked tree languages. In *Implementation and Application of Automata - 24th International Conference, CIAA 2019, Košice, Slovakia, July 22-25, 2019, Proceedings*, volume 11601 of *Lecture Notes in Computer Science*, pages 83–94. Springer.

Hubert Comon, Max Dauchet, Rémi Gilleron, Florent Jacquemard, Denis Lugiez, Sophie Tison, and Marc Tommasi. 2002. *Tree Automata Techniques and Applications*. Online publication available at `http://www.grappa.univ-lille3.fr/tata`.

Marco Damonte, B. Shay Cohen, and Giorgio Satta. 2017. An incremental parser for abstract meaning representation. In *Proceedings of the 15th Conference of the European Chapter of the Association for Computational Linguistics: Volume 1, Long Papers*, pages 536–546. Association for Computational Linguistics.

Joost Engelfriet and Heiko Vogler. 1994. The translation power of top-down tree-to-graph transducers. *Journal of Computer and System Sciences*, 49:258–305.

Joost Engelfriet and Heiko Vogler. 1998. The equivalence of bottom-up and top-down tree-to-graph transducers. *Journal of Computer and System Sciences*, 56(3):332–356.

Jonas Groschwitz, Matthias Lindemann, Meaghan Fowlie, Mark Johnson, and Alexander Koller. 2018. AMR dependency parsing with a typed semantic algebra. In *Proceedings of the 56th Annual Meeting of the Association for Computational Linguistics (Volume 1: Long Papers)*, pages 1831–1841, Melbourne, Australia. Association for Computational Linguistics.

Daniel Hershcovich, Omri Abend, and Ari Rappoport. 2017. A transition-based directed acyclic graph parser for UCCA. In *Proceedings of the 55th Annual Meeting of the Association for Computational Linguistics (Volume 1: Long Papers)*, pages 1127–1138, Vancouver, Canada. Association for Computational Linguistics.

Bevan Jones, Jacob Andreas, Daniel Bauer, Karl Moritz Hermann, and Kevin Knight. 2012. Semantics-based machine translation with hyperedge replacement grammars. In *Proceedings of COLING 2012*, pages 1359–1376. The COLING 2012 Organizing Committee.

Donald E. Knuth. 1977. A generalization of dijkstra's algorithm. *Information Processing Letters*, 6:1–5.

Marco Kuhlmann and Peter Jonsson. 2015. Parsing to noncrossing dependency graphs. *Transactions of the Association for Computational Linguistics*, 3:559–570.

Marco Kuhlmann and Stephan Oepen. 2016. Towards a catalogue of linguistic graph banks. *Computational Linguistics*, 42(4):819–827.

Andreas Maletti, Jonathan Graehl, Mark Hopkins, and Kevin Knight. 2009. The power of extended top-down tree transducers. *SIAM J. Comput.*, 39(2):410–430.

Wim Martens and Joachim Niehren. 2005. Minimizing tree automata for unranked trees. In *Database Programming Languages*, pages 232–246, Berlin, Heidelberg. Springer Berlin Heidelberg.

Rebecca Nesson and Stuart M. Shieber. 2006. Simpler TAG semantics through synchronization. In *Proceedings of the 11th Conference on Formal Grammar*, Malaga, Spain.

Stephan Oepen, Marco Kuhlmann, Yusuke Miyao, Daniel Zeman, Silvie Cinkova, Dan Flickinger, Jan Hajic, and Zdenka Uresova. 2015. Semeval 2015 task 18: Broad-coverage semantic dependency parsing. In *Proceedings of the 9th Intl. Workshop on Semantic Evaluation (SemEval 2015)*, pages 915–926.

Stephan Oepen, Marco Kuhlmann, Yusuke Miyao, Daniel Zeman, Dan Flickinger, Jan Hajic, Angelina Ivanova, and Yi Zhang. 2014. Semeval 2014 task 8: Broad-coverage semantic dependency parsing. In *Proc. 8th International Workshop on Semantic Evaluation (SemEval 2014)*, pages 63–72.

Xiaochang Peng, Daniel Gildea, and Giorgio Satta. 2018. AMR parsing with cache transition systems. In *Proceedings of the Thirty-Second AAAI Conference on Artificial Intelligence, (AAAI-18), New Orleans, Louisiana, USA, February 2-7, 2018*, pages 4897–4904. AAAI Press.

Xiaochang Peng, Linfeng Song, and Daniel Gildea. 2015. A synchronous hyperedge replacement grammar based approach for amr parsing. In *Proceedings of the Nineteenth Conference on Computational*

Natural Language Learning, pages 32–41. Association for Computational Linguistics.

Natalie Schluter. 2015. The complexity of finding the maximum spanning DAG and other restrictions for DAG parsing of natural language. In *Proceedings of the Fourth Joint Conference on Lexical and Computational Semantics, *SEM 2015, June 4-5, 2015, Denver, Colorado, USA.*, pages 259–268.

James W. Thatcher. 1973. Tree automata: An informal survey. In A. V. Aho, editor, *Currents in the Theory of Computing*, pages 143–172. Prentice Hall, New York.

David Vilares and Carlos Gómez-Rodríguez. 2018. A transition-based algorithm for unrestricted AMR parsing. In *Proceedings of the 2018 Conference of the North American Chapter of the Association for Computational Linguistics: Human Language Technologies, Volume 2 (Short Papers)*, pages 142–149. Association for Computational Linguistics.

Chuan Wang, Nianwen Xue, and Sameer Pradhan. 2015a. Boosting transition-based AMR parsing with refined actions and auxiliary analyzers. In *Proc. 53rd Annual Meeting of the Association for Computational Linguistics and the 7th Intl. Joint Conf. on Natural Language Processing (Short Papers)*, pages 857–862.

Chuan Wang, Nianwen Xue, and Sameer Pradhan. 2015b. A transition-based algorithm for AMR parsing. In *Proc. 2015 Conference of the North American Chapter of the Association for Computational Linguistics: Human Language Technologies, (NAACL HLT 2015), Denver, Colorado, USA, 2015*, pages 366–375.

On the Compression of Lexicon Transducers

Marco Cognetta, Cyril Allauzen, Michael Riley
{cognetta,allauzen,riley}@google.com
Google

Abstract

In finite-state language processing pipelines, a lexicon is often a key component. It needs to be comprehensive to ensure accuracy, reducing out-of-vocabulary misses. However, in memory-constrained environments (e.g., mobile phones), the size of the component automata must be kept small. Indeed, a delicate balance between comprehensiveness, speed, and memory must be struck to conform to device requirements while providing a good user experience.

In this paper, we describe a compression scheme for lexicons when represented as finite-state transducers. We efficiently encode the *graph* of the transducer while storing transition labels separately. The graph encoding scheme is based on the LOUDS (Level Order Unary Degree Sequence) tree representation, which has constant time tree traversal for queries while being information-theoretically optimal in space. We find that our encoding is near the theoretical lower bound for such graphs and substantially outperforms more traditional representations in space while remaining competitive in latency benchmarks.

1 Introduction

Modern finite-state language processing pipelines often consist of several finite-state transducers in composition. For example, a virtual keyboard pipeline, used for decoding on mobile devices, can consist of a context dependency transducer C, a lexicon L, and an n-gram language model G (Ouyang et al., 2017). A *bikey* C transducer is used to encode context in gesture decoding, the lexicon transducer L maps from a character string to the corresponding word ID, and the language model G gives the a priori probability of a word sequence. A similar decomposition is often used in speech recognition decoding (Mohri et al., 1996).

These models are then composed as

$$C \circ L \circ G.$$

The application of this combined model to an input character string outputs the corresponding word string and probability. Unfortunately, in order to be accurate, these models may need to be large. This problem is aggravated when the composition is performed statically since the state space grows with the product of the input automata sizes. In practice, *on-the-fly composition* is often used to save space (Mohri et al., 1996; Hori et al., 2004; Caseiro and Trancoso, 2006). Additionally, it is of practical importance to have compact and efficient finite-state language model component representations.

There are a variety of compression schemes available for automata (Daciuk, 2000). These range from general compression algorithms, which do not depend on a specific underlying structure (Daciuk and van Noord, 2001; Daciuk and Weiss, 2011; Mohri et al., 2015) to schemes that try to heavily exploit specific structural properties of the inputs (Watanabe et al., 2009; Sorensen and Allauzen, 2011). Another important consideration is whether the automata can be decompressed just for a queried portion or need to be more fully decompressed. Generic compression algorithms often have relatively good compression ratios over a wide class of machines, but they sacrifice speed and space in use since they often do not admit such selective decompression. In contrast, structurally-specific compression algorithms can have an attractive balance between the compression ratio and query performance, but are limited to precise subclasses of machines. In real-time production systems, the latter method often proves more desirable since a user should not have to wait long or waste space when a query is answered.

Proceedings of the 14th International Conference on Finite-State Methods and Natural Language Processing, pages 18–26
Dresden, Germany, September 23-25, 2019. ©2019 Association for Computational Linguistics

Among the transducers mentioned above, the context-dependency transducer C can be represented implicitly (in code) and structurally-specific compression algorithms for the n-gram language model G have previously been developed (Sorensen and Allauzen, 2011). This leads us to investigate the compression of the lexicon L.

This paper is organized as follows. Section 2 introduces the formal algebraic structures and notation that we will use. Section 3 describes different representations for these algebraic structures. In Section 4, we formally define a lexicon and explore its possible representations. Section 5 develops an information-theoretic bound on the number of bits needed to encode a lexicon, Section 6 presents our encoding, and Section 7 presents experiments on the quality of that encoding. Finally, we offer concluding remarks in Section 8.

2 Preliminaries

2.1 Graphs and Trees

A *directed graph* (or *digraph*) $G = (V, A)$ has a finite set of *nodes* (or *vertices*) V and a finite set of directed *arcs* (or *edges*) $A \subseteq V \times V$. An arc $a = (p[a], n[a])$ spans from a *source* node $p[a]$ to a *destination* node $n[a]$. A path π is a non-empty list of consecutive arcs $a_1, a_2, \ldots, a_n$ where $p[a_{i+1}] = n[a_i]$. We write $p[\pi] = p[a_1]$, $n[\pi] = n[a_n]$. A cycle is a path π with $p[\pi] = n[\pi]$. A digraph is acyclic if it has no cycles. The *out-degree* of a node $v \in V$ is $|\{w \in V \mid (v, w) \in A\}|$ and the *in-degree* is $|\{w \in V \mid (w, v) \in A\}|$.

We distinguish several specific digraph cases:

- An *out-tree* (V, A, i) is an acyclic digraph for which the in-degree of every node is 1 except for the distinguished *root* node $i \in V$, which has in-degree 0. The nodes with out-degree 0 are called *leaves*.

- An *in-tree* (V, A, f) is an acyclic digraph for which the out-degree of every node is 1 except for the distinguished *root* node $f \in V$, which has out-degree 0. The nodes with in-degree 0 are called *leaves*.

- A directed *bipartite digraph* $(V_1 \cup V_2, A)$ partitions the nodes into two disjoint sets V_1 and V_2 with $A \subseteq (V_1 \times V_2) \cup (V_2 \times V_1)$.

2.2 Finite-State Transducers

A finite-state transducer $T = (\Sigma, \Gamma, Q, E, i, F)$ has a finite input alphabet Σ, a finite output alphabet Γ, a finite set of states Q, a finite set of transitions $E \subseteq Q \times (\Sigma \cup \{\epsilon\}) \times \Gamma^* \times Q$, an initial state i and a final set of states $F \subseteq Q$. The symbol ϵ represents the empty string. A transition $e = (p[e], i[e], o[e], n[e]) \in E$ represents a move from the *source* state $p[e]$ to the *destination* state $n[e]$ with the *input label* $i[e]$ and *output label* $o[e]$. Associated with any transducer is a directed graph $G(T) = (Q, A)$ where $A = \{(q, q') \in Q \times Q : (q, x, y, q') \in E\}$. Thus, there is a 1:1 correspondence between states and nodes but there may be multiple transitions, with different labelings, that correspond to the same digraph arc. In that case, we say the transition is a digraph *multiarc*.

A path $\pi = e_1, \ldots, e_n$, a cycle, $p[\pi]$ and $n[\pi]$ are analogously defined to digraphs and define $i[\pi] = i[e_1] \ldots i[e_n]$ and $o[\pi] = o[e_1] \ldots o[e_n]$. $P(q, q')$ denotes the set of all paths in T from state q to q'. We extend this to sets in the obvious way: $P(q, R)$ denotes the set of all paths from state q to $q' \in R$ and so forth. A path π is successful if it is in $P(i, F)$ and in that case the transducer is said to accept the input string $i[\pi]$ and output $o[\pi]$.

A finite-state transducer is *subsequential* if it is input deterministic, that is, no two outgoing transitions at the same state share the same input label, and the destination state of any epsilon transition is a final state with no outgoing transitions.

3 Representations

3.1 Graph and Tree Representations

Basic Graph and Tree Representation. A simple digraph representation uses *adjacency lists*: denote the nodes V by integers from 1 to N, let a be an array indexed by the node number, and let $a[q] = (q_1, \ldots, q_n)$ be a list of the nodes $\{q_j \in V : (q, q_j) \in A\}$. An in-tree and out-tree can use this representation where a distinguished integer such as 1 or $|V|$ is used to denote the root. A directed bipartite graph can also use this representation where it may be convenient to number the nodes in V_1 from 1 to $|V_1|$ and V_2 from $|V_1| + 1$ to $|V|$.

Compact Tree Representation. In the case of trees, there is a particularly compact representation known as LOUDS (Level Order Unary Degree Sequence). We can quantify compactness as follows.

For a finite set with M elements, we require at least $N = \log M$ bits to uniquely encode each element. We call an encoding scheme *succinct* if it takes at most $N + o(N)$ bits to encode any element uniquely.

The LOUDS tree encoding is a succinct representation of ordinal trees (where a node's children have a total ordering). Given an ordinal tree of N nodes, it encodes it in $2N + 1$ bits, while the information-theoretic lower bound is $2N - O(\log N)$ (Jacobson, 1989). Moreover, $O(1)$ time parent-child traversals can be implemented using $o(N)$ extras bits of storage (Geary et al., 2004).

Let b be a bitstring where $b[i]$ is the element at index i when starting from 0. Then, we define $Rank_x$ and $Select_x$, where $x \in \{0, 1\}$, as

$$Rank_x^{\text{b}}(n) = |\{i \mid \text{b}[i] = x, \, 0 \le i < n\}|$$
$$Select_x^{\text{b}}(n) = \text{the index of the } n\text{-th } x \text{ in b.}$$

These operations can be performed in constant time using $o(|\text{b}|)$ extra bits of space (Vigna, 2008).

The LOUDS encoding is then constructed as follows. We start with the bitstring **10**. Then, from the root in breadth-first order, we append $\mathbf{1^d 0}$, where **d** is the number of children of the current node. Here, we assume the graph is labeled in breadth-first order. Then, a node n corresponds to the n-th 1 in the bitstring (or, equivalently, the $(n + 1)$-th 0). We can find the parent or first/last child (if any) using a combination of *Rank* and *Select* queries:

$$Parent^{\text{b}}(n) = Rank_0^{\text{b}}(Select_1^{\text{b}}(n))$$
$$FirstChild^{\text{b}}(n) = Rank_1^{\text{b}}(Select_0^{\text{b}}(n) + 1)$$
$$LastChild^{\text{b}}(n) = Rank_1^{\text{b}}(Select_0^{\text{b}}(n + 1) - 1).$$

From these, we can retrieve the number of children of a node, the i-th child, whether or not a node is a leaf, and many other operations in a constant number of queries (Geary et al., 2004; Delpratt et al., 2006). It is known that *Select* and *Rank* can be performed in constant time in the length of the bitstring by augmenting the bitstring with $o(N)$ additional bits of information (thus retaining any succinctness properties) (Kim et al., 2005; Vigna, 2008).

3.2 Transducer Representations

Basic Transducer Representation. A simple transducer representation uses adjacency lists as well, stored in an array a indexed by states that are denoted by integers from 0 to $|Q| - 1$, The value $a[q] = ((i_1, o_1, q_1), \ldots, (i_n, o_n, q_n))$ is a list

of the elements of $\{(i_j, o_j, q_j) \in \Sigma \times \Gamma \times Q : (q, i_j, o_j, q_j) \in E\}$. The initial state can be denoted by 0 and the final states can be stored separately. We will call this representation `AdjList` in our experiments where we use 32 bits for each of the input label, output label, and destination state of each transition.

Compact Transducer Representation. A more compact transducer representation stores the $|Q|$ adjacency lists across 2 global arrays as follows. First an array `I`, indexed by integers from 0 to $|Q|$, holds the values $\text{I}[q] = \sum_{0 \le i < q} |a[q]|$. Second an array `A`, indexed by integers from 0 to $|E| - 1$, holds the concatenation of the adjacency lists $a[0] \cdots a[|Q| - 1]$. The adjacency list for a given state q can be recovered from `I` and `A` as

$$a[q] = \bigcup_{i=\text{I}[q]}^{\text{I}[q+1]-1} \{\text{A}[i]\}.$$

Observe that `I` stores a monotonic nondecreasing sequence of integers, hence we encode using a differential coding approach similar to PForDelta (Zukowski et al., 2006). We store `A` using a variable-length encoding that ensures that $\log |Q| + \log |\Sigma| + \log |\Gamma|$ bits are used per entry in `A` on average. Final states are stored as superfinal transitions. We will call this representation `CmpAdjList` in our experiments.

4 Lexicons

Lexicon Definition. We define a *lexicon* as a finite binary relation $L \subset \Sigma^+ \times \Gamma$ that pairs nonempty character strings from the finite alphabet Σ to a *word* symbol in the finite alphabet Γ. This terminology matches our keyboard application described above. For the speech recognition application, the Σ alphabet represents phonemes. We will assume the relation L is functional and one-to-one. In other words, each character string in the domain of L maps to only one word (i.e., no homonyms) and each word maps to only one character string (i.e., unique spellings). This is natural for the keyboard application.[1]

Lexicon Representation While there are many ways to represent a lexicon, we focus on using a character-to-word finite-state transducer. An advantage of this approach is that we can use trans-

---

[1] For the speech application the alphabets may need to be extended to eliminate any homophones and non-unique pronunciations (Mohri et al., 1996).

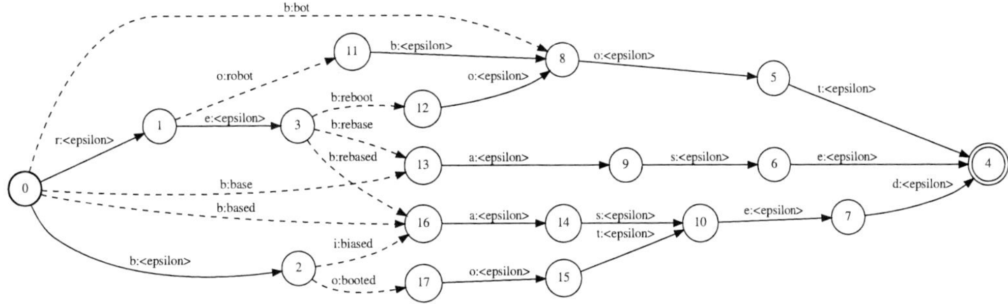

Figure 1: A character-to-word lexicon transducer in canonical form. The dashed arcs are special *bridge arcs*. Notice that removing the bridge arcs disconnects the graph while leaving two tree structures.

ducer determinization and minimization to put the transducer into a minimal canonical form (possible since L is finite and thus has an acyclic transducer representation) (Mohri et al., 2002). Figure 1 gives an example of a character-to-word lexicon transducer in this canonical form. Each word in a canonical lexicon corresponds to exactly one successful path (by subsequentiality) and every successful path has exactly one transition with an non-ϵ output label (by definition of a lexicon). Further, there is only one final state (by acyclicity and minimality) which we will denote by f. What remains is to store this representation compactly. We will do so by storing the transducer graph and its labels separately.

Given a minimal lexicon transducer T, we will now show that we can decompose the graph $G(T)$ into three sub-graphs: a *prefix graph* $G_p(T)$, a *suffix graph* $G_s(T)$, and a *bridge graph* $G_b(T)$. We further show that $G_p(T)$ is an out-tree, $G_s(T)$ is an in-tree, and $G_b(T)$ is a directed bipartite graph. We will use this decomposition in our stored representation.

Formally, let $G(T) = (Q, A)$ as defined above. Then define $G_p(T) = (Q_p, A_p)$, $G_s(T) = (Q_s, A_s)$, and $G_b(T) = (Q_b, A_b)$ as

$$Q_p = \{q \in Q : \pi \in P(i, q) \land o[\pi] = \epsilon\}$$
$$Q_s = \{q \in Q : \pi \in P(q, F) \land o[\pi] = \epsilon\}$$
$$Q_b = \{q \in Q : (q, q') \in A_b \lor (q', q) \in A_b\}$$
$$A_p = \{(q, q') \in A : q, q' \in Q_u\}$$
$$A_s = \{(q, q') \in A : q, q' \in Q_s\}$$
$$A_b = \{(q, q') \in A : (q, x, y, q') \in E \land y \neq \epsilon\}.$$

In other words, the prefix graph corresponds to transitions on paths in T before the output label, the suffix graph to those after the output label, and the bridge graph to those with the output label. It is easy to see a transition in T corresponds to an arc in exactly one of these sub-graphs. Further, Q_p and Q_s partition Q.

The prefix graph is an out-tree rooted at $i \in Q_p$. Suppose there are two arcs entering some state $q \in Q_p$. Then there must be two successful paths in T that pass through q with the same word label, which is a contradiction.

Similarly, the suffix graph is an in-tree rooted at $f \in Q_s$. For example, suppose there are two arcs leaving some state $q \in Q_s$. Then again there must be two successful paths in T that pass through q with the same word label, which is a contradiction.

Finally, the bridge graph is a directed bipartite graph with arcs that span from Q_p to Q_s because for any successful path in T the transition with a non-ϵ output label is preceded by a subpath with all ϵ output labels from the initial state i and followed by a subpath with all ϵ output labels to the final state f. Observe that only bridge arcs in A_b can be multiarcs of $G(T)$ since L is one-to-one.

Figure 1 shows this decomposition for our example with the bridge arcs specially marked.

5 The Optimal Graph Encoding

Now that we have described the canonical form of our lexicon transducer and its graph decomposition, we can begin to devise a compression scheme. We first wish to find the information-theoretic bound on the number of bits required to uniquely encode any lexicon graph. That is, among all lexicon transducers with given prefix out-tree and suffix in-tree sizes (and a given number of leaves in each) and k bridge arcs, how many bits is sufficient to encode them so that they are all pairwise distinguishable?

In this section, we let n and n_ℓ be the number of nodes and leaves in the prefix out-tree and m and m_ℓ be the same for the suffix in-tree.

The LOUDS tree encoding is optimal for all n node ordinal trees up to lower order terms (Jacobson, 1989). This is because there are

$$\frac{\binom{2n}{n}}{n}$$

ordinal trees on n nodes, and

$$\log \frac{\binom{2n}{n}}{n} = 2n - O(\log n).$$

This is compared to the $2n + 1$ bits used by LOUDS. However, when the number of leaves is known, this bound can be reduced. There are

$$\frac{\binom{n-2}{n_\ell-1}\binom{n-1}{n_\ell-1}}{n_\ell}$$

ordinal trees with n nodes and n_ℓ leaves (Yamanaka et al., 2012).

We are left with the task of counting the number of valid bridge graphs with k arcs. Each bridge graph is uniquely defined by choosing a set of k bridge arcs, i.e., a k element subset of $Q_p \times Q_s$. Every state in a minimal lexicon transducer must belong to a successful path, hence every node in its graph must belong to a path from the root of Q_p to the root of Q_s. A leaf in Q_p (resp. Q_s) belongs to such a path if and only if it is the origin (resp. destination) of a bridge arc. Hence, a set of k bridge arcs $A_b \in \mathcal{P}_k(Q_p \times Q_s)$ is *valid* iff for every leaf q there exists a bridge arc $a \in A_b$ such that $q = p[a]$ or $q = n[a]$. Let Q_p^ℓ and Q_s^ℓ be the set of leaves in the prefix and suffix graphs respectively, and $Q^\ell = Q_p^\ell \cup Q_s^\ell$.

Let $\mathcal{A}_q$ denote the set of sets of k bridge arcs where the leaf $q \in Q^\ell$ is not part of an arc:

$$\mathcal{A}_q = \begin{cases} \mathcal{P}_k((Q_p \setminus \{q\}) \times Q_s) & \text{if } q \in Q_p^\ell, \\ \mathcal{P}_k(Q_p \times (Q_s \setminus \{q\})) & \text{otherwise.} \end{cases}$$

A set of bridge arcs is valid if and only if it does not belong to any of $\mathcal{A}_q$. Hence, the number of valid sets of bridge arcs is

$$\left| \mathcal{P}_k(Q_p \times Q_s) \setminus \bigcup_{q \in Q^\ell} \mathcal{A}_q \right| = \binom{nm}{k} - \left| \bigcup_{q \in Q^\ell} \mathcal{A}_q \right|.$$

We can now apply the inclusion-exclusion principle to compute the cardinality of the union in that last term:

$$\left| \bigcup_{q \in Q^\ell} \mathcal{A}_q \right| = \sum_{\emptyset \neq X \subseteq Q^\ell} (-1)^{|X|+1} \left| \bigcap_{x \in X} \mathcal{A}_x \right|.$$

Observe that, for a non-empty subset X of Q^ℓ,

$$\bigcap_{x \in X} \mathcal{A}_x = \mathcal{P}_k((Q_p \setminus X) \times (Q_s \setminus X))$$

and the cardinality of that intersection is:

$$\left| \bigcap_{x \in X} \mathcal{A}_x \right| = \binom{(n-i)(m-j)}{k}$$

where $i = |X \cap Q_p|$ and $j = |X \cap Q_s|$. Hence, the cardinality of the intersection defined by a given X depends only on the number of leaves from Q_p and Q_s in X. We can continue the inclusion-exclusion computation using

$$\left| \bigcup_{q \in Q^\ell} \mathcal{A}_q \right| = \sum_{\substack{i=0 \\ i+j>0}}^{n_\ell} \sum_{j=0}^{m_\ell} (-1)^{i+j+1} \sum_{\substack{X \subseteq Q^\ell \\ |X \cap Q_p^\ell|=i \\ |X \cap Q_s^\ell|=j}} \left| \bigcap_{x \in X} \mathcal{A}_x \right| =$$

$$\sum_{\substack{i=0 \\ i+j>0}}^{n_\ell} \sum_{j=0}^{m_\ell} (-1)^{i+j+1} \binom{n_\ell}{i}\binom{m_\ell}{j}\binom{(n-i)(m-j)}{k},$$

the last derivation following from

$$\left| \left\{ X \subseteq Q^\ell \,\middle|\, \begin{array}{l} i = |X \cap Q_p|, \\ j = |X \cap Q_s| \end{array} \right\} \right| = \binom{n_\ell}{i}\binom{m_\ell}{j}.$$

We can now complete the computation of the number of valid bridge graphs:

$$\binom{mn}{k} - \sum_{\substack{i=0 \\ i+j>0}}^{n_\ell} \sum_{j=0}^{m_\ell} (-1)^{i+j+1} \binom{n_\ell}{i}\binom{m_\ell}{j}\binom{(n-i)(m-j)}{k}$$

$$= \sum_{i=0}^{n_\ell} \sum_{j=0}^{m_\ell} (-1)^{i+j} \binom{n_\ell}{i}\binom{m_\ell}{j}\binom{(n-i)(m-j)}{k}.$$

We are unaware of any asymptotic analysis of this summation or a way to closely estimate its logarithm. To compare it with our encoding, we use a loose upper bound of $\binom{nm}{k}$ and Stirling's approximation to get

$$\log\binom{nm}{k} \approx nm \log nm - k \log k$$

$$- (nm - k) \log(nm - k).$$

Overall, the number of possible lexicon graphs given n, m, k, n_ℓ, and m_ℓ can be found by multiplying the number of n (m) node, n_ℓ (m_ℓ) leaf trees

$$\frac{\binom{n-2}{n_\ell-1}\binom{n-1}{n_\ell-1}}{n_\ell}\frac{\binom{m-2}{m_\ell-1}\binom{m-1}{m_\ell-1}}{m_\ell}$$

by the number of valid bridge graphs.

Finally, we note that by choosing any out-tree as a prefix graph, any in-tree as a suffix graph, and any valid bridge graph, we obtain a graph that is a valid lexicon graph. A minimal lexicon transducer can be derived from that graph by labeling each non-bridge arc with a unique input label (and epsilon output) and each bridge arc with a unique input and output label.[2]

6 Compact Lexicon Encoding

6.1 Encoding the Graph

We encode the prefix, suffix, and bridge graphs separately. Encoding the prefix out-tree and suffix in-tree using LOUDS leads to a natural numbering of the nodes in Q: nodes in Q_p are numbered from 0 to $n-1$ in BFS order and nodes in Q_s from n to $|Q|-1$ in BFS order using the *reverse* of A_s, $\{(q', q) \mid (q, q') \in A_s\}$, with 0 and n denoting the roots of Q_p and Q_s, respectively. The LOUDS representation of the prefix and suffix graphs consists of two bitstrings, b_p of length $n+1$ and b_s of length $m+1$, using $2(n+m+1)$ bits combined.

We represent the bridge graph using a compact adjacency list approach. We use an array A_b indexed from 0 to $n-1$ holding the concatenation of the bridge-arc adjacency lists of the prefix nodes $a_b[0] \cdots a_b[n-1]$. We use a bitmap b_b with $n+k$ bits, one for each prefix node and bridge arc, to implement an index into A_b as follows. The bitmap b_b is encoded by concatenating $\mathbf{1^d 0}$ for each prefix node q, where[3]

$$\mathbf{d} = \left|\{q' \in Q_s \mid (q, q') \in A_b\}\right| = |a[q]|.$$

We retrieve the number of bridge arcs originating at a node $q \in Q_p$ by computing

$$N_b(q) = Select_0^{\mathsf{b}_b}(q) - Select_0^{\mathsf{b}_b}(q-1),$$

and the index in the dense array A_b to the position where the adjacency list for q starts by

$$I_b(q) = Rank_1^{\mathsf{b}_b}(Select_0^{\mathsf{b}_b}(q-1)).$$

The variable-length encoding mentioned in Section 3.2 is used to compress A_b in $k \log m$ bits, since the k entries in A_b can take at most m values.

It is possible to reduce the bridge arc adjacency list and multiplicity encoding to

$$\min(n + k \log m, m + k \log n) + k + 1$$

bits by noting that the bridge arcs travel unidirectionally from the prefix out-tree to suffix in-tree so we can represent them in either the forward or reverse direction, depending on which uses less space. However, we choose not to do this as it would incur an additional traversal time cost.

In total, our encoding uses

$$2(n + m + 1) + n + k + k\lceil \log m\rceil$$

bits to store the graph. We note that this is asymptotically worse than the best possible from Section 5. Nevertheless, in Section 7, we show empirically that it performs substantially better than the `CmpAdjList` format and is useful in practice.

6.2 Encoding the Labeling

We now encode the arc labels for each of the three component graphs using four ancillary arrays.

The arrays L_p and L_s store the input labels for each of the $n-1$ prefix arcs and $m-1$ suffix arcs. For $q \in Q_p \setminus \{0\}$, $\mathsf{L}_p[q-1]$ holds the input label for the unique incoming prefix arc to q. Likewise, for $q \in Q_s \setminus n$, $\mathsf{L}_s[q-n-1]$ holds the input label for the unique outgoing suffix arc to q. Recall that arcs in the prefix out-tree or suffix in-tree always have output label ϵ.

The arrays L_b^i and L_b^o store the input and output label for each of the k bridge arcs, using the same indexing as A_b: the bridge arc corresponding to the j-th entry in A_b, has input label $\mathsf{L}_b^i[j]$, output label $\mathsf{L}_b^o[j]$ and destination $\mathsf{A}_b[j]$.

Each of the arrays L_p, L_s, L_b^i, and L_b^o is compressed using the same variable-length encoding scheme as `CmpAdjList`. This allows us to directly compare the effect of encoding the graph separately from the arc label data. Encoding finality is simple – only one node, the root of the suffix in-tree, is final.

---

[2] Since a minimal transducer is labeled-pushed (Mohri, 2000), a bridge arc that is the only outgoing arc at a given node must be a multiarc that becomes 2 (or more) transitions with the same source and destination but with distinct input and output labels.

[3] In the case where multiarcs are present, which is extremely rare in practice, their multiplicities are encoded by using $\mathbf{d} = |\{e \in E \mid p[e] = q \wedge (q, n[e]) \in A_b\}|$.

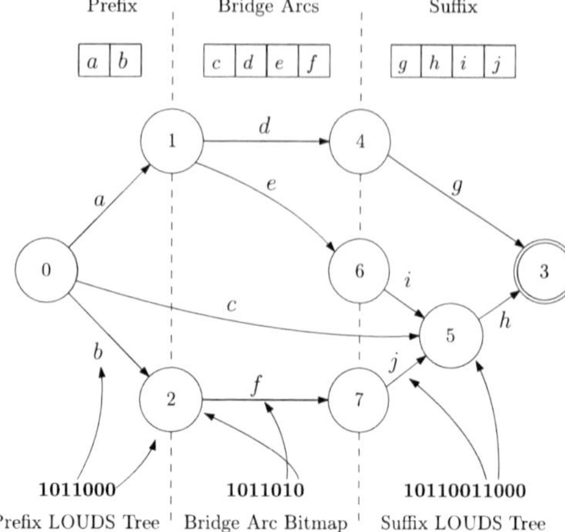

Figure 2: An example memory layout of our character-to-word lexicon transducer. The arrows demonstrate which nodes and arcs are encoded by which bits in the bridge arc and LOUDS tree bitmaps.

An overview of the memory layout of our encoding is given in Figure 2. We discuss the practical space savings in Section 7. All together, we call this representation the `LOUDS` lexicon format in our experiments.

6.3 Traversing the Transducer

We traverse the transducer by constructing the transitions originating at a given state q on demand.

When $q \in Q_p$, the set $E[q]$ of outgoing transitions in q can be decomposed as

$$E[q] = E_p[q] \cup E_b[q]$$

where $E_p[q]$ represents the transitions corresponding to prefix arcs and $E_b[q]$ the ones corresponding to bridge arcs. The first component can be computed from the prefix LOUDS tree by

$$E_p[q] = \bigcup_{q'=FirstChild^{b_p}(q)}^{LastChild^{b_p}(q)} \{(q, \mathrm{L}_p[q'-1], \epsilon, q')\}$$

and the second component can be recovered from the compact adjacency representation of the bridge graph as

$$E_b[q] = \bigcup_{j=I_b(q)}^{I_b(q)+N_b(q)-1} \{(q, \mathrm{L}_b^i[j], \mathrm{L}_b^o[j], \mathrm{A}_b[j])\}.$$

When $q \in Q_s \setminus \{n\}$, there is a single outgoing transition in q that can be computed from the suffix

LOUDS tree as

$$(q, \mathrm{L}_s[q - n - 1], \epsilon, n + Parent^{b_s}(q - n)).$$

Finally, when $q = n$, q is the root of the suffix out-tree. There are no outgoing transitions in q but q is final.

6.4 Closure

In practice, we often use a modified lexicon transducer representing its *closure* T^+, which accepts one or more words from the lexicon. For this, an ϵ-labeled transition from the final state to the initial state can be added to the canonical transducer.[4]

7 Experiments

We compare our lexicon encoding to the two other transducer representations in Section 3.2. We measure the memory size of the resulting machines as well as their runtimes on a decoding task. We prepare a set of lexicons using the most common $500k$ words in the Google keyboard (GBoard) Russian language model. We extract the $50k$, $100k$, ..., $500k$ most frequent words to create a total of 10 lexicons.

We first compare the space used by the `AdjList`, the `CmpAdjList`, and the `LOUDS` lexicon formats. The results are shown in Figure 3. The `LOUDS` lexicon outperforms the other two formats in every case. On the $500k$ word lexicon, it is 90.8% smaller than the `AdjList` format and 58.8% smaller than the `CmpAdjList` format.

Figure 4 shows the number of bits required to encode the Russian lexicons using our encoding and the upper bound of the optimal encoding. We use the parameters from Table 1 along with the upper bound described in Section 5 and the number of bits for our representation from Section 6. Our graph encoding nearly matches the upper bound approximation in all situations. For the $500k$ lexicon, the difference between our encoding and the upper bound is less than 2%. In contrast, the standard adjacency list format graph requires ten times more space across all test cases. We now consider the performance of our encoding on a benchmark decoding task consisting of on-the-fly composition with an n-gram language model followed by shortest path computation, which simulates a typical pipeline in applications. For the language model, we use a $244k$ state n-gram model trained

---

[4]In the keyboard example, this transition might instead be labeled with the space symbol on input.

# Words	50k	100k	150k	200k	250k	300k	350k	400k	450k	500k
Prefix Nodes	76207	148026	219494	292499	360911	429080	494766	558619	620429	670232
Suffix Nodes	7867	12548	15964	18187	20634	22454	23850	25059	25955	26977
Prefix Leaves	13402	26371	39300	52288	64894	77462	89881	102067	114228	124097
Suffix Leaves	1602	2560	3266	3732	4182	4512	4754	4989	5221	5421

Table 1: The size of the prefix out-tree and suffix in-tree as well as the number of leaves in each for all of the Russian lexicons. Note that the number of bridge arcs is the same as the number of words.

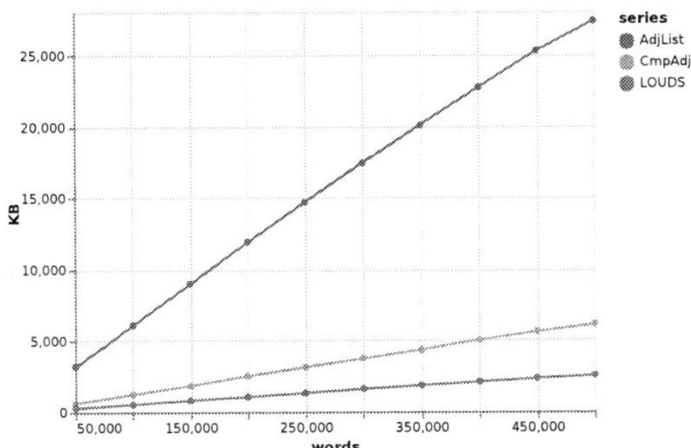

Figure 3: The amount of disk space required by each of the FST formats on our Russian language lexicon test set.

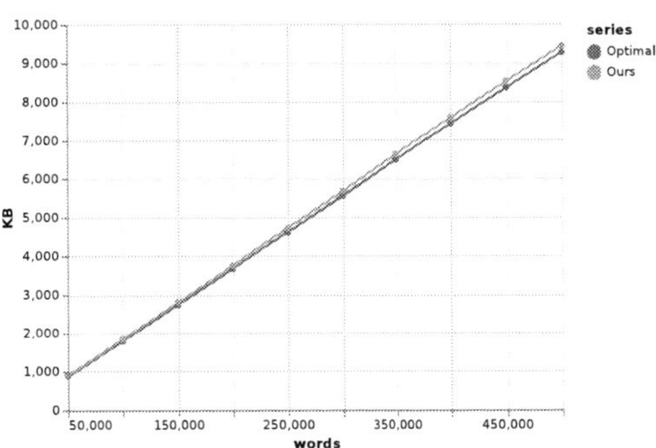

Figure 4: The theoretical number of bits required to encode the graphs of the Russian lexicons. We compare our encoding's exact space requirements with the upper bound as discussed in Section 5.

on Russian language data. Figure 5 shows the speed of this benchmark for each of the lexicon formats. At its worst, the LOUDS format was $\sim$ 20% slower than the CmpAdjList format. However, for the $500k$ word case, the difference between the LOUDS format and the CmpAdjList format was only 8.6%. In these experiments, no pre-processing (transition sorting, caching, etc.) of the transducers was done so that the raw access time for each format could be measured more accurately.

8 Conclusion

In this paper, we described a compact encoding for character-to-word lexicon transducers in canonical minimal form. The transducer graph is decomposed into simpler subgraphs, exploited in the encoding. The arc label data is encoded separately using variable-length compression schemes. We presented an information-theoretic lower bound for the graph encoding and compare the encoding to an asymptotic upper bound approximation.

Our encoding is compared to two alternative formats – adjacency lists with and without variable length compression. Ours is more than 58% smaller while being only $\sim$9% slower in tests on a decoding benchmark. Furthermore, this encod-

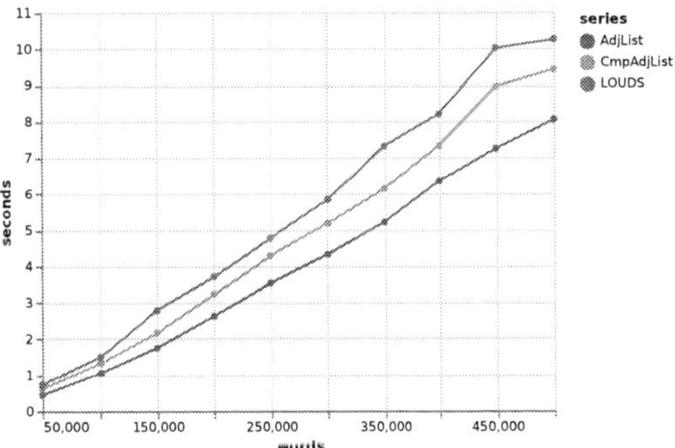

Figure 5: The time for the decoding task with a 244k state n-gram model. The average over 50 trials is given.

ing is very close to the information-theoretic upper bound on all the test cases.

References

Diamantino Caseiro and Isabel Trancoso. 2006. A specialized on-the-fly algorithm for lexicon and language model composition. *IEEE Trans. Audio, Speech & Language Processing*, 14(4):1281–1291.

Jan Daciuk. 2000. Experiments with automata compression. In *Implementation and Application of Automata, 5th International Conference, CIAA 2000,*

London, Ontario, Canada, July 24-25, 2000, Revised Papers, pages 105–112.

Jan Daciuk and Gertjan van Noord. 2001. Finite automata for compact representation of language models in NLP. In *Implementation and Application of Automata, 6th International Conference, CIAA 2001, Pretoria, South Africa, July 23-25, 2001, Revised Papers*, pages 65–73.

Jan Daciuk and Dawid Weiss. 2011. Smaller representation of finite state automata. In *Implementation and Application of Automata - 16th International Conference, CIAA 2011, Blois, France, July 13-16, 2011. Proceedings*, pages 118–129.

O'Neil Delpratt, Naila Rahman, and Rajeev Raman. 2006. Engineering the LOUDS succinct tree representation. In *Experimental Algorithms, 5th International Workshop, WEA 2006, Cala Galdana, Menorca, Spain, May 24-27, 2006, Proceedings*, pages 134–145.

Richard F. Geary, Rajeev Raman, and Venkatesh Raman. 2004. Succinct ordinal trees with level-ancestor queries. In *Proceedings of the Fifteenth Annual ACM-SIAM Symposium on Discrete Algorithms, SODA 2004, New Orleans, Louisiana, USA, January 11-14, 2004*, pages 1–10.

Takaaki Hori, Chiori Hori, and Yasuhiro Minami. 2004. Fast on-the-fly composition for weighted finite-state transducers in 1.8 million-word vocabulary continuous speech recognition. In *INTERSPEECH 2004 - ICSLP, 8th International Conference on Spoken Language Processing, Jeju Island, Korea, October 4-8, 2004*.

Guy Jacobson. 1989. Space-efficient static trees and graphs. In *30th Annual Symposium on Foundations of Computer Science, Research Triangle Park, North Carolina, USA, 30 October - 1 November 1989*, pages 549–554.

Dong Kyue Kim, Joong Chae Na, Ji Eun Kim, and Kunsoo Park. 2005. Efficient implementation of rank and select functions for succinct representation. In *Experimental and Efficient Algorithms, 4th International Workshop, WEA 2005, Santorini Island, Greece, May 10-13, 2005, Proceedings*, pages 315–327.

Mehryar Mohri. 2000. Minimization algorithms for sequential transducers. *Theoretical Computer Science*, 234:177–201.

Mehryar Mohri, Fernando Pereira, and Michael Riley. 2002. Weighted finite-state transducers in speech recognition. *Computer Speech & Language*, 16(1):69–88.

Mehryar Mohri, Fernando C. N. Pereira, and Michael Riley. 1996. Weighted automata in text and speech processing. In *ECAI 96, 12th European Conference on Artificial Intelligence, Workshop on Extended Finite State Models of Language*. John Wiley & Sons.

Mehryar Mohri, Michael Riley, and Ananda Theertha Suresh. 2015. Automata and graph compression. In *IEEE International Symposium on Information Theory, ISIT 2015, Hong Kong, China, June 14-19, 2015*, pages 2989–2993.

Tom Ouyang, David Rybach, Françoise Beaufays, and Michael Riley. 2017. Mobile keyboard input decoding with finite-state transducers. *CoRR*, abs/1704.03987.

Jeffrey Sorensen and Cyril Allauzen. 2011. Unary data structures for language models. In *INTERSPEECH 2011, 12th Annual Conference of the International Speech Communication Association, Florence, Italy, August 27-31, 2011*, pages 1425–1428.

Sebastiano Vigna. 2008. Broadword implementation of rank/select queries. In *Experimental Algorithms, 7th International Workshop, WEA 2008, Provincetown, MA, USA, May 30-June 1, 2008, Proceedings*, pages 154–168.

Taro Watanabe, Hajime Tsukada, and Hideki Isozaki. 2009. A succinct n-gram language model. In *ACL 2009, Proceedings of the 47th Annual Meeting of the Association for Computational Linguistics and the 4th International Joint Conference on Natural Language Processing of the AFNLP, 2-7 August 2009, Singapore, Short Papers*, pages 341–344.

Katsuhisa Yamanaka, Yota Otachi, and Shin-Ichi Nakano. 2012. Efficient enumeration of ordered trees with k leaves. *Theor. Comput. Sci.*, 442:22–27.

Marcin Zukowski, Sandor Heman, Niels Nes, and Peter Boncz. 2006. Super-scalar ram-cpu cache compression. In *Proceedings of the 22nd International Conference on Data Engineering, ICDE 2006*. IEEE.

MSO with tests and reducts

Tim Fernando and **David Woods** and **Carl Vogel**
School of Computer Science and Statistics
Trinity College Dublin, Ireland
`{tim.fernando,dwoods,carl.vogel}@tcd.ie`

Abstract

Tests added to Kleene algebra (by Kozen and others) are considered within Monadic Second Order logic over strings, where they are likened to statives in natural language. Reducts are formed over tests and non-tests alike, specifying what is observable. Notions of temporal granularity are based on observable change, under the assumption that a finite set bounds what is observable (with the possibility of stretching such bounds by moving to a larger finite set). String projections at different granularities are conjoined by superpositions that provide another variant of concatenation for Booleans.

1 Introduction

Regular languages can be studied declaratively through formulas of Monadic Second-Order logic over strings (MSO; e.g., Libkin, 2010) or through equations built with the constructs $+, \cdot, {}^{*}, 0, 1$ of a Kleene algebra (KA; e.g., Kozen, 1994). A KA with a subalgebra of *tests* forming a Boolean algebra is a KA with tests (KAT; e.g., Kozen, 1997). Tests are identified below with *statives* that serve as a basis for the approach to temporal semantics in linguistics initiated in Dowty (1979). This identification is justified by

(i) a guarded string interpretation of KAT (Kozen and Smith, 1996), in which tests form states, as conceived in Propositional Dynamic Logic (PDL, Fischer and Ladner, 1979), and

(ii) a notion of homogeneity associated (by Dowty and other linguists) with statives, and linked below to tests under a conception of time as observable change.

These two points are developed below in MSO using reducts. Kozen and Smith's definition of guarded strings is reformulated so that

(†) the MSO-sentence φ picking out guarded strings over actions Σ and tests B does *not* mention B (or their Boolean complements), asserting only that exactly one action occurs at every position except for the final one, where no action occurs.

Precisely what (†) means is taken up in section 2, with the help of reducts. Why (†) is significant becomes plain in section 3, where the reformulation is used to clarify the connection with tests and states in PDL.[1] A notion of temporal granularity based on observable change in MSO is built on projections that compress reducts. These projections are applied in section 4 to generalize interval networks from (Allen, 1983).

2 Guarded strings, MSO and reducts

For any finite set Σ, let Reg_Σ be the set of languages over the alphabet Σ accepted by finite automata. Then $\langle \text{Reg}_\Sigma, \cup, \cdot, {}^{*}, \emptyset, \epsilon \rangle$ is a KA — arguably, the Σ-canonical KA. For a KA with tests, we start in §2.1 with a finite set B of tests, and present the free Boolean algebra generated by B in terms of powersets 2^X of sets X. Strings over the alphabet $2^{B \cup \Sigma}$ are then used in §2.2 for an extension to a KA. This deviates tellingly from Kozen and Smith (1996)'s presentation of guarded strings over the alphabet $\Sigma \cup B \cup \overline{B}$ with Boolean complements $\overline{B}$ of B, reviewed in §2.3. The deviation is natural from the perspective of MSO, which is brought into the picture along with reducts in §2.4.

2.1 Finite free Boolean algebras

Given a set B, the set T_B of *Boolean terms over* B is the smallest set $\supseteq$-containing $B \cup \{0, 1\}$ that is closed under the binary connectives $+, \cdot$ and the unary connective c (for complements). Assuming

---

[1] We focus throughout on semantic intuitions relevant to our present purposes, leaving out details such as the equational axioms of KA or the precise language of PDL.

27

Proceedings of the 14th International Conference on Finite-State Methods and Natural Language Processing, pages 27–36
Dresden, Germany, September 23-25, 2019. ©2019 Association for Computational Linguistics

B is finite, the *free Boolean algebra generated by* B is

$$F(B) = \langle 2^{(2^B)}, \cup, \cap, \emptyset, 2^B, 2^B \setminus \cdot \rangle$$

(with addition $\cup$, multiplication $\cap$, and complement $2^B \setminus X$ of a subset X of 2^B). A *B-atom* is a subset q of B, and is used to interpret Boolean terms over B as follows

$$[\![b]\!]_B := \{q \subseteq B \mid b \in q\} \text{ for } b \in B$$
$$[\![0]\!]_B := \emptyset \qquad\qquad [\![1]\!]_B := 2^B$$

and for terms $t, t' \in T_B$,

$$[\![t + t']\!]_B := [\![t]\!]_B \cup [\![t']\!]_B$$
$$[\![t \cdot t']\!]_B := [\![t]\!]_B \cap [\![t']\!]_B$$
$$[\![c(t)]\!]_B := [\![1]\!]_B \setminus [\![t]\!]_B.$$

2.2 Guarded strings of sets

Next, given a set Σ disjoint from T_B, $\Sigma \cap T_B = \emptyset$, let the set $T_{\Sigma,B}$ of *(Σ, B)-terms* be the smallest set containing $\Sigma \cup T_B$ that is closed under the binary connectives $+, \cdot$ and the unary connective *. To extend the interpretation $[\![t]\!]_B$ of Boolean terms t over B to (Σ, B)-terms, we weaken the notion of a B-atom as follows. Let 2^B_Σ be the set

$$2^B_\Sigma := \{q \cup \{p\} \mid q \subseteq B \text{ and } p \in \Sigma\}$$

of sets obtained from a subset of B by adjoining an element of Σ. The set

$$\mathcal{G}^B_\Sigma := (2^B_\Sigma)^* 2^B \quad (\subset (2^{B \cup \Sigma})^+)$$

is generated by the rules

$$\frac{q \subseteq B}{q \in \mathcal{G}^B_\Sigma} \qquad \frac{q \subseteq B \quad p \in \Sigma \quad s \in \mathcal{G}^B_\Sigma}{(q \cup \{p\})s \in \mathcal{G}^B_\Sigma}$$

to produce strings

$$(q_1 \cup \{p_1\}) \cdots (q_n \cup \{p_n\})q_{n+1}$$

of length $n + 1$ (for $n \geq 0$), formed from $q_1 \cdots q_{n+1} \in (2^B)^{n+1}$ and $p_1 \cdots p_n \in \Sigma^n$. Let us call elements of $\mathcal{G}^B_\Sigma$ *(Σ, B)-guarded strings* (making B-atoms (Σ, B)-guarded strings of length 1). To interpret a (Σ, B)-term as a set of (Σ, B)-guarded strings, two bits of notation are handy.

(i) For any string s of length > 0, let α_s be the symbol that occurs first in s.

(ii) For any symbol q and language L, let $L[q]$ be the set of strings that, with q attached to the right, belong to L

$$L[q] := \{s \mid sq \in L\}.$$

Now, given sets L and L' of strings of length > 0, the *Σ-fused product of L and L'* is the set

$$L \bullet_\Sigma L' := \{ss' \mid s' \in L' \text{ and } s \in L[\alpha_{s'} \setminus \Sigma]\}$$

of strings ss' from $s' \in L'$ and s such that $sq \in L$ where q is $\alpha_{s'} \setminus \Sigma$. That is,

$$L \bullet_\Sigma L' = \{s \cdot_\Sigma s' \mid s \in L, \ s' \in L' \text{ and}$$
$$s \cdot_\Sigma s' \text{ is defined}\}$$

where $\cdot_\Sigma$ is a partial binary function on strings of length > 0 such that

$$sq \cdot_\Sigma \alpha s' \text{ is defined} \iff q = \alpha \setminus \Sigma$$
$$\implies sq \cdot_\Sigma \alpha s' = s\alpha s'.$$

Notice that if L and L' are both sets of B-atoms, then their Σ-fused product is just their intersection

$$L \bullet_\Sigma L' = L \cap L'.$$

Consequently, we can extend $[\![\cdot]\!]_B : T_B \to 2^{2^B}$ to an interpretation $[\![\cdot]\!]_{\Sigma,B} : T_{\Sigma,B} \to 2^{\mathcal{G}^B_\Sigma}$, setting

$$[\![t]\!]_{\Sigma,B} := [\![t]\!]_B \quad \text{for } t \in T_B$$
$$[\![p]\!]_{\Sigma,B} := \{(q \cup \{p\})q' \mid q, q' \subseteq B\} \quad \text{for } p \in \Sigma$$

and for all $t, t' \in T_{\Sigma,B}$,

$$[\![t + t']\!]_{\Sigma,B} := [\![t]\!]_{\Sigma,B} \cup [\![t']\!]_{\Sigma,B}$$
$$[\![t \cdot t']\!]_{\Sigma,B} := [\![t]\!]_{\Sigma,B} \bullet_\Sigma [\![t']\!]_{\Sigma,B}$$
$$[\![t^*]\!]_{\Sigma,B} := ([\![t]\!]_{\Sigma,B})^{\star\Sigma}$$

where the Σ-asterate $^{\star\Sigma}$ is the Σ-fused analog of Kleene star

$$L^{\star\Sigma} := \bigcup_{n \geq 0} L_n$$

with $L_0 := 2^B$ (the $\bullet_\Sigma$-identity for $2^{\mathcal{G}^B_\Sigma}$) and $L_{n+1} := L \bullet_\Sigma L_n$.

2.3 Strings in place of sets

Guarded strings in Kozen and Smith (1996) are conceived over an alphabet different from $2^{B \cup \Sigma}$ by fixing a string $b_1 \cdots b_n$ that enumerates

$$B = \{b_1, \ldots, b_n\}$$

	B-atom	alphabet	product
$\mathcal{G}_\Sigma^B$	$q \subseteq B$	$2^{\Sigma \cup B}$	$\bullet_\Sigma$
$\mathcal{G}_{\Sigma,B}$	$c_1 \cdots c_n \in \mathcal{A}_B$	$\Sigma \cup B \cup \overline{B}$	$\diamond_n$

Table 1: Guarded strings 2 ways, given Σ and B

without repetition (making n the cardinality of B). Each $b \in B$ is paired with a fresh test $\overline{b}$, relative to which a B-atom $q \subseteq B$ can be understood as n choices $c_1 \cdots c_n$ between b_i and $\overline{b_i}$, with

$$c_i := \begin{cases} b_i & \text{if } b_i \in q \\ \overline{b_i} & \text{otherwise.} \end{cases}$$

2^B is repackaged as the language

$$\mathcal{A}_B := (b_1 + \overline{b_1})(b_2 + \overline{b_2}) \cdots (b_n + \overline{b_n})$$

to turn $\mathcal{G}_\Sigma^B$ from §2.2 into the set

$$\mathcal{G}_{\Sigma,B} := (\mathcal{A}_B \Sigma)^* \mathcal{A}_B$$

of *guarded strings over Σ and B*, with alphabet

$$\Sigma \cup B \cup \overline{B} \quad \text{where} \quad \overline{B} := \{\overline{b_1}, \ldots, \overline{b_n}\}.$$

Every (Σ, B)-term t is then interpretable as a subset $[\![t]\!]$ of $\mathcal{G}_{\Sigma,B}$, with

$$[\![p]\!] = \{sps' \mid s, s' \in \mathcal{A}_B\} \qquad \text{for } p \in \Sigma$$

and for $b \in B$,

$$[\![b]\!] = \{s \in \mathcal{A}_B \mid s \in (B \cup \overline{B} - \{\overline{b}\})^+\}.$$

In place of the Σ-fused product $\bullet_\Sigma$, we have the *coalesced product* $\diamond_n$

$$L \diamond_n L' := \{s\hat{s}s' \mid s\hat{s} \in L, \ \hat{s}s' \in L'$$
$$\text{and length}(\hat{s}) = n\}.$$

Inasmuch as the two KATs over $2^{\mathcal{G}_\Sigma^B}$ and $2^{\mathcal{G}_{\Sigma,B}}$ are isomorphic, it is tempting to dismiss the difference recorded in Table 1 as cosmetic. Nonetheless, there are reasons for preferring 2^B over $\mathcal{A}_B$ from the perspective of MSO, a natural home for Boolean tests, with or without atoms.

2.4 MSO and reducts

Given a finite set A, an *MSO$_A$-model* is understood (in this paper) to be a structure

$$\langle [n], S_n, \{U_a\}_{a \in A} \rangle$$

over the set $[n] := \{1, \ldots, n\}$ of integers from 1 to n (for some positive integer n), with the successor relation

$$S_n := \{(i, i+1) \mid i \in [n-1]\}$$

on $[n]$, and for each $a \in A$, a subset U_a of $[n]$. We can identify $\langle [n], S_n, \{U_a\}_{a \in A} \rangle$ with the string $\alpha_1 \cdots \alpha_n$ over the alphabet 2^A given by

$$\alpha_i := \{a \in A \mid i \in U_a\} \qquad \text{for } i \in [n]$$

making U_a the set of positions where a occurs

$$U_a = \{i \in [n] \mid a \in \alpha_i\}.$$

To construe a string $a_1 \cdots a_n \in A^+$ as an MSO$_A$-model, we lift it to $\boxed{a_1} \cdots \boxed{a_n} \in (2^A)^+$, drawing boxes instead of curly braces $\{, \}$ for sets *qua* string symbols, as opposed to sets *qua* languages.[2] Given a string s over the alphabet 2^A and a subset A' of A, the A'-reduct of s, $\rho_{A'}(s)$, is s intersected componentwise with A'

$$\rho_{A'}(\alpha_1 \cdots \alpha_n) := (\alpha_1 \cap A') \cdots (\alpha_n \cap A')$$

(Fernando, 2016). To illustrate, for $A = \Sigma \cup B$, the Σ-reduct of a string

$$(q_1 \cup \boxed{p_1}) \cdots (q_n \cup \boxed{p_n}) q_{n+1}$$

in $\mathcal{G}_\Sigma^B$ is

$$\boxed{p_1} \cdots \boxed{p_n} \boxed{}.$$

Indeed, we can describe $\mathcal{G}_\Sigma^B$ by embedding Σ into $2^{\Sigma \cup B}$ via

$$\Sigma_\square := \{\boxed{p} \mid p \in \Sigma\}.$$

or by MSO$_A$-formulas built with unary predicate symbols P_a labeled by $a \in A$ and the binary predicate symbol S (for successors).

Proposition 1. *For any disjoint sets Σ and B,*

$$\mathcal{G}_\Sigma^B = \{s \in (2^{B \cup \Sigma})^+ \mid \rho_\Sigma(s) \in \Sigma_\square^* \square\}$$
$$= \{s \in (2^{B \cup \Sigma})^+ \mid s \models \forall x \chi_\Sigma(x)\}$$

where $\chi_\Sigma(x)$ is the MSO$_\Sigma(x)$-formula

$$\exists y(xSy) \equiv \bigvee_{a \in \Sigma} P_a(x)$$

(saying x is non-final iff some $a \in \Sigma$ occurs at x)

---

[2] Although conflating a string s with the singleton language $\{s\}$ is usually harmless, it is dangerous to confuse, for instance, the empty language $\emptyset$ with the string $\square$ (of length 1), or the language of two strings $\{a, a'\}$ with the single string $\boxed{a, a'}$.

conjoined with the $MSO_\Sigma(x)$-formula

$$\neg \bigvee_{a \in \Sigma} \left(P_a(x) \wedge \bigvee_{a' \in \Sigma \setminus \{a\}} P_{a'}(x) \right)$$

(saying no two symbols from Σ occur at x).

Note that $\forall x\, \chi_\Sigma(x)$ is an MSO_Σ-sentence stating

($\dagger$) exactly one symbol from Σ occurs at every string position except for the last position, where no symbol from Σ occurs.

Inasmuch as ($\dagger$) describes a very particular encoding of guarded strings (applicable to $\mathcal{G}_\Sigma^B$ but not to $\mathcal{G}_{\Sigma,B}$), it is natural to ask: can we motivate ($\dagger$) without resorting to details of encoding? We will argue in section 3 that we can, observing for now that $\chi_\Sigma(x)$ makes no mention of B (belonging, as it does, to MSO_Σ).

The price for working with

$$\langle \mathcal{G}_\Sigma^B, \cup, \bullet_\Sigma, \emptyset, 2^B, 2^B \setminus \cdot \rangle$$

as opposed to Kozen and Smith (1996)'s KAT

$$\langle \mathcal{G}_{\Sigma,B}, \cup, \diamond_n, \emptyset, \mathcal{A}_B, \mathcal{A}_B \setminus \cdot \rangle$$

is a complication in the alphabet of strings interpreting MSO_A from A to 2^A. But since MSO_A-models are already strings over 2^A, that price has already been paid. Rather it is the step from $\mathcal{G}_\Sigma^B$ to $\mathcal{G}_{\Sigma,B}$ that is costly, complicating the label set A with a set $\overline{B}$ of labels for complements of B. It is telling that a string in $\mathcal{G}_{\Sigma,B}$ satisfies the $MSO_{\{b,\overline{b}\}}$-biconditionals

$$P_{\overline{b}}(x) \equiv \neg P_b(x)$$

only at positions x where b or $\overline{b}$ occurs. By contrast, every string in $\mathcal{G}_\Sigma^B$ can be expanded to a $MSO_{\Sigma \cup B \cup \overline{B}}$-model satisfying

$$\forall x\, (P_{\overline{b}}(x) \equiv \neg P_b(x)) \quad \text{for every } b \in B$$

(not that $\overline{b}$ is needed to interpret $T_{\Sigma,B}$ in $2^{\mathcal{G}_\Sigma^B}$).

A crude measure of the complexity of a regular language $L \subseteq (2^A)^+$ is given by

Proposition 2. *For any finite set A and regular language $L \subseteq (2^A)^+$, there is a smallest subset A' of A such that for some $MSO_{A'}$-formula φ,*

$$L = \{s \in (2^A)^+ \mid s \models \varphi\}.$$

Proposition 2 follows from

($\ddagger$) for all strings $s \in (2^A)^+$, subsets A' of A and $MSO_{A'}$-formulas φ,

$$s \models \varphi \iff \rho_{A'}(s) \models \varphi$$

and the fact that if A'' is another subset of A,

$$\rho_{A''}(\rho_{A'}(s)) = \rho_{A' \cap A''}(s).$$

Provable by induction on φ, ($\ddagger$) is an instance of the *satisfaction condition* characteristic of *institutions* (Goguen and Burstall, 1992), to which we shall return in §3.3 below.

If the least set A' that Proposition 2 associates with L is called the *grain of L*, then $\mathcal{G}_\Sigma^B$ has grain Σ (by Proposition 1 and a moment's reflection). Not so the regular language $\mathcal{G}_{\Sigma,B}$, whose image under the map

$$a_1 \cdots a_n \;\mapsto\; \boxed{a_1} \cdots \boxed{a_n}$$

has grain $\Sigma \cup B \cup \overline{B}$. Proposition 1 consigns B to the background (using MSO's propositional connectives to interpret the Boolean structure of a KAT), drawing all attention to Σ. Indeed, as conceived in PDL, tests belong in Σ — or so we argue in the next section (*pace* Kozen)

The remainder of this section fleshes out, for $A = \Sigma \cup B \cup \overline{B}$, an MSO_A-definition ψ_Σ^B of $\mathcal{G}_{\Sigma,B}$

$$\mathcal{G}_{\Sigma,B} \;=\; \{s \in A^+ \mid s \models \psi_\Sigma^B\}$$

and is best skipped by readers for whom $\chi_\Sigma(x)$ is ugly enough. We let ψ_Σ^B be $\forall x\, \psi_{\Sigma,B}(x)$ for $\psi_{\Sigma,B}(x)$ given with the help of some abbreviations. For $A' \subseteq A$, let $\mathrm{one}_{A'}(x)$ be the MSO disjunction

$$\mathrm{one}_{A'}(x) \;:=\; \bigvee_{a \in A'} P_a(x)$$

saying some symbol from A' occurs in position x, and let $\mathrm{atm}_B(x_1 \ldots x_n)$ abbreviate

$$\bigwedge_{1 \leq i < n} x_i S x_{i+1} \wedge \bigwedge_{1 \leq i \leq n} \mathrm{one}_{\{b_i, \overline{b_i}\}}(x_i)$$

putting a string from $\mathcal{A}_B$ in $x_1 \ldots x_n$. Now, $\psi_{\Sigma,B}(x)$ is the conjunction of (1), (2) and (3) below, where (1) ensures $b_i + \overline{b_i}$ is followed by $b_{i+1} + \overline{b_{i+1}}$ for i from 1 to $n-1$

$$\bigwedge_{i=1}^{n-1} (\mathrm{one}_{\{b_i, \overline{b_i}\}}(x) \supset \exists y (x S y \wedge$$

$$\mathrm{one}_{\{b_{i+1}, \overline{b_{i+1}}\}}(y))) \quad (1)$$

KAT	PDL
Boolean in B	formula φ
action in Σ	program (e.g., test $\varphi?$)
B-atom $\subseteq B$	state $\in Q$
guarded string	input/output pair $\in Q \times Q$

Table 2: KAT vs PDL

while (2) says $b_n + \overline{b_n}$ can only be followed by a symbol from Σ

$$\forall y(\mathrm{one}_{\{b_n, \overline{b_n}\}}(x) \wedge xSy \supset \mathrm{one}_\Sigma(y)) \qquad (2)$$

(allowing for the case where x is the last position of the string), and (3) puts atoms before and after x whenever a symbol from Σ occurs at x

$$\mathrm{one}_\Sigma(x) \supset (\mathrm{before}_B(x) \wedge \mathrm{after}_B(x)) \qquad (3)$$

where $\mathrm{before}_B(x)$ abbreviates

$$\exists x_1 \cdots \exists x_n \, (x_n Sx \wedge \mathrm{atm}_B(x_1 \ldots x_n))$$

and $\mathrm{after}_B(x)$ abbreviates

$$\exists x_1 \cdots \exists x_n \, (xSx_1 \wedge \mathrm{atm}_B(x_1 \ldots x_n)).$$

3 Tests and observable change

A *test* in PDL is a program $\varphi?$ built from a proposition φ, where, given a set Q of states,

(i) φ is interpreted as the set $[\![\varphi]\!] \subseteq Q$ of states *satisfying* φ, and

(ii) a program p is interpreted as a binary relation $[\![p]\!]$ on Q consisting of pairs (q, q') such that

$$\text{on input } q, p \text{ can output } q'$$

(iii) $\varphi?$ is a side-effect free test of φ that aborts on states that do not satisfy ψ

$$[\![\varphi?]\!] := \{(q, q) \mid q \in [\![\varphi]\!]\}.$$

A cursory comparison of PDL with KAT, summarised in Table 2, suggests KAT Booleans form PDL states (or B-atoms), raising the question:

> where is the KAT counterpart of $\varphi?$ in Σ, which is assumed disjoint from the set B of Booleans?

The present section fills this gap by introducing for every $b \in B$, a test $?b$ that is interpreted the way an action p in Σ is in KAT, albeit with more care than the "anything-goes" clause

$$[\![p]\!]_{\Sigma, B} := \{(q \cup \boxed{p})q' \mid q, q' \subseteq B\}$$

that accepts any input/output pair q, q'. To regulate the changes effected by an action in Σ, we introduce a labeled transition relation

$$E \subseteq 2^B \times \Sigma \times 2^B$$

and interpret each $p \in \Sigma$ as the subset

$$\{(q \cup \boxed{p})q' \mid E(q, p, q')\}$$

of $\mathcal{G}_\Sigma^B$ (writing $E(q, p, q')$ and $(q, p, q') \in E$ interchangably). The "anything-goes" interpretation is the special case

$$E = 2^B \times \Sigma \times 2^B.$$

But to capture the meaning of a test $?b$ in the manner PDL does for $\varphi?$, we require that

$$E(q, ?b, q') \implies b \in q \text{ and } q = q'$$

for all $q, q' \subseteq B$. To align the interpretation closer to the input/output semantics of PDL programs, we will interpret $[\![?b]\!]$ as

$$\{(q \cup \boxed{?b})q \mid q \subseteq B \text{ and } b \in q\}$$

and form B-reducts (removing actions $p \in \Sigma$ buried in guarded strings) before compressing them (according to bc from §3.1).

3.1 Regulated programs including tests

Given sets Σ and B, and for every $b \in B$, a label $?b \notin \Sigma \cup B$ such that

$$?b = ?b' \text{ only if } b = b',$$

let

$$\Sigma[B] := \Sigma \cup \{?b \mid b \in B\}.$$

We can then extend any set $E \subseteq 2^B \times \Sigma \times 2^B$ to

$$E_B := E \cup \{(q, ?b, q) \mid q \subseteq B \text{ and } b \in q\}$$

and pick out the subset $\mathcal{G}_{|E}$ (pronounced "G restricted by E") of $\mathcal{G}_B^{\Sigma[B]}$ generated by

$$\frac{q \subseteq B}{q \in \mathcal{G}_{|E}} \qquad \frac{sq \in \mathcal{G}_{|E} \quad E_B(q, p, q')}{s(q \cup \boxed{p})q' \in \mathcal{G}_{|E}}.$$

to interpret a term t from $T_{\Sigma[B], B}$ as a subset $[\![t]\!]_{|E}$ of $\mathcal{G}_{|E}$ by suitable adjustments to $[\![\cdot]\!]_{\Sigma, B}$. In particular, for $b \in B$,

$$[\![b]\!]_{|E} = \{q \mid q \subseteq B \text{ and } b \in B\}$$

and for $p \in \Sigma[B]$,

$$[\![p]\!]_{|E} \;=\; \{(q \cup \{p\})q' \mid q, q' \subseteq B \text{ and } \\ E_B(q, p, q')\}$$

and for $\bullet_\Sigma$ as defined in §2.2,

$$[\![t \cdot t']\!]_{|E} \;=\; [\![t]\!]_{|E} \bullet_\Sigma [\![t']\!]_{|E}.$$

Now, whereas

$$L \bullet_\Sigma L' = L \cap L' \text{ for } L, L' \subseteq 2^B,$$

the interpretation $[\![?b]\!]_{|E}$ of a test $?b$ is not a subset of 2^B unless it is $\emptyset$.

To relate $[\![?b]\!]_{|E}$ back to $[\![b]\!]_{|E}$, a few definitions are helpful. Let us call a string $\alpha_1 \cdots \alpha_n$ *stutterless* if $\alpha_i \neq \alpha_{i+1}$ for all $i \in [n-1]$. The *block compression* $bc(s)$ *of* a string $s = \alpha_1 \cdots \alpha_n$ deletes from s every α_i such that $\alpha_i = \alpha_{i+1}$

$$bc(s) \;:=\; s \text{ if length}(s) < 2$$
$$bc(\alpha \alpha' s) \;:=\; \begin{cases} bc(\alpha' s) & \text{if } \alpha = \alpha' \\ \alpha \, bc(\alpha' s) & \text{otherwise.} \end{cases}$$

Clearly, $bc(s)$ is stutterless and

$$s \text{ is stutterless} \iff s = bc(s).$$

Moreover, if $?b$ were removed from the strings in $[\![?b]\!]_{|E}$, then we would be left with strings qq such that $b \in q$, to which we can apply bc to get $[\![b]\!]_{|E}$. We systematise the removal of elements of $\Sigma[B]$ from strings in $[\![t]\!]_{|E}$ next, aligning our semantics with PDL's.

3.2 Observable change

For terms $t \in T_{\Sigma[B],B}$ and subsets C of $\Sigma[B] \cup B$, let us apply block compression bc to the C-reducts of strings in $[\![t]\!]_{|E}$ for

$$[t]_{E,C} \;:=\; \{bc(\rho_C(s)) \mid s \in [\![t]\!]_{|E}\}$$

and observe that for all $b \in B$,

$$[?b]_{E,B} \;=\; [b]_{E,B} \;=\; [\![b]\!]_{|E}.$$

More generally, let us define a translation

$$\theta : T_{\Sigma[B],B} \to T_{\Sigma,B}$$

translating tests $?b$ back to b

$$\theta(?b) \;:=\; b \qquad \text{for } b \in B$$

otherwise leaving t as is

$$\theta(a) := a \qquad \text{for } a \in \Sigma \cup B$$
$$\theta(t + t') := \theta(t) + \theta(t') \qquad \theta(t^*) := \theta(t)^*$$
$$\theta(t \cdot t') := \theta(t) \cdot \theta(t') \qquad \theta(c(t)) := c(\theta(t)).$$

Also, let us say Σ is *E-active* if for every $p \in \Sigma$,

$$E(q, p, q') \implies q \neq q'$$

for all $q, q' \subseteq B$ (requiring that states change under p).

Proposition 3. *For all* $t \in T_{\Sigma[B],B}$,

$$[t]_{E,B} \;=\; [\theta(t)]_{E,B}$$

and assuming Σ *is E-active,*

$$[\theta(t)]_{E,B} \;=\; \{\rho_B(s) \mid s \in [\![\theta(t)]\!]_{|E}\}.$$

The two parts of Proposition 3 can be sharpened at the cost of complicating the notation.

Part 1 For all $t \in T_{\Sigma[B],B}$,

$$[t]_{E,C} = [\theta(t)]_{E,C}$$

for any set C disjoint from $\Sigma[B]$.

Given $p \in \Sigma$, let us say p is (E, C)-*observable* if

$$E(q, p, q') \implies q \cap C \neq q' \cap C$$

for all $q, q' \subseteq B$ (so that p is C-observably E-active).

Part 2 For all $t \in T_{\Sigma,B}$,

$$[t]_{E,C} = \{\rho_C(s) \mid s \in [\![t]\!]_{|E}\}$$

assuming that every $p \in \Sigma$ from which t is formed is (E, C)-observable.

3.3 Actions for a specific Boolean

The condition that p is (E, C)-observable can be formulated in $\text{MSO}_{C \cup \{p\}}$ as

$$\forall x \forall y \, ((P_p(x) \wedge xSy) \supset \text{diff}_C(x, y)) \qquad (4)$$

where $\text{diff}_C(x, y)$ abbreviates the MSO-formula

$$\text{diff}_C(x, y) \;:=\; \bigvee_{b \in C} \neg(P_b(x) \equiv P_b(y))$$

saying x and y can be separated by a unary predicate with label from C. Dropping the action p from (4) results in the requirement that every temporal step S change C

$$\forall x \forall y \, (xSy \supset \text{diff}_C(x, y)) \qquad (\text{ntc}_C)$$

designated (ntc_C) for the slogan

no time without change$_C$.

This slogan is behind the function bc_C that maps a string s to the block compression of its C-reduct

$$bc_C(s) := bc(\rho_C(s))$$

(turning $[\![t]\!]_{|E}$ to $[\![t]\!]_{E,C}$ in §3.2).

Proposition 4. *For any $C \subseteq A$ and $s \in (2^A)^*$,*

$$s \models (ntc_C) \iff bc_C(s) = s$$

and

$$bc_C(bc_C(s)) = bc_C(s).$$

To understand the importance of the subscript C, recall that MSO satisfaction $\models$ has the property
(‡) for all strings $s \in (2^A)^+$, subsets C of A and MSO$_C$-sentences φ,

$$s \models \varphi \iff \rho_C(s) \models \varphi.$$

(‡) brings out a fundamental limitation of an MSO$_C$-sentence φ, its insensitivity to differences between strings with the same C-reduct.

The significance of the subscript C is easy to overlook when describing $\mathcal{G}_{|E}$ in MSO. Consider from Proposition 1, the $\chi_\Sigma(x)$ conjunct

$$\neg two_\Sigma(x) := \neg \bigvee_{a \in \Sigma} \left(P_a(x) \wedge \bigvee_{a' \in \Sigma \setminus \{a\}} P_{a'}(x) \right)$$

banning two programs in Σ from occurring simultaneously at x. The problem with running $p \in \Sigma$ simultaneously with $?b \notin \Sigma$ at x is that the state transitions they describe under E_B may clash. Indeed, programs in PDL and more generally, Dynamic Logic (Harel et al., 2000) are interpreted as executing in isolation; for instance, the PDL test $\varphi?$ ensures the input state does not change, and a random assignment $x :=?$ changes at most the value of x. In both cases, any change from a program running concurrently is ruled out. Put another way, $\chi_\Sigma(x)$'s conjunct $\neg two_\Sigma(x)$ expresses the assumption that each program in Σ is to be understood as covering all programs that might run at x.

By contrast, actions described in everyday speech are invariably partial in that
(i) their effects are bounded, and
(ii) they never occur in isolation.

Keeping (i) and (ii) in mind, and zeroing in on a specific Boolean $b \in B$, let us add labels $l(b)$ and $r(b)$ to Σ for actions that mark the *left* and *right* borders of b as follows. Let $\Delta_b^l(x)$ be the MSO$_{\{b\}}(x)$-formula

$$\Delta_b^l(x) := (\exists y)(xSy \wedge P_b(y)) \wedge \neg P_b(x)$$

putting x just before b becomes true, and let $\Delta_b^r(x)$ be the MSO$_{\{b\}}(x)$-formula

$$\Delta_b^r(x) := P_b(x) \wedge \neg(\exists y)(xSy \wedge P_b(y))$$

putting x at b's right border. We then use $\Delta_b^l(x)$ to define $P_{l(b)}$

$$\forall x \, (P_{l(b)}(x) \equiv \Delta_b^l(x)) \qquad (l_b)$$

and $\Delta_v^r(x)$ for $P_{r(v)}$

$$\forall x \, (P_{r(b)}(x) \equiv \Delta_b^r(x)) \qquad (r_b)$$

(Fernando, 2019). Now, replacing diff$_C(x,y)$ in (ntc$_C$) by

$$\text{border}_C(x) := \bigvee_{b \in C} (P_{l(b)}(x) \vee P_{r(b)}(x))$$

yields: no time without *borders$_C$*

$$\forall x \forall y \, (xSy \supset \text{border}_C(x)). \qquad (ntb_C)$$

More precisely,

$$\left(\bigwedge_{b \in C} (l_b) \wedge (r_b) \right) \supset ((ntc_C) \equiv (ntb_C))$$

since for every $b \in C$,

$$((l_b) \wedge (r_b) \wedge xSy) \supset$$
$$(P_b(x) \equiv P_b(y)) \equiv (P_{l(b)}(x) \vee P_{r(b)}(x))$$

suppressing $\forall x \forall y$ to simplify the notation. Returning now to points (i) and (ii) above, notice that under (l_b) and (r_b),
(i) the effects of $l(b)$ and $r(b)$ are confined to b and although

$$((l_b) \wedge (r_b)) \supset \neg \exists x (P_{l(b)}(x) \wedge P_{r(b)}(x))$$

means $l(b)$ cannot occur with $r(b)$,
(ii) $l(b)$ can occur with $l(b')$ or $r(b')$ for $b' \neq b$. [3]
Complex actions can be built from a finite set of b-specific actions $l(b)$ and $r(b)$, provided we stay away from the $\mathcal{G}_\Sigma^B$ postulate $\neg two_\Sigma(x)$, which effectively pretends actions are indivisible atoms.

---

[3] Approximating $l(b)$ by the Dynamic Logic program

$$(b = \text{false})?; b :=?; (b = \text{true})?$$

overshoots badly, having unbounded effects that go beyond $l(b)$ in banning any changes to b' different from b.

4 Projections and superpositions

Having re-interpreted concatenation $\cdot$ as $\bullet_\Sigma$ and $\diamond_n$ in section 2 so that its restriction to tests is Boolean conjunction, we present in this section yet another notion of conjunction for combining descriptions of change at varying granularities. We start with the descriptions in §4.1, computing their conjunctions in §4.2.

4.1 Some star-free descriptions

Given a subset C of some fixed set A (determining a fragment MSO_A) and a string s of subsets of C, let us agree the pair (C, s) describes the set of stutterless strings over the alphabet 2^A that $\textit{lc}_C$ maps to s.[4] That is, if we gather together all stutterless strings over 2^A in

$$\mathcal{L}_A := \{ \textit{lc}(s) \mid s \in (2^A)^* \}$$

then

$$[\![(C, s)]\!]_A := \{ s' \in \mathcal{L}_A \mid \textit{lc}_C(s') = s \}.$$

To illustrate, for

$$s_1 = \boxed{\ }\boxed{1}\boxed{\ },$$

$[\![(\{1\}, s_1)]\!]_{\{1,2\}}$ consists of s_1, all strings from

$$\boxed{\ }(\boxed{2}\,)^{*}\boxed{1}\boxed{\ }$$

and many more, including $\boxed{2 \mid 2{,}1 \mid \ \mid 2}$. In general, for $s \in \mathcal{L}_A$, $[\![(A, s)]\!]_A$ is $\{s\}$. Otherwise, if C is a proper subset of A, then $[\![(C, s)]\!]_A$ is infinite. In either case, $[\![(C, s)]\!]_A$ is first-order definable with the transitive closure $<$ of S. That is, $[\![(C, s)]\!]_A$ is star-free.

Next, we interpret a finite subset $\mathcal{C}$ of $2^A \times \mathcal{L}_A$ as the intersection

$$[\![\mathcal{C}]\!]_A = \bigcap_{(C,s)\in\mathcal{C}} [\![(C, s)]\!]_A$$

of the interpretations of pairs (C, s) in $\mathcal{C}$. Notice $[\![\mathcal{C}]\!]_A$ is also star-free. Continuing the example above, if

$$\mathcal{C}_2 = \{(\{1\}, s_1), (\{2\}, s_2)\}$$

where $s_i = \boxed{\ }\boxed{i}\boxed{\ }$ then $[\![\mathcal{C}_2]\!]_{\{1,2\}}$ consists of exactly 13 strings, one for each of the interval relations from Allen (1983), such as

$$\boxed{\ \mid 2 \mid 1{,}2 \mid 2 \mid\ }\quad \text{depicting}\quad 1\ \textit{during}\ 2$$

---

[4] The restriction here to stutterless strings is motivated by the Aristotelian dictum, *no time without change*, a C-relativization of which is enforced by $\textit{lc}_C$ (Proposition 4).

(e.g., Fernando, 2016). Generalizing from 2 intervals to any integer $n \geq 2$, we can extend the set

$$\{(\{i\}, s_i) \mid i \in [n]\}$$

to a partial function $\mathcal{C}$ from $2^{[n]}$ to $\mathcal{L}_{[n]}$, defined on certain pairs $\{i, j\}$ which $\mathcal{C}$ maps to a string $\mathcal{C}(\{i, j\})$ depicting an Allen relation between i and j. The result is an interval network with node set $[n]$ and edge set

$$\{C \in domain(\mathcal{C}) \mid |C| = 2\},$$

each C in which is labeled by the Allen relation depicted by $\mathcal{C}(C)$. We can label the edge C by a set $L \subseteq \mathcal{L}_C$ if we loosen (C, s) to the pair (C, L), interpreted as the inverse image of L under $\textit{lc}_C$ restricted to $\mathcal{L}_A$

$$\begin{aligned}
[\![(C, L)]\!]_A &:= \{ s \in \mathcal{L}_A \mid \textit{lc}_C(s) \in L \} \\
&= \bigcup_{s \in L} [\![(C, s)]\!]_A.
\end{aligned}$$

For $A \subseteq A'$,

$$\begin{aligned}
[\![\mathcal{C}]\!]_{A'} &= \{ s \in \mathcal{L}_{A'} \mid \textit{lc}_A(s) \in [\![\mathcal{C}]\!]_A \} \\
&= [\![(A, [\![\mathcal{C}]\!]_A)]\!]_{A'}
\end{aligned}$$

since

$$\textit{lc}_C(s) = \textit{lc}_C(\textit{lc}_{C'}(s)) \quad \text{when } C \subseteq C' \subseteq A.$$

Thus, we can calculate $[\![\mathcal{C}]\!]_A$ by concentrating on $\bigcup domain([\![\mathcal{C}]\!])$ before attending to the full set A

$$[\![\mathcal{C}]\!]_A = [\![(\hat{C}, [\![\mathcal{C}]\!]_{\hat{C}})]\!]_A \quad \text{for } \hat{C} := \bigcup domain(\mathcal{C}).$$

As §4.2 makes clear, $[\![\mathcal{C}]\!]_{\hat{C}}$ is always finite (unlike $[\![\mathcal{C}]\!]_A \supseteq [\![\mathcal{C}]\!]_{\hat{C}}$).

4.2 Conjunction as superposition

We now define, for any subsets C and C' of A, a binary operation $\&_{C,C'}$ on languages such that for all $s \in \mathcal{L}_C$ and $s' \in \mathcal{L}_{C'}$,

$$[\![\{(C, s), (C', s')\}]\!]_{C\cup C'} = \{s\}\,\&_{C,C'}\,\{s'\}$$

and more generally, for all $L \subseteq \mathcal{L}_C$ and $L' \subseteq \mathcal{L}_{C'}$,

$$L\,\&_{C,C'}\,L' = [\![(C, L)]\!]_{C\cup C'} \cap [\![(C', L')]\!]_{C\cup C'}.$$

As a first stab, observe that if $\&_\circ$ forms the componentwise union of strings of the same length

$$\alpha_1 \cdots \alpha_n \,\&_\circ\, \alpha_1' \cdots \alpha_n' := (\alpha_1 \cup \alpha_1') \cdots (\alpha_n \cup \alpha_n')$$

then

$$\rho_{C \cup C'}(s) \;=\; \rho_C(s) \;\&_\circ\; \rho_{C'}(s).$$

It will be useful to introduce rules (s0) and (s1)

$$\frac{}{\&(\epsilon, \epsilon, \epsilon)} \;(\text{s0}) \qquad \frac{\&(s, s', \hat{s})}{\&(\alpha s, \alpha' s, (\alpha \cup \alpha')\hat{s})} \;(\text{s1})$$

that together generate $\&_\circ$ as the set of triples $(s, s', \hat{s})$ such that

$$\&(s, s', \hat{s}) \text{ is derivable from (s0) and (s1)}.$$

To factor in $\textit{bc}$ for $\textit{bc}_C$, we add the two rules (b1) and (b2)

$$\frac{\&(\alpha s, s', \hat{s})}{\&(\alpha s, \alpha' s', (\alpha \cup \alpha')\hat{s})} \;(\text{b1})$$

$$\frac{\&(s, \alpha' s', \hat{s})}{\&(\alpha s, \alpha' s', (\alpha \cup \alpha')\hat{s})} \;(\text{b2})$$

so that, for example, the language

$$[\!(\{1\}, \boxed{1}\,)]\!]_{\{1,2\}} \;\cap\; [\!(\{2\}, \boxed{2}\,)]\!]_{\{1,2\}}$$

of Allen relations between 1 and 2 (from §4.1) is the set of strings s such that

$$\&(\boxed{1}, \boxed{2}, s)$$

is derivable from (s0), (s1), (b1) and (b2). The intersection $[\![(C, s)]\!]_{C \cup C'} \cap [\![(C', s')]\!]_{C \cup C'}$ becomes trickier when $C \cap C' \neq \emptyset$ (as with the transitivity table in Allen (1983)). Accordingly, we refine the rules (s1), (b1) and (b2), adding the side conditions

$$\alpha \cap C' \subseteq \alpha' \quad \text{and} \quad \alpha' \cap C \subseteq \alpha$$

to these rules for

$$\frac{\&(s, s', \hat{s}) \quad \alpha \cap C' \subseteq \alpha' \quad \alpha' \cap C \subseteq \alpha}{\&(\alpha s, \alpha' s, (\alpha \cup \alpha')\hat{s})} \;(\text{s1})_{C,C'}$$

and similarly for $(\text{b1})_{C,C'}$ and $(\text{b2})_{C,C'}$. Now, let $\&_{C'}^{C}(s, s', \hat{s})$ abbreviate:

$$\&(s, s', \hat{s}) \text{ is derivable from (s0)},$$
$$(\text{s1})_{C,C'}, (\text{b1})_{C,C'} \text{ and } (\text{b2})_{C,C'}.$$

Then for all $s \in \mathcal{L}_C$, $s' \in \mathcal{L}_{C'}$ and $\hat{s} \in \mathcal{L}_{C \cup C'}$,

$$\&_{C'}^{C}(s, s', \hat{s}) \iff \hat{s} \in [\![\{(C, s), (C', s')\}]\!]_{C \cup C'}$$

and indeed, the definition we require is

$$L \;\&_{C,C'}\; L' := \{\hat{s} \in \mathcal{L}_{C \cup C'} \mid (\exists s \in L)(\exists s' \in L')$$
$$\&_{C'}^{C}(s, s', \hat{s})\}$$

(Woods and Fernando, 2018).

4.3 More projections

Recalling the KAT dichotomy between Booleans in B and actions in Σ (paralleling that between formulas and programs in Dynamic Logic[5]) it should be noted that the sets C and C' have been construed throughout to be subsets of B. The MSO-formulas $\Delta_b^l(x)$ and $\Delta_b^r(x)$ introducing the actions $l(b)$ and $r(b)$ in §3.3 define a border translation from B to Σ under which $\textit{bc}$ becomes the removal $d_\square$ of empty boxes underlying projections in the S-strings of Durand and Schwer (2008), with, for instance, the Allen relation 1 *during* 2 recast as

$$\boxed{l(2)} \; \boxed{l(1)} \; \boxed{r(1)} \; \boxed{r(2)}$$

(Fernando, 2019; Fernando and Vogel, 2019). This section has focused on $\textit{bc}$ (for tests/statives) to lighten the notation. We can adapt §§4.1, 4.2 for $C, C' \subseteq \Sigma$, putting $d_\square$ in place of $\textit{bc}$.

5 Conclusion

The present paper is essentially an argument for interpreting MSO_A relative to strings over the alphabet 2^A, rather than strings over the alphabet A. The latter smuggles in an assumption $\forall x \, \text{spec}_A(x)$ where $\text{spec}_A(x)$ is the $\text{MSO}_A(x)$-formula

$$\bigvee_{a \in A} \left(P_a(x) \wedge \bigwedge_{a' \in A \setminus \{a\}} \neg P_{a'}(x) \right)$$

specifying exactly one label from A for the string position x. For a KAT generated by Booleans B and actions Σ, the alphabet A may contain $B \cup \Sigma$ (not to mention $\overline{B}$), with the guarded string interpretation in (Kozen and Smith, 1996) imposing $\text{spec}_B(x)$ and $\text{spec}_\Sigma(x)$ at various positions x, treating states as Boolean atoms (absent in an infinite free Boolean algebra) and actions as programs running in isolation (as in Dynamic Logic). Neither $\text{spec}_B(x)$ nor $\text{spec}_\Sigma(x)$ is necessary or desirable for applications where descriptions of states and actions are partial. Section 2 challenges $\text{spec}_B(x)$, slighting B with a Σ-reduct (Proposition 1), while section 3 puts notions of observable change (described in Propositions 3 and 4) ahead of $\text{spec}_\Sigma(x)$ to account for tests. Casting spec aside, section 4 compresses C-reducts, for $C \subseteq B$, and conjoins them by superposition. (More in Fernando, To appear.)

---

[5]Linguistic papers applying Dynamic Logic to temporal semantics include Naumann (2001); Pustejovsky and Moszkowicz (2011).

Acknowledgments

Thanks to three anonymous referees for their comments, and to Heiko Vogler for encouragement. This research is supported by Science Foundation Ireland (SFI) through the CNGL Programme (Grant 12/CE/I2267) in the ADAPT Centre, https://www.adaptcentre.ie. The ADAPT Centre for Digital Content Technology is funded under the SFI Research Centres Programme (Grant 13/RC/2106) and is co-funded under the European Regional Development Fund.

References

J. Allen. 1983. Maintaining knowledge about temporal intervals. *Communications of the ACM*, 26(11):832–843.

D.R. Dowty. 1979. *Word Meaning and Montague Grammar*. Reidel, Dordrecht.

I.A. Durand and S.R. Schwer. 2008. A tool for reasoning about qualitative temporal information: the theory of S-languages with a Lisp implementation. *Journal of Universal Computer Science*, 14(20):3282–3306.

T. Fernando. 2016. On regular languages over power sets. *Journal of Language Modelling*, 4(1):29–56.

T. Fernando. 2019. Projecting temporal properties, events and actions. In *Proceedings 13th International Conference on Computational Semantics*, pages 1–12. www.aclweb.org/anthology/W19-0401.

T. Fernando. To appear. Pictorial narratives and temporal refinement. In *Proc 29th Semantics and Linguistic Theory (SALT)*. UCLA/Cornell.

T. Fernando and C. Vogel. 2019. Prior probabilities of Allen interval relations over finite orders. In *Proc 11th International Conference on Agents and Artificial Intelligence (ICAART 2019), Special Session on Natural Language Processing in AI*. Prague, available in www.scss.tcd.ie/Tim.Fernando/NLPinAI_2019.pdf.

M.J. Fischer and R.E. Ladner. 1979. Propositional dynamic logic of regular programs. *J. Comput. Syst. Sci.*, 18(2):194–211.

J.A. Goguen and R.M. Burstall. 1992. Institutions: abstract model theory for specification and programming. *Journal of the ACM*, 39(1):95–146.

D. Harel, D. Kozen, and J. Tiuryn. 2000. *Dynamic Logic*. MIT Press.

D. Kozen. 1994. A completeness theorem for Kleene algebras and the algebra of regular events. *Information and Computation*, 110(2):366–390.

D. Kozen. 1997. Kleene algebra with tests. *Transactions on Programming Languages and Systems*, 19(3):427–443.

D. Kozen and F. Smith. 1996. Kleene algebra with tests: Completeness and decidability. In *Proc. 10th Int. Workshop Computer Science Logic (CSL'96)*, LNCS 1258, pages 244–259. Springer-Verlag.

L. Libkin. 2010. *Elements of Finite Model Theory*. Springer.

R. Naumann. 2001. Aspects of changes: a dynamic event semantics. *Journal of Semantics*, 18:27–81.

J. Pustejovsky and J.L. Moszkowicz. 2011. The qualitative spatial dynamics of motion in language. *Spatial Cognition and Computation*, 11:15–44.

D. Woods and T. Fernando. 2018. Improving string processing for temporal relations. *Proc. 14th Joint ACL-ISO Workshop on Interoperable Semantic Annotation (ISA-2018)*, pages 76–86.

Finite State Transducer Calculus for Whole Word Morphology

Maciej Janicki
NLP Group, University of Leipzig
Augustusplatz 10, 04109 Leipzig, Germany
`macjan@o2.pl`

Abstract

The research on machine learning of morphology often involves formulating morphological descriptions directly on surface forms of words. As the established two-level morphology paradigm requires the knowledge of the underlying structure, it is not widely used in such settings. In this paper, we propose a formalism describing structural relationships between words based on theories of morphology that reject the notions of internal word structure and morpheme. The formalism covers a wide variety of morphological phenomena (including non-concatenative ones like stem vowel alternation) without the need of workarounds and extensions. Furthermore, we show that morphological rules formulated in such way can be easily translated to FSTs, which enables us to derive performant approaches to morphological analysis, generation and automatic rule discovery.

1 Introduction

In computational linguistics, morphological analysis is usually understood as segmenting words into smaller meaningful units, called *morphs*. There exists a well-established computational model for such analysis, called two-level morphology (Koskenniemi, 1983; Beesley and Karttunen, 2003). It models the mapping between the surface forms of words and the morph sequences using handwritten rules, which are compiled to Finite State Transducers. This allows for a composition of lexicon and rules to an efficient morphological analyzer. Examples of such analyzers include Omorfi for Finnish (Pirinen, 2015), Morphisto for German (Zielinski and Simon, 2008) and TRMorph for Turkish (Çöltekin, 2010).

However, the research coming from the machine learning side often requires models that describe string transformations between surface forms directly, without referring to any underlying structures which cannot be observed in the data and are difficult to infer by a learning algorithm. Such transformations can also be described and implemented as finite-state transducers. Despite that, a standardized model of this kind of morphological description seems to be lacking. Instead, many authors develop their own models and implementations for the purpose of a concrete learning algorithm. With some exceptions, the design, implementation and performance of the string processing algorithms is usually not described in detail and the approaches used for that are sometimes suboptimal.

In this paper, we present a finite-state computational model of string transformations on surface forms based on a linguistic theory called Whole Word Morphology. We first review research on machine learning of morphology which motivates the need for such a model (Sec. 2). In Sec. 3, we describe the formalism and its linguistic foundations, and in Sec. 4, we present the implementation of the formalism within the FST calculus. Sec. 5 contains a procedure for automatic rule discovery from unannotated data, while in Sec. 6, we measure the performance of our implementation of the model.

2 Motivation and Related Work

The recent research on machine learning of morphology tends more and more often towards models describing transformations on whole words, instead of representing words as concatenations of morphs. Arguably the most important reason for this is that morph boundaries are often not clearly visible in surface forms due to morphophonology and orthography.[1] In the following, we review

---

[1] This was also the reason for the emergence of two-level morphology. However, two-level morphology was de-

Proceedings of the 14th International Conference on Finite-State Methods and Natural Language Processing, pages 37–45
Dresden, Germany, September 23-25, 2019. ©2019 Association for Computational Linguistics

some of the papers utilizing such transformational models. Our focus here is not the learning algorithm (which is usually the main focus of the respective paper), but the assumed model of morphology, together with its linguistic and computational foundations.

(Neuvel and Fulop, 2002) present a computational model of morphology based on Whole Word Morphology (Ford et al., 1997). Morphology is described in terms of patterns which summarize structural similarities and differences between pairs of words. The patterns consist of constant elements and wildcards: for example, the relationship within the pair (*receive*, *reception*) would be expressed as $/X\text{ceive}/ \leftrightarrow /X\text{ception}/$. In order to discover such rules automatically, the authors use rather simple string processing algorithms: they try matching every word to every other and check whether the beginnings or the ends of the words match. They subsequently compute an alignment by anchoring the words either at their beginning or end.

(Wicentowski, 2002) proposes a transformational model designed for learning mappings between inflected forms and lemmas. It is based on splitting words into seven parts and describing the changes in each part separately. In addition to prefixation and suffixation, it aims to cover phenomena such as internal vowel changes or changes at the boundary between stem and prefix/suffix (e.g. *hop* $\sim$ *hopping*), which are attributed to a separate segment. (Lindén, 2008, 2009) likewise attempts to model the transformation between base and inflected form part by part, but adopts a simpler, three-way split into prefix, stem and suffix. (Lindén, 2009) mentions that the model was implemented as a cascade of Finite State Transducers.

(Botha and Blunsom, 2013) propose a model of morphology aimed at capturing especially the templatic morphology found in Semitic languages. The model is based on Simple Range Concatenating Grammars (SRCGs), which are a mildly context-sensitive class of formal grammars. It is thought as an extension of the purely concatenative model, which can be represented by a context-free (or perhaps even regular) grammar.

(Durrett and DeNero, 2013) and (Ahlberg et al., 2014) present two different approaches to learning inflection from complete paradigm tables. The input data in such setting are lists of tuples (b, w, t), where b is the base word (lemma), w the inflected word and t a tag, i.e. a bundle of inflectional features. An important point of learning algorithms for this task is an appropriate model of string transformations from b to w. (Durrett and DeNero, 2013) use a semi-Markov log-linear model to model the probability of application of individual transformations (like prefix, stem or suffix change) independently, while (Ahlberg et al., 2014) model string transformations on whole words in form of patterns with wildcards. We note that the string transformation model of (Durrett and DeNero, 2013) is tightly coupled to the machine learning method applied by the authors, while the model of (Ahlberg et al., 2014) is more general and independent of the classification method (in this case, memory-based classification).

With works like (Soricut and Och, 2015; Narasimhan et al., 2015; Luo et al., 2017), we can observe a shift from segmentation to word-based string transformations also in the area of unsupervised learning of morphology. Currently, they appear to adopt very simple transformation models that only involve affixation. On the other hand, (Janicki, 2015) and (Sumalvico, 2017) present a probabilistic model suitable for unsupervised learning, which is based on Whole Word Morphology and describes morphology in terms of whole-word transformation patterns.

As a conclusion from the above literature review, we recognize a need for a standardized model of morphological relationship between surface forms of words. As most of the models presented above are motivated by the need to cover non-concatenative phenomena, especially internal vowel changes and Semitic templatic morphology, the model we aim at should be able to handle those phenomena in a natural and general fashion. Following (Neuvel and Fulop, 2002), we see Whole Word Morphology as the right linguistic foundation for such formalism, and following (Lindén, 2008, 2009), we consider FSTs to be the right tool for implementing string transformations efficiently. Thus, the contribution of the present paper is twofold:

1. A formal definition of a transformational model of morphology, similar to the ones em-

---

signed with the goal of efficient implementation of handwritten grammars and, despite some research in this direction (Theron and Cloete, 1997; Koskenniemi, 2013), is rather not suitable for the machine learning scenario.

ployed by (Neuvel and Fulop, 2002; Ahlberg et al., 2014; Janicki, 2015),

2. An implementation of the model based on the FST calculus.

3 The Formalism

3.1 Definitions

We base our formalism on the linguistic theory of Whole Word Morphology (henceforth, WWM) introduced by (Ford et al., 1997; Neuvel and Singh, 2002). It models structural similarities in form and meaning between words in form of rules, which are expressed as patterns containing wildcards. For example, the relationship within the French pair (*chanteur*, *chanteuse*) can be expressed by the following rule:[2]

$$/X\text{œr}/_{\text{N.MASC}} \leftrightarrow /X\text{øz}/_{\text{N.FEM}} \tag{1}$$

In the above rule, X denotes a variable which can be instantiated with any string of phonemes and represents the common part of both words. The units inside slashes refer to whole words in their surface forms.

In general, we express a *morphological rule with n variables* as follows:

$$/a_0X_1a_1 \ldots X_na_n/ \mapsto /b_0X_1b_1 \ldots X_nb_n/ \tag{2}$$

The elements a_i and b_i are constants (literal strings), which usually represent the differing parts of words on the left-hand and right-hand side of the rule.[3] The elements X_i are variables (wildcards), which represent the part that is preserved by the rule, but varies from pair to pair. Additionally, the following conditions must be satisfied:

1. The variables must be retained in the same order on both sides of the rule.

2. For $0 < i < n$, either a_i or b_i has to be non-empty.

Because of the first condition, we can represent such rule as a vector of $2n + 2$ strings: $\langle a_0, a_1, \ldots, a_n, b_0, b_1, \ldots, b_n \rangle$.

Contrary to (1), which is a relational description and thus uses a bidirectional arrow, we formulate our rules as having a privileged direction. Although most rules can be applied in both directions, the productivity of back-formation is mostly much lower, so that specifying a direction seems linguistically plausible. Modeling rules which are similarly productive in both directions can be achieved by including the reverse rule separately in the grammar.

As an illustration of (2), the rule expressing the relationship between the German pairs (*singen*, *gesungen*), (*klingen*, *geklungen*), (*trinken*, *getrunken*) could have the following form:

$$/X_1\text{i}X_2/ \mapsto /\text{ge}X_1\text{u}X_2/ \tag{3}$$

The rule could also contain more constant elements to express the necessary conditions for its application:

$$/X_1\text{in}X_2\text{en}/ \mapsto /\text{ge}X_1\text{un}X_2\text{en}/ \tag{4}$$

With each rule, we can associate a function r, which transforms a word fitting to the left-hand side of the rule into a set of corresponding words fitting to the right-hand side:

$$r(v) = \{b_0x_1b_1 \ldots x_nb_n : x_1, \ldots, x_n \in \Sigma^+ \\ \wedge v = a_0x_1a_1 \ldots x_na_n\} \tag{5}$$

Note that the outcome of the rule application is a *set* of words, rather than a single word. In general, the rule application might result in multiple different words, because there might be different ways of splitting the word into the sequence $a_0X_1a_1 \ldots X_na_n$. For example, the application of the rule $/X_1\text{a}X_2/ \rightarrow /X_1\text{ä}X_2\text{e}/$ to the German word *Kanal* results in the set: $\{K\ddot{a}nale, Kan\ddot{a}le\}$. In case the word does not fit to the left-hand side of the rule, the rightmost condition is never fulfilled and the result is an empty set. Thus, the function r is defined on the whole of Σ^+.

3.2 Coverage of Morphological Phenomena

In addition to covering affixation, circumfixation and stem vowel alternations, as shown already in the previous section, the following further morphological phenomena can be handled by the formalism:

---

[2]The example comes from (Ford et al., 1997), which is a linguistic monography, thus it represents words in form of phonemic transcriptions. All further examples use written representations.

[3]However, the constants a_i, b_i for a given position i do not have to differ. By being equal or containing a common part, they might also represent the context necessary for the rule to apply. For example, in the rule $/X\text{ate}/ \mapsto /X\text{ation}/$, both constants contain the common prefix 'at'. Formulating this rule as $/X\text{e}/ \mapsto /X\text{ion}/$ would correspond to the same string transformation, but would extend its coverage to a few further cases, like (*deplete*, *depletion*).

Templatic morphology. A relationship between pairs like the Arabic (*kataba*, *kutiba*) can be generalized as the following rule:

$$/X_1aX_2aX_3a/ \mapsto /X_1uX_2iX_3a/ \qquad (6)$$

Although the formalism does not provide a way to restrict the instantiations of variables to a single consonant, it could be easily extended to express such restrictions on variables in a form similar to regular expressions.

Compounding. The proponents of Whole Word Morphology and similar theories explicitly reject the analysis of compounds as 'words composed of multiple words' (Singh and Dasgupta, 2003; Starosta, 2003). In consequence, compounds are also analyzed as related to a *single* word, while the other part is considered to be a morphological constant. For example, the English word *blackberry* would be related to *black* via the following rule:

$$/X/_{\text{N/ADJ}} \mapsto /X\text{berry}/_{\text{N}} \qquad (7)$$

According to (Singh and Dasgupta, 2003; Starosta, 2003), the relationship between the a rule like (7) and the word 'berry' is purely etymological and thus not a part of a synchronic description of morphology. This claim is supported by the fact that newly coined compounds (in languages that exhibit compounding) virtually always involve at least one part that is already known as 'compound-forming', rather than combining two arbitrary words. Indeed, in morphological analyzers based on two-level morphology, the cyclicity used to model compouding often causes massive overgeneration.

4 WWM Rules as FSTs

A rule defined as in (2) can be easily converted to an FST. The general scheme for that is given in Fig. 1. The arrows represent concatenation and each rectangular block represents a transducer. There are two kinds of blocks: transducers mapping corresponding constants, like $a_0 : b_0$, and transducers representing the variables. The latter are simply identity transducers accepting Σ^+. Figure 2 shows a concrete FST corresponding to the rule (4).

4.1 Analysis

There is no concept of a 'morphological analysis' in WWM. Each word is treated as an independent unit of language. However, given a word, we might be interested in its structural relationships to other words.

Let R be the set of rules found in the morphology of a language of interest and let T_r be a transducer corresponding to rule r. The disjunction of all rules, T_R, yields a transducer accepting morphologically related pairs:

$$T_R = \bigcup_{r \in R} T_r \qquad (8)$$

Further, let V denote a vocabulary and T_V the identity transducer corresponding to V. With the following composition, we obtain a transducer capable of mapping all words from V to all their possible derivations:

$$T_A = T_V \circ T_R \qquad (9)$$

T_A can be called a 'WWM analyzer'. A lookup of an unknown word v in T_A yields all words from the known vocabulary from which v can be derived. Furthermore, a three-way composition $T_V \circ T_R \circ T_V$ gives us all pairs of related words from V.

4.2 Generation

Another common question of morphology is: Given a vocabulary V and a set of rules R, what further words can be postulated? The identity transducer for such new words, T_N, is obtained from the following formula:

$$T_N = T_A \downarrow \backslash T_V \qquad (10)$$

where $T_A \downarrow$ denotes the output projection of T_A and $\backslash$ denotes subtraction.

5 Automatic Rule Discovery

As shown in Sec. 3, our definition of rule is general enough to capture many morphological phenomena, including some important non-concatenative ones. On the other hand, the resulting computational model is simple enough to allow for completely unsupervised rule discovery without prior linguistic knowledge. In this section, we show how to achieve this in two stages: first, we identify pairs of string-similar words in the vocabulary. Then, we extract candidate rules from each such pair. Frequent patterns are good candidates for rules, which can be passed to a further statistical model, like the one of (Janicki, 2015; Sumalvico, 2017).

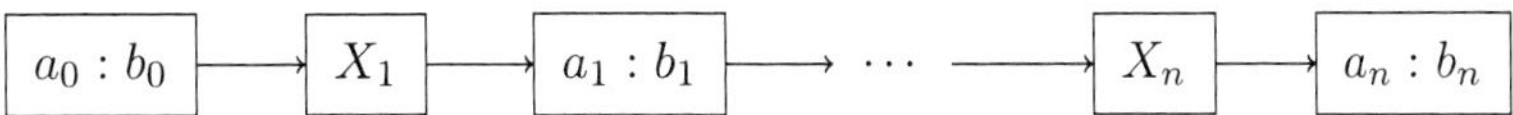

Figure 1: A scheme for converting morphological rules into FSTs.

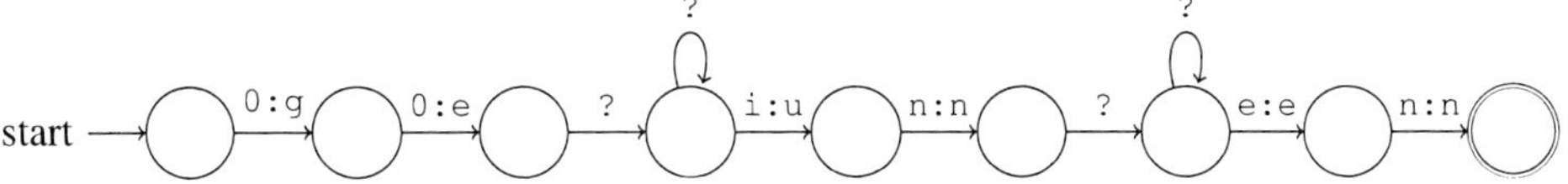

Figure 2: The transducer corresponding to rule (4).

5.1 Finding Pairs of Similar Words

A plausible and widely used string similarity measure is edit distance (Levenshtein, 1966). Using the Fast Similarity Search algorithm (Bocek et al., 2007), we are able to identify pairs of words with edit distance at most k without comparing each word to every other. The algorithm works by generating a *deletion neighborhood* of each word, consisting of strings that can be obtained from that word by deleting up to k characters. The resulting list of pairs (word, substring) is sorted according to the substring. Observe that words with edit distance $\leq k$ are guaranteed to share a common substring, although words sharing a common substring might also have edit distance $> k$. Thus, we treat pairs of words sharing a common substring as candidates, for which edit distance has to be computed with usual means.

For the purpose of discovering potential morphological rules, it is reasonable to modify the notion of edit distance. Firstly, morphological rules usually operate on groups of consecutive letters, rather than single letters independently, so deletion or substitution of a segment of consecutive letters should yield higher similarity than deletion or substitution of the same number of non-consecutive letters. Secondly, although we are going to permit word-internal alternations, more change should be permitted at the beginning and at the end of words, since that is where most morphological rules operate. Bearing in mind the representation (2), let l_{affix} denote the maximum length of a morphological constant at the beginning or the end of a word (a_0, b_0, a_n, b_n in (2)), l_{infix} the maximum length of a morphological constant inside the word (a_i, b_i for $0 < i < n$ in (2)) and k_{max} the maximum number of variables. In order to generate pairs which are related by a rule satisfying this constraint, we obtain the following constraints on a deletion environment: deleting up to l_{affix} con-

secutive letters at the beginning and end of the word, and up to l_{infix} consecutive letters in at most $k_{\text{max}} - 1$ slots inside the word. The usual setting for those parameters, which covers a vast majority of morphological rules encountered in practice, is $l_{\text{affix}} = 5, l_{\text{infix}} = 3, k_{\text{max}} = 2$.

Such settings allow for deletion of up to 13 letters in total, so that even for middle-length words it would consider all pairs to be similar. In order to prevent this, we introduce an additional constraint: the total amount of deleted characters must be smaller than half of the word's length. In this way, we can consider long affixes, but only if enough of the word is still left to form a recognizable stem.

With all those constraints, computing a deletion neighborhood of a word becomes a complex operation. It is therefore helpful to visualize and implement it using transducers. We will construct the transducer S mapping words to their deletion neighborhoods as a composition of two simpler transducers: $S = S_1 \circ S_2$. The transducer S_1 (Fig. 3) performs the deletions, substituting a special symbol δ for each deleted character. The transducer consists of segments, corresponding to the deleted sequences: states 0-5 represent the prefix, 10-15 the suffix and 7-9 the infix. Between each pair of segments, an arbitrary number of identity mappings is performed (state sequences 5-6 and 9-10). The epsilon transitions, for example from states 0-4 to 5, correspond to a less-than-maximum number of deletions in a given slot. It can easily be seen that changing e.g. the parameter l_{affix} simply corresponds to altering the length of the top and bottom chains, just as l_{infix} correspond to the length of the middle chain and $k_{\text{max}} - 1$ to the number of such middle chains.

The transducer S_2 (Fig. 4) takes the output of S_1 and checks whether the number of deletions is smaller than the number of remaining characters. As the general formulation of this problem cannot be solved by a finite-state machine, it requires

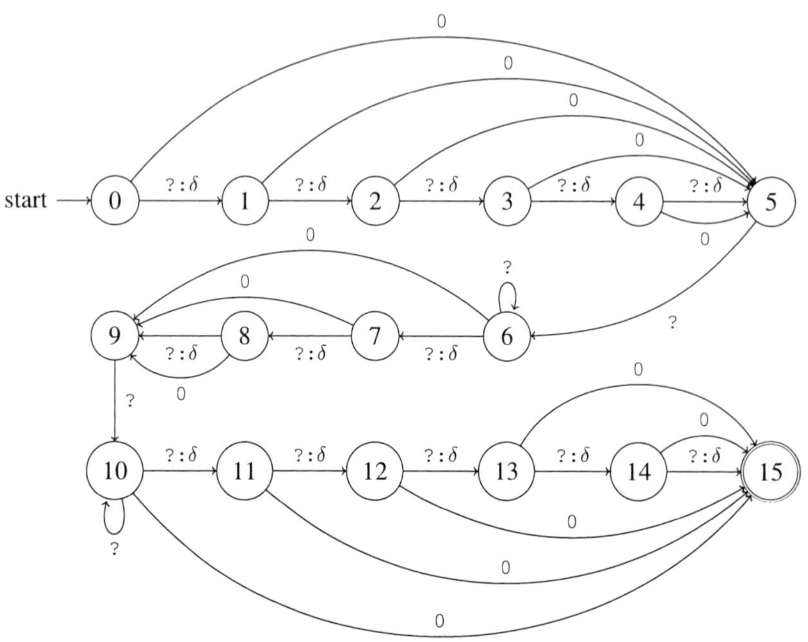

Figure 3: The transducer S_1 for generating a deletion neighborhood.

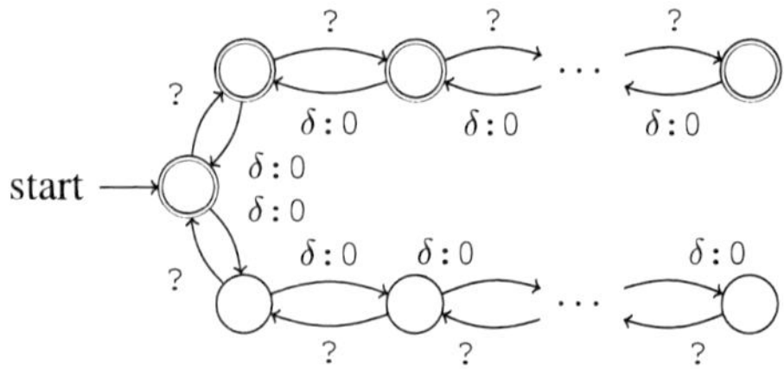

Figure 4: The filter S_2 ensuring that no more than the half of a word is deleted.

a bound on word length. In my implementation, I restrict the maximum word length to 20 characters, but it is easy to change this parameter. The states of S_2 correspond to the difference between the number of letters and the number of deletions seen so far. The states above the initial state correspond to positive, and the ones below to negative values. Furthermore, S_2 removes the deletion symbols and returns the substring consisting of the remaining letters.

We can now generate all pairs of similar words from a lexicon automaton L by performing the following composition:

$$P = (L \circ S) \circ (L \circ S)^{-1} \qquad (11)$$

There are various ways to implement this in prac-tice. Computing the composition directly is usu-ally not feasible because of high memory com-plexity. One possibility is to use S for substring generation, but otherwise proceed as in the orig-inal FastSS algorithm: store the words and sub-strings in an index structure, either on disk or in memory, then retrieve words for each substring. Another possibility is to use S to generate sub-strings for a given word and then look the sub-strings up in the transducer $(L \circ S)^{-1}$ to obtain similar words. The latter composition can be com-puted statically. We additionally convert the re-sulting transducer to HFST optimized lookup for-mat (Silfverberg and Lindén, 2009). While the lookup approach is still significantly slower, it has an advantage in providing a way to retrieve *all* words w' similar to a given word w at once. It is thus better suited for parallelization, especially in case the pairs (w, w') are subject to further pro-cessing.

5.2 Extraction of Rule Candidates

Given a pair (w, w') of string-similar words, we want to extract morphological rules modeling the difference between those words. For this purpose, we first align the words on character-to-character basis using the well-known dynamic programming algorithm for computing edit distance (Wagner and Fischer, 1974). Then, we attribute each character mapping either to a morphological constant or a variable, in a way that fulfills the constraints on l_{affix}, l_{infix} and k. The candidate rules are constructed incrementally while iterating over the alignment and unfinished rules are stored in a priority queue. In case an aligned character pair can be attributed either to a constant or to a variable, both possibilities are stored in a queue, so that at the end we obtain multiple rules with varying degrees of generality. For example, the rules extracted from the German pair (*trifft*, *getroffen*) include $/X_1 i X_2 t/ \rightarrow /ge X_1 o X_2 en/$ (the most general rule), as well as e.g. $/X \text{ifft}/ \rightarrow /ge X \text{offen}/$.

Table 1 shows example rules extracted from a word list coming from German Wikipedia. While the top of the list consists entirely of morphological patterns, the bottom of the table shows that patterns resulting from accidental word similarities can also become frequent enough to be confused with morphological rules. Thus, this approach identifies rule *candidates*, which have to be further filtered based on other criteria than mere frequency.

6 Experiments

We have implemented the algorithms described in the previous section using the HFST library (Lindén et al., 2011). Furthermore, we conducted experiments realizing the algebraic operations described in Sec. 4 and the rule discovery procedure described in Sec. 5. The results demonstrate that our model is suitable for building analyzers based on the Whole Word Morphology paradigm and the required computational resources are easily achievable.

First, we run the rule discovery procedure on word lists extracted from German Wikipedia.[4] The generation of pairs of similar words and the subsequent rule extraction is implemented in a parallelized fashion. Table 2 shows the computation times for various sizes of input vocabulary and numbers of processes. The results demonstrate that this step is feasible for input data of as much as 150,000 words (and probably even somewhat larger). In our view, this is enough to discover the

vast majority of productive morphological rules.

We disjunct several thousand most frequent rules to construct a rule transducer T_R, which is used in algebraic operations shown in Table 3. Most operations are realized within at most several minutes, the longest one being the construction of the largest generator in slightly above 11 minutes.

Note that the computation times reported in Table 3 are much shorter than the ones in Table 2. Moreover, the former appear to increase linearly in both $|V|$ and $|R|$. Thus, although the limits on the vocabulary size in the rule discovery procedure are quite tight, once we have discovered the rules (or obtained them in another way, e.g. manually written), we can apply the transducer to find pairs of related words in much larger lexica. Using 3-way composition (Allauzen and Mohri, 2008) for computing $T_A \circ T_V$ could probably further improve the analysis of a new lexicon.

7 Conclusion

We have presented a formalism allowing for the description of morphological regularities as transformational patterns on whole words in their surface forms. The formalism is grounded in linguistic theories rejecting the notion of internal structure of words and can be especially useful in the context of machine learning, where descriptions of such underlying structures are not available. It captures non-concatenative phenomena naturally and allows for representing rules as FSTs, so that performant algorithms for morphological analysis and generation are readily available as algebraic operations on transducers. We suggest that such standardized formalism can present an alternative to models of morphology and string processing algorithms developed for a specific machine learning method, which are common in the literature.

References

Malin Ahlberg, Markus Forsberg, and Mans Hulden. 2014. Semi-supervised learning of morphological paradigms and lexicons. In *Proceedings of the EACL*, pages 569–578.

Cyril Allauzen and Mehryar Mohri. 2008. 3-way composition of weighted finite-state transducers. In *International Conference on Implementation and Application of Automata (CIAA 2008)*, pages 262–273, San Francisco, CA, USA.

Kenneth R. Beesley and Lauri Karttunen. 2003. *Fi-*

---

[4]Note that unsupervised learning of morphology *per se* is not our focus in this paper. The rule discovery procedure would constitute only a preprocessing step to proper learning. However, we use the resulting rule transducer T_R in further compositions to demonstrate their computational feasibility.

rank	rule	frequency	example
1	$/X\mathrm{n}/ \to /X/$	8555	Epoche $\to$ Epochen
2	$/X/ \to /X\mathrm{n}/$	8555	Epochen $\to$ Epoche
3	$/X\mathrm{en}/ \to /X\mathrm{e}/$	7465	aufgehenden $\to$ aufgehende
4	$/X\mathrm{e}/ \to /X\mathrm{en}/$	7465	aufgehende $\to$ aufgehenden
5	$/X\mathrm{en}/ \to /X/$	6030	Abkürzungen $\to$ Abkürzung
6	$/X/ \to /X\mathrm{en}/$	6030	Abkürzung $\to$ Abkürzungen
7	$/X\mathrm{e}/ \to /X/$	5640	niedrige $\to$ niedrig
8	$/X/ \to /X\mathrm{e}/$	5640	niedrig $\to$ niedrige
9	$/X\mathrm{s}/ \to /X/$	4917	Erdbebens $\to$ Erdbeben
10	$/X/ \to /X\mathrm{s}/$	4917	Erdbeben $\to$ Erdbebens
		$\ldots$	
53	$/X\mathrm{en}/ \to /X\mathrm{t}/$	1194	nutzen $\to$ nutzt
54	$/X\mathrm{en}/ \to /X\mathrm{es}/$	1194	einfachen $\to$ einfaches
		$\ldots$	
746	$/X_1\mathrm{a}X_2/ \to /X_1\mathrm{o}X_2/$	196	unterbrachen $\to$ unterbrochen
747	$/X_1\mathrm{t}X_2/ \to /X_1\mathrm{m}X_2/$	195	warten $\to$ warmen
748	$/X_1\mathrm{n}X_2/ \to /X_1\mathrm{l}X_2/$	195	Zähnen $\to$ Zählen
749	$/X_1\mathrm{m}X_2/ \to /X_1\mathrm{t}X_2/$	195	warmen $\to$ warten
750	$/X_1\mathrm{l}X_2/ \to /X_1\mathrm{n}X_2/$	195	Zählen $\to$ Zähnen
751	$/X_1\mathrm{ge}X_2\mathrm{t}/ \to /X_1X_2\mathrm{en}/$	195	zugefügt $\to$ zufügen
752	$/\{\mathrm{CAP}\}X_1X_2/ \to /X_1\mathrm{sch}X_2/$	195	Allergie $\to$ allergische
753	$/X_1\mathrm{sch}X_2/ \to /\{\mathrm{CAP}\}X_1X_2/$	195	allergische $\to$ Allergie
754	$/X_1\ddot{\mathrm{a}}X_2\mathrm{er}/ \to /X_1\mathrm{a}X_2/$	195	Häuser $\to$ Haus
755	$/X_1\mathrm{a}X_2/ \to /X_1\ddot{\mathrm{a}}X_2\mathrm{er}/$	195	Haus $\to$ Häuser
756	$/\mathrm{g}X/ \to /\mathrm{ausg}X/$	194	gegraben $\to$ ausgegraben
757	$/\mathrm{ausg}X/ \to /\mathrm{g}X/$	194	ausgegraben $\to$ gegraben

Table 1: Example rules extracted from the German Wikipedia.

$|V|$	num. processes			
	1	2	4	6
10k	426	238	146	134
50k	8757	5273	4128	3657
100k	33629	22981	18624	15297
150k	82287	55268	41827	37623

Table 2: Computation times (in seconds) for the rule discovery procedure.

Computation	$|V|$	$|R|$			
		1k	2k	5k	10k
$T_V \circ T_R$	10k	2.86	5.72	13.6	22.8
	50k	13.4	28.7	67.2	115
	100k	26.9	56.3	137	237
	150k	41.3	86.6	208	355
$T_A \circ T_V$	10k	0.68	1.17	2.36	3.77
	50k	3.58	5.82	11.4	18.0
	100k	7.21	11.6	22.9	35.3
	150k	10.9	16.8	33.7	51.7
$T_A \downarrow \backslash T_V$	10k	5.39	10.0	23.1	40.4
	50k	28.6	51.9	125	219
	100k	57.9	107	266	452
	150k	88.6	159	397	682

Table 3: Computation times (in seconds) for various operations related to the WWM analyzer. All algebraic operations include the minimization of the resulting transducer.

nite State Morphology. Center for the Study of Language and Information.

Thomas Bocek, Ela Hunt, and Burkhard Stiller. 2007. Fast similarity search in large dictionaries. Technical report, University of Zurich.

Jan A. Botha and Phil Blunsom. 2013. Adaptor grammars for learning non-concatenative morphology. In *Proceedings of the 2013 Conference on Empirical Methods in Natural Language Processing*, pages 345–356, Seattle, Washington.

Çağrı Çöltekin. 2010. A freely available morphological analyzer for Turkish. In *LREC 2010, Seventh International Conference on Language Resources and Evaluation*.

Greg Durrett and John DeNero. 2013. Supervised learning of complete morphological paradigms. In *Proceedings of NAACL-HLT*, pages 1185–1195.

Alan Ford, Rajendra Singh, and Gita Martohardjono. 1997. *Pace Pāṇini: Towards a word-based theory of morphology*. American University Studies. Series XIII, Linguistics, Vol. 34. Peter Lang Publishing, Incorporated.

Maciej Janicki. 2015. A multi-purpose bayesian model for word-based morphology. In *Systems and Frameworks for Computational Morphology – Fourth International Workshop, SFCM 2015*. Springer.

Kimmo Koskenniemi. 1983. *Two-Level Morphology: A General Computational Model for Word-Form Recognition and Production*. Ph.D. thesis, University of Helsinki.

Kimmo Koskenniemi. 2013. An informal discovery procedure for two-level morphological rules.

Vladimir I. Levenshtein. 1966. Binary codes capable of correcting deletions, insertions, and reversals. *Soviet Physics Doklady*, 10(8):707–710.

Krister Lindén. 2008. A probabilistic model for guessing base forms of new words by analogy. In *CICling-2008, 9th International Conference on Intelligent Text Processing and Computational Linguistics*, Haifa, Israel.

Krister Lindén. 2009. Entry generation by analogy – encoding new words for morphological lexicons. *Northern European Journal of Language Technology*, 1:1–25.

Krister Lindén, Erik Axelson, Sam Hardwick, Tommi A. Pirinen, and Miikka Silfverberg. 2011. HFST – framework for compiling and applying morphologies. In *Systems and Frameworks for Computational Morphology – Second International Workshop, SFCM 2011*. Springer.

Jiaming Luo, Karthik Narasimhan, and Regina Barzilay. 2017. Unsupervised learning of morphological forests. *TACL*.

Karthik Narasimhan, Regina Barzilay, and Tommi Jaakkola. 2015. An unsupervised method for uncovering morphological chains. *TACL*.

Sylvain Neuvel and Sean A. Fulop. 2002. Unsupervised learning of morphology without morphemes. In *Proceedings of the 6th Workshop of the ACL Special Interest Group in Computational Phonology (SIGPHON)*, pages 31–40.

Sylvain Neuvel and Rajendra Singh. 2002. Vive la différence! What morphology is about. *Folia Linguistica*, 35(3-4):313–320.

Tommi A. Pirinen. 2015. Development and use of computational morphology of Finnish in the open source and open science era: Notes on experiences with Omorfi development. *SKY Journal of Linguistics*, 28:381–393.

Miikka Silfverberg and Krister Lindén. 2009. Hfst runtime format - a compacted transducer format allowing for fast lookup. In *Finite-State Methods and Natural Language Processing - FSMNLP 2009 Eight International Workshop*.

Rajendra Singh and Probal Dasgupta. 2003. On so-called compounds. In (Singh and Starosta, 2003), pages 77–89.

Rajendra Singh and Stanley Starosta, editors. 2003. *Explorations in Seamless Morphology*. SAGE Publications, New Delhi.

Radu Soricut and Franz Josef Och. 2015. Unsupervised morphology induction using word embeddings. In *NAACL 2015*, pages 1626–1636.

Stanley Starosta. 2003. Do compounds have internal structure? A seamless analysis. In (Singh and Starosta, 2003), pages 116–147.

Maciej Sumalvico. 2017. Unsupervised learning of morphology with graph sampling. In *Proceedings to RANLP 2017*, Varna, Bulgaria.

Pieter Theron and Ian Cloete. 1997. Automatic acquisition of two-level morphological rules. In *Fifth Conference on Applied Natural Language Processing*, Washington, DC, USA.

Robert A. Wagner and Michael J. Fischer. 1974. The string-to-string correction problem. *Journal of the ACM*, 21(I):168–173.

Robert Wicentowski. 2002. *Modeling and Learning Multilingual Inflectional Morphology in a Minimally Supervised Framework*. Ph.D. thesis, Johns Hopkins University.

Andrea Zielinski and Christian Simon. 2008. Morphisto – an open source morphological analyzer for German. In *Finite State Methods and Natural Language Processing, 7th International Workshop, FSMNLP 2008*, Ispra, Italy.

Weighted parsing for grammar-based language models

Richard Mörbitz
Faculty of Computer Science
Technische Universität Dresden
01062 Dresden
richard.moerbitz@tu-dresden.de

Heiko Vogler
Faculty of Computer Science
Technische Universität Dresden
01062 Dresden
heiko.vogler@tu-dresden.de

Abstract

We develop a general framework for weighted parsing which is built on top of grammar-based language models and employs flexible weight algebras. It generalizes previous work in that area (semiring parsing, weighted deductive parsing) and also covers applications outside the classical scope of parsing, e.g., algebraic dynamic programming. We show an algorithm which terminates and is correct for a large class of weighted grammar-based language models.

1 Introduction

The weighted parsing problem takes as input a weighted language model (LM) and a syntactic object a. For instance, the LM can be given by some grammar G, e.g., a context-free grammar (CFG) or a linear context-free rewriting system (LCFRS), and a can be some string. Each rule r of G has a value (*weight of r*); the weight is an element of some *weight algebra* $\mathbb{K}$. That algebra has a binary commutative and associative operation $\oplus$ on its carrier set, which is used to handle ambiguity of G. As output we expect an element $\mathbb{k} \in \mathbb{K}$ which is the $\oplus$-accumulation of the weight $\mathrm{wt}(d)_\mathbb{K}$ of each abstract syntax tree (AST) d of a in G, i.e.,

$$\mathbb{k} = \sum_{d \in \mathrm{AST}(G,a)}^{\oplus} \mathrm{wt}(d)_\mathbb{K}$$

where $\mathrm{wt}(d)_\mathbb{K}$ is computed by other operations of the algebra $\mathbb{K}$ (using the weights of the occurring rules) and $\sum^{\oplus}$ is an extension of $\oplus$ to infinitely many summands (*infinitary sum operation*). For instance, if $\mathbb{K} = [0,1]$ is the set of probabilities, $\oplus = \max$, $\sum^{\oplus} = \sup$, and $\mathrm{wt}(d)_\mathbb{K}$ is the product of all weights of occurrences of rules in d, then $\mathbb{k}$ is the maximal probability of an AST of a in G.

Goodman (1999) developed a formal framework for weighted parsing, called *semiring parsing*. As weight algebras he used complete semirings $(\mathbb{K}, \oplus, \otimes, \mathbb{0}, \mathbb{1}, \sum^{\oplus})$ (Eilenberg, 1974), i.e., $\sum^{\oplus}$

is the infinitary sum operation extending $\oplus$. The binary operation $\otimes$ is used to compute $\mathrm{wt}(d)_\mathbb{K}$. By appropriate choices of the complete semiring, he formalized the following problems as weighted parsing problems for a CFG G and a: the calculation of recognition, string probabilities, number of derivations, derivation forests, probability of best derivation, best derivation, and best n derivations. The algorithm which he proposed for solving the weighted parsing problem is a pipeline with two phases. In the first phase, the CFG G, a deduction system I (Shieber et al., 1995), and the syntactic object a (i.e., a string) are combined into a single CFG G' (using a construction idea of Bar-Hillel et al., 1961). In the second phase, the value $\mathbb{k}$ (from above) is calculated, if G' is acyclic.[1]

Nederhof (2003) developed a similar framework, called *weighted deductive parsing*. As weight algebras he employed algebras of the form $(\mathbb{K}, \min, \mathbb{0}, \Omega, \sum^{\min})$ where $\mathbb{K}$ is a totally ordered set, $\sum^{\min} = \inf$ (infimum), $\inf(\mathbb{K}) \in \mathbb{K}$, and Ω is a set of superior functions; a superior function f is an operation on $\mathbb{K}$ which is monotone non-decreasing in each argument and $f(\mathbb{k}_1, \ldots, \mathbb{k}_m) \geq \max(\mathbb{k}_1, \ldots, \mathbb{k}_m)$ holds. The algorithm which he proposed for solving the weighted parsing problem is again a pipeline with two phases, where the first phase is the same as in the framework of Goodman (1999) and the resulting CFG G' is denoted by $c(G, a)$. In the second phase, he employed the algorithm of Knuth (1977), which generalizes the shortest distance algorithm of Dijkstra (1959) from graphs to hypergraphs and also works if G' is cyclic. If the CFG G' is non-branching, i.e., a linear grammar (Khabbaz, 1974, Def. 1), then in the second phase a graph algorithm can

---

[1]Goodman (1999) actually defines the algorithm so that it attempts to compute an infinite sum. He states that in applications, this computation needs to be replaced by instructions specific to the used semiring.

Proceedings of the 14th International Conference on Finite-State Methods and Natural Language Processing, pages 46–55
Dresden, Germany, September 23-25, 2019. ©2019 Association for Computational Linguistics

be used as an alternative to Knuth's algorithm; e.g., the single source shortest distance algorithm of Mohri (2002) if the weight algebra $\mathbb{K}$ is a complete semiring which is *closed for G'*.

In this paper, we generalize the two-phase pipeline approach of Goodman (1999) and Nederhof (2003) as follows. We specify the LM by using the general approach of initial algebra semantics (Goguen et al., 1977). For this, we employ weighted regular tree grammars (wRTG) and evaluate the generated trees (by the unique homomorphism) in some language algebra $\mathcal{L}$, which provides the set of syntactic objects as carrier set. This approach is very flexible and covers LMs for strings (CFG, LCFRS), but also trees and graphs (Drewes et al., 2016). Our second generalization concerns the weight algebra. We consider complete multioperator monoids (Kuich, 1999) which are algebras of the form $(\mathbb{K}, \oplus, \mathbb{0}, \Omega, \sum^{\oplus})$, where Ω is a set of operations on $\mathbb{K}$ and $\sum^{\oplus}$ is the infinitary sum operation which extends $\oplus$. We call the combination of such an LM and weight algebra *weighted RTG-based language model* (wRTG-LM). These combinations are very general and even exceed the scope of parsing; e.g., each algebraic dynamic programming problem (Giegerich et al., 2004), like minimum edit distance or matrix chain multiplication, can be formalized within this framework.

For solving the weighted parsing problem, given a wRTG-LM and a syntactic object a, we formalize the first phase as *canonical weighted deduction system*, which uses a CYK-like deduction system. For the second phase (*value computation algorithm*), we propose a generalization of Mohri's approach to hypergraphs, in the spirit of Knuth's generalization of Dijkstra's algorithm. We prove (in sketches) that our weighted parsing algorithm is terminating and solves the weighted parsing problem for every *closed wRTG-LM* with a *finitely decomposing* language algebra. This covers the approaches of Goodman (1999) and Nederhof (2003); our value computation algorithm subsumes the algorithms of Knuth (1977) and Mohri (2002). Due to space restrictions, we cannot show our detailed proofs of the theorems in this paper.

2 Preliminaries

Mathematical notions. We let $\mathbb{N} = \{0, 1, 2, \ldots\}$ be the set of natural numbers and $[m] = \{1, \ldots, m\}$ for each $m \in \mathbb{N}$. An *alphabet* is a finite, nonempty set. The powerset of a set A is denoted by $\mathcal{P}(A)$. Let $f: A \rightarrow B$ be a mapping; we extend it to the mapping $f': \mathcal{P}(A) \rightarrow \mathcal{P}(B)$ by letting $f(U) = \{f(a) \mid a \in U\}$, and we denote f' also by f. A *family over A* is a mapping $f: I \rightarrow A$, where I is a countable set (index set). As usual, we represent each family f over A by $(f(i) \mid i \in I)$ and abbreviate $f(i)$ by f_i.

Ranked sets, trees, and regular tree grammars. A *ranked set* is a set Γ such that each $\gamma \in \Gamma$ is associated with a natural number $\mathrm{rk}_\Gamma(\gamma)$, its *rank*. The set of all elements of Γ with rank $m \in \mathbb{N}$ is denoted by Γ_m. A ranked set Σ with $\Sigma \subseteq \Gamma$ is *rank preserving (in Γ)* if $\Sigma_m \subseteq \Gamma_m$ for each $m \in \mathbb{N}$. Let H be a set. The set of *trees over Γ and H* is defined in the usual way, where elements of H may only occur at leaves. We denote this set by $T_\Gamma(H)$ and abbreviate $T_\Gamma(\emptyset)$ by T_Γ. Let $t \in T_\Gamma(H)$. A *path in t* is a sequence of positions of d from the root to a leaf. Let p be a path in t. The sequence of labels of d along p is denoted by $\mathrm{seq}(d, p)$. A *ranked alphabet* is a ranked set which is an alphabet.

A *regular tree grammar* (RTG) (Brainerd, 1969) is a tuple $G = (N, \Sigma, A_0, R)$ where N is an alphabet (nonterminals), Σ is a ranked alphabet (terminals) with $N \cap \Sigma = \emptyset$, $A_0 \in N$ (initial nonterminal), and R is finite set of rules where each rule has the form $A \rightarrow \sigma(A_1, \ldots, A_m)$ with $m \in \mathbb{N}$, $A, A_1, \ldots, A_m \in N$, and $\sigma \in \Sigma_m$. Each RTG G can be considered as a context-free grammar G' (with terminal alphabet $\Sigma \cup \{(,), \text{comma}\}$), which generates well-formed expressions. Thus the derivation relation $\Rightarrow_G$ is the usual derivation relation of G'. The *tree language generated by G* is the set $L(G) = \{t \in T_\Sigma \mid A_0 \Rightarrow_G^* t\}$.

By viewing each rule $A \rightarrow \sigma(A_1, \ldots, A_m)$ of R as symbol with rank m, we can define the set $\mathrm{AST}(G)$ of *abstract syntax trees of G* to be the set of all $d \in T_R$ such that for each position w of d the following holds: if d has label $A \rightarrow \sigma(A_1, \ldots, A_m)$ at w, then the i-th successor of w ($i \in [m]$) is labeled by a rule with left-hand side A_i (cf. Fig. 2). We define the mapping $\pi_\Sigma: \mathrm{AST}(G) \rightarrow T_\Sigma$ such that $\pi_\Sigma(d)$ is obtained from d by replacing each label $A \rightarrow \sigma(A_1, \ldots, A_m)$ by σ (cf. Fig. 2). Hence $\pi_\Sigma(\mathrm{AST}(G)) = L(G)$.

Γ-algebras. Let Γ be a ranked set. A *Γ-algebra* (or: algebra) is a pair $(\mathcal{A}, \phi)$ where $\mathcal{A}$ is a set (*carrier set*) and ϕ is a mapping (*interpretation map-*

ping) which maps each $\gamma \in \Gamma_m$ ($m \in \mathbb{N}$) to an m-ary operation $\phi(\gamma)$ over $\mathcal{A}$, i.e., $\phi(\gamma): \mathcal{A}^m \to \mathcal{A}$. In the sequel, we will sometimes identify $\phi(\gamma)$ and γ (as it is usual in algebra).

The *Γ-term algebra* is the Γ-algebra (T_Γ, ϕ_Γ) where $\phi_\Gamma(\gamma)(t_1, \ldots, t_m) = \gamma(t_1, \ldots, t_m)$ for every $m \in \mathbb{N}$, $\gamma \in \Gamma_m$, and $t_1, \ldots, t_m \in T_\Gamma$. For each Γ-algebra $(\mathcal{A}, \phi)$ there is exactly one homomorphism, denoted by $(.)_\mathcal{A}$, from the Γ-term algebra to $(\mathcal{A}, \phi)$ (Wechler, 1992). We write its application to an argument $t \in T_\Gamma$ as $t_\mathcal{A}$. Intuitively, $(.)_\mathcal{A}$ evaluates a tree t in $(\mathcal{A}, \phi)$, in the same way as arithmetic expressions (e.g., $3 + 2 \cdot (4 + 5)$) are evaluated in the $\{+, \cdot\}$-algebra $(\mathbb{Z}, +, \cdot)$ to some values (here: 21). Often we abbreviate an algebra $(\mathcal{A}, \phi)$ by its carrier set $\mathcal{A}$. For every $a \in \mathcal{A}$ we let $\mathrm{factors}(a) = \{b \in \mathcal{A} \mid b <_{\mathrm{factor}}^* a\}$, where for every $a, b \in \mathcal{A}$, $b <_{\mathrm{factor}} a$ if there is a $\gamma \in \Gamma$ such that b occurs in some tuple $(b_1, \ldots, b_m)$ with $\phi(\gamma)(b_1, \ldots, b_m) = a$. We call $(\mathcal{A}, \phi)$ *finitely decomposable* if $\mathrm{factors}(a)$ is finite for every $a \in \mathcal{A}$.

Monoids. A *monoid* is an algebra $(\mathbb{K}, \oplus, \mathbb{0})$ such that $\oplus$ is a binary, associative operation on $\mathbb{K}$ and $\mathbb{0} \oplus \Bbbk = \Bbbk = \Bbbk \oplus \mathbb{0}$ for each $\Bbbk \in \mathbb{K}$. In the rest of this paper, each occurrence of $\Bbbk, \Bbbk_1, \Bbbk_2, \ldots$ is assumed to be universally quantified over $\mathbb{K}$ if not specified otherwise. The monoid is *commutative* if $\oplus$ is commutative; it is *extremal* (Mahr, 1984) if $\Bbbk_1 \oplus \Bbbk_2 \in \{\Bbbk_1, \Bbbk_2\}$; it is *idempotent* if $\Bbbk \oplus \Bbbk = \Bbbk$. It is *naturally ordered* if the binary relation $\preceq \subseteq \mathbb{K} \times \mathbb{K}$ (defined by $\Bbbk_1 \preceq \Bbbk_2$ if there is a $\Bbbk \in \mathbb{K}$ such that $\Bbbk_1 \oplus \Bbbk = \Bbbk_2$) is anti-symmetric (in which case it is a partial order, since reflexivity and transitivity hold by definition). It is *complete* if for each countable set I, there is an operation $\sum_I^\oplus$ which maps each family $(\Bbbk_i \mid i \in I)$ to an element of $\mathbb{K}$, coincides with $\oplus$ when I is finite, and otherwise satisfies axioms which guarantee commutativity and associativity (Eilenberg, 1974, p. 124). We abbreviate $\sum_I^\oplus(\Bbbk_i \mid i \in I)$ by $\sum_{i \in I}^\oplus \Bbbk_i$. A complete monoid is *d-complete* (Karner, 1992) if for every $\Bbbk \in \mathbb{K}$ and family $(\Bbbk_i \mid i \in \mathbb{N})$ of elements of $\mathbb{K}$ the following holds: if there is an $n_0 \in \mathbb{N}$ such that for every $n \in \mathbb{N}$ with $n \geq n_0$, $\sum_{i \in \mathbb{N}: i \leq n}^\oplus \Bbbk_i = \Bbbk$, then $\sum_{i \in \mathbb{N}}^\oplus \Bbbk_i = \Bbbk$. A complete monoid is *completely idempotent* if for every $\Bbbk \in \mathbb{K}$ and countable set I it holds that $\sum_{i \in I}^\oplus \Bbbk = \Bbbk$.

By easy calculations we obtain the following implications: (1) if $\mathbb{K}$ is extremal, then it is idempotent, (2) if $\mathbb{K}$ is completely idempotent, then it is d-complete, and (3) if $\mathbb{K}$ is d-complete, then it

is naturally ordered.

Multioperator monoids. A *multioperator monoid* (M-monoid) (Kuich, 1999) is an algebra $(\mathbb{K}, \oplus, \mathbb{0}, \Omega)$ such that $(\mathbb{K}, \oplus, \mathbb{0})$ is a commutative monoid and Ω is a set of operations on $\mathbb{K}$ which contains at least the unary identity $\mathrm{id}: \mathbb{K} \to \mathbb{K}$. We view Ω as a ranked set, and hence $(\mathbb{K}, \phi)$ as an Ω-algebra where $\phi(\omega) = \omega$ for each $\omega \in \Omega$. Thus $t_\mathbb{K} \in \mathbb{K}$ is the evaluation of $t \in T_\Omega$ in the algebra $(\mathbb{K}, \phi)$. An M-monoid inherits the properties of its monoid (e.g., being complete). We denote a complete M-monoid by $(\mathbb{K}, \oplus, \mathbb{0}, \Omega, \sum^\oplus)$.

An M-monoid is *distributive* if for each m-ary $\omega \in \Omega$ and every $i \in [m]$,

$$\omega(\Bbbk_{1,i-1}, \Bbbk_i \oplus \Bbbk, \Bbbk_{i+1,m})$$
$$= \omega(\Bbbk_{1,i-1}, \Bbbk_i, \Bbbk_{i+1,m}) \oplus \omega(\Bbbk_{1,i-1}, \Bbbk, \Bbbk_{i+1,m})$$

where $\Bbbk_{1,i-1}$ and $\Bbbk_{i+1,m}$ abbreviate $\Bbbk_1, \ldots, \Bbbk_{i-1}$ and $\Bbbk_{i+1}, \ldots, \Bbbk_m$, respectively. If $\mathbb{K}$ is complete, then we additionally require that the above equation also holds for each countable set of summands.

Next we show examples of M-monoids.

- Each semiring $(\mathbb{K}, \oplus, \otimes, \mathbb{0}, \mathbb{1})$ can be considered as the M-monoid $(\mathbb{K}, \oplus, \mathbb{0}, \Omega_\otimes)$ (Fülöp et al., 2009) where $\Omega_\otimes = \{\mathrm{mul}_\Bbbk^{(m)} \mid m \in \mathbb{N}, \Bbbk \in \mathbb{K}\}$ and for every $m \in \mathbb{N}$ we define

$$\mathrm{mul}_\Bbbk^{(m)}(\Bbbk_1, \ldots, \Bbbk_m) = \Bbbk \otimes \Bbbk_1 \otimes \cdots \otimes \Bbbk_m \ .$$

  Note that $\mathbb{1} = \mathrm{mul}_\mathbb{1}^{(0)}()$.

- Knuth (1977) uses complete, distributive M-monoids of the form $(\mathbb{K}, \min, \mathbb{0}, \Omega, \sum^{\min})$ where $\mathbb{K}$ is a totally ordered set, $\inf(\mathbb{K}) \in \mathbb{K}$, and the operations in Ω are superior functions. We will call such M-monoids *superior M-monoids*. We note that each superior M-monoid is d-complete.

3 Weighted RTG-based language models and the weighted parsing problem

As framework for the definition of our language models we use the initial algebra approach (Goguen et al., 1977). An *RTG-based language model* (RTG-LM) is a tuple $(G, (\mathcal{L}, \phi))$ where

- $G = (N, \Sigma, A_0, R)$ is an RTG and

- $(\mathcal{L}, \phi)$ is a Γ-algebra (*language algebra*) such that $\Sigma \subseteq \Gamma$ is rank preserving; the elements of $\mathcal{L}$ are called *syntactic objects*.

The *language generated by* $(G, (\mathcal{L}, \phi))$ is the set

$$L(G)_\mathcal{L} = \{t_\mathcal{L} \mid t \in L(G)\} \subseteq \mathcal{L} \ ,$$

i.e., the set of all syntactic objects which result

$$r_1: \quad \text{S} \xrightarrow{1.0} \langle x_1 x_2 \rangle (\text{NP}, \text{VP}) \qquad r_8: \quad \text{NN} \xrightarrow{1.0} \langle \textit{fruit} \rangle$$

$$r_2: \quad \text{NP} \xrightarrow{0.2} \langle x_1 \rangle (\text{NN}) \qquad r_9: \quad \text{NNS} \xrightarrow{0.4} \langle \textit{flies} \rangle$$

$$r_3: \quad \text{NP} \xrightarrow{0.5} \langle x_1 x_2 \rangle (\text{NN}, \text{NNS}) \quad r_{10}: \quad \text{NNS} \xrightarrow{0.6} \langle \textit{bananas} \rangle$$

$$r_4: \quad \text{NP} \xrightarrow{0.3} \langle x_1 \rangle (\text{NNS}) \qquad r_{11}: \quad \text{VBZ} \xrightarrow{1.0} \langle \textit{flies} \rangle$$

$$r_5: \quad \text{VP} \xrightarrow{0.4} \langle x_1 x_2 \rangle (\text{VBZ}, \text{PP}) \quad r_{12}: \quad \text{VBP} \xrightarrow{1.0} \langle \textit{like} \rangle$$

$$r_6: \quad \text{VP} \xrightarrow{0.6} \langle x_1 x_2 \rangle (\text{VBP}, \text{NP}) \quad r_{13}: \quad \text{IN} \xrightarrow{1.0} \langle \textit{like} \rangle$$

$$r_7: \quad \text{PP} \xrightarrow{1.0} \langle x_1 x_2 \rangle (\text{IN}, \text{NP})$$

Figure 1: Rules of RTG of Ex. 1.

from evaluating trees of $L(G)$ in the language algebra $\mathcal{L}$. For each $a \in \mathcal{L}$, we let

$$\text{AST}(G, a) = \{d \in \text{AST}(G) \mid \pi_\Sigma(d)_\mathcal{L} = a\} \ .$$

Example 1. We consider the Γ-algebra $CFG^\Delta = (\Delta^*, \phi)$ as language algebra where $\Delta = \{\textit{fruit}, \textit{flies}, \textit{like}, \textit{bananas}\}$, $\Gamma = \bigcup_{m \in \mathbb{N}} \Gamma_m$, and $\Gamma_m = \{\langle u_0 x_1 u_1 \cdots x_m u_m \rangle \mid u_i \in \Delta^*\}$. We define

$$\phi(\langle u_0 x_1 u_1 \cdots x_m u_m \rangle)(a_1, \ldots, a_m)$$
$$= u_0 a_1 u_1 \cdots a_m u_m$$

for every $a_1, \ldots, a_m \in \Delta^*$.

We consider the RTG $G = (N, \Sigma, S, R)$ with $N = \{\text{S}, \text{NP}, \text{VP}, \text{PP}, \text{NN}, \text{NNS}, \text{VBZ}, \text{VBP}, \text{IN}\}$ and $\Sigma = \{\langle \delta \rangle \mid \delta \in \Delta\} \cup \{\langle x_1 \rangle, \langle x_1 x_2 \rangle\} \subseteq \Gamma$, and R contains the rules shown in Fig. 1 (ignoring the numbers above the arrows for the time being).

The tree in the middle of the upper row of Fig. 2 is an abstract syntax tree $d \in \text{AST}(G)$. It expresses that certain insects (*fruit flies*) like something (*bananas*). We obtain $\pi_\Sigma(d)$ by dropping the non-highlighted parts of d (left of upper row). The application of the homomorphism $(.)_{CFG^\Delta}: \text{T}_\Sigma \to CFG^\Delta$ to $\pi_\Sigma(d)$ yields the string $a = \textit{fruit flies like bananas}$. We note that there is another abstract syntax tree $d' \in \text{AST}(G)$, viz., $d' = r_1(r_2(r_8), r_5(r_{11}, r_7(r_{13}, r_4(r_{10}))))$ such that $\pi_\Sigma(d')_{CFG^\Delta} = a$. It expresses how *fruit* performs a certain activity (to fly like bananas). Hence this RTG-LM is ambiguous. $\quad \Box$

It should be clear from Ex. 1 that each context-free grammar with terminal alphabet Δ can be represented as an RTG-LM (G, CFG^Δ), and vice versa, each RTG-LM (G, CFG^Δ) represents a CFG. In the same way, one can characterize LCFRS and tree adjoining grammars by (1) superposing sorts to the set N of nonterminals of the RTG (in order to represent fanout and the characteristic "substitution tree / adjoining tree" of arguments, respectively), and (2) by defining appropriate Γ-algebras $\mathcal{LCFRS}^\Delta$ (Kallmeyer, 2010, Def. 6.2+6.3) and $\mathcal{TAG}^\Delta$ (Büchse et al., 2012; Koller and Kuhlmann, 2012), respectively. The language algebras CFG^Δ, $\mathcal{LCFRS}^\Delta$, and $\mathcal{TAG}^\Delta$ are finitely decomposable.

A *weighted RTG-based language model* (wRTG-LM) is a tuple

$$\big((G, (\mathcal{L}, \phi)), \ (\mathbb{K}, \oplus, \mathbb{0}, \Omega, \textstyle\sum^\oplus), \ \text{wt} \big) \ ,$$

where

- $(G, (\mathcal{L}, \phi))$ is an RTG-LM,

- $(\mathbb{K}, \oplus, \mathbb{0}, \Omega, \sum^\oplus)$ is a complete M-monoid (*weight algebra*), and

- wt maps each rule of G with rank m to an m-ary operation in Ω. We lift wt to the mapping $\text{wt}': \text{T}_R \to \text{T}_\Omega$ and denote wt' also by wt.

Definition 2. The *weighted parsing problem* is the following problem: given a wRTG-LM $((G, (\mathcal{L}, \phi)), (\mathbb{K}, \oplus, \mathbb{0}, \Omega, \sum^\oplus), \text{wt})$ and an $a \in \mathcal{L}$, compute the value $\text{parse}(a) \in \mathbb{K}$ where

$$\text{parse}(a) = \sum_{d \in \text{AST}(G,a)}^\oplus \text{wt}(d)_\mathbb{K} \ . \qquad \Box$$

Example 3. (Ex. 1 cont.) The best derivation problem of (Goodman, 1999) consists of computing, given a syntactic object a and a grammar, the abstract syntax trees of a with maximal probability (and this probability). Let R_∞ be a ranked set such that $(R_\infty)_m$ is infinite for each $m \in \mathbb{N}$. In analogy to Goodman, we define the *best derivation M-monoid* to be the d-complete M-monoid

$$\mathbb{BD} = (V, \ \max_{\mathbb{BD}}, \ (0, \emptyset), \ \Omega_{\mathbb{BD}}, \ \textstyle\sum^{\max_{\mathbb{BD}}}),$$

where $V = [0, 1] \times \mathcal{P}(\text{T}_{R_\infty})$ and $[0, 1]$ is the interval of real numbers from 0 to 1 and

- for every $(p_1, D_1), (p_2, D_2) \in V$, the value $\max_{\mathbb{BD}}((p_1, D_1), (p_2, D_2))$ is (p_i, D_i) if $p_i > p_j$ for $i, j \in \{1, 2\}$, and $(p_1, D_1 \cup D_2)$ if $p_1 = p_2$,

- $\Omega_{\mathbb{BD}} = \{\text{tc}_{p,r} \mid p \in [0, 1] \text{ and } r \in R_\infty\}$, where for each $p \in [0, 1]$ and $r \in R_\infty$ of rank m, we define $\text{tc}_{p,r}: V^m \to V$ (tc abbreviates top concatenation) such that for every $(p_1, D_1), \ldots, (p_m, D_m) \in V$

$$\text{tc}_{p,r}((p_1, D_1), \ldots, (p_m, D_m)) = (p', D')$$

where $p' = p \cdot p_1 \cdot \ldots \cdot p_m$ and $D' = \{r(d_1, \ldots, d_m) \mid d_i \in D_i, 1 \leq i \leq m\}$, and

- for every family $((p_i, D_i) \mid i \in I)$ over V, we define $\sum^{\max_{\mathbb{BD}}}_{i \in I} (p_i, D_i) = (p, D)$, where $p = \sup\{p_i \mid i \in I\}$ and $D = \bigcup_{i \in I : p_i = p} D_i$.

Since $\mathbb{BD}$ is completely idempotent, it is also d-complete.

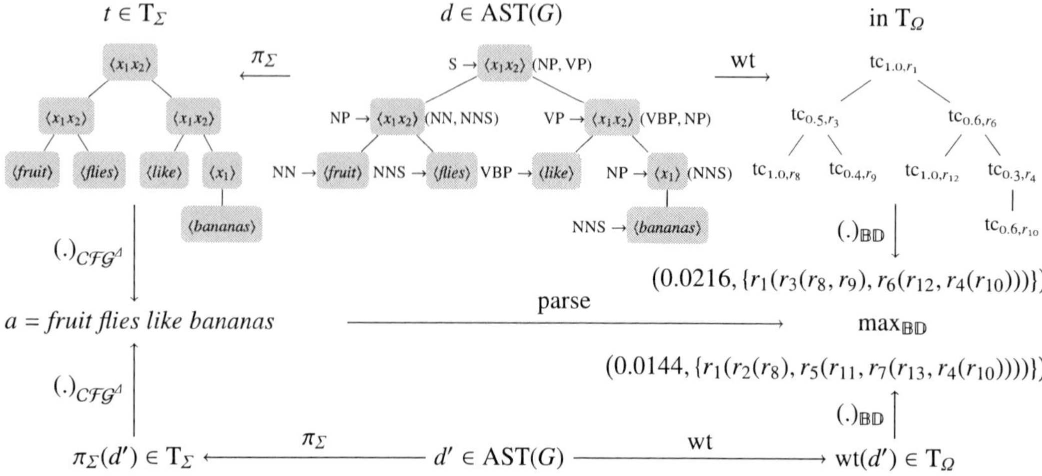

Figure 2: Illustration of the weighted parsing problem for the wRTG-LM $((G, C\!\mathcal{F}\mathcal{G}^\Delta), \mathbb{BD}, \mathrm{wt})$ and the syntactic object $a = \textit{fruit flies like bananas}$ of Δ^*, see Ex. 3.

Now we consider the finite set R of rules of the RTG G given in Ex. 1. We can assume that $R \subseteq R_\infty$ is rank preserving. We define the mapping $\mathrm{wt}\colon R \to \Omega_{\mathbb{BD}}$ by $\mathrm{wt}(r_i) = \mathrm{tc}_{p_i, r_i}$ where p_i is shown in Fig. 1 above the arrow of r_i. For each $d \in \mathrm{AST}(G, a)$, the second component of $\mathrm{wt}(d)_{\mathbb{BD}}$ has exactly one element. Recall d' from Ex. 1, a second AST which is evaluated to a. We obtain $\mathrm{wt}(d')_{\mathbb{BD}} = (0.0144, \{r_1(r_2(r_8), r_5(r_{11}, r_7(r_{13}, r_4(r_{10}))))\})$. Thus

$$\mathrm{max}_{\mathbb{BD}}\left(\mathrm{wt}(d)_{\mathbb{BD}}, \mathrm{wt}(d')_{\mathbb{BD}}\right) = \mathrm{wt}(d)_{\mathbb{BD}} \ .$$

As one might expect, it is more likely that a refers to the preferences (to *like bananas*) of certain insects (*fruit flies*). Fig. 2 illustrates the parsing problem for the wRTG-LM $((G, C\!\mathcal{F}\mathcal{G}^\Delta), \mathbb{BD}, \mathrm{wt})$ and $a = \textit{fruit flies like bananas}$. $\square$

In summary, each wRTG-LM consists of two components: a *syntax component* and a *weight component*. The syntax component (cf. the left of Fig. 2) contains the language algebra $(\mathcal{L}, \phi)$. This is a Γ-algebra whose carrier set is the set of syntactic objects. The mapping π_Σ maps each abstract syntax tree to a tree in the Σ-term algebra T_Σ, which is then evaluated to a syntactic object by the unique homomorphism $(.)_\mathcal{L}$ (recall that $\Sigma \subseteq \Gamma$).

The weight component (cf. the right of Fig. 2) contains a complete M-monoid $(\mathbb{K}, \oplus, \mathbb{0}, \Omega, \sum^\oplus)$ whose carrier set is the set of weights. The mapping wt maps each abstract syntax tree to a tree in the Ω-term algebra T_Ω, which is then evaluated to a weight in $\mathbb{K}$ by the unique homomorphism $(.)_\mathbb{K}$. Weights in $\mathbb{K}$ are accumulated using $\oplus$.

$$
\begin{array}{lll}
A \to \mathrm{del}_a(A) & \phi(\mathrm{del}_a)(w) = aw & \mathrm{del}_a(n) = n + 1 \\
A \to \mathrm{ins}_a(A) & \phi(\mathrm{ins}_a)(w) = wa & \mathrm{ins}_a(n) = n + 1 \\
A \to \mathrm{rep}_{a,b}(A) & \phi(\mathrm{rep}_{a,b})(w) = awb & \mathrm{rep}_{a,b}(n) = n' \\
A \to \mathrm{nil} & \phi(\mathrm{nil})() = \$ & \mathrm{nil}() = 0
\end{array}
$$

Figure 3: Rules of G for each $a, b \in \Delta$, the interpretation ϕ, and the operations in Ω where $n' = n + 1$ if $a \neq b$, and n otherwise.

The weighted parsing problem takes as input a wRTG-LM and a syntactic object a, and it computes the $\oplus$-accumulation of the weights of each AST of a.

Example 4. Giegerich et al. (2004) formalized dynamic programming (Bellman, 1952, 1954) in an algebraic setting, called *algebraic dynamic programming* (ADP). We claim that each ADP problem is a weighted parsing problem. To support this statement, we consider the computation of the minimum edit distance (med) between two words over some alphabet Δ by deletion, insertion, and replacement, and we "simulate" its ADP-specification as wRTG-LM $((G, (\mathcal{L}, \phi)), \mathbb{K}, \mathrm{wt})$. The rules of the RTG G and the interpretation ϕ are shown in the first and second columns of Fig. 3, respectively. Thus, for each tree $t \in L(G)$, $t_\mathcal{L} = u\$v$ for some $u, v \in \Delta^*$. We choose the complete, distributive M-monoid $(\mathbb{K}, \oplus, \emptyset, \Omega, \sum^\oplus)$ with $\mathbb{K} = \{h(F) \mid F \in \mathcal{P}(\mathbb{N})\}$ for the single-valued objective function $h\colon \mathcal{P}(\mathbb{N}) \to \mathcal{P}(\mathbb{N})$ with $h(F) = \{\min(F)\}$. We let $F_1 \oplus F_2 = h(F_1 \cup F_2)$ for every $F_1, F_2 \in \mathbb{K}$, and $\sum^\oplus_{i \in \mathbb{N}} F_i = \{\inf(\bigcup_{i \in \mathbb{N}} F_i)\}$. The set Ω is shown in the third column of Fig. 3.

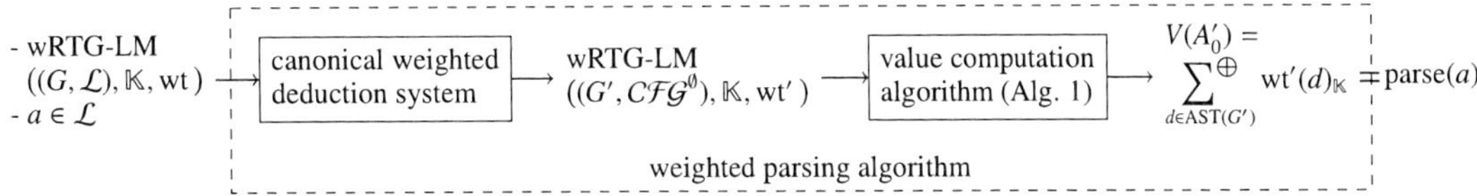

Figure 4: Two-phase pipeline for solving the weighted parsing problem (A_0' is the initial nonterminal of G').

Note that h satisfies Bellman's principle of optimality: $h(\omega(F)) = h(\omega(h(F)))$ for each unary $\omega \in \Omega$ and $F \in \mathbb{K}$. Then $\mathrm{med}(u, v) = \mathrm{parse}(u\$v^{-1})$ for every $u, v \in \Delta^*$, where v^{-1} is the reversal of v.

This construction can be generalized to a procedure which turns every specification of an ADP problem into a weighted parsing problem. Due to space restrictions, we cannot present this procedure in its entirety. $\qquad\square$

4   The weighted parsing algorithm

The weighted parsing algorithm is supposed to solve the weighted parsing problem. As input, it takes a wRTG-LM $\mathcal{G}$ and a syntactic object a. Its output is intended to be $\mathrm{parse}(a)$. The algorithm is a pipeline with two phases (cf. Fig. 4) and follows the modular approach of Nederhof (2003). First, a *canonical weighted deduction system* computes from $\mathcal{G}$ and a a new wRTG-LM $\mathcal{G}'$ with the same weight structure as $\mathcal{G}$, but a different RTG and the language algebra $C\mathcal{F}\mathcal{G}^\emptyset$. Second, $\mathcal{G}'$ is the input to the *value computation algorithm* (Alg. 1), which computes the value $V(A_0')$; this is supposed to be $\sum^{\oplus}_{d\in\mathrm{AST}(G')} \mathrm{wt}(d)_{\mathbb{K}} = \mathrm{parse}(a)$.

Weighted deduction systems.   Parsing of some string w with some grammar G can be formalized as a deduction system $\mathcal{D}$ (Shieber et al., 1995). $\mathcal{D}$ consists of a set of inference rules

$$\frac{I_1 \ldots I_m}{I} \{c_1, \ldots, c_p\}$$

where $m \in \mathbb{N}$, $I, I_1, \ldots, I_m$ are *items*, and $c_1, \ldots, c_p$ are side conditions. Each item represents a Boolean-valued property (of some combination of nonterminals of G and/or substrings of $a = w$). The meaning of an inference rule is: given that $I_1, \ldots, I_m$ and $c_1, \ldots, c_p$ are true, I is true as well. Nederhof (2003) pointed out that "a deduction system having a grammar G [...] and input string w in the side conditions can be seen as a construction c of a context-free grammar $c(G, w)$ [...]"; also, he extended $\mathcal{D}$ and $c(G, a)$ with weights.

Inspired by this, we define the *canonical weighted deduction system* as a mapping cwds which takes two arguments: (a) a wRTG-LM

$\mathcal{G} = ((G, \mathcal{L}), \mathbb{K}, \mathrm{wt})$ such that the language algebra $(\mathcal{L}, \phi)$ is finitely decomposable and (b) a syntactic object $a \in \mathcal{L}$. Let $G = (N, \Sigma, A_0, R)$. Then we define

$$\mathrm{cwds}(\mathcal{G}, a) = ((G', C\mathcal{F}\mathcal{G}^\emptyset), \mathbb{K}, \mathrm{wt}') ,$$

where $G' = (N', \Sigma', A_0', R')$ and

- $N' = \{(A_0, a)\} \cup (N \times \Sigma \times \mathrm{factors}(a))$; N' is finite, because $\mathcal{L}$ is finitely decomposable,

- $\Sigma' = \{\langle x_1 \ldots x_m \rangle \mid$ a rule with rank m is in $R\}$,

- $A_0' = (A_0, a)$, and

- for each $\sigma \in \Sigma$, the rule $r' = (A_0, a) \to (A_0, \sigma, a)$ is in R' and $\mathrm{wt}'(r') = \mathrm{id}$; for each $r = (A \to \sigma(A_1, \ldots, A_m))$ in R and $a_0, a_1, \ldots, a_m \in \mathrm{factors}(a)$ with $\phi(\sigma)(a_1, \ldots, a_m) = a_0$ and every rule $A_i \to \sigma_i(\ldots)$ ($i \in [m]$) in R, the rule r'
  $$(A, \sigma, a_0) \to \langle x_1 \ldots x_m \rangle ((A_1, \sigma_1, a_1), \ldots, (A_m, \sigma_m, a_m))$$
  is in R' and we let $\mathrm{wt}'(r') = \mathrm{wt}(r)$.

Note that cwds implements a CYK-like deduction system. The elements of N' have a very general form. Depending on $\mathcal{L}$, they can be understood as, e.g., spans of strings, occurrences of patterns in trees, or occurrences of subgraphs in graphs. We note that for every $d \in \mathrm{AST}(G')$ it holds that $\pi_\Sigma(d)_{C\mathcal{F}\mathcal{G}^\emptyset} = \varepsilon$, i.e., each abstract syntax tree is evaluated to the empty string. Moreover, cwds is *weight-preserving* in the following sense:

(1) there is a bijective mapping ψ from the set $\mathrm{AST}(G, a)$ to $\mathrm{AST}(G')$ and

(2) for every $d \in \mathrm{AST}(G, a)$ we have that $\mathrm{wt}(d)_{\mathbb{K}} = \mathrm{wt}'(\psi(d))_{\mathbb{K}}$.

Value computation algorithm.   This is Alg. 1. Its input is a wRTG-LM $\mathcal{G}'$ with language algebra $C\mathcal{F}\mathcal{G}^\emptyset$. It maintains a mapping V, which assigns a weight to each nonterminal, and a Boolean variable *changed*. The output is the value $V(A_0')$. The algorithm starts by assigning the weight $\mathbb{0}$ to each nonterminal (lines 1–2). Then, in a *repeat-until loop* (lines 3–12), the weight of each nonterminal is recomputed in every iteration of that loop as follows (where $\langle x_{1,m}\rangle$ abbreviates $\langle x_1, \ldots, x_m \rangle$):

$$V(A) = \bigoplus_{\substack{r\in R': \\ r=(A\to\langle x_{1,m}\rangle(A_1,\ldots,A_m))}} \mathrm{wt}'(r)(V(A_1), \ldots, V(A_m)) .$$

Algorithm 1 Value computation algorithm

Input: $((G', CFG^0), (\mathbb{K}, \oplus, \mathbb{0}, \Omega, \sum^{\oplus}), \mathrm{wt}')$ which is a wRTG-LM with $G' = (N', \Sigma', A'_0, R')$
Variables: $V: N' \to \mathbb{K}, V' \in \mathbb{K}, changed \in \mathbb{B}$
Output: $V(A'_0)$

1: **for each** $A \in N'$ **do**
2:     $V(A) \leftarrow \mathbb{0}$
3: **repeat**
4:     $changed \leftarrow$ false
5:     **for each** $A \in N'$ **do**
6:        $V' \leftarrow \mathbb{0}$
7:        **for each** $r = (A \to \langle x_{1,m}\rangle(A_1, \ldots, A_m))$ in R' **do**
8:           $V' \leftarrow V' \oplus \mathrm{wt}'(r)(V(A_1), \ldots, V(A_m))$
9:        **if** $V(A) \neq V'$ **then**
10:           $changed \leftarrow$ true
11:           $V(A) \leftarrow V'$
12: **until** $changed =$ false

The algorithm terminates after the first iteration in which no nonterminal has changed its weight.

We note that in practice, a complete computation of $\mathrm{cwds}(G, a)$ prior to the execution of the value computation algorithm (Alg. 1) is impossible. Similar to Nederhof (2003), we execute the value computation algorithm on an incomplete input which is extended on demand (lazy evaluation). More precisely, G' is initialized so that it only contains the rules of rank 0 (and the nonterminals in their left-hand sides). Then, each time a value different from $\mathbb{0}$ is first assigned to a nonterminal A in line 11, we compute the following set of rules: each rule whose right-hand side only contains A and other nonterminals for which this computation has already been done is in that set. These new rules (and the nonterminals in their left-hand sides) are added to G'.

5 Termination and correctness

We are interested in two formal properties of the value computation algorithm (Alg. 1) and of the weighted parsing algorithm (Fig. 4): termination and correctness.

The value computation algorithm computes the weights of the ASTs bottom-up and reuses the results of common subtrees (as in dynamic programming); this requires distributivity of the weight algebra. Moreover, solving the weighted parsing problem by a terminating algorithm involves the following difficulty: there may be infinitely many ASTs (due to cycles) which are evaluated to the

same syntactic object a. Thus $\mathrm{parse}(a)$ is an infinite sum, which in general cannot be computed in finite time. Hence, a terminating algorithm can only solve the weighted parsing problem if the infinite sum is equal to the sum over some finite subset of the infinite sum's index set.

We have organized this section as follows. In Subsection 5.1 we define the class of *closed* wRTG-LMs (similar to Mohri, 2002) and prove that the value computation algorithm (Alg. 1) is terminating and correct for closed wRTG-LMs as input. We say that the value computation algorithm is *correct* if after termination

$$V(A'_0) = \sum_{d \in \mathrm{AST}(G')}^{\oplus} \mathrm{wt}'(d)_{\mathbb{K}} \ .$$

In Subsection 5.2 we prove that the weighted parsing algorithm (Fig. 4) is terminating and correct for two classes of inputs. We say that the weighted parsing algorithm is *correct* if it computes $\mathrm{parse}(a)$.

5.1 Properties of the value computation algorithm

Since each wRTG-LM has a finite set of rules, an infinite set of ASTs is only possible if the ASTs are cyclic in the following sense. Recall that R' is the set of rules of the input G' to the value computation algorithm (Alg. 1). Let $\rho \in (R')^*$. We call ρ *cyclic* if $|\rho| \geq 2$, $\rho_1 = \rho_{|\rho|}$, and for every $i, j \in \mathbb{N}$, if $1 \leq i < j < |\rho|$, then $\rho_i \neq \rho_j$. From now on, let $\rho \in (R')^*$ be cyclic, $d \in T_{R'}$, and $c \in \mathbb{N}$. A path p in d is (c, ρ)-*cyclic* if ρ occurs exactly c times in $\mathrm{seq}(d, p)$. We define the set $\mathrm{cutout}(d, \rho)$ which contains every tree obtained from d by cutting out at least one occurrence of ρ. We illustrate cutout by an example in Fig. 5.

Definition 5. Let $c \in \mathbb{N}$. A wRTG-LM $G' = ((G', CFG^0), \mathbb{K}, \mathrm{wt}')$ is *c-closed* if $\mathbb{K}$ is distributive and d-complete, and for each $d \in T_{R'}$ and cyclic string $\rho \in (R')^*$ the following holds: if there is a (c, ρ)-cyclic path in d, then

$$\mathrm{wt}'(d)_{\mathbb{K}} \oplus \bigoplus_{d' \in \mathrm{cutout}(d, \rho)} \mathrm{wt}'(d')_{\mathbb{K}} = \bigoplus_{d' \in \mathrm{cutout}(d, \rho)} \mathrm{wt}'(d')_{\mathbb{K}} \ .$$

G' is *closed* if it is c-closed for some $c \in \mathbb{N}$.   □

For every $c \in \mathbb{N}$ and ranked set R', we let $T_{R'}^{(c)}$ be the set of all those $d \in T_{R'}$ such that for every cyclic $\rho \in (R')^*$ and $c' > c$, no path in d is (ρ, c')-cyclic. In other words, $T_{R'}^{(c)}$ contains all those trees of $T_{R'}$ which have at most c occurrences of some cycle in some of their paths. Clearly $T_{R'}^{(c)}$ is finite, $T_{R'}^{(c)} \subseteq T_{R'}^{(c+1)}$ for every $c \in \mathbb{N}$,

$$r_3 - \boxed{r_1 - r_2 - r_1} - r_3 - \boxed{r_1 - r_2 - r_1} - r_4$$

with subtrees r_4; $r_2 - r_4$; $r_2 - r_4$; r_4.

$$r_3 - \boxed{r_1 - r_2 - r_1} - r_3 - \boxed{r_1} - r_4 \qquad r_3 - \boxed{r_1} - r_3 - \boxed{r_1 - r_2 - r_1} - r_4 \qquad r_3 - \boxed{r_1} - r_3 - \boxed{r_1} - r_4$$

Figure 5: Top: tree d over the ranked set $R' = \{r_1^{(2)}, r_2^{(1)}, r_3^{(1)}, r_4^{(0)}\}$ with a $(2, \rho)$-cyclic path (horizontal line) for $\rho = r_1 r_2 r_1$. Bottom: the set $\mathrm{cutout}(d, \rho)$. Please do not confuse the elements of R' with the rules of Ex. 1 and 3.

and $\bigcup_{c \in \mathbb{N}} T_{R'}^{(c)} = T_{R'}$. Given a wRTG-LM $G' = ((G', CFG^{\emptyset}), \mathbb{K}, \mathrm{wt}')$ with set of rules R', we let $\mathrm{AST}(G')^{(c)} = T_{R'}^{(c)} \cap \mathrm{AST}(G')$ for every $c \in \mathbb{N}$.

Theorem 6. For every $c \in \mathbb{N}$ and c-closed wRTG-LM $((G', CFG^{\emptyset}), \mathbb{K}, \mathrm{wt}')$ the following holds:

$$\sum_{d \in \mathrm{AST}(G')}^{\oplus} \mathrm{wt}'(d)_{\mathbb{K}} = \bigoplus_{d \in \mathrm{AST}(G')^{(c)}} \mathrm{wt}'(d)_{\mathbb{K}} \ .$$

Proof (sketch). As $\mathbb{K}$ is distributive, we can show by induction on $n \in \mathbb{N}$ that for every $B \subseteq \mathrm{AST}(G') \setminus \mathrm{AST}(G')^{(c)}$ with $|B| = n$, adding B to the index set of $\oplus$ does not change the sum's value. Then, as $\mathbb{K}$ is d-complete, the equality holds. ∎

This theorem reflects the desired property: given that our wRTG-LM is c-closed (with $c \in \mathbb{N}$), each (possibly infinite) sum over all ASTs can be computed as a sum over the finite set $\mathrm{AST}(G')^{(c)}$.

Theorem 7. The value computation algorithm (Alg. 1) is terminating and correct for every closed wRTG-LM G' with language algebra $CFG^{\emptyset}$.

Proof (sketch). Let G' be c-closed. We note that in line 8, the value in the right-hand side of $\oplus$ always corresponds to the sum over the weights of some trees in $(T_{R'})_A$; this is due to the fact that $\mathbb{K}$ is distributive. By the form of recomputation in lines 3–12, each $d \in (T_{R'})_A$ contributes to that sum at most once. Furthermore, V' only differs from $V(A)$ if a tree from the finite set $T_{R'}^{(c)}$ has been used to compute V', but not $V(A)$ (this is a consequence of G' being closed). Thus, *changed* is only set to true finitely often and the algorithm eventually terminates. Then, after termination, $V(A_0') = \bigoplus_{d \in \mathrm{AST}(G')^{(c)}} \mathrm{wt}'(d)_{\mathbb{K}}$ and Theorem 6 implies correctness. ∎

5.2 Properties of the weighted parsing algorithm

We discuss two classes of wRTG-LMs for which the weighted parsing algorithm (Fig. 4) is termi-

nating and correct.

(1) Closed wRTG-LMs with arbitrary language algebras. Each of them is a wRTG-LM $((G, (\mathcal{L}, \phi)), (\mathbb{K}, \oplus, 0, \Omega, \sum^{\oplus}), \mathrm{wt})$ which is c-closed for some $c \in \mathbb{N}$, and c-*closed* is defined as in Def. 5. (We note that this generalization is possible because Def. 5 does not use any property of $CFG^{\emptyset}$.) The following particular wRTG-LMs are closed:

- wRTG-LMs with acyclic RTG, where an RTG G is acyclic if $\mathrm{AST}(G) = \mathrm{AST}(G)^{(0)}$,

- wRTG-LMs with superior, d-complete M-monoids as weight algebras, and

- wRTG-LMs with weight algebra $\mathbb{BD}$ if no chain rule and ε-rule has probability 1.0 (as in Ex. 3).

(2) Non-looping wRTG-LMs with distributive M-monoids as weight algebras. A wRTG-LM G is *non-looping* if for every syntactic object a and tree d over the set of rules of G which is evaluated to a the following holds: no proper subtree of d is evaluated to a. ADP problems can be specified by non-looping wRTG-LMs, because the syntactic objects of ADP represent (sub-)problems which have to be solved. Thus, if G is looping, then the solution of a subproblem would depend on itself, which contradicts dynamic programming. In general, non-looping is not decidable, but it is for particular language algebras, e.g., CFG^{Δ}.

Lemma 8. For every closed or nonlooping wRTG-LM G with finitely decomposable language algebra and syntactic object a, the wRTG-LM $\mathrm{cwds}(G, a)$ is closed.

Theorem 9. The weighted parsing algorithm (Fig. 4) is terminating and correct for every closed or nonlooping wRTG-LM with finitely decomposable language algebra.

Proof. The weighted parsing algorithm terminates because (a) the computation of cwds is terminating

algorithm	class of valid inputs	class C_1 of RTG	class C_2 of weight algebras
(a) Knuth (1977)	$C_1 \times C_2$	RTG	superior M-monoid
(b) Goodman (1999)	$C_1 \times C_2$	acyclic RTG	complete semiring
(c) Mohri (2002)	C_2 closed for C_1	monadic RTG	commutative, d-complete semiring
(d) Alg. 1	closed wRTG-LM	RTG	distributive, d-complete M-monoid

Table 1: Comparison of four value computation algorithms. The second column represents the class of wRTG-LMs to which the corresponding algorithm is applicable. The expression $C_1 \times C_2$ denotes the class of all wRTG-LMs with RTGs in C_1 and weight algebras in C_2.

for every wRTG-LM with finitely decomposable language algebra and (b) the value computation algorithm (Alg. 1) is terminating by Theorem 7, which we can be applied due to Lemma 8. The weighted parsing algorithm is correct because (a) cwds is weight-preserving and (b) the value computation algorithm is correct by Theorem 7 (which is applicable again due to Lemma 8), hence

$$\text{parse}(a) \overset{(a)}{=} \sum_{d \in \text{AST}(G')}^{\oplus} \text{wt}'(d)_{\mathbb{K}} \overset{(b)}{=} V(A_0') \ . \quad \blacksquare$$

6 Comparison of value computation algorithms

Here we compare our value computation algorithm (Alg. 1) to the algorithm of Knuth (1977), the second phase of Goodman (1999), and the algorithm of Mohri (2002).

We focus on the question of applicability of the algorithms, i.e., we identify the classes of inputs for which the algorithms are terminating and correct (*class of valid inputs*). In order to have a basis for a fair comparison, we understand the inputs of the algorithms of Knuth (1977), Goodman (1999), and Mohri (2002) as particular wRTG-LMs of the form $((G', C\mathcal{F}\mathcal{G}^\emptyset), (\mathbb{K}, \oplus, \mathbb{0}, \Omega, \sum^\oplus), \text{wt}')$ with $G' = (N', \Sigma', A_0', R')$. An algorithm is correct for such a wRTG-LM if it returns $\sum_{d \in \text{AST}(G')}^{\oplus} \text{wt}'(d)_{\mathbb{K}}$.

We employ two parameters: C_1 (subset of the class of all RTGs) and C_2 (subset of the class of all weight algebras). Tab. 1 shows the classes of valid inputs parameterized with values for C_1 and C_2. Each valid input in rows (a)–(d) is a closed wRTG-LM. Thus, if one of the value computation algorithms (a)–(c) is applicable, then our value computation algorithm (Alg. 1) is applicable too. In particular, Alg. 1 is applicable to wRTG-LMs with the best derivation M-monoid $\mathbb{BD}$ as weight algebra (cf. Ex. 3), which in general is the case for neither of algorithms (a)–(c). The reason for this is that $\mathbb{BD}$ is not superior (opposing (a)) and RTG-LMs are in general neither acyclic (opposing (b))

nor monadic (opposing (c)). The same holds for ADP problems.

We cannot give a general statement about the complexity of our value computation algorithm (Alg. 1), because the operations in the weight algebra of a wRTG-LM can be undecidable. If we abstract from the costs of particular operations, then we obtain the complexity of Mohri's algorithm. This complexity depends on the number of times the value of a nonterminal changes, which in general is not polynomial in the size of the input wRTG-LM. Mohri circumvents this problem by specifying the order in which nonterminals are processed for well-known classes of inputs, e.g., acyclic graphs or superior weight algebras. We can adapt this idea by imposing such an ordering on the iteration over the nonterminals in line 5. Thus our value computation algorithm achieves the same complexity as Knuth's algorithm (if the input is restricted to superior wRTG-LMs) or the algorithm in Goodman's second phase (if the input is restricted to acyclic wRTG-LMs), respectively.

We note that although our value computation algorithm (Alg. 1) has the same complexity as the other algorithms, in average it performs more computations than those. This is because in each iteration of lines 5–11, the values of all nonterminals are recomputed. This could be avoided by using a direct generalization of Mohri's algorithm to the branching case rather than Alg. 1. However, the intricacies of such a generalization would exceed the scope of this paper.

Acknowledgements

We thank the anonymous reviewers for their helpful comments and our colleagues Kilian Gebhardt and Frederic Dörband for fruitful discussions.

References

Y. Bar-Hillel, M. Perles, and E. Shamir. 1961. On formal properties of simple phrase structure grammars. 14:143–172. Reprinted in Y. Bar-Hillel. (1964). *Language and Information: Selected Essays on their Theory and Application*, Addison-Wesley 1964, 116–150.

R. Bellman. 1952. On the theory of dynamic programming. *Proceedings of the National Academy of Sciences*, 38(8):716–719.

R. Bellman. 1954. The theory of dynamic programming. Technical report, RAND Corp Santa Monica CA.

W. S. Brainerd. 1969. Tree generating regular systems.

M. Büchse, M.-J. Nederhof, and H. Vogler. 2012. Tree parsing for tree-adjoining machine translation. *Journal of Logic and Computation*, 22(6).

E. Dijkstra. 1959. A note on two problems in connexion with graphs. *Numer. Math.*, 1:269–271.

F. Drewes, K. Gebhardt, and H. Vogler. 2016. EM-training for weighted aligned hypergraph bimorphisms. In *Proceedings of the SIGFSM Workshop on Statistical NLP and Weighted Automata*, pages 60–69, Berlin, Germany. Association for Computational Linguistics.

S. Eilenberg. 1974. *Automata, languages, and machines*. Academic press.

Z. Fülöp, A. Maletti, and H. Vogler. 2009. A Kleene theorem for weighted tree automata over distributive multioperator monoids. *Theory of Computing Systems*, 44(3):455–499.

R. Giegerich, C. Meyer, and P. Steffen. 2004. A discipline of dynamic programming over sequence data. *Science of Computer Programming*, 51:215–263.

J. A. Goguen, J. W. Thatcher, E. G. Wagner, and J. B. Wright. 1977. Initial algebra semantics and continuous algebras. *Journal of the ACM (JACM)*, 24(1):68–95.

J. Goodman. 1999. Semiring parsing. *Computational Linguistics*, 25(4):573–605.

L. Kallmeyer. 2010. *Parsing beyond context-free grammars*. Springer.

G. Karner. 1992. On limits in complete semirings. *Semigroup Forum*, 45(1):148–165.

N. A. Khabbaz. 1974. Control sets on linear grammars. *Information and Control*, 25(3):206–221.

D. E. Knuth. 1977. A Generalization of Dijkstra's Algorithm. *Inform. Process. Lett.*, 6(1):1–5.

A. Koller and M. Kuhlmann. 2012. Decomposing TAG algorithms using simple algebraizations. In *Proceedings of the 11th TAG+ Workshop*, Paris.

W. Kuich. 1999. Linear systems of equations and automata on distributive multioperator monoids. *Contributions to general algebra*, 12:247–256.

B. Mahr. 1984. Iteration and summability in semirings. *Annals of Discrete Mathematics*, pages 229–256.

M. Mohri. 2002. Semiring frameworks and algorithms for shortest-distance problems. *Journal of Automata, Languages and Combinatorics*, 7(3):321–350.

M.-J. Nederhof. 2003. Squibs and discussions: Weighted deductive parsing and Knuth's algorithm. *Computational Linguistics*, 29(1):135–143.

S. Shieber, Y. Schabes, and F. Pereira. 1995. Principles and implementation of deductive parsing. *The Journal of Logic Programming*, 24(12):3–36.

W. Wechler. 1992. *Universal Algebra for Computer Scientists*, first edition, volume 25 of *Monogr. Theoret. Comput. Sci. EATCS Ser.* Springer-Verlag, Heidelberg/Berlin.

Regular transductions with MCFG input syntax

Mark-Jan Nederhof
University of St Andrews

Heiko Vogler
Technische Universität Dresden

Abstract

We show that regular transductions for which the input part is generated by some multiple context-free grammar can be simulated by synchronous multiple context-free grammars. We prove that synchronous multiple context-free grammars are strictly more powerful than this combination of regular transductions and multiple context-free grammars.

1 Introduction

In machine translation, one is interested in automatically translating sentences of one natural language into sentences of another natural language. Such translations can be considered as string-to-string transductions by viewing the words of a natural language as symbols of a formal language, and viewing sentences as strings. Several formal models for such transductions have been proposed, e.g., syntax-directed translation schemata (Lewis and Stearns, 1968), also known as synchronous context-free grammars (Chiang, 2007), two-way generalized sequential machines (2gsm) (Sheperdson, 1959; Aho and Ullman, 1970), MSO definable string-to-string transductions (MSO-sst) (Courcelle and Engelfriet, 2012), and streaming string transducers (SST) (Alur and Černý, 2010).

It has been established that the deterministic versions of 2gsm, MSO-sst, and SST generate the same class of string-to-string transductions (Alur and Černý, 2010; Engelfriet and Hoogeboom, 2001); the same is true for the nondeterministic versions of MSO-sst and SST (Alur and Deshmukh, 2011). Due to these characterizations, the involved transducers and the corresponding transductions are called *regular transducers* and *regular transductions*, respectively.

In statistical machine translation (Lopez, 2008), one aims at automatically inferring a translation model from some bilingual corpus, where the translation model is chosen from some class of formal devices, e.g., the class of regular transducers. In the seminal paper by Brown et al. (1993), the inference is based on the concept of *alignment graph* (used as hidden random variable in the EM-algorithm (Dempster et al., 1977)); each such graph consists of an input sentence w, an output sentence v, and a binary relation between the set $\mathrm{pos}(v)$ of positions of v and the set $\mathrm{pos}(w)$ of positions of w. In the particular case of the IBM models each alignment graph is a partial mapping from $\mathrm{pos}(v)$ to $\mathrm{pos}(w)$. These have almost the same mathematical structure as the *origin graphs* of Bojańczyk (2013), except that in the latter, the mapping is total.

Bojańczyk (2013) and Bojańczyk et al. (2017a,b) investigated the concept of regular transductions with origin semantics, where the origin semantics of a regular transducer $\mathcal{A}$ is a set of the origin graphs that $\mathcal{A}$ can create: if $\mathcal{A}$ produces a portion v' of the output while reading the input symbol at position i, then each position of v' is aligned to i.

Since the domain of each regular transduction is a regular string language, it cannot capture non-regular syntactic phenomena on the source side of the translation. To enhance this capability, this paper investigates imposing additional syntactic restrictions on the input of a regular transducer, through intersection with a multiple context-free grammar (Seki et al., 1991) (MCFG). We prove that the resulting transduction can also be generated by a synchronous MCFG, which is a pair of MCFGs with synchronized nonterminals, much as in, e.g., synchronous context-free grammars. We further give an example of a synchronous MCFG whose transduction cannot be represented as the intersection of a regular transducer and a MCFG.

Proceedings of the 14th International Conference on Finite-State Methods and Natural Language Processing, pages 56–64
Dresden, Germany, September 23-25, 2019. ©2019 Association for Computational Linguistics

2 Preliminaries

We let $\mathbb{N} = \{0, 1, 2, \ldots\}$, $\mathbb{N}_+ = \mathbb{N} \setminus \{0\}$, and $[i, j] = \{k \in \mathbb{N} \mid i \leq k \leq j\}$ for every $i, j \in \mathbb{N}$. We abbreviate $[1, j]$ by $[j]$. We abbreviate sequences of objects, like $a_1 \cdots a_n$ and $a_1, \ldots, a_n$, by $a_{1,n}$. We denote the powerset of a set A by $\mathcal{P}(A)$. We abbreviate a set $\{a\}$ with one element by a. An alphabet A is a nonempty and finite set.

For functions $f : A \to B$ and $g : B \to C$, we denote their composition by $f \circ g$, i.e., $(f \circ g)(a) = g(f(a))$ for each $a \in A$.

We let $X = \{x_1, x_2, x_3, \ldots\}$ be a set of *variables* and $X_k = \{x_1, \ldots, x_k\}$ for each $k \in \mathbb{N}$.

Let Σ_1 and Σ_2 be alphabets. An *origin graph* (over Σ_1 and Σ_2) is a triple (w, v, g) where $w \in \Sigma_1^*$, $v \in \Sigma_2^*$, and g (*origin mapping*) maps each position j of v to a position i of w. Intuitively, the pair $(j, i) \in g$ indicates that the symbol at position j of v originated from position i of w. Let A be a set of origin graphs and L_1 and L_2 formal languages. Then we define

$$A \text{\Large$\cap$} (L_1 \times L_2) =$$
$$\{(w, v, g) \mid (w, v, g) \in A, w \in L_1, v \in L_2\} \ .$$

We generally refer to Σ_1 as the *input alphabet* and Σ_2 as the *output alphabet*. For a set $L \subseteq L_1 \times L_2$ we define the *input projection* as $\mathrm{proj}_1(L) = \{w \mid (w, v) \in L\}$ and the *output projection* as $\mathrm{proj}_2(L) = \{v \mid (w, v) \in L\}$.

3 Streaming String Transducers

Here we recall the definition of streaming transducer from Alur and Deshmukh (2011), with some slight modifications that refer to the final output of a string.

Let $\mathcal{R}$ be a finite set of *registers*, and let $\rho = |\mathcal{R}|$. Let Γ be an alphabet. A *copyless assignment to $\mathcal{R}$ over Γ* (or short: *assignment*) is a mapping $\alpha : \mathcal{R} \to (\mathcal{R} \cup \Gamma)^*$ such that any $r \in \mathcal{R}$ occurs at most once in the set $\{\alpha(r') \mid r' \in \mathcal{R}\}$. We assume there is a fixed total ordering $r_1, \ldots, r_\rho$ of the ρ registers in $\mathcal{R}$. This allows us to specify an assignment α in the form $(r_1, \ldots, r_\rho) := (\alpha(r_1), \ldots, \alpha(r_\rho))$. The *identity assignment* is the mapping $\mathrm{id} : \mathcal{R} \to (\mathcal{R} \cup \Gamma)^*$ such that $\mathrm{id}(r) = r$ for each $r \in \mathcal{R}$. The set of all copyless assignments to $\mathcal{R}$ over Γ is denoted by $\mathrm{Ass}(\mathcal{R}, \Gamma)$. The composition of two copyless assignments $\alpha_1, \alpha_2 \in \mathrm{Ass}(\mathcal{R}, \Gamma)$ is the mapping $\alpha_1 \circ \alpha_2' : \mathcal{R} \to (\mathcal{R} \cup \Gamma)^*$, where α_2' is the canonical extension of α_2 to a mapping of type $(\mathcal{R} \cup \Gamma)^* \to (\mathcal{R} \cup \Gamma)^*$. For convenience, we drop the prime and write $\alpha_1 \circ \alpha_2$ instead of $\alpha_1 \circ \alpha_2'$. Clearly, $\alpha_1 \circ \alpha_2$ is a copyless assignment to $\mathcal{R}$ over Γ, and $(\mathrm{Ass}(\mathcal{R}, \Gamma), \circ, \mathrm{id})$ is a monoid.

A *nondeterministic streaming string transducer* (*over Σ_1 and Σ_2*) (for short: NSST) is a tuple $\mathcal{A} = (Q, \Sigma_1, \Sigma_2, \mathcal{R}, r_o, T, q_0, F)$ where Q is a finite, nonempty set of *states*, Σ_1 and Σ_2 are the input alphabet and the output alphabet, respectively, $\mathcal{R}$ is a finite set of *registers*, $r_o \in \mathcal{R}$ is the *output register*, $T \subseteq Q \times \Sigma_1 \times \mathrm{Ass}(\mathcal{R}, \Sigma_2) \times Q$ is a finite set of *transitions*, $q_0 \in Q$ is the *initial state*, and $F \subseteq Q$ is the set of *final states*.

The *summary of $\mathcal{A}$* is the mapping

$$\Delta : (Q \times \Sigma_1^*) \to \mathcal{P}(\mathrm{Ass}(\mathcal{R}, \Sigma_2) \times Q)$$

defined inductively as follows.

$$\Delta(q, \varepsilon) = \{(\mathrm{id}, q)\}$$
$$\Delta(q, wa) = \{(\alpha \circ \alpha_w, q'') \mid$$
$$(\exists q' \in Q) : (\alpha_w, q') \in \Delta(q, w),$$
$$(q', a, \alpha, q'') \in T\}$$

for each $q \in Q$, $w \in \Sigma_1^*$, and $a \in \Sigma_1$.

The string-to-string transduction *computed by $\mathcal{A}$* is the set $[\![\mathcal{A}]\!] \subseteq \Sigma_1^* \times \Sigma_2^*$ defined by

$$[\![\mathcal{A}]\!] = \{(w, (\alpha \circ \alpha_\varepsilon')(r_o)) \mid$$
$$w \in \Sigma_1^*, (\exists q' \in F) : (\alpha, q') \in \Delta(q_0, w)\}$$

where $\alpha_\varepsilon \in \mathrm{Ass}(\mathcal{R}, \Sigma_2)$ is defined by $\alpha_\varepsilon(r) = \varepsilon$. Clearly, $\mathrm{proj}_1([\![\mathcal{A}]\!])$ is a regular language. We note that $q_0 \in F$ if and only if $\{v \in \Sigma_2^* \mid (\varepsilon, v) \in [\![\mathcal{A}]\!]\} = \{\varepsilon\}$.

Each $(w, v) \in [\![\mathcal{A}]\!]$ is obtained by at least one sequence of transitions, and possibly more than one due to nondeterminism. For a given such sequence, each symbol occurrence in v is obtained by application of a transition (q', a, α, q''), and this links the index of that symbol occurrence in v to the index of the corresponding occurrence of a in w. Thereby the sequence of transitions corresponds in a natural way to an origin graph. The set of such origin graphs is denoted by $[\![\mathcal{A}]\!]^o$, and will be called the *origin semantics of $\mathcal{A}$*.

Example 3.1. Let $\Sigma = \{a, b, \#\}$. We consider the transformation

$$\tau = \{(w, w\#w) \mid w \in \{a, b\}^*,$$
$$|w| = 2 \cdot n \text{ for some } n \in \mathbb{N}_+\} \ .$$

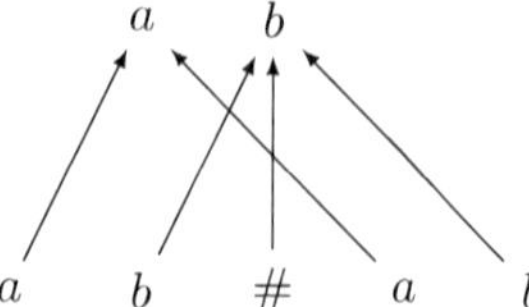

Figure 1: Origin graph of $(ab, ab\#ab)$ in Example 3.1.

For instance $(ab, ab\#ab) \in \tau$. The transformation τ can be computed by the NSST $\mathcal{A} = (Q, \Sigma, \Sigma, \mathcal{R}, r_1, T, q_0, F)$ where $Q = \{q_0, q_1, q_f\}$, $F = \{q_f\}$, $\mathcal{R} = \{r_1, r_2\}$, T contains, for every $i \in \{0, 1\}$ and $\gamma \in \{a, b\}$, the transitions

$$\big(q_i, \gamma, (r_1, r_2) := (r_1\gamma, r_2\gamma), q_{1-i}\big) \quad \text{and}$$
$$\big(q_1, \gamma, (r_1, r_2) := (r_1\gamma\#r_2\gamma, \varepsilon), q_f\big) \ .$$

For instance,

$$\Delta(q_0, \varepsilon) = \{(\mathrm{id}, q_0)\}$$
$$\Delta(q_0, a) = \{((r_1, r_2) := (r_1a, r_2a), q_1)\}$$
$$\Delta(q_0, ab) = \{((r_1, r_2) := (r_1ab, r_2ab), q_0),$$
$$((r_1, r_2) := (r_1ab\#r_2ab, \varepsilon), q_f)\} \ .$$

Let α denote $(r_1, r_2) := (r_1ab\#r_2ab, \varepsilon)$. Then

$$(\alpha \circ \alpha_\varepsilon)(r_1) = \alpha_\varepsilon(\alpha(r_1)) = \alpha_\varepsilon(r_1ab\#r_2ab)$$
$$= ab\#ab \ .$$

Since q_0 is the initial state and q_f is the final state, we obtain $(ab, ab\#ab) \in [\![\mathcal{A}]\!]$. The corresponding origin graph is shown in Figure 1. □

We call a NSST *nondeleting* if for each assignment α occurring in a transition, each register r occurs exactly once in $\{\alpha(r') \mid r' \in \mathcal{R}\}$. For each NSST $\mathcal{A}$, there is a nondeleting NSST $\mathcal{A}'$ such that $[\![\mathcal{A}]\!] = [\![\mathcal{A}']\!]$. The proof is very similar to the proof of a similar result for MCFG by Seki et al. (1991), which we will mention again in Section 4. We outline how $\mathcal{A}' = (Q', \Sigma_1, \Sigma_2, \mathcal{R}', r_o, T', q_0', F')$ is constructed from $\mathcal{A} = (Q, \Sigma_1, \Sigma_2, \mathcal{R}, r_o, T, q_0, F)$.

First, Q' contains a new state q_0' plus states of the form q_D where $q \in Q$ and $D \subseteq \mathcal{R}$. The intuition is that the registers in D are those that must remain empty in $\mathcal{A}'$, as in a corresponding computation in $\mathcal{A}$ their contents would later appear as part of a register that is deleted (or that is not the output register when the end of the input is reached). By keeping those registers empty, they no longer need

to be deleted, and instead can be added in an arbitrary way to assignments without changing the semantics. We let $q_D \in F'$ if and only if $q \in F$ and $r_o \notin D$, and $q_0' \in F'$ if and only if $q_0 \in F$.

For each $D \subseteq \mathcal{R}$ and $(q, a, \alpha, q') \in T$, we have $(q_{D'}, a, \alpha', q_D') \in T'$, where D' and α' are defined as follows. The registers in D' are obtained in one of two ways. First, if $r \in D$, then every register in $\alpha(r)$ is in D', and secondly, if a register r' does not occur in $\alpha(r)$ for any r, then it is in D'.

In the first instance, $\alpha'(r)$ is a copy of $\alpha(r)$ for each $r \notin D$, and $\alpha'(r)$ is obtained from $\alpha(r)$ by omitting all output symbols for each $r \in D$. However, each register r' that does not occur in $\alpha(r)$, for any r, is added to $\alpha'(r'')$ in an arbitrary place for an arbitrary r''. Moreover, if $q = q_0$, then T' also contains (q_0', a, α', q_D').

For example, if

$$(q, a, (r_1, r_2, r_3, r_4) := (r_2br_3, c, d, er_1), q')$$

is in T, then for $D = \{r_1, r_3\}$, we have $D' = \{r_2, r_3, r_4\}$, where D' contains r_2 and r_3 because r_2br_3 is assumed to be deleted later, and D' contains r_4 because it is deleted here. Further, T' would include

$$(q_{D'}, a, (r_1, r_2, r_3, r_4) := (r_2r_3, cr_4, \varepsilon, er_1), q_D')$$

where we have added r_4 to the right-hand side of the assignment in an arbitrary place.

4 Synchronous Multiple Context-Free Grammars

A *multiple context-free grammar (over Σ)* (for short: MCFG) is a tuple $\mathcal{G} = (N, S, \Sigma, P)$ where N is an alphabet of *nonterminals*, each nonterminal A has a *fanout* in $\mathbb{N}$ (denoted by $\mathrm{fo}(A)$), $S \in N$ is an *initial nonterminal* with $\mathrm{fo}(S) = 1$, Σ is an alphabet of *terminals*, and P is a finite set of *rules*, where each rule has the form

$$A_0(w_{1,\ell_0}) \to A_1(x_{1,\ell_1}^{(1)}) \cdots A_n(x_{1,\ell_n}^{(n)})$$

where $n \in \mathbb{N}$, $A_0, A_1, \ldots, A_n$ are nonterminals with $\mathrm{fo}(A_i) = \ell_i$ for each $i \in [0, n]$; for each $i \in [n]$, $x_{1,\ell_i}^{(i)}$ is a sequence of ℓ_i variables in X such that the set of all variables occurring in $x_{1,\ell_1}^{(1)}, \ldots, x_{1,\ell_n}^{(n)}$ is X_m where $m = \sum_{i=1}^{n} \ell_i$; for each $j \in [\ell_0]$, each w_j is in $(\Sigma \cup X_m)^*$; finally, the rule is *linear in X*, i.e., each variable in X occurs at most once in

$w_1 \cdots w_{\ell_0}$. The *rank* of this rule is n. The rank of $\mathcal{G}$ is the maximal rank of its rules.

Rules can be instantiated by consistent substitution of variables. The derivation relation $\Rightarrow$ of $\mathcal{G}$ is defined in the usual way, by applying instantiated rules. The language over Σ generated by $\mathcal{G}$ is defined to be the set of strings w such that $S(w) \Rightarrow^* \varepsilon$, and is denoted by $L(\mathcal{G})$. Two MCFGs are *equivalent* if they generate the same language.

A MCFG is called *uni-lexicalized* if there is exactly one terminal in each rule. For each MCFG there is an equivalent uni-lexicalized MCFG. A MCFG is called *nondeleting* if each variable that occurs in the right-hand side occurs exactly once in the left-hand side. For each MCFG there is an equivalent nondeleting MCFG (Seki et al., 1991).

A *synchronous multiple context-free grammar* (for short: synchronous MCFG) is a tuple $\mathcal{G} = (N, S, \Sigma_1, \Sigma_2, P)$ such that $\mathcal{G}' = (N, S, \Sigma_1 \cup \Sigma_2, P)$ is an MCFG (called *underlying MCFG*) except that S has fanout 2. Moreover, for each nonterminal A we split its fanout ℓ into an *input fanout* ℓ_1 and an *output fanout* ℓ_2 such that $\ell = \ell_1 + \ell_2$, and denote this by $\mathrm{fo}(A) = (\ell_1, \ell_2)$. In particular, we let $\mathrm{fo}(S) = (1, 1)$. We call the first ℓ_1 arguments of A its *input arguments* and the remaining ℓ_2 arguments its *output arguments*, and we separate these two blocks by a semicolon. We require that elements of Σ_1 and Σ_2 may only occur in input arguments and output arguments, respectively. Finally, we require that no variable may simultaneously occur in an input and in an output argument. We implement this requirement by choosing X as set of input variables and $Y = \{y_1, y_2, \ldots\}$ as set of output variables. Hence, a rule of a synchronous MCFG has the form

$$A_0(w_{1,\ell_0}; v_{1,m_0}) \rightarrow$$
$$A_1(x_{1,\ell_1}^{(1)}; y_{1,m_1}^{(1)}) \cdots A_n(x_{1,\ell_n}^{(n)}; y_{1,m_n}^{(n)})$$

where $n \in \mathbb{N}$, $A_0, A_1, \ldots, A_n$ are nonterminals and each A_i has fanout (ℓ_i, m_i); for each $i \in [n]$, $x_{1,\ell_i}^{(i)}$ and $y_{1,m_i}^{(i)}$ are sequences of variables in X and Y, respectively; for each $j \in [\ell_0]$, string w_j is in $(\Sigma_1 \cup \{x_{1,\ell_1}^{(1)}, \ldots, x_{1,\ell_n}^{(n)}\})^*$, and for each $j \in [m_0]$, string v_j is in $(\Sigma_2 \cup \{y_{1,m_1}^{(1)}, \ldots, y_{1,m_n}^{(n)}\})^*$; finally, the rule is linear in X and Y.

The MCFG $\mathcal{G}_1 = (N, S, \Sigma_1, P_1)$ is the *input component of* $\mathcal{G}$, where the fanout of each nonterminal of N is its input fanout in $\mathcal{G}$, and P_1 is the set of all rules of P in which the output arguments are dropped. Similary, we define the *output component of* $\mathcal{G}$.

Let $\mathcal{G}$ be a synchronous MCFG. We define the derivation relation $\Rightarrow_{\mathcal{G}}$ of $\mathcal{G}$ to be the derivation relation of its underlying MCFG. The *string-to-string transduction computed by* $\mathcal{G}$ is the set

$$[\![\mathcal{G}]\!] = \{(w, v) \in \Sigma_1^* \times \Sigma_2^* \mid S(w; v) \Rightarrow^* \varepsilon\} \ .$$

A *uni-lexicalized* synchronous MCFG is a synchronous MCFG in which each rule either contains exactly one input symbol or contains neither input symbols nor output symbols. In a straightforward way, we can associate with each uni-lexicalized synchronous MCFG $\mathcal{G}$ a set $[\![\mathcal{G}]\!]^o$ of origin graphs by linking each occurrence of an output terminal of a rule to the unique input terminal of that rule.

5 Intersecting the Input of NSST with MCFG

Lemma 5.1. For every NSST $\mathcal{A}$ over Σ_1 and Σ_2 and every MCFG $\mathcal{G}$ over Σ_1, there is a uni-lexicalized synchronous MCFG $\mathcal{G}'$ over Σ_1 and Σ_2 such that $[\![\mathcal{A}]\!]^o \sqcap ([\![\mathcal{G}]\!] \times \Sigma_2^*) = [\![\mathcal{G}']\!]^o$.

Proof. Let $\mathcal{A} = (Q, \Sigma_1, \Sigma_2, \mathcal{R}, r_o, T, q_0, F)$, where $\mathcal{R}$ consists of the registers $r_1, \ldots, r_\rho$, and let $\mathcal{G} = (N, S, \Sigma_1, P)$ be an MCFG. Without loss of generality we may assume that $\mathcal{A}$ is nondeleting and that $\mathcal{G}$ is uni-lexicalized.

The intuition behind the construction of $\mathcal{G}'$ covers two aspects. Starting from the MCFG $\mathcal{G}$, we impose the state behaviour of $\mathcal{A}$ onto the nonterminal behaviour of $\mathcal{G}$ by a type of construction that can be traced back to Bar-Hillel et al. (1964). This aspect of the construction achieves $\mathrm{proj}_1([\![\mathcal{G}']\!]) = \mathrm{proj}_1([\![\mathcal{A}]\!]) \cap [\![\mathcal{G}]\!]$. The second aspect concerns the manipulation of the registers of $\mathcal{A}$. We let $\mathcal{G}'$ simulate the assignments in its output component, while its input component processes the input string.

The number of relevant assignments is in general infinite. In order to be able to simulate these assignments using a finite set of rules of $\mathcal{G}'$, we split up each assignment into a finite part, called "pattern", and a potentially infinite part, called "residue". The pattern represents ρ register occurrences in the image of the assignment, while the residue consists of the 2ρ strings that are interlaced with the register occurrences. The patterns are maintained as annotations of the nonterminals of $\mathcal{G}'$ and the residues appear in the output arguments of $\mathcal{G}'$. The residues of the left-hand side of a rule will be expressed in terms of residues that appear as output variables in the right-hand side. For this purpose, we introduce assignments that have output variables in their image.

For instance, let $\mathcal{G}$ contain the rule $A(ax_1^{(2)}x_1^{(1)}) \rightarrow B(x_1^{(1)})\ C(x_1^{(2)})$ and $\mathcal{A}$ have states $q_1,\ldots,q_5$. Assume that there is a transition (q_5,a,α,q_3), and that there are strings $w_1^{(2)},w_1^{(1)} \in \Sigma_1^*$ such that $(\alpha_2,q_1) \in \Delta(q_3,w_1^{(2)})$ and $(\alpha_1,q_2) \in \Delta(q_1,w_1^{(1)})$. Then $\mathcal{G}'$ will have a rule of the form

$$A_{(q_5,p_1^{(0)},q_2)}(ax_1^{(2)}x_1^{(1)};\ldots) \rightarrow$$
$$B_{(q_1,p_1^{(1)},q_2)}(x_1^{(1)};\ldots)\ C_{(q_3,p_1^{(2)},q_1)}(x_1^{(2)};\ldots)$$

where $p_1^{(1)}$ and $p_1^{(2)}$ are patterns corresponding to α_1 and α_2, respectively, and $p_1^{(0)}$ corresponds to $\alpha_1 \circ \alpha_2 \circ \alpha$. Hence there is a corresponding pattern for each argument in the right-hand sided and in the left-hand side.

Formally, a *pattern over* $\mathcal{R}$ is an assignment $p \in \mathrm{Ass}(\mathcal{R},\emptyset)$. Obviously, $\mathrm{Ass}(\mathcal{R},\emptyset)$ is finite. Now assume a rule $A_0(w_{1,\ell_0}) \rightarrow A_1(x_{1,\ell_1}^{(1)}) \cdots A_n(x_{1,\ell_n}^{(n)})$. Let $\vec{\ell} = (\ell_1,\ldots,\ell_n)$, $X_{\vec{\ell}} = \{x_i^{(k)} \mid k \in [n], i \in [\ell_k]\}$, and $Y_{\vec{\ell}} = \{y_i^{(k)} \mid k \in [n], i \in [2\rho\ell_k]\}$. For each $\alpha \in \mathrm{Ass}(\mathcal{R},\Sigma_2 \cup Y_{\vec{\ell}})$ we define the *pattern* $\mathrm{p}(\alpha)$ and the *residue* $\mathrm{r}(\alpha) \in ((\Sigma_2 \cup Y_{\vec{\ell}})^*)^*$ as follows. Assume that for each $j \in [\rho]$ the string $\alpha(r_j)$ has the form $v_{j,0}r_{j,1}v_{j,1}\cdots r_{j,\mu_j}v_{j,\mu_j}$ for some $\mu_j \in [0,\rho]$, $v_{j,k} \in (\Sigma_2 \cup Y_{\vec{\ell}})^*$ ($k \in [0,\mu_j]$), and $\{r_{j,1},\ldots,r_{j,\mu_j}\} \subseteq \mathcal{R}$. Then

$$\mathrm{p}(\alpha) = ((r_1,\ldots,r_\rho) :=$$
$$(r_{1,1}\cdots r_{1,\mu_1},\ \ldots,\ r_{\rho,1}\cdots r_{\rho,\mu_\rho}))$$
$$\mathrm{r}(\alpha) = (v_{1,0},v_{1,1},\ldots,v_{1,\mu_1},\ \ldots,$$
$$v_{\rho,0},v_{\rho,1},\ldots,v_{\rho,\mu_\rho})\ .$$

For example, let α be the assignment

$$(r_1,r_2,r_3,r_4) :=$$
$$(ay_3br_4,\ r_2y_2cr_3,\ dey_4,\ fy_1r_1)\ .$$

Then

$$\mathrm{p}(\alpha) = ((r_1,r_2,r_3,r_4) := (r_4,\ r_2r_3,\ \varepsilon,\ r_1))$$
$$\mathrm{r}(\alpha) = (ay_3b,\varepsilon,\ \varepsilon,y_2c,\varepsilon,\ dey_4,\ fy_1,\varepsilon)\ .$$

For a pattern $p_i^{(k)}$ corresponding to $x_i^{(k)}$, we define an assignment $[p_i^{(k)}] \in \mathrm{Ass}(\mathcal{R},Y_{\vec{\ell}})$, which introduces output variables next to register occurrences. Assume that

$$p_i^{(k)} = ((r_1,\ldots,r_\rho) := (s_1\cdots s_{\mu_1},$$
$$s_{\mu_1+1}\cdots s_{\mu_2},\ \ldots,$$
$$s_{\mu_{\rho-1}+1}\cdots s_{\mu_\rho}))$$

for some $\mu_1,\ldots,\mu_\rho \in [0,\rho]$, $\mu_i \leq \mu_{i+1}$ ($i \in [\rho-1]$), and $s_j \in \mathcal{R}$ ($j \in [\mu_\rho]$). Let $\mu_0 = 0$ and $\kappa_j = 2\rho(i-1) + \mu_j + j$ ($j \in [0,\mu_\rho]$). Then

$$[p_i^{(k)}](r_j) =$$
$$y_{\kappa_{j-1}+1}^{(k)}\ s_{\mu_{j-1}+1}\ y_{\kappa_{j-1}+2}^{(k)}\ \cdots\ s_{\mu_j}\ y_{\kappa_j}^{(k)}\ .$$

For instance, if $\rho = 4$ and $p_3^{(2)}$ is the pattern

$$(r_1,r_2,r_3,r_4) := (r_4,\ r_2r_3,\ \varepsilon,\ r_1)$$

then $\mu_1 = 1$, $\mu_2 = 3$, $\mu_3 = 3$, $\mu_4 = 4$, $\kappa_0 = 2\rho(i-1) = 16$, $\kappa_1 = \kappa_0 + \mu_1 + 1 = 18$, $\kappa_2 = \kappa_0 + \mu_2 + 2 = 21$, $\kappa_3 = \kappa_0 + \mu_3 + 3 = 22$, $\kappa_4 = \kappa_0 + \mu_4 + 4 = 24$, and

$$[p_3^{(2)}] = ((r_1,r_2,r_3,r_4) :=$$
$$(y_{17}^{(2)}r_4y_{18}^{(2)}, y_{19}^{(2)}r_2y_{20}^{(2)}r_3y_{21}^{(2)}, y_{22}^{(2)}, y_{23}^{(2)}r_1y_{24}^{(2)}))\ .$$

We construct the synchronous MCFG $\mathcal{G}' = (N',S',\Sigma_1,\Sigma_2,P')$ as follows. We let

$$N' = \{S'\} \cup \{A_c \mid A \in N, \mathrm{fo}_\mathcal{G}(A) = \ell,$$
$$c \in (Q \times \mathrm{Ass}(\mathcal{R},\emptyset) \times Q)^\ell\}$$

where $\mathrm{fo}_{\mathcal{G}'}(S') = (1,1)$ and $\mathrm{fo}_{\mathcal{G}'}(A_c) = (\mathrm{fo}_\mathcal{G}(A), 2\rho \cdot \mathrm{fo}_\mathcal{G}(A))$.

Let $A_0(w_{1,\ell_0}) \rightarrow A_1(x_{1,\ell_1}^{(1)}) \cdots A_n(x_{1,\ell_n}^{(n)})$ be a rule in P. For every $k \in [0,n]$ and $i \in [\ell_k]$ let $q_{i,1}^{(k)},q_{i,2}^{(k)} \in Q$ and $p_i^{(k)} \in \mathrm{Ass}(\mathcal{R},\emptyset)$. We abbreviate $(q_{i,1}^{(k)},p_i^{(k)},q_{i,2}^{(k)})$ by $c_i^{(k)}$.

We extend Δ to a function

$$\Delta' : Q \times (\Sigma_1 \cup X_{\vec{\ell}})^* \rightarrow \mathcal{P}(\mathrm{Ass}(\mathcal{R},\Sigma_2 \cup Y_{\vec{\ell}}) \times Q)$$

by defining

$$\Delta'(q,\varepsilon) = \{(\mathrm{id},q)\}$$
$$\Delta'(q,wa) = \{(\alpha \circ \alpha_w, q'') \mid$$
$$(\exists q' \in Q):(\alpha_w,q') \in \Delta'(q,w),$$
$$(q',a,\alpha,q'') \in T\}$$
$$\Delta'(q,wx_i^{(k)}) = \{([p_i^{(k)}] \circ \alpha_w, q_{i,2}^{(k)}) \mid$$
$$(\alpha_w,q_{i,1}^{(k)}) \in \Delta'(q,w)\}$$

Then the set P' contains the rule

$$(A_0)_{c_{1,\ell_0}^{(0)}} (w_{1,\ell_0}; v_{1,2\rho\ell_0}) \rightarrow$$
$$(A_1)_{c_{1,\ell_1}^{(1)}} (x_{1,\ell_1}^{(1)}; y_{1,2\rho\ell_1}^{(1)}) \cdots$$
$$(A_n)_{c_{1,\ell_n}^{(n)}} (x_{1,\ell_n}^{(n)}; y_{1,2\rho\ell_n}^{(n)})$$

for each choice of α_{1,ℓ_0} such that $(\alpha_i, q_{i,2}^{(0)}) \in \Delta'(q_{i,1}^{(0)}, w_i)$ and $\mathrm{p}(\alpha_i) = p_i^{(0)}$, for each $i \in [\ell_0]$, where $\mathrm{r}(\alpha_i) = (v_{2\rho(i-1)+1, 2\rho i})$. This is illustrated in Figure 2.

In addition, for each $c \in \{(q_0, p_1^{(1)}, q) \mid p \in \mathrm{Ass}(\mathcal{R}, \emptyset), q \in F\}$ the rule

$$S'(x_1; \alpha_\varepsilon([p_1^{(1)}](r_\circ))) \rightarrow S_c(x_1; y_{1,2\rho}^{(1)})$$

is in P'. Note that if $\mathcal{G}$ is uni-lexicalized, then so is $\mathcal{G}'$.

We can prove the following invariant. For every $A \in N$, $\ell = \mathrm{fo}(A)$, $w_1, \ldots, w_\ell \in \Sigma_1^*$, $v_1, \ldots, v_{2\rho\ell} \in \Sigma_2^*$, $c = (c_1, \ldots, c_\ell)$ with $c_i = (q_{i1}, p_i, q_{i2}) \in Q \times \mathrm{Ass}(\mathcal{R}, \emptyset) \times Q$ for each $i \in [\ell]$, we have

$$A_c(w_{1,\ell}; v_{1,2\rho\ell}) \Rightarrow_{\mathcal{G}'}^* \varepsilon \quad \text{if and only if}$$
$$A(w_{1,\ell}) \Rightarrow_{\mathcal{G}}^* \varepsilon \wedge$$
$$(\forall i \in [\ell]) : (\exists \alpha) : (\alpha, q_{i2}) \in \Delta(q_{i1}, w_i) \wedge$$
$$\mathrm{r}(\alpha) = v_{2\rho(i-1)+1, 2\rho i} \ .$$

This invariant implies that for every $w \in \Sigma_1^*$ and $v \in \Sigma_2^*$: $S'(w; v) \Rightarrow_{\mathcal{G}'}^* \varepsilon$ if and only if $S(w) \Rightarrow_{\mathcal{G}}^* \varepsilon \wedge (w, v) \in [\![\mathcal{A}]\!]$. Thus $[\![\mathcal{G}']\!] = [\![\mathcal{A}]\!] \cap ([\![\mathcal{G}]\!] \times \Sigma_2^*)$. By the assumption that $\mathcal{G}$ is uni-lexicalized, furthermore $[\![\mathcal{G}']\!]^o = [\![\mathcal{A}]\!]^o \cap ([\![\mathcal{G}]\!] \times \Sigma_2^*)$. $\square$

Example 5.2. We consider the NSST $\mathcal{A}$ of Example 3.1 and the MCFG $\mathcal{G} = (N, A, \Sigma, P)$ with $N = \{A\}$, $\mathrm{fo}(A) = 1$, and for each $\gamma \in \Sigma$, P contains the rules

$$A(\gamma x_1) \rightarrow A(x_1) \quad \text{and} \quad A(\gamma) \rightarrow \varepsilon \ .$$

Obviously, $[\![\mathcal{G}]\!] = \Sigma^*$. We apply the construction of Lemma 5.1 to $\mathcal{A}$ and $\mathcal{G}$ and we obtain the uni-lexicalized synchronous MCFG $\mathcal{G}'$ which contains for each $\gamma \in \Sigma$ and $i \in \{0, 1\}$ at least the following rules.

$$S'(x_1; y_1y_2y_3) \rightarrow A_{(q_0,p,q_f)}(x_1; y_{1,4})$$
$$A_{(q_i,p,q_f)}(\gamma x_1; y_1, \gamma y_2, \gamma y_3, y_4) \rightarrow$$
$$A_{(q_{1-i},p,q_f)}(x_1; y_{1,4})$$
$$A_{(q_1,p,q_f)}(\gamma; \varepsilon, \gamma\#, \gamma, \varepsilon) \rightarrow \varepsilon$$

where $p = ((r_1, r_2) := (r_1r_2, \varepsilon))$. For instance, $\Delta'(q_0, \gamma x_1)$ contains $([p_1^{(1)}] \circ \alpha, q_f)$ where $\alpha = ((r_1, r_2) := (r_1\gamma, r_2\gamma))$ is the assignment in the transition $(q_0, \gamma, \alpha, q_1)$ of $\mathcal{A}$. The calculation of $[p_1^{(1)}] \circ \alpha$ is

$$\begin{pmatrix} r_1 \\ r_2 \end{pmatrix} \xrightarrow{[p_1^{(1)}]} \begin{pmatrix} y_1 r_1 y_2 r_2 y_3 \\ y_4 \end{pmatrix} \xrightarrow{\alpha}$$
$$\begin{pmatrix} y_1 r_1 \gamma y_2 r_2 \gamma y_3 \\ y_4 \end{pmatrix}$$

hence $\mathrm{p}([p_1^{(1)}] \circ \alpha) = ((r_1, r_2) := (r_1r_2, \varepsilon))$ and $\mathrm{r}([p_1^{(1)}] \circ \alpha) = (y_1, \gamma y_2, \gamma y_3, y_4)$.

An example of a derivation is

$$S'(ab; ab\#ab) \Rightarrow_{\mathcal{G}'} A_{(q_0,p,q_f)}(ab; \varepsilon, ab\#, ab, \varepsilon)$$
$$\Rightarrow_{\mathcal{G}'} A_{(q_1,p,q_f)}(b; \varepsilon, b\#, b, \varepsilon)$$
$$\Rightarrow_{\mathcal{G}'} \varepsilon \ .$$

$\square$

This example can be easily generalized:

Lemma 5.3. For every NSST $\mathcal{A}$ there is a uni-lexicalized synchronous MCFG $\mathcal{G}'$ such that $[\![\mathcal{A}]\!]^o = [\![\mathcal{G}']\!]^o$.

Proof. Let $\mathcal{A}$ be a NSST over Σ_1 and Σ_2. As illustrated by Example 5.2, we can construct a MCFG $\mathcal{G}$ such that $[\![\mathcal{G}]\!] = \Sigma_1^*$. The result then follows from Lemma 5.1. $\square$

On the basis of Lemma 5.3, one can obtain complexity bounds on typical tasks involving NSST, such as deciding whether $(w, v) \in [\![\mathcal{A}]\!]$ for given strings w and v and NSST $\mathcal{A}$, relying on known complexity results for synchronous MCFG, and related formalisms such as synchronous LCFRS (Kaeshammer, 2013).

However, the relation between NSST and synchronous MCFG does not in any obvious way suggest a practical algorithm to do inference of NSST on the basis of sets of origin graphs, and this problem must remain outside the scope of the present paper.[1]

6 A Proper Subclass of Synchronous MCFG

In the light of Lemma 5.1 one may ask whether for *every* synchronous MCFG $\mathcal{G}$ one may find NSST $\mathcal{A}$

---

[1] We thank an anonymous reviewer for the suggestion to consider the problem of inference of NSST.

$$A_{(q_5,p_1^{(0)},q_2)}\left(ax_1^{(2)}x_1^{(1)};\ y_1^{(1)}y_3^{(2)}b,\ cy_4^{(2)}y_2^{(1)}y_1^{(2)}de,\ y_2^{(2)}y_3^{(1)},\ y_4^{(1)}\right)$$

$(\alpha_1,q_2)\in\Delta'(q_5,ax_1^{(2)}x_1^{(1)})$
$\alpha_1=[p_1^{(1)}]\circ[p_1^{(2)}]\circ\alpha=((r_1,r_2):=(y_1^{(1)}y_3^{(2)}b\,r_1\,cy_4^{(2)}y_2^{(1)}y_1^{(2)}de\,r_2\,y_2^{(2)}y_3^{(1)},\ y_4^{(1)}))$
$\mathrm{p}(\alpha_1)=((r_1,r_2):=(r_1r_2,\varepsilon))=p_1^{(0)}$
$\mathrm{r}(\alpha_1)=(y_1^{(1)}y_3^{(2)}b,\ cy_4^{(2)}y_2^{(1)}y_1^{(2)}de,\ y_2^{(2)}y_3^{(1)},\ y_4^{(1)})$

$$B_{(q_1,p_1^{(1)},q_2)}\left(x_1^{(1)};y_1^{(1)},y_2^{(1)},y_3^{(1)},y_4^{(1)}\right)\qquad\qquad C_{(q_3,p_1^{(2)},q_1)}\left(x_1^{(2)};y_1^{(2)},y_2^{(2)},y_3^{(2)},y_4^{(2)}\right)$$

$p_1^{(1)}=((r_1,r_2):=(r_2r_1,\varepsilon))$
$[p_1^{(1)}]=((r_1,r_2):=(y_1^{(1)}r_2y_2^{(1)}r_1y_3^{(1)},\ y_4^{(1)}))$

$p_1^{(2)}=((r_1,r_2):=(r_2,r_1))$
$[p_1^{(2)}]=((r_1,r_2):=(y_1^{(2)}r_2y_2^{(2)},\ y_3^{(2)}r_1y_4^{(2)}))$

Figure 2: The construction in the proof of Lemma 5.3, for an NSST with two registers, $A(ax_1^{(2)}x_1^{(1)})\to B(x_1^{(1)})\,C(x_1^{(2)})$, and transition (q_5,a,α,q_3) with $\alpha=((r_1,r_2):=(br_1c,der_2))$.

and MCFG $\mathcal{G}'$ such that $[\![\mathcal{G}]\!]=[\![\mathcal{A}]\!]\cap([\![\mathcal{G}']\!]\times\Sigma_2^*)$, for the shared output alphabet Σ_2, and perhaps even that $[\![\mathcal{G}]\!]^o=[\![\mathcal{A}]\!]^o\cap([\![\mathcal{G}']\!]\times\Sigma_2^*)$. In this section we show the answer to the former question is negative, whereby it is negative for the latter question as well. This holds even if the rank of $\mathcal{G}$ is restricted to 1 and $[\![\mathcal{G}]\!]$ is a function, that is, if $(w,v_1),(w,v_2)\in[\![\mathcal{G}]\!]$ implies $v_1=v_2$.

To see this, consider the synchronous MCFG $\mathcal{G}$ of rank 1 with $N=\{S,A\}$, $\Sigma_1=\Sigma_2=\{a,b,a',b'\}$, and the following rules.

$$S(x_1x_2;\ y)\to A(x_1,x_2;\ y)$$
$$A(x_1a,x_2a';\ yaa')\to A(x_1,x_2;\ y)$$
$$A(x_1a,x_2b';\ yab')\to A(x_1,x_2;\ y)$$
$$A(x_1b,x_2a';\ yba')\to A(x_1,x_2;\ y)$$
$$A(x_1b,x_2b';\ ybb')\to A(x_1,x_2;\ y)$$
$$A(\varepsilon,\varepsilon;\ \varepsilon)\to\varepsilon$$

For two strings $w=a_1\cdots a_n$ and $w'=a_1'\cdots a_n'$ of identical length n, we define $\mathrm{shuffle}(w,w')$ to be the string $a_1a_1'\cdots a_na_n'$. The string-to-string transduction computed by $\mathcal{G}$ can now be written as

$$[\![\mathcal{G}]\!]=\{(ww',\mathrm{shuffle}(w,w'))\mid(\exists n\in\mathbb{N}):$$
$$w\in\{a,b\}^n\wedge w'\in\{a',b'\}^n\}$$

which is clearly a function. Suppose $[\![\mathcal{G}]\!]$ were $[\![\mathcal{A}]\!]\cap([\![\mathcal{G}']\!]\times\Sigma_2^*)$ for some NSST $\mathcal{A}=(Q,\Sigma_1,\Sigma_2,\mathcal{R},c_o,T,q_0,F)$ and MCFG $\mathcal{G}'$. Then

$$[\![\mathcal{G}]\!]=[\![\mathcal{A}]\!]\cap(\{ww'\mid(\exists n\in\mathbb{N}):$$
$$w\in\{a,b\}^n\wedge w'\in\{a',b'\}^n\}\times\Sigma_2^*)\ .$$

For each $(w,w')\in\{a,b\}^n\times\{a',b'\}^n$, there are $q\in Q$, $q'\in F$, and assignments α_1 and α_2 such that $(\alpha_1,q)\in\Delta(q_0,w)$ and $(\alpha_2,q')\in\Delta(q,w')$. We then have $(\alpha_2\circ\alpha_1\circ\alpha_\varepsilon)(r_o)=\mathrm{shuffle}(w,w')$.

As illustrated in Figure 3, we want to capture how the contents that the registers have just after reading w eventually become substrings of register r_o, after also w' has been read. To formalize this, we first define $\Phi_{\alpha_1}(r)=r^{|(\alpha_1\circ\alpha_\varepsilon)(r)|}$ for $r\in\mathcal{R}$. In words, each register r is mapped to $|(\alpha_1\circ\alpha_\varepsilon)(r)|$ copies of its own name, to encode the size of its contents after reading w. Secondly, we introduce a new symbol $\dagger$, and define Ψ to be the assignment such that $\Psi(r)=r$ for $r\in\mathcal{R}$ and $\Psi(c)=\dagger$ for $c\in\Sigma_2$. We now define $\sigma(\alpha_1,\alpha_2)=(\alpha_2\circ\Psi\circ\Phi_{\alpha_1})(r_o)\in(\{\dagger\}\cup\mathcal{R})^{2n}$. We call $\sigma(\alpha_1,\alpha_2)$ the *schema* of α_1 and α_2.

If we fix $n>0$, to be determined later, then the number of possible schemas $\sigma(\alpha_1,\alpha_2)$ is bounded by $(2n)^{2\rho}$, where $\rho=|\mathcal{R}|$ as before. This follows from the fact that each schema is determined by a set of pairs of indices. There is one such pair for each register r, consisting of the index in the schema where the substring $r^{|(\alpha_1\circ\alpha_\varepsilon)(r)|}$ starts, and another index where it ends. If this substring is empty, this can be encoded by a starting index that is greater than the ending index.

We define the predicate G as

$$G(w,w',q,s)\equiv$$
$$(\exists\alpha_1,\alpha_2,q'\in F):(\alpha_1,q)\in\Delta(q_0,w)\wedge$$
$$(\alpha_2,q')\in\Delta(q,w')\wedge$$
$$\sigma(\alpha_1,\alpha_2)=s$$

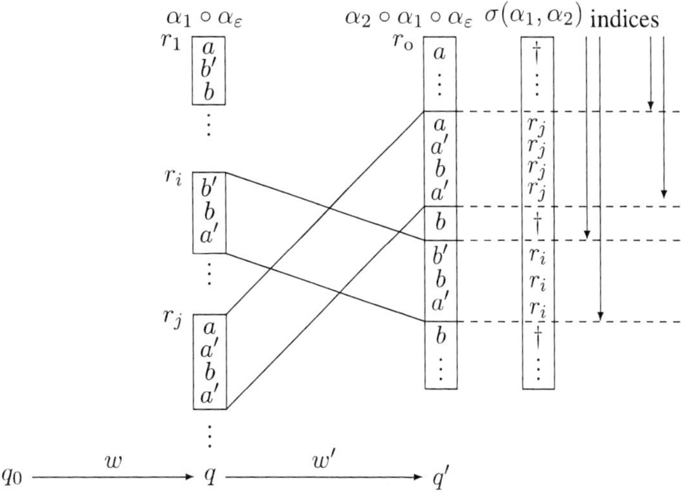

Figure 3: The processing of ww' and corresponding schema $\sigma(\alpha_1, \alpha_2)$. A set of indices, one pair per register, determines a schema.

for $(w, w') \in \{a, b\}^n \times \{a', b'\}^n$, $q \in Q$ and schema s. For each $(w, w') \in \{a, b\}^n \times \{a', b'\}^n$, there is at least one combination of q and s such that $G(w, w', q, s)$.

For each $q \in Q$, let $C(q)$ be the number of pairs $(w, w') \in \{a, b\}^n \times \{a', b'\}^n$ such that $G(w, w', q, s)$ for some s. Now fix q to be such that $C(q)$ is maximal among the κ states of $\mathcal{A}$. This means that there are at least $2^{2n}/\kappa$ pairs $(w, w') \in \{a, b\}^n \times \{a', b'\}^n$ such that $G(w, w', q, s)$ for some s.

For each schema s, let $C(q, s)$ be the number of pairs $(w, w') \in \{a, b\}^n \times \{a', b'\}^n$ such that $G(w, w', q, s)$. Now fix s to be such that $C(q, s)$ is maximal among the at most $(2n)^{2\rho}$ schemas. This means that there are at least $\frac{2^{2n}}{\kappa \cdot (2n)^{2\rho}}$ pairs $(w, w') \in \{a, b\}^n \times \{a', b'\}^n$ such that $G(w, w', q, s)$.

There is a string $w' \in \{a', b'\}^n$ such that there are at least $\frac{2^{2n}}{\kappa \cdot (2n)^{2\rho}}/2^n = \frac{2^n}{\kappa \cdot (2n)^{2\rho}}$ strings $w \in \{a, b\}^n$ such that $G(w, w', q, s)$. For this w' and α_2 fixed, there are at least $\log_2(\frac{2^n}{\kappa \cdot (2n)^{2\rho}}) = n - \log_2 \kappa - 2\rho(1 + \log_2 n) \geq n - \log_2 \kappa - 2\rho n$ positions in shuffle(w, w') where we may find both a and b, depending on the choice of $w \in \{a, b\}^n$. This means the schema s contains at least $2n - 2\log_2 \kappa - 4\rho n - \rho$ occurrences of symbols from $\mathcal{R}$; note that in the output string, symbols from $\{a', b'\}$ are interlaced with symbols from $\{a, b\}$.

Similarly, there is a string $w \in \{a, b\}^n$ such that there are at least $\frac{2^n}{\kappa \cdot (2n)^{2\rho}}$ strings $w' \in \{a', b'\}^n$ such that $G(w, w', q, s)$. For this w and α_1 fixed, there are at least $n - \log_2 \kappa - 2\rho n$ positions in shuffle(w, w') where we may find both a' and b', depending on the choice of $w' \in \{a, b\}^n$. This means the schema s contains at least $2n - 2\log_2 \kappa - 4\rho n - \rho$ occurrences of $\dagger$.

Altogether, this requires the length of the schema, and thereby of the output string, to be at least $4n - 4\log_2 \kappa - 8\rho n - 2\rho$. We now obtain the contradiction $4n - 4\log_2 \kappa - 8\rho n - 2\rho > 2n$ by choosing $n > \frac{\rho + 2\log_2 \kappa}{1 - 4\rho}$.

The transduction $[\![\mathcal{G}]\!]$ above is almost the same as the transduction called *merge* by Alur and Černý (2010), who also present a proof that this is beyond the power of deterministic SST (DSST). Because this transduction is a function, and because functional NSSTs are equivalent to DSSTs (Alur and Deshmukh, 2011), this could be used to produce an alternative to our proof above. However, the proof by Alur and Černý (2010) appears to contain at least one mistake, which is why we chose to present our own.[2]

---

[2]The proof by Alur and Černý (2010) considers "short configurations". These represent the contents of the registers after reading the first half of an input string, but replacing the contents of a register by a special symbol $*$ if its length is greater than some number t such that $2^t > \rho$. (Here we use our own variable names rather than those of op. cit.) It is then argued that the number of distinct short configurations is bounded by $\kappa \rho 2^t$. It appears to us this should have been

7 Conclusions

Motivated by potential applications of origin graphs for machine translation, we have considered NSSTs. We have shown that when their input languages are restricted by MCFGs, then transducers with origin semantics are obtained that can also be generated by synchronous MCFGs. We have further shown that not every synchronous MCFG can be obtained by such a combination of a NSST and a MCFG.

Acknowledgments

Anonymous reviewers provided valuable comments.

References

A.V. Aho and J.D. Ullman. 1970. A characterization of two-way deterministic classes of languages. *J. Comput. Syst. Sci.*, 4(6):523—538.

R. Alur and P. Černý. 2010. Expressiveness of streaming string transducers. In *FSTTCS, volume 8 of LIPIcs*, pages 1—12. Schloss Dagstuhl - Leibniz-Zentrum für Informatik.

R. Alur and J.V. Deshmukh. 2011. Nondeterministic streaming transducers. In *International Colloquium on Automata, Languages, and Programming (ICALP 2011)*, volume 6756 of *LNCS*, pages 1–20. Springer-Verlag.

Y. Bar-Hillel, M. Perles, and E. Shamir. 1964. On formal properties of simple phrase structure grammars. In Y. Bar-Hillel, editor, *Language and Information: Selected Essays on their Theory and Application*, chapter 9, pages 116–150. Addison-Wesley, Reading, Massachusetts.

M. Bojańczyk. 2013. Transducers with origin semantics. Technical report, arXiv:1309.6124, 24. Sep 2013.

M. Bojańczyk, L. Daviaud, B. Guillon, and V. Penelle. 2017a. Which classes of origin graphs are generated by transducers? In *44th Int. Colloquium on Automata, Languages, and Programming (ICALP 2017)*, pages 114:1–114:13.

M. Bojańczyk, L. Daviaud, B. Guillon, and V. Penelle. 2017b. Which classes of origin graphs are generated by transducers? http://guillon.di.unimi.it/files/automatic/pdf/gb_2017_oxford.pdf.

P.F. Brown, V.J. della Pietra, S.A. della Pietra, and R.L. Mercer. 1993. The mathematics of statistical machine translation: parameter estimation. *Computational Linguistics*, 19(3)(2):263–311.

D. Chiang. 2007. Hierarchical phrase-based translation. *Computational Linguistics*, 33(2):201–228.

B. Courcelle and J. Engelfriet. 2012. *Graph structure and monadic second-order logic*. Cambridge University Press.

A.P. Dempster, N.M. Laird, and D. Rubin. 1977. Maximum likelihood from incomplete data via the EM algorithm. *Journal of the Royal Statistical Society. Series B (Methodological)*, 39(1):1–38.

J. Engelfriet and H.-J. Hoogeboom. 2001. MSO definable string transductions and two-way finite state transducers. *ACM Transactions on Computational Logic (TOCL)*, 2(2):216–254.

M. Kaeshammer. 2013. Synchronous linear context-free rewriting systems for machine translation. In *Proceedings of the Seventh Workshop on Syntax, Semantics and Structure in Statistical Translation*, pages 68–77, Atlanta, Georgia. Association for Computational Linguistics.

P. Lewis and R. Stearns. 1968. Syntax-directed transduction. *Journal of the ACM*, 15(3):465–488.

A. Lopez. 2008. Statistical machine translation. *ACM Computing Surveys*, 40(3):8:1–8:9.

H. Seki, T. Matsumura, M. Fujii, and T. Kasami. 1991. On multiple context-free grammars. *Theoretical Computer Science*, 88:191–229.

J.C. Sheperdson. 1959. The reduction of two-way automata to one-way automata. IBM J. Res. Development 3.

$\kappa(1 + \sum_{t' \leq t} 4^{t'})^\rho$, as for each register, the short configuration contains either $*$ or a string of length up to t over an alphabet of 4 symbols; their assumption that registers at that point cannot contain symbols a' or b' is insufficiently motivated, and even if it were, there is a discrepancy between $\kappa(1 + \sum_{t' \leq t} 2^{t'})^\rho$ and $\kappa\rho 2^t$, which places the correctness of the proof as a whole in doubt.

A Syntactically Expressive Morphological Analyzer for Turkish

Adnan Öztürel
Google Research
ozturel@google.com

Tolga Kayadelen
Google Research
tkayadelen@google.com

Işın Demirşahin
Google Research
isin@google.com

Abstract

We present a broad coverage model of Turkish
morphology and an open-source morphological analyzer that implements it. The model
captures intricacies of Turkish morphology-
syntax interface, thus could be used as a baseline that guides language model development.
It introduces a novel fine part-of-speech tagset,
a fine-grained affix inventory and represents
morphotactics without zero-derivations. The
morphological analyzer is freely available. It
consists of modular reusable components of
human-annotated gold standard lexicons, implements Turkish morphotactics as finite-state
transducers using OpenFst and morphophonemic processes as Thrax grammars.[1]

1 Introduction

The agglutinative morphology of Turkish is complex, due to rich inflectional and derivational morphotactics, a considerably large affix inventory,
and morphophonemic processes with potential irregularities. Therefore, morphology processing is
an integral part of Turkish NLP in devising sublexical representations to serve the needs of language
model development (Oflazer et al., 2003; Çakıcı,
2005; Sulubacak et al., 2016).

From a theoretical standpoint, Bozşahin (2002)
claims that transparent integration of morphology
to syntactic processing is essential in order to over-
come phrasal scope conflicts. They propose that
morphology-syntax integration can be attained in
architectural level using: (i) a lexemic grammar
where morphological parsing is the precursor of
syntactic analysis to resolve sublexical hypothesis space for syntax to operate on lexemic constituents, or (ii) a morphemic grammar with lexical items of root forms and affixes that has adequate lexical categories to capture correct seman-

tic bracketing, for a transparent morphology-syntax interface. They illustrate latter approach on a
linear fragment of Turkish inflectional paradigms
using a lexicalized grammar formalism.

The former approach is studied mainly over
two-level models (Koskenniemi, 1984). Oflazer
(1994) presents the first two-level description of
Turkish morphology, Sak et al. (2009) adapts this
definition to build a stochastic finite-state transducer (FST) that is trained on 200 million words
and Şahin et al. (2013) utilize flag diacritics in
limiting illicit morphological parses. Consider-
ing the restricted availability of these morphological analyzers, open-source alternatives have been
proposed by Akın and Akın (2007) and Çöltekin
(2010, 2014).

In this paper we present a morphology model
for Turkish that improves the above-mentioned
models in a number of ways. Our model captures
all syntactic processes that are handled by morphology at the word level over a sufficiently elaborate representation. It uses a gold standard human-
annotated lexicon which, to our knowledge, is the
first in the literature. We introduce a fine part-
of-speech tagset which provides finer control in
modeling morphotactics for lexical categories, and
represent productive derivational morphology in a
level of comprehensive scrutiny that none of the
previous models do. Finally, we present novel
methods to represent named entities in morphological analysis, eliminate zero-derivations from
morphotactics and a linguistically sound approach
to handle some intricacies around case morphology.

The model is implemented as an FST, it is open-
source, thus extensible. It can be used in building
lexemic syntactic processors that depend on morphological analysis, and also in morphemic grammar development and treebank induction.

---

[1] https://github.com/google-research/
turkish-morphology

65

Proceedings of the 14th International Conference on Finite-State Methods and Natural Language Processing, pages 65–75
Dresden, Germany, September 23-25, 2019. ©2019 Association for Computational Linguistics

Input:	affıyla
Intermediate:	af"+SH+YlA
Output:	(af[NN]+[PersonNumber=A3sg]+SH[Possessive=P3sg] +YlA[Case=Ins])+[Proper=False]

Figure 1: Levels of analysis for the word *affıyla* '*with their exemption*'. For illustrative purposes ambiguous interpretations on both intermediate and output tape is omitted and only a single parse is presented.

2 Levels of Analysis

Morphological analysis is composed of morphophonemic and morphotactic analysis layers. As illustrated in Fig. 1 the morphophonemic layer acts as the first level of analysis. It resolves phonetic processes that work at the morphology level by mapping input surface forms to an intermediate representation (see Section 3). The intermediate representation consists of an annotation of the morphophonemic irregularities of the root followed by the meta-morphemes that correspond to the affixes that are realized in the surface form.[2] The morphotactic layer is composed of the lexicon of root forms (see Section 4), affix inventory, and a word-internal grammar that defines affixation paths for each lexical category (see Section 5). It maps the intermediate representation into a morphological parse, which represents the sublexical segmentation and marks the root form with its lexical category, and inflectional and derivational affixes with their functional feature tags.

3 Morphophonemics

The morphophonemic layer is implemented as 9 Thrax grammars (Roark et al., 2012) which are formed of regular expressions and word-internal context-dependent rewrite rules that are compiled into FSTs. Composing the FSTs defined by these grammars yields the morphophonemic model. We handle all known phonological phenomena that play a role in Turkish word formation and that manifest itself in word orthography (Oflazer et al., 1994; Göksel and Kerslake, 2004).

A vowel harmony grammar maps back/front vowels into the meta-phoneme A and high vowels to H given the preceeding vowels (e.g. *evinde* → *evHndA*). A vowel change grammar implements the alteration of root final '*e*' to '*i*' when a suffix that starts with '*y*' is affixed (e.g. *diyecek* →

deyecek). A vowel drop grammar implements elision, i.e. /vowel/ - /∅/ alteration (e.g. *burnu* → *bur**u**nu*).

A consonant voicing grammar handles sonorization and respectively maps root final {'*t*', '*d*'} into {'*p*', '*b*'} and {'*c*', '*ğ*', '*ng*'} into {'*ç*', '*k*', '*nk*'} if a suffix starting with a vowel is affixed (e.g. *kitabının* → *kita**p**~ının*, or *rengi* → *ren**k**i*). A consonant change grammar maps suffix initial dental consonants {'*d*', '*t*'} into the meta-phoneme D by referring whether the morpheme to its left ends with {'*f*', '*s*', '*t*', '*k*', '*ç*', '*ş*', '*h*', '*p*'} (e.g. *evde* → *ev**D**e*, or *uçakta* → *uçak**D**a*). A consonant drop grammar captures elision of affix initial consonants when the morpheme that preceeds the affix ends with a consonant (e.g. *evinin* → *ev**S**i**N**in*). A gemination grammar implements duplication of the root final consonants {'*b*', '*d*', '*k*', '*l*', '*m*', '*n*', '*s*', '*t*', '*z*'} when a suffix that starts with a vowel is affixed to the root (e.g. *affıyla* → *af"ıyla*). A y-insertion grammar implements insertion of root final '*y*' to roots that end with '*su*' when a suffix starting with a dropping consonant or high vowel is affixed to them (e.g. *akarsuyuyla* → *akarsu^uyla*).

Finally, a dedicated morpheme segmentation grammar marks morpheme boundaries (e.g. *evlerinde* → *ev+ler+i+nde*). Most of these phonological processes (except vowel harmony and some of the consonant voicing/change processes with certain irregularities) are not generalized but only apply to a small set of roots from certain lexical categories. Therefore, they are annotated on root forms (see Section 4.3).

4 Lexicon of Root Forms

Our lexicon consists of 47,202 entries.[3] An entry is a 5-tuple of root form (or word stem), its part-of-speech (PoS), annotation of morphophonemic irregularities, morphosyntactic and semantic

---

[2] We represent meta-phonemes in capitals (e.g. **H** represents the set of high vowels {'*u*', '*ü*', '*ı*', '*i*'}), and fully realized phonemes that appear in the surface form in lowercase. **+** is used in the intermediate representation to denote morpheme boundaries. On the output tape inflectional morphemes are marked with **+** delimeter and derivational morphemes are marked with **-**.

[3] The base lexicon can be extended through open-source contributions especially with lexical items of open class categories. See annotation guidelines on `https://github.com/google-research/turkish-morphology/blob/master/analyzer/src/lexicon/README.md`.

Tag	Root	Morphophonemics	Features	Compound
NN	af	af"	-	false
NN	milletvekili	milletvekil	-	true
CC	velevki	-	+[ConjunctionType=Sub]	false

Figure 2: Structure of the lexicon.

features, and a boolean denoting whether the root form is a compound (see Fig. 2).

Each lexicon entry was annotated by 3 human annotators, where one of the annotators was the tie-breaker on 2-way annotation. Thus the lexicon is expected to have higher consistency and quality in compared with those that are acquired through semi-automatic extraction and labeling of lexical items over web-based corpora (Çöltekin, 2014) and affix stripping algorithms (Eryiğit and Adalı, 2004), which do not guarantee gold standard annotations due to the ambiguity that morphophonemic processes introduce in the surface form of the affixes.

4.1 Root Form

By *root form* (or *word stem*) we mean the part of a word form that remains when all inflectional and derivational morphemes are stripped. We assume any productive affixation process should be represented in morphotactics and respective affixes should be members of the affix inventory, but not part of the root form. This includes all morphemes that interact with syntactic processes. Morphosyntactic productivity is not a sole indicator of such processes. Affixes that compositonally alter the semantics of the root form should also be a part of the affix inventory. Our morpheme segmentation scheme, which is based on these principles, is presented in Section 5.2.

4.2 Part-of-Speech Tagset

All previous models of Turkish morphology and labelled corpora assume coarse PoS tagsets (Oflazer et al., 2003; Sulubacak et al., 2016). Distinctively, we use a more elaborate subcategorization of coarse lexical types, the fine PoS tagset that is presented in Table 1. The reason to use a fine categorization is two-fold. It provides control in modeling morphotactics so that we can define a custom grammar of affixation for each lexical category which captures the true inflectional and derivational paradigms of the category in order to restrict overgeneration. Second, the morphological parse incorporates a realistic representation of

Coarse Tag	Fine Tag	Description
ADJ	JJ	Adjective
	VJ	Verb in participle form
ADP	IN	Postposition
ADV	CRB	Converb
	RB	Adverb
	WRB	Interrogative adverb
AFFIX	PFX	Prefix
CONJ	CC	Coordinating conjunct
DET	DT	Determiner
	PDT	Prediterminer
	WDT	Wh-determiner
EXS	EX	Existential verb
NOUN	ADD	Electronic address
	NN	Common noun
	NNP	Proper noun
	VN	Verbal noun
NUM	CD	Cardinal number
ONOM	DUP	Onomatopoeic
PRON	PRD	Demonstrative pronoun
	PRF	Derived pronoun
	PRI	Indefinite pronoun
	PRP	Personal pronoun
	PRP$	Possessive pronoun
	PRR	Reflexive pronoun
	WP	Wh-pronoun
PRT	EP	Final particle
	OP	Coordinative particle
	RPC	Clitic particle
	RPNEG	Negation particle
	RPQ	Question particle
VERB	NOMP	Nominal predicate
	VB	Verb

Table 1: Fine PoS tagset that is used in lexical categorization. As a reference for comparisong we present their mapping to coarse tags, which is aligned with Universal Dependecies (UD) (Petrov et al., 2012; Nivre et al., 2016) except the bold marked Turkish-specific additions. Due to space considerations we do not present the tags '.' (punctuation) and 'X' (catch-all for abbreviations, etc.). For the complete PoS tagset that we use, refer to `https://github.com/google-research/turkish-morphology/blob/master/analyzer/src/lexicon/README.md`.

lexical types and thus it is more informative of the actual syntactic structure.

The tags are categorized into two mutually exclusive sets. Those that are lexical (used in annotating the PoS of roots in the lexicon), and those that arise due to derivational morphology. The second set is {CRB, PRF, VJ, VN}. Fig. 3-a-d presents an example of their use in sentence-level

(a) **Pronominalization** '*Ali took (the one) that is with the child*'
    Ali   çocuktakini   aldı
    Ali   çocuk+DA-ki+NH   al[VB]+DH
    Ali[NNP] (child[NN]+Loc)([**PRF**]-Pron+Acc) take[VB]+Past

(b) **Noun Clause** '*Ali knows that you stole the money*'
    Ali   parayı   senin   çaldığını   biliyor
    Ali   para+YH   sen+NHn   çal-DHk+SH+NH   bil+Hyor
    Ali[NNP] money[NN]+Acc you[PRP$]+Gen (steal[NN])([**VN**]-PastNom+P3sg+Acc) know[VB]+Prog1

(c) **Relative Clause** '*Ali knows the money that you stole since three years*'
    Ali   senin   çaldığın   parayı
    Ali   sen+NHn   çal-DHk+Hn   para+YH
    Ali[NNP] you[PRP$]+Gen (steal[VB])([**VJ**]-PastPart+P2sg) money[NN]+Acc

    üç   yıldır   biliyor
    üç   yıl-DHr   bil+Hyor
    3[CD]   (year[NN])([RB]-Since) know[VB]+Prog1

(d) **Adverbial Clause** '*I went home running*'
    Eve   koşarak   gittim
    Ev+YA   koş-YArAk   git+DH+m
    Home[NN]+Dat (run[VB])([**CRB**]-Ger) go[VB]+Past+V1sg

(e) **Nominal Predicate** '*(that is) Ali's child*'
    Ali'nin   çocuğudur
    Ali+'+NHn   çocuk+SH+DHr
    Ali[NNP]+Apos+Gen child[**NOMP**]+P3sg+GenCop

Figure 3: Morphological feature and PoS labeling of sentences that illustrate the use of morphologically derived lexical categories and nominal predicates in sentence-level context.

context. Fig. 3-e illustrates an example for the NOMP (nominal predicate) category. It captures cases where non-verbal roots are affixed with copula markers and act as the main predicate of the sentence. Unlike previous models, we differentiate between verbal and non-verbal predicates in terms of PoS labels.

4.3 Morphophonemic Irregularities

Consonant voicing irregularities apply to roots whose final voiceless consonant fails to get voiced despite attachment of an affix that starts with a vowel. It only applies to sounds that are [-voiced][+plosive]. We annotate final voiceless plosives { '*k*', '*p*', '*t*', '*ç*'} on roots that do not follow this process with **K**, ~ and **Ç** (e.g. *meş***K**, *tehdit*~, *gö***Ç**). Likewise, roots that undergo gemination and y-insertion are respectively annotated with " and ^ (e.g. *af*" or *akarsu*^).

The lateral '*l*' has allophones when it occurs in root final position after back vowels. When an affix beginning with a vowel is attached to roots with palatalized root final '*l*', affix form is resolved as if the vowel in the last syllable of the root is a front vowel. Hence, we respectively annotate back vowels { '*a*', '*â*', '*o*', '*u*'} that appear in the last syllable of such roots with {, [, %, and } (e.g. *ihtim*{*l* or *metrop*%*l*). Similarly, last vowel of the roots that undergo epenthesis and vowel closing are an-

notated with **?** and **E** (e.g. *buru***?***n* or *y***E**).

In case of code-switching foreign words are used in Turkish sentences and get inflected according to the lexical category that they hold in sentence-level context while root form is preserved on surface. Last syllable of the Turkish pronunciation of these roots are annotated to guide morpophonemics model to resolve surface form of the affixes that attach to them (e.g. *charter****ır***). Abbreviations are handled in the same manner.

4.4 Lexical Features

Besides the morphological features described in Section 5 we represent certain syntactic agreement, semantic and sentence-level segmentation features in morphological parse. These features are lexically conditioned, thus annotated in the root form lexicon. They can be used in feature-engineering for morphological disambiguation, PoS tagging and syntactic parsing. There are 5 such feature categories:

Apostrophe marks optional apostrophes that separate affixes from nominal and nominal predicate roots (e.g. *Ankara'da* '*Ankara*+Apostrophe+Loc').

Temporal is used to mark common nouns and adverbs that denote temporality (e.g. *süre* '(for some) *duration*' or *akşamüzeri* '*towards evening*').

Input: kitaplık
Output: (kitap[NN]+[PersonNumber=A3sg]+[Possessive=Pnon] +[Case=Bare])([NN]-lHk[Derivation=For]
                      +[PersonNumber=A3sg]+[Possessive=Pnon]+[Case=Bare])+[Proper=False]

Figure 4: Morphological parse of the word *kitaplık* '*bookshelf*'. Composed of two IGs, each enclosed in parantheses. First one consisting of the root *kitap* '*book*' and its inflections and second consisting of the derivational morpheme -lHk (which derives '*bookshelf*' from '*book*') and its inflectional features.

ConjunctionType specifies subcategorization of conjunct roots, denoting whether they are adverbial, coordinating, parallel or subordinating given the sentence and/or discourse-level context (e.g. *ya* '*either*+Parallel' or *ile* '*with*+Coordinating').

DeterminerType marks determiner roots as definite, indefinite, demonstrative or directional (e.g. *çoğu* '*most of*+Indefinite').

ComplementType indicates whether the complement of a postposition is a number, finite verb, or nominal which is marked for a certain case. This feature is inherited from the METU-Sabancı Treebank (MST) (Atalay et al., 2003; Oflazer et al., 2003). Unlike MST, we distinguish postpositions with number and finite verb complements from those that have nominative case marked nominal counterparts (e.g. (gitti 'went') *diye*+FiniteComplement, or (yatırımcı 'investor') *için*+NominativeComplement).

4.5   Compound Nouns

Certain noun roots end with compounding marker +SH, which is ambiguous with 3rd person possessive inflection morpheme (e.g. *milletvekil(i)* '*member of parliament*+SH'). These roots have irregular nominal inflectional morphotactics. When inflected for 3rd person plural (A3pl), inflectional morpheme +lAr precedes +SH as in Fig. 5. Such noun roots are annotated in the lexicon as shown in Fig. 2 and we define a custom inflectional paradigm for them to capture this behaviour in the morphotactics model.

(a)   milletvekil+lAr+SH
       milletvekil+ler+i
       milletvekilleri
(b)   *milletvekil(i)+lAr+SH
       *milletvekil(i)+ler+i
       *milletvekilileri

Figure 5: 3rd person singular inflections on compound noun roots.

5   Morphotactics

The morphotactic layer is implemented using the OpenFst library (Allauzen et al., 2007). We define 15 FSTs, where each reflects a custom affixation grammar per coarse lexical category (Section 4.2). The overall morphotactics model is obtained by composing those 15 FSTs.

5.1   Segmentation And Inflectional Groups

Following Hakkani-Tür et al. (2002) and Oflazer (2003), we segment a word into its root and inflectional groups (IG). IGs tokenize a word into subsegments based on the derivational boundaries that are in the word. As illustrated in Fig. 4 it is a complex segmental unit comprising of the derivational morpheme, lexical category of the derived form and inflections that might occur after that derivation.

In IG-based modeling last IG determines the final lexical category of the word and inflectional features of the last IG apply to the whole word in determining its grammatical function in sentence-level context. While building cascaded NLP architectures with lexemic syntactic processing units morphological features of the last IG are informative in PoS tagging and syntactic parsing to constraint data sparsity. We do not employ IG-based segmentation as a theoretical construct in our model, but rather include it as part of the morphological analysis representation. Together with IG boundaries we also represent segmentation of individual morphemes which is helpful in extracting morphemic grammars and assigning individual lexical categories to each morpheme.

5.2   Affix Inventory and Feature Tagset

Our affix inventory is composed of 51 inflectional and 72 derivational morphemes (excluding morphemes that are not realized in surface and by generalizing allophones over meta-phonemes). Inflectional morphemes are categorized over 8 feature categories (e.g. *Case* or *Possessive* on nominals, *Copula* or *TenseAspectMood* on verbals) and 42 feature values (e.g. *Case=Abl* or *TenseAspectMood=Aor*), whereas a single feature category is used to mark all derivations (*Derivation*) which can take 62 feature values (e.g. *Derivation=PastPart*). Compared to the models reported

(a) çaldığını *'that you stole (it)'*
(çal[VB]+[Polarity=Pos])([VN]-DHk[Derivation=PastNom]+[PersonNumber=A3sg] +SH[Possessive=P3sg]
+NH[Case=Acc])+[Proper=False]

(b) çaldığın *'(the thing) that you stole'*
(çal[VB]+[Polarity=Pos])([VJ]-DHk[Derivation=PastPart]+Hn[Possessive=P2sg]) +[Proper=False]

(c) koşarak *'(by) running'*
(koş[VB]+[Polarity=Pos])([CRB]-YArAk[Derivation=Ger])+[Proper=False]

Figure 6: PoS and derivational feature labeling for nominalizers, participles and converbials.

in the literature this is the most fine-grained morpheme segmentation model for Turkish.[4]

Çakıcı (2012) reports an affix inventory of 53 inflectional and 29 derivational morphemes, which is inherited from Oflazer et al. (1994) and used in extracting morpheme segmentations from MST. An investigation into the affix inventory of Şahin et al. (2013) shows that they do not represent some productive derivational processes (see Table 2). An example is -lA (Make), which creates denominal and deadjectival verbs in Turkish. According to Nakipoğlu and Üntak (2008) verbs derived by this suffix make up the largest portion of Turkish verb lexicon (excluding light verb constructions), accounting for about 21% of the verbs that are found in Turkish dictionaries. Çöltekin (2014) also does not represent -CAk (Coll), -CAnAk (Coll), -izm (Doct) -gil (Fam), -ist (Foll), -lA (Make), -lArcA (Of), -vari(Sim), -Hmtrak (Sim), -dA (Snd). Akın and Akın (2007) and Sak et al. (2009) does not segment infinitive markers from the root form. Sulubacak et al. (2016) consider verbal derivational morphemes -lAn (Acquire), -lAş (Become) and nominal derivational morphemes -CH (Agentive), -CHk and -CAğHz (Diminutive) on noun roots as a part of the root form, although they are semantically productive.

To represent the adequate phrasal scope of these affixes in morphemic syntactic processing and to recover clausal architecture in sentence-level disambiguation tasks in lexemic syntactic processing it is essential to explicitly segment and mark them. One example is Turkish subordination, which is handled through morphology. As illustrated in Fig. 3-b-d, noun, relative and adverbial clauses are created with an affix that attaches to the base verb to create a clause out of the sentence headed by the verb, which can then function as an argument or adjunct of the matrix verb.

Feature	Description	Morpheme	Example
Rcp	Reciprocal	-Hş	söyleş
Rfx	Reflexive	-Hn	süslen
Nonf	Nonfinite	-YHş	tüken-iş
Dim	Diminutive	-cAğHz	çocuk-cağız
Doct	Doctrine	-izm	komün-izm
Fam	Family	-gil, -lAr	annem-gil
Foll	Follower	-ist, -st	komün-ist
From	From	-lH	Ankara-lı
Lang	Language	-CA	Alman-ca
Ness	Ness	-lHk	insan-lık
Make	Make	-lA	işaret-le
Aff	Affinity	-CHl	et-çil
Of	Of	-lArcA	ton-larca
Sim	Similar	-Hmtrak, -vari	sarı-mtrak
Coll	Collective	-CAk, -CAnAk	toplu-canak
Ly	Adverbial	-CAsHnA	aptal-casına
Bcm	Become	-lAş	iyi-leş
Snd	Sound	-dA	fokur-da

Table 2: Derivational morphemes in our affix inventory distinct from Şahin et al. (2013).

We segment subordinating affixes that are described in Göksel and Kerslake (2004). They can be subcategorized into: (i) *Nominalizers* which create noun clauses (or verbal nouns), (ii) *Participles* which create adjectival clauses, (iii) *Converbials* which create adverbial clauses. A subset of these suffixal forms are ambiguous between two functions, they both create noun and adjectival clauses (e.g. -DHk affix in Fig. 3-b and Fig. 3-c). We explicitly mark differing functions of these in sentence-level context. Morphological feature tags for morphemes that create a noun clause end with -Nom (short for nominalizer, e.g. PastNom), and feature tags for those that create an adjectival clause end with -Part (short for Participle, e.g. PastPart). Words derived via attachment of subordinating affixes are also differentiated at the level of PoS. If they are derived by *Nominalizers* they receive the fine tag VN (verbal noun), words derived by *Participles* receive the tag VJ (verbal adjective) and those that are derived by *Converbials* are tagged as CRB (short for converbial). This brings in further syntactic expressivity to the morphological analyses as shown in Fig. 6.

---

[4] For an exhaustive list of morphemes segmented and tagged by our model, refer to `https://github.com/google-research/turkish-morphology/blob/master/analyzer/src/morphotactics/README.md`.

(a)   *İyi* ile kötünün savaşı. *'The battle between the good and the bad.'*
(iyi[NN]+[PersonNumber=A3sg]+[Possessive=Pnon]+[Case=Bare]) +[Proper=False]

(b)   1000 liraya tablet baktım ama *iyisini* bulamadım.
'I have searched for a tablet to buy for 1000 liras but couldn't find a good one.'
(iyi[PRI]+[PersonNumber=A3sg]+SH[Possessive=P3sg]+NH[Case=Acc]) +[Proper=False]

(c)   *İyi* bir insan. *'A good person.'*
(iyi[JJ])+[Proper=False]

(d)   İlaç bana *iyi* geldi. *'The medicine made me feel well.'*
(iyi[RB])+[Proper=False]

(e)   Bugün *iyiyim*. *'I am well today.'*
(iyi[NOMP]+[PersonNumber=A3sg]+[Possessive=Pnon]+[Case=Bare] +[Copula=PresCop]
+YHm[PersonNumber=V1sg])+[Proper=False]

Figure 7: Morphological parses for root form *iyi* *'good'* in 5 distinct sentence-level context.

5.3 Eliminating Zero-Derivation

The distinction between lexical categories is blurry in Turkish. Previous models employ a zero-derivation mechanism to capture this ambiguity, which is syntactic type shifting of a word through affixation of a so-called *empty morpheme* that does not realize in surface form. Instead, we cross-categorize lexical entries of root forms in the lexicon according to the syntactic functions they can take. This method ensures all derivational morphemes to have a corresponding realization in the surface. Representation-wise morphological parse ends up being significantly simplified and more tractable without empty morphemes while the base lexicon is kept compact and maintainable.

Fig. 7 presents disambiguated analyses for the word *iyi* *'good'* in context. In its root form the word is 5-way ambiguous between categories NN, PRI, JJ, RB, and NOMP. As a preprocessing step prior to FST compilation such categorically ambiguous root forms are cross-categorized by adding new lexical items to the lexicon with a tag from the set of ambiguous lexical categories. We utilize a comprehensive set of cross-categorization rules that capture all ambiguous lexical category pairs.[5] This method enables us to strip lexical ambiguity handling from morphotactic model development while keeping morphotactic models for each lexical category generic. For example, word form *iyisi* (iyi+si, 'good+SH[3Psg]') will only be parsed as NN, NOMP, and PRI, where JJ and RB interpretations are pruned, even though the root form is cross-categorized for those tags. This is because the morphotactic model for JJ and RB

would not allow root form *iyi* to be inflected for 3rd person possessive (P3sg).

5.4 Case Marking

Turkish is a nominative-accusative language where subjects are marked with nominative case (not realized in surface form) and direct objects with accusative (+YH and +NH). It is also shown to exhibit a grammatical phenomenon called *Head Incorporation*, which results in the verb forming a complex grammatical unit with its direct object (Kornfilt, 2003). In such cases direct object nominals do not have any case marking and they exhibit different behaviour from their cased counterparts in terms of syntactic and semantic properties.

Turkish is considered a free word order language where direct objects can be scrambled within the sentence from their canonical (preverbal) position (Bozşahin, 1998, 2000). However, as illustrated by Fig. 8-c caseless direct objects are less flexible to scramble and leave their preverbal positions.[6] Besides scrambling, caseless direct objects are also shown to be invisible to syntax in terms of binding and passivization (Aydemir, 2004; Öztürk, 2005, 2009). Furthermore, Aydemir (2004) shows that depending on whether the direct object has accusative case, the item that occurs before it can either be interpreted as an adjective or adverb. In Fig. 9-a, the noun *araba* has accusative marking, and modifier *iyi* is interpreted as an adjectival modifier of the noun. In Fig. 9-b, *araba* does not have any case and therefore invisible for syntactic modification, *iyi* is interpreted as an adverb and modifies the whole verb phrase. These

---

[5] For the complete set of cross-categorization rules that we use, refer to `https://github.com/google-research/turkish-morphology/blob/master/analyzer/src/morphotactics/README.md`.

[6] A detailed investigation into the extent of flexibility by which caseless objects can move from their preverbal positions is beyond the scope of this paper. For a thorough linguistic analysis, refer to Gračanin-Yüksek and İşsever (2011).

pieces of evidence are taken to indicate that case-less direct objects might not be forming syntactic arguments on their own.

(a) Ahmet   dün   akşam   pasta   ye+di
    Ahmet   yesterday evening cake+Nom   eat+Past

(b) Ahmet   pasta+yı   dün   akşam   ye+di
    Ahmet   cake+Acc   yesterday evening eat+Past

(c) *Ahmet pasta   dün   akşam   ye+di
    *Ahmet cake   yesterday evening eat+Past

Figure 8: Scrambling, adopted from Kornfilt (2003).

(a) Ahmet   iyi   arabayı   kullanır
    Ahmet   iyi   araba+YH   kullan+Hr
    Ahmet[NNP]good[JJ]car[NN]+Accdrive[VB]+Aor
    'Ahmet drives the good car'

(b) Ahmet   iyi   araba   kullanır
    Ahmet   iyi   araba   kullan+Hr
    Ahmet[NNP]good[RB]car[NN]+Baredrive[VB]+Aor
    'Ahmet drives well'
    (lit. *'Ahmet does good car-driving'*)

Figure 9: Modification of caseless direct objects.

Previous Turkish morphology models mark such caseless objects with subjective case (nominative). They also extend application of subjective case to all other caseless nominals in the sentence, even to those that are caseless objects of postpositional phrases. We find this treatment syntactically problematic, because grammatical properties of subjects and caseless objects are completely different, so we label them distinctively. While a subject is marked with nominative case (Nom), caseless objects are marked to bear no case (Bare). These distinctive case features can be useful in downstream NLP tasks, especially in adequately disambiguating subjects from caseless objects in syntactic parsing.

5.5 Agreement

In Turkish a predicate agrees with its subject in Person and Number. As shown in Lewis (1967), Good and Alan (2000) and Göksel and Kerslake (2004) there are four suffixal paradigms for this agreement. The predicate can combine with affixes in one of these paradigms depending on its Tense-Aspect-Mood properties. Predicates having past tense (+YDH) or conditional (+YsA) are inflected with -k paradigm, those that are in imperative and optative mood are respectively inflected with imperative and optative paradigms, and all others are inflected with -z paradigm. Our model is sufficiently expressive of these paradigms based on agreement properties of predicates.

TenseAspectMood verbal inflectional feature that is marked on predicates clarifies which paradigm needs to be used in agreement morphology. Agreement itself is encoded in the *PersonNumber* feature of the morphological parse of verbals and nominals. Verbal agreement feature tags start with '*V*' prefix (e.g. V3sg), whereas for nominals prefix '*A*' is used (e.g. A3sg). Fig. 10 presents a scrambled raising construction, where embedded clause subject *seni* receives objective (accusative) case from the matrix verb *san*. Since the sentence is scrambled, word order is not a reliable indicator of which noun phrase is the subject of which clause. However, this information is easily recoverable from the morphological analyses using the agreement between *PersonNumber* features of the verbs and noun phrases.

5.6 Proper Nouns

We represent named entities as part of the morphological parse with the boolean feature *Proper*. All words that are part of a multi-word named entity are marked as *Proper=True*. This method allows us to label internal structure (PoS and morphological features) of multi-word named entities and spans of tokens that form them in sentence-level context (see Fig. 11). Trained over a representative corpus, a disambiguator based on such features of our model can output predictions whether a sequence of words form a named entity in context.

6   Testing and Evaluation

In order to test correctness of generated morphological analyses and identify possible gaps in the root form lexicon, we utilized a human-annotation based iterative development and testing scheme. 6 annotators, who are linguistically trained Turkish native speakers disambiguated morphological analyses that are output by our morphological analyzer by referring to sentence-level context. Annotation is done on a corpora of 2,200 sentences which are randomly extracted from Turkish Wikipedia pages. Annotators iteratively annotated batches of 200 sentences, reported illicit morphological analyses and word forms that cannot be parsed. Analyses for every word in the corpora is annotated by 2 annotators. The model and the root form lexicon is improved by taking account of syntactic constructions that are observed

Seni	ben	akıllısın	sandım
sen+YH	ben	akıllı+sHn	san+DH+m
you[PRP]+A2sg+Acc	I[PRP]+A1sg+Nom	smart[NOMP]+V2sg	consider[VB]+Past+V1sg

'I considered you smart'

Figure 10: Person and number agreement in scrambled raising construction.

Yüzüklerin	Efendisini	izledim
Yüzük+lAr+NHn	Efendi+SH+NH	izle+DH+m
Ring[NN]+A3pl+Gen+**Proper=True**	Lord[NN]+P3sg+Acc+**Proper=True**	watch[VB]+Past+V1sg+**Proper=False**

'I watched Lord of the Rings'

Figure 11: *Proper* feature labeling on named entities that span across multiple tokens.

in the corpora until no illicit analysis is reported and a satisfactory level of coverage is attained. Our improvements also aimed to refactor affixation grammars that are defined by the morphotactics model to limit overgeneration by disallowing affixation of certain derivational morphemes to a set of inflectional morphemes (e.g. -gil (Family) nominal derivation morpheme can only follow common and proper noun word stems or possessive inflections).

Table 3 shows coverage statistics of our model on a data set that is different than our development corpora. We define coverage as the fraction of word forms that our model can parse among the set of unique observed word forms. We calculate it over a merge of training and test set sentences of Turkish section of the CoNLL 2007 Shared Task of Dependency Parsing data set (Nivre et al., 2007), which contains 60,310 tokens and 18,443 unique word forms (after case-folding). On contrary to Çöltekin (2010) we do not remove tags, punctuation and numbers from the data set. The analyzer can parse 17,624 word forms, yielding 95.56% coverage, while generating 24.96 analyses and 2.06 IGs on average per word form. When we remove *Proper* morphological feature from the morphological parse, which generates duplicate analyses that only differ by this feature, the average number of analyses per word form is reduced to 12.82. Note that the coverage we report is not directly comparable with Şahin et al. (2013) since we do not employ any fallback mechanisms that depend on affix stripping. Such fallback methods potentially result in higher coverage with occasionally incorrect morphological parses.

7 Conclusions and Future Work

In this paper we presented a syntactically expressive morphology model for Turkish, a human-annotated gold lexicon of root forms and a fine-

Coverage statistics	
Tokens	60,130
Unique word forms	18,443
Accepted word forms	17,624
Unrecognized word forms	819
Coverage	95.56%
Average number of analyses	
With *Proper* feature	24.96
Without *Proper* feature	12.82
Average number of inflectional groups	
With *Proper* feature	2.06
Without *Proper* feature	2.05

Table 3: Statistics on analyzer coverage and average number of analyses and inflectional groups that it generates.

grained affix inventory. While doing so, we also introduced a novel method to eliminate zero-derivations, a fine part-of-speech tagset and elaborate representations of inflectional/derivational features. We have shown that the implemented model has high coverage and does not overgenerate. In terms of lexemic syntactic processing, we would like to investigate implications of our representation in building morphological disambiguators and syntactic parsers. In parallel, we would also like to experiment with fully morphemic grammar induction, since our fine-grained morpheme segmentation scheme can be used in capturing adequate phrasal scope.

Acknowledgments

We would like to thank Martin Jansche for helping with Thrax and OpenFst integration; Haşim Sak for sharing their implementation; Ryan McDonald, Jan Botha and Bernd Bohnet for their comments; Savaş Çetin, Nihal Meriç Atilla, Eda Aydın Oktay, Faruk Büyüktckin, Hakan Keser, Hilal Yıldırım, İlmiye Karakimseli and Ozan Mahir Yıldırım for their meticulous work on data annotation.

References

Ahmet Afşin Akın and Mehmet Dündar Akın. 2007. Zemberek, an open source NLP framework for Turkic languages. *Structure*, 10:1–5.

Cyril Allauzen, Michael Riley, Johan Schalkwyk, Wojciech Skut, and Mehryar Mohri. 2007. OpenFst: A general and efficient weighted finite-state transducer library. In *International Conference on Implementation and Application of Automata*, pages 11–23. Springer.

Nart Bedin Atalay, Kemal Oflazer, and Bilge Say. 2003. The annotation process in the Turkish treebank. In *Proceedings of 4th International Workshop on Linguistically Interpreted Corpora (LINC-03) at EACL 2003*.

Yasemin Aydemir. 2004. Are Turkish preverbal bare nouns syntactic arguments? *Linguistic Inquiry*, 35(3):465–474.

Cem Bozşahin. 1998. Deriving the predicate-argument structure for a free word order language. In *Proceedings of the 36th Annual Meeting of the Association for Computational Linguistics and 17th International Conference on Computational Linguistics-Volume 1*, pages 167–173. Association for Computational Linguistics.

Cem Bozşahin. 2000. Gapping and word order in Turkish. In *Proceedings of the 10th International Conference on Turkish Linguistics*, pages 58–66.

Cem Bozşahin. 2002. The combinatory morphemic lexicon. *Computational Linguistics*, 28(2):145–186.

Ruket Çakıcı. 2005. Automatic induction of a CCG grammar for Turkish. In *Proceedings of the ACL student research workshop*, pages 73–78. Association for Computational Linguistics.

Ruket Çakıcı. 2012. Morpheme segmentation in the METU-Sabancı Turkish treebank. In *Proceedings of the Sixth Linguistic Annotation Workshop*, pages 144–148. Association for Computational Linguistics.

Çağrı Çöltekin. 2010. A freely available morphological analyzer for turkish. In *LREC*, volume 2, pages 19–28.

Çağrı Çöltekin. 2014. A set of open source tools for Turkish natural language processing. In *LREC*, pages 1079–1086.

Muhammet Şahin, Umut Sulubacak, and Gülşen Eryiğit. 2013. Redefinition of Turkish morphology using flag diacritics. In *Proceedings of The Tenth Symposium on Natural Language Processing (SNLP-2013), Phuket, Thailand, October*.

Gülşen Eryiğit and Eşref Adalı. 2004. An affix stripping morphological analyzer for Turkish. In *Proceedings of the IASTED International Conference on Artificial Intelligence and Applications*.

Aslı Göksel and Celia Kerslake. 2004. *Turkish: A comprehensive grammar*. Routledge.

Jeff Good and CL Alan. 2000. Affix-placement variation in Turkish. In *Proceedings of the 25th Annual Meeting of the Berkeley Linguistics Society: Special Session on Caucasian, Dravidian, and Turkic Linguistics*, pages 63–74.

Martina Gračanin-Yüksek and Selçuk İşsever. 2011. Movement of bare objects in Turkish. *Dilbilim Araştırmaları*, 22(1):33–49.

Dilek Z Hakkani-Tür, Kemal Oflazer, and Gökhan Tür. 2002. Statistical morphological disambiguation for agglutinative languages. *Computers and the Humanities*, 36(4):381–410.

Jaklin Kornfilt. 2003. Scrambling, subscrambling, and case in Turkish. *Word order and scrambling*, 125155.

Kimmo Koskenniemi. 1984. A general computational model for word-form recognition and production. In *Proceedings of the 10th International Conference on Computational Linguistics and 22nd Annual Meeting on Association for Computational Linguistics*. Association for Computational Linguistics.

Geoffrey L Lewis. 1967. *Turkish grammar*. Oxford University Press.

Mine Nakipoğlu and Aslı Üntak. 2008. A complete verb lexicon of Turkish based on morphemic analysis. *Turkic Languages*, 12:221–280.

Joakim Nivre, Marie-Catherine De Marneffe, Filip Ginter, Yoav Goldberg, Jan Hajic, Christopher D Manning, Ryan T McDonald, Slav Petrov, Sampo Pyysalo, Natalia Silveira, et al. 2016. Universal Dependencies v1: A Multilingual Treebank Collection. In *LREC*.

Joakim Nivre, Johan Hall, Sandra Kübler, Ryan McDonald, Jens Nilsson, Sebastian Riedel, and Deniz Yuret. 2007. The CoNLL 2007 shared task on dependency parsing. In *Proceedings of the 2007 Joint Conference on Empirical Methods in Natural Language Processing and Computational Natural Language Learning (EMNLP-CoNLL)*.

Kemal Oflazer. 1994. Two-level description of Turkish morphology. *Literary and Linguistic Computing*, 9(2):137–148.

Kemal Oflazer. 2003. Dependency parsing with an extended finite-state approach. *Computational Linguistics*, 29(4):515–544.

Kemal Oflazer, Elvan Göçmen, and Cem Bozşahin. 1994. An outline of Turkish morphology. *Report to NATO Science Division SfS III (TU-LANGUAGE), Brussels*.

Kemal Oflazer, Bilge Say, Dilek Zeynep Hakkani-Tür, and Gökhan Tür. 2003. Building a Turkish treebank. In *Treebanks*, pages 261–277. Springer.

Balkız Öztürk. 2005. *Case, referentiality and phrase structure*. John Benjamins.

Balkız Öztürk. 2009. Incorporating agents. *Lingua*, 119(2):334–358.

Slav Petrov, Dipanjan Das, and Ryan McDonald. 2012. A Universal Part-of-Speech Tagset. In *LREC*.

Brian Roark, Richard Sproat, Cyril Allauzen, Michael Riley, Jeffrey Sorensen, and Terry Tai. 2012. The OpenGrm open-source finite-state grammar software libraries. In *Proceedings of the ACL 2012 System Demonstrations*, pages 61–66. Association for Computational Linguistics.

Haşim Sak, Tunga Güngör, and Murat Saraçlar. 2009. A stochastic finite-state morphological parser for Turkish. In *Proceedings of the ACL-IJCNLP 2009 Conference short papers*, pages 273–276. Association for Computational Linguistics.

Umut Sulubacak, Memduh Gökırmak, Francis Tyers, Çağrı Çöltekin, Joakim Nivre, and Gülşen Eryiğit. 2016. Universal dependencies for Turkish. In *Proceedings of COLING 2016, the 26th International Conference on Computational Linguistics: Technical Papers*, pages 3444–3454.

Using Meta-Morph Rules to develop Morphological Analysers:
A case study concerning Tamil

K Sarveswaran
University of Moratuwa
Sri Lanka
`sarvesk@uom.lk`

Gihan Dias
University of Moratuwa
Sri Lanka
`gihan@uom.lk`

Miriam Butt
University of Konstanz
Germany
`miriam.butt@uni-konstanz.de`

Abstract

This paper describes a new and larger coverage Finite-State Morphological Analyser (FSM) and Generator for the Dravidian language Tamil. The FSM has been developed in the context of computational grammar engineering, adhering to the standards of the ParGram effort. Tamil is a morphologically rich language and the interaction between linguistic analysis and formal implementation is complex, resulting in a challenging task. In order to allow the development of the FSM to focus more on the linguistic analysis and less on the formal details, we have developed a system of meta-morph(ology) rules along with a script which translates these rules into FSM processable representations. The introduction of meta-morph rules makes it possible for computationally naive linguists to interact with the system and to expand it in future work. We found that the meta-morph rules help to express linguistic generalisations and reduce the manual effort of writing lexical classes for morphological analysis. Our Tamil FSM currently handles mainly the inflectional morphology of 3,300 verb roots and their 260 forms. Further, it also has a lexicon of approximately 100,000 nouns along with a guesser to handle out-of-vocabulary items. Although the Tamil FSM was primarily developed to be part of a computational grammar, it can also be used as a web or stand-alone application for other NLP tasks, as per general ParGram practice.

1   Introduction

A morphological analyser and generator is a crucial tool for Natural Language Processing (NLP), especially for processing morphologically rich languages like Tamil, in which morphemes are used to mark various types of information like tense, aspect, mood, person, number and, gender, *etc*. Our use of Finite-State Morphology (FSM) is based on the two-level approach to morphology in which there are two layers, namely surface and lexical (Karttunen and Beesley, 2001). The surface layer represents the actual word, and the lexical layer has a string, also called a lexical string, which shows the morphological analysis. For a language like Tamil, this analysis string is generally complex and may be long.

Designing and writing out a large number of lexical strings is not only tedious but also complicated for a morphologically rich language like Tamil. On the other hand, Tamil is morphologically well structured, in other words, the order of morphemes is generally rather templatic (Lehmann, 1993), though there are a few exceptions. For instance, simple indicative verbs consist of a root that is then followed by a tense marker and finally the person-number-gender (PNG) marker. Because of the complex, yet templatic nature of the morphological system, we decided to aid and speed up the development of the Tamil FSM via the innovation of a set of meta-morph(ology) rules. We further found that our meta-morph approach can also be extended to other structured languages by performing some initial experimentation with Sinhala, an Indo-Aryan language.

Our FSM is being developed in the context of the construction of a computational grammar for Tamil. For this, we are using the Xerox Linguistic Environment (XLE) using Lexical Functional Grammar (LFG), adhering to standards and methods set within the international ParGram effort (Butt et al., 1999).[1]

---

[1] https://typo.uni-konstanz.de/redmine/projects/pargram/wiki

76

Proceedings of the 14th International Conference on Finite-State Methods and Natural Language Processing, pages 76–86
Dresden, Germany, September 23-25, 2019. ©2019 Association for Computational Linguistics

2 Background

2.1 The Tamil language

Tamil is a Dravidian language, specifically a Southern Dravidian language that is spoken natively by more than 80 million people across the world. It has been recognised as a classical language by the government of India since it has more than 2000 years of a continuous and unbroken literary tradition (George, 2000). It is an official language of Sri Lanka and Singapore, and has regional official status in Tamil Nadu and Pondichchery, India. It has also been recognised as a minority or indigenous language in several countries including Malaysia, Mauritius and South Africa and is taught as a second language in several other countries, including Canada, Australia and United Kingdom.

Tamil is an agglutinative language where a set of morphemes are generally suffixed to a lemma. However, there are a few exceptions where morphemes are prefixed to lemmas. Words in Tamil take both inflectional and derivational suffixes, and engage in compounding. Nouns in Tamil are primarily marked for case and number. Verbs, on the other hand, display complex morphological paradigms that express a range of information relevant for syntactic and semantic analysis.

2.2 Morphology of Tamil

2.2.1 Verb morphology

Verbs in Tamil realise a range of information including tense, mood, aspect, negation, interrogation, information about emphasis, speaker perspective, sentience or rationality, and conditional and causal relations (Annamalai et al., 2014). Entities in Tamil are fundamentally classified into rational vs. irrational. Entities are termed rational if they are perceived as being able to think on their own. The rest are termed irrational. Further, it has been claimed that a weak vs. strong distinction found exists in the verbal paradigms that can be used to determine transitivity, ergativity, volitivity and affectedness (Paramasivam, 2011).

All of these properties are realised via suffixation. For instance, *he has been coming* can be translated by the Tamil verb form வந்துகொண்டிருந்திருக்கிறான் (vantukoṇṭiruntirukkirāṉ). This word consists of the following morphs: வா (vā) (lemma: 'come') + கொண்டு (koṇṭu) (continuous) + இருந்து (iruntu) (has) + இரு (iru) (be) + கிறு (kiru) (present tense) + ஆன் (āṉ) (3rd person + singular + masculine + rational). In Tamil, PNG and rationality are expressed via a single portmanteau form (Nuhman, 1999; Sarveswaran et al., 2018). For instance, in the above example it is the morph ஆன் (āṉ) that marks all of these features.

Tamil verbs can be classified on the basis of criteria that can be either morphological, syntactic or semantic (Paramasivam, 2011; Agesthialingom, 1971). Many scholars, including Lisker (1951); Graul (1855); Arden (1962) have classified verbs based on their morphology, specifically, based on how morphemes conjugate. Graul (1855) has provided an early classification on which other scholars have built their proposals (e.g., Irākavaiyaṅkār 1958; Sithiraputhiran 2004). His classification was also adapted for the Tamil lexicon project (Rajaram, 1986). Graul's classification of Tamil verbal lemmas includes 12 categories, and is based on the future tense markers in the verbs. His basic classification is also adopted in our work. In addition, Tamil also contains a set of auxiliaries, derived verbs and compound verbs.

2.3 Noun morphology

Nouns in Tamil display the morphological processes of inflection, derivation and compounding. Nouns are inflected for number and cases (Rajendran, 2012; Nuhman, 1999). In our FSM, we have so far tackled the inflectional morphology. We have also implemented a guesser which handles the inflections of out-of-lexicon nouns, including compound nouns. Compound nouns are handled as a single unit in our current system.

Rajendran (2012) has proposed a paradigm for noun morphology with 26 classes based on the morphophonological changes, also called *canti* (Sandhi). Among these 26 classes, 9 classes are used to capture the morphophonological rules pertaining to pronouns. Pronouns take different forms (different from their nominative forms) when inflecting for a case suffix. Currently, we are handling a subset of all of the possible pronoun categories.

In our noun paradigm, we have identified 38

classes for pronouns, including personal, possessive, and interrogative pronouns. We found that though many pronouns are subject to the same morphophonological rules, these result in different analyses or lexical strings. Therefore, these have been sorted into different classes. Overall, we followed the same classification as proposed by Rajendran (2012) for other noun classes.

2.4 Finite-State Morphology

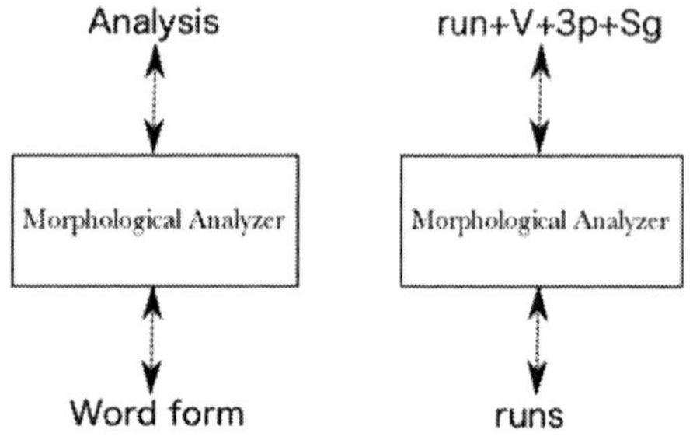

Figure 1: Word form (or Surface form) and Analysis form (or Lexical form)
Source : https://fomafst.github.io/morphtut.html

The theory of two-level morphology saw successful early applications for morphologically rich languages like Finnish, Russian and Sanskrit (Koskenniemi, 1983; Karttunen and Beesley, 2001). Subsequently, it has been taken up by researchers developing morphological analysers for other languages, including the South Asian languages Urdu, Sindhi and Nepali (Bögel et al., 2007; Prasain, 2011; Rahman, 2016) (see also Seiss 2012 for the morphologically extremely complex Australian language Murrinh-patha). In the two-level morphological analysis, a word is represented at two levels, namely the lexical level or lexical form, and the surface level or surface form, as shown in Figure 1.

Several tools have been developed to model FSM. Proprietary tools like the Xerox Finite-State Transducer (XFST) (Beesley and Karttunen, 2003) and the FSM Library from AT&T (now in OpenFST) have been widely used in the past. Open source solutions like OpenFST (Allauzen et al., 2007), HFST (Lindén et al., 2009) and Foma (Hulden, 2009) are also employed. XFST has been used widely as an aid to grammar engineering in the LFG/XLE context (Beesley and Karttunen, 2003; Butt et al., 1999; Rahman, 2016) as part of the ParGram effort. However, we found that in addition to licensing issues, XFST also has issues in rendering the scripts of South Asian languages, including Tamil, Sinhala and Devanagari. Among the available open source solutions, Foma complies with XFST standards, and has built-in support for the Unicode processing and proper rendering of South Asian scripts. We therefore decided to work with this software.

3 Related work

3.1 Meta-model / Meta-grammar development

Fokkens and Bender (2013) argue strongly that humans are better suited to the task of developing linguistic analyses than machines. We also believe that it is specifically better for the analysis of a language like Tamil, which is computationally under-resourced and which displays complex and interacting patterns of linguistic structure that need to be made transparent for down-stream NLP applications.

Bender et al. (2011) and Butt and King (2003) point out that regression testing is important for grammar engineering to be able to manage complex models when extended. This is also true for the development of a morphological analyser for a morphologically complex language like Tamil, where a continuous development is required, and where each time the system should be checked for possible errors. In order to facilitate the regression testing, Fokkens and Bender (2013) proposed a meta-grammar layer for grammar development, which places the customisation of source code under the control of grammar engineers while other users are then encouraged to do whatever changes may be necessary for their language specific needs. Otherwise, engineers need to engage with in-depth linguistic knowledge, and in turn, linguists need to engage with engineering issues.

The concept of meta-modelling has also been used in domains such as information mining. For instance, Ruiz et al. (2016) have proposed meta-association rules to compile new information from data extracted from multiple data sets, in order to provide a summarised representation. Similarly, the meta-rules proposed here also provide a summary of how words are formed.

3.2 Morphological analysers

A number of studies have been done on FSMs for South Asian languages. One of the earliest was Bögel et al. (2007) for Urdu that includes a transliteration component so that the morphological analyzer and generator can also be used for the structurally almost identical language Hindi. In addition to inflectional and derivational morphology, it also tackles complex problems such as reduplication and compounding. Prasain (2011) has developed an FSM for Nepali using the two-level morphology approach and XFST tool. Rahman (2016) has developed an analyser and generator for Sindhi as a part of his work on grammar development for Sindhi. He also used XFST, which he then integrated within his grammar.

Antony and Soman (2012) have carried out a survey on the state of affairs of computational morphology of Indian languages, and have documented 17 efforts of morphological analysers and/or generators for Tamil. 12 of them were carried out before 2007 and the relevant papers, data sets and/or software are not retrievable. The remainder have been carried out since 2010. Among those five efforts (Anand Kumar et al., 2010b,a; Menaka et al., 2010) are available for download in binary form yet without any data sets.

Menaka et al. (2010) and Anand Kumar et al. (2010b) have used rule-based approaches which only perform morphological generations. Anand Kumar et al. (2010a) have, on the other hand, applied a machine learning approach for the morphological analysis and generation of Tamil. Anand Kumar et al. (2010a) claim that the system was tested using 40,000 verbs and 30,000 nouns, and that the machine learning system was trained using 130,000 verbs and 70,000 nouns from their own corpus. However, data sets, sources or any detailed documentation are not available except for a sample corpus with 270,000 tokens. The extendability of this work to aid grammar development is also questionable, and would yet need to be researched. An email exchange with the authors has established that they do not work on this domain anymore.

Parameshwari (2011) has implemented a morphological analyser and generator for Tamil using a rule-based approach which covers verbs, nouns, adjectives, pronouns, numerals and non-standard Tamil words, with the use of the Apertium tool. The author claims that the system shows an accuracy of 84%. There are no associated data sets or rules available and the authors are also not contactable.

Lushanthan et al. (2014) have proposed a morphological analyser and generator for Tamil and have implemented it using XFST. The authors have used transliteration to handle the Tamil script given that XFST has issues in rendering, although it supports Unicode internally. The authors have considered 2,000 noun and 96 verb stems for the analysis and generation. They have tested the proposed system using their own data set consisting of 3,500 nouns and 500 verbs with a success rate of 78%. However, the data sets and XFST rules have not been made available.

Anna University, India has developed a morphological analyser in 2001 called *Atcharam* that has recently been added to the GitHub repository.[2] It is developed for TAB (TAmil Bilingual) encoded text as a stand-alone application using Java. Further, there is no detailed technical documentation or rule set. Some data in the form of a list of words are available in the repository. However, those are encoded using TAB, and an attempt to convert them to Unicode was also not successful.

There are also some morphological tools available in the GitHub code repository without corresponding academic publications. Pranavan and *et al.*[3] have provided work on a basic morphological analyser developed as a stand-alone application using Java. However, as also claimed by the developers, it is a basic analyser which handles only 20 words with 28 conjugation forms.

Yet another code repository is that by tacola-aucse.[4] This is also developed as a stand-alone application using Java, covering the analysis of verbs and nouns. However, no

---

[2] https://github.com/tacola-auceg/morpha_ta
[3] https://github.com/Pranavan135/Tamil_Morphological_Analyzer
[4] https://github.com/tacola-aucse/Morphological-Analyzer-For-Tamil

information about the data set or the rules developed, were found. We managed to run the tool with an older version of Java, but, irregular verbs like செத்தான் (cettāṉ) 'he died' do not give any analysis. In some cases, the given analysis is very confusing, especially when an out-of-vocabulary word is fed in. For instance, the analysis of சர்வேஸ்வரன் (carvēśvaraṉ), a proper noun, showed that it has the root of சர்வே (carvē) and a future tense marker வ் (v) and the past tense marker ன் (n). That is, it not only mistakes a proper noun for a verb, it also provides a completely wrong analysis with two tense markers. Furthermore, if the text is not Unicode normalised, then the tool produces unexpected results. Finally, when there are multiple analyses for a word, only one is provided. In comparison to the other tools available, however, this tool works well, but the extendability of the stand-alone Java tool is not very straightforward, unless a complete documentation can be found.

4 Development of Tamil FSM

4.1 Need for a Tamil FSM

Our research conducted on existing Tamil morphological analysers has demonstrated that none of the analysers developed in the past are complete or maintained anymore and that most of the existing applications do not support Unicode encoding. Our target task of constructing a computational grammar requires a morphological analyser with good accuracy with a specific type of interface to the grammar. None of the existing efforts fulfill these requirements.

On the other hand, we found that the open source software Foma fulfils our requirements; while rendering our scripts correctly, it also complies with XFST and can be easily integrated to the grammar we develop.

4.2 Methodology

Lexicons of verbs and nouns were compiled from various sources and classified on the basis of their inflected classes. Thereafter, a set of labels was identified and a parser to parse the meta-morph rules was developed. Next, orthographic rules were written for the identified classes. The FSM was then evaluated. In order to evaluate, a data set was also compiled, since there were no existing benchmark data sets found. All the inputs were preprocessed before being analysed. The Tamil FSM has been developed as a web-based system (parsers.projects.uom.lk) so that anyone can check or use it, where a word can be fed in, and an analysis produced as an output.

4.2.1 Pre-processing

Due to the nature of the Tamil Unicode encoding and input methods, all the inputs needed to be Unicode normalised before being fed to the web interface for analysis or generation. In Tamil, the same character can be formed by multiple code sequences if it is not controlled or handled by the keyboard input driver. For instance, the letter கொ can be entered by users using the following sequences: க + ொ or க + ெ + ா . However, it is only the first sequence is acceptable and logical. Because, in Tamil, a composite character like கொ is formed by adding a vowel to a consonant. In Unicode, vowels are denoted by vowel modifiers. Therefore, a consonant cannot be followed by two vowel modifiers (actually two vowels). However, in the case of க + ெ + ா , there are two vowel modifiers are followed by a consonant. This is impossible in Tamil. Therefore, it is important to convert all the unacceptable formations to acceptable formations; the process of converting other forms to Unicode normalised form is called Unicode normalisation. Otherwise, this would lead to issues when passing through the FST. We therefore developed a script that enables the Unicode normalisation of Tamil text.

4.2.2 Compiling lexicons

A lexicon of 3,300 lemmata of Tamil verbs was compiled from the following two verified sources:

- Annamalai et al. (2014) identified 369 of the most frequently used verbs in Modern Tamil. Their analysis is based on a corpus of 7 million tokens compiled from the web and took into account expert advice on linguistic matters. Their list has been included in the contemporary Tamil dictionary Cre-A (Ramakrishnana, 2014).

- Irākavaiyaṅkār (1958) surveyed Tamil literature up until 1958, where he identified 3,124 lemmas and categorised these into 12 classes as per the classification proposed by Graul (1855) (Sithiraputhiran, 2004). However, some of these forms are not used in the contemporary language. Nevertheless, since the analysis of those verbs is necessary for processing the historical Tamil text, the entire list has been considered for the development of our FSM.

In Tamil, complex verbs are formed on the basis of infinitival forms, verbal participles and verbal nouns (Boologarambai, 1986). Therefore, in addition to the verbal lemmata collected, auxiliary classes were also constructed manually, using the infinitival and verbal participle forms of the lemmata.

Tamil nouns were collected from various databases online, glossaries and corpora. An initial level of cleaning was additionally conducted in order to ensure that the list has only lemmata.

4.2.3 Verb Paradigm

Instead of handling words individually, a paradigmatic approach is used to reduce the volume of the problem. Anand Kumar et al. (2010b) have proposed a paradigm with 32 classes in their data-driven morphological analyser, while Menaka et al. (2010) identified a verb paradigm with 34 classes in their Tamil morphological generator study. However, we have here chose to use the widely accepted 12 verb paradigm proposed by Graul (1855). In addition to these 12 categories, each of the 7 irregular verbs defined in (Annamalai et al., 2014) is considered as a separate category. Further, 15 auxiliaries, identified from the literature, were also implemented as 15 separate classes. Altogether, a taxonomy of 34 classes has been used to develop the FSM for verbal forms.

4.2.4 Conjugation forms

Annamalai et al. (2014) have identified 254 forms for each Tamil verb after a rigorous analysis of their corpus of contemporary texts. Some verbs may not take all of the 254 forms. Further, Rajaram (1986) has also identified 21 forms for each verb from a pedagogical perspective. On the other hand, Anand Kumar et al. (2010a) claim that a Tamil verb lemma can take up to 8,000 forms though not all are listed or found in the literature. In our FSM 260 inflectional forms are considered. These forms are the set common to Annamalai et al. (2014) and Rajaram (1986). For each lemma, these 260 forms are generated and analysed. However, more forms can easily be added to the system without the need of any additional programming.

4.2.5 Morpheme labels

There are different sets of labels used to mark the morphemes in the morphological analysers of Anand Kumar et al. (2010a); Menaka et al. (2010). Kirov et al. (2016) attempt to unify the morphological labels under the brand of Unimorph to facilitate the cross-lingual morphological transfer.

However, in our Tamil FSM, we have developed a set of our own morpheme labels. Because PNG and rationality are marked by a single morph in Tamil, it is more efficient from a grammar engineering perspective to handle them together, thus reducing the number of lexical rules in the grammar (Butt et al., 1999). While we have decided to develop and use our own labelling, we plan to implement an interface that will facilitate exporting information in the Unimorph format (Kirov et al., 2016).

5 Meta-morph rules

From the review of Tamil morphological analysers, it is evident that most of the efforts in defining morphological structure or morphotactics are deeply coupled with the programming logic. In some other efforts, people have spent a considerable amount of time writing rules.

Snippet 1 Snippet of meta-morph rules

```
1.classes=C1,C2,C3,C4,C5,C17,C18,C19
2.commonLabels=+fin+sim+ind
3.v-ind=root+tense+png
4.v-euph=root+past+euph+pngeuph
```

On the other hand, arguments have been presented that a meta-representation of the formal implementational details will allow and encourage computationally naive linguists to contribute to the development of linguistic resources for language processing.

The meta-morph rules outlined in this paper successfully hide the programming details of the morphological analysis and help to focus only on the analysis of the language. Further, this also automates the generation of lexical entries, which when done manually is not only a tedious and time-consuming task, but also one where people can easily make mistakes. This is particularly true for a language like Tamil in which each verb may undergo several hundred inflections. Therefore, even if a paradigm approach is used, it is challenging to write rules, maintain them and perform a regression testing without the aid of a meta-grammar.

To achieve this we have developed meta-morph rules. Consider Snippet-1 of the meta-morph rules example. Line number 3 shows how finite, simple and indicative verbs are formed for the classes listed in line number 1. The order of conjugation also matters, where it shows that with a verb root, first, it is a tense marker that is coined, and finally a PNG marker follows. These rules can also be applied in other studies to see how words are conjugated in Tamil. Further, the rules can be defined at different levels. For instance, line number 3 shows that all the finite, simple and indicative verbs are formed by conjugating a tense and a PNG, where tense stands for the realisation of one of the three tenses available. However, line number 4 shows that verbs which consist of euphonic markers (material used to fulfill phonological phrasing requirements) are constructed only with past tense verbs, and with a specific PNG marker. Snippet-1 thus exemplifies the type of meta-morph rules that we have devised.[5]

The corresponding values for the labels in the meta-morph rules are stored in JSON[6] files. Data are stored in JSON as key-value pairs which are also human readable. The above rules and JSON entries can be written in a plain text file. For instance, Snippet-2 shows how tense labels are defined and stored in a JSON file. As shown here, there can be different past tense markers for different classes of verbs. For general cases, the tense marking

can be done as shown in line 3. However, if required, a particular tense marker can also be used, as shown in line number 4 of the above Snippet-1. In addition to labels, values corresponding to each morph can also be stored in the JSON file, as shown in Snippet-2. For instance, in the above example for "past1", the label is *past* and the morph த் (which marks the verb as past) is also included as a part of the label. This information becomes part of the lexical analysis. Further, as shown in the Snippet-2, the proposed data structure provides the flexibility for defining different tense markers and labels for different classes, and these data can be referred at different levels when writing the meta-morph rules. For instance, it can be either referred as "past" or "past1" rule-base.

Snippet 2 Snippet of data in a JSON file

```
"tense": {
"past": {
        "past1": {
                "label":"+past=த்",
                "marker":"த",
                "classes":["C1","C15"]
                },
        "past2": {
                "label":"+past=ண்ட்",
                "marker":"ண்ட",
                "classes":["C2"]
        }
},
"pres":{
        "pres1": {
                "label":"+pres=கிற்",
                "marker":"கிற",
                "classes":["C2","C3"]
        }
},
"fut": {
        "fut1": {
                "label": "+fut=வ்",
                "marker": "வ",
                "classes": ["C3","C4"]
        }
}
}
```

---

[5]A reviewer asks about the formal power of the meta-morph rules. Essentially they replace the continuation classes found in LEXC.

[6]https://www.json.org/

In case a mistake in the labelling, or in the

value of a marker, is found, it can be easily corrected in the JSON text file without needing to engage with FSM programming.

Once the meta-morph rules are finalised, they can be parsed to produce the actual lexical strings that are then fed to Foma to compile an FST. A parser is developed using Python to parse these morph-rules to generate lexical rules for Foma. A sample of compiled meta-morph rules will look as shown in Snippet-3. We use the pipe "|" symbol to mark morpheme boundaries, as inspired by Beesley and Karttunen (2003), who use "TB" to mark the token boundary. "|" is used in Universal Dependencies to separate features.[7] The % is allowed to escape special characters in the lexical string.

Apart from the generation of these intermediate entries, orthographical rules were written for each class in the paradigm as necessary. If a new class needs to be introduced, then a new set of entries needs to be added to the orthographical file. Otherwise, there is no need to touch the lexical strings or the orthographical files.

Snippet 3 Snippet of lexical string or analysis string

%|+fin %|+sim %|+ind %|+strong
%|+past %= த் %|+3sgn %=அது

We initially developed a Tamil FSM by entering all of the necessary lexical strings manually, yet found this to be tedious task that took time and energy away from understanding the more generalised overall structure of the language morphology. In evaluating our progress, we found that correcting errors was complicated and time-consuming, since we always had to engage with the details of the Foma specifications. The frustration with these time-consuming tasks led us to experiment with meta-morph rules. We found writing rules in the meta-morph and defining feature-value pairs using JSON to be easy and quick. It also helped us to accelerate the process of developing our FSM for Tamil, where for instance the identification of mistakes could be corrected easily. Adding a

lexical string or new conjugational form also became very straightforward. We need to just list the classes which will take those new forms and then define a generalised rule for the formation of that word as shown in Snippet-1.

6 Evaluation and Discussion

There are no benchmark data sets available to evaluate a morphological analyser in Tamil. Therefore, the 500K corpus from AUKBC[8] was used for evaluation. This corpus is compiled from a popular Tamil historical novel written by an Indian author. From the 19,250 unique verbs found in the corpus, only the finite, infinitives, relative participles, verbal participles and conditional verbs were extracted. However, the finite verbs compiled also comprised of compound and derivational verbs, which cannot be separated from the finite list as there are no tags to identify them. In addition 26,000 tokens which were marked as nouns also extracted from the corpus to evaluate the noun morphology. However, the list had a significant number of compound nouns, nominal complex (for instance, noun + conjunction), personal names, and borrowed words from Sanskrit. Table 1 shows the outcome of the evaluations.

Derivational verbs, spelling mistakes, nominal complex words, and personal names, as well as errors in the tagging, were the primary causes for the failure of the Tamil FSM. The guesser provided an analysis for the compound verbs and nouns.

7 Conclusion

We conclude that meta-morph rules are useful for the acceleration of the development of FSMs. At the same time, they allow the statement of linguistic generalisations in a form that is easily human readable and provides an interface for computationally naive linguists to interact with the FSM and to potentially help extend and improve it.

The Tamil FSM outlined in this paper has also been developed as a web-based system: `parsers.projects.uom.lk`. The evaluation in Table 1 shows that the Tamil FSM already provides a high accuracy for the analysis of verbs and a reportable accuracy for the

---

[7]https://universaldependencies.org/format.html

[8]http://www.au-kbc.org/nlp/corpusrelease.html

Word type	Found in the Corpus	Analysed	Percentage
Verbs - Finite	10,269	10,142	98.7
Verbs - Infinitive	1,615	1,540	95.4
Verbs - Relative participle	2,677	2,525	94.3
Verbs - Verbal participle	3,339	3,110	93.1
Nouns	26,000	19,990	76.5

Table 1: Evaluation results

analysis of nouns. Further, the system also shows if there are multiple analyses for a word; for instance, an analysis for a word செய்யும் (*ceyyum*) is shown in the Figure 2.

In future work, we intend to explore whether the meta-morph rule interface can be further generalised and used for other languages, at least for other South Asian Languages. We already have performed an initial work on this for the Indo-Aryan language Sinhala and the results are encouraging. We will also extend the existing Tamil FSM by fully incorporating derivational morphology.

Analysis of செய்யும்

Root : செய்
+nonfin
+sim
+futANDadjpart=உம்

Root : செய்
+fin
+sim
+ind
+strong
+fut=உம்
+3sgn=∅

Root : செய்
+fin
+sim
+ind
+strong
+fut=உம்
+3pln=∅

Figure 2: Screenshot of the analysis from the web interface

Acknowledgement

This research was supported by the Accelerating Higher Education Expansion and Development (AHEAD) Operation of the Ministry of Higher Education, Sri Lanka funded by the World Bank and the DAAD (German Academic Exchange Office). We also thank Lauri Karttunen for his time and provision of several helpful pointers.

References

S Agesthialingom. 1971. A Note on Tamil Verbs. *Anthropological Linguistics*, pages 121–125.

Cyril Allauzen, Michael Riley, Johan Schalkwyk, Wojciech Skut, and Mehryar Mohri. 2007. OpenFst: A general and efficient weighted finite-state transducer library. In *International Conference on Implementation and Application of Automata*, pages 11–23. Springer.

M Anand Kumar, V Dhanalakshmi, KP Soman, and S Rajendran. 2010a. A sequence labeling approach to morphological analyzer for Tamil language. *International Journal on Computer Science and Engineering (IJCSE)*, 2(06):1944–195.

M Anand Kumar, VV Dhanalakshmi, and S Rajendran. 2010b. A novel data driven algorithm for Tamil morphological generator. *International Journal of Computer Applications*, 6:52–56.

E Annamalai, A Dhamotharan, and A Ramakrishnan. 2014. *Akarātiyin putiya patippil taṟkālat tamil ilakkaṇa viḷakkam*, pages xxxi–xlvii. Crea-A Publishers, India.

PJ Antony and KP Soman. 2012. Computational morphology and natural language parsing for Indian languages: a literature survey. *International Journal of Scientific and Engineering Research*, 3.

Albert Henry Arden. 1962. *A progressive grammar of common Tamil*. Christian Literature Society.

Kenneth R Beesley and Lauri Karttunen. 2003. Finite-state morphology: Xerox tools and techniques. *CSLI Publications, Stanford*.

Emily M Bender, Dan Flickinger, and Stephan Oepen. 2011. Grammar engineering and linguistic hypothesis testing: Computational support for complexity in syntactic analysis. *Language from a cognitive perspective: grammar, usage and processing*, pages 5–29.

Tina Bögel, Miriam Butt, Annette Hautli, and Sebastian Sulger. 2007. Developing a Finite-State Morphological Analyzer for Urdu and Hindi. In *Finite-State Methods and Natural Language Processing*, pages 86–96. Potsdam University Press. Revised Papers of the Sixth International Workshop on Finite-State Methods and Natural Language Processing.

A Boologarambai. 1986. *A Study of Auxiliaries in the Old and the Middle Tamil*. Ph.D. thesis, Centre of Advanced study in linguistics, Annamalai University, India.

Miriam Butt and Tracy H. King. 2003. Grammar writing, testing and evaluation. In Ali Farghaly, editor, *A Handbook for Language Engineers*, pages 129–179. CSLI Publications, Stanford.

Miriam Butt, Tracy Holloway King, Maria-Eugenia Nino, and Frederique Segond. 1999. *A Grammar Writer's Cookbook*. CSLI Publications, Stanford.

Antske Fokkens and Emily M Bender. 2013. Time travel in grammar engineering: Using a metagrammar to broaden the search space. In *Proceedings of the ESSLLI Workshop on High-Level Methodologies in Grammar Engineering*, pages 105–116.

L. Hart George. 2000. Statement on the Status of Tamil as a Classical Language. Available: https://southasia.berkeley.edu/tamil-classes. Accessed on: 2017-11-12.

Karl Graul. 1855. *Outline of Tamil grammar*. Leipzig University.

Mans Hulden. 2009. Foma: a finite-state compiler and library. In *Proceedings of the 12th Conference of the European Chapter of the Association for Computational Linguistics: Demonstrations Session*, pages 29–32. Association for Computational Linguistics.

M Irākavaiyaṅkār. 1958. *'Viṉaittiripu vilakkam' (conjugation of Tamil verbs) (in Tamil)*. Eighty year anniversary publication.

Lauri Karttunen and Kenneth R Beesley. 2001. A short history of two-level morphology. *ESSLLI-2001 Special Event titled" Twenty Years of Finite-State Morphology*. Available. http://www.helsinki.fi/esslli/.

Christo Kirov, John Sylak-Glassman, Roger Que, and David Yarowsky. 2016. Very-large scale parsing and normalization of wiktionary morphological paradigms. In *Proceedings of the Tenth International Conference on Language Resources and Evaluation (LREC 2016)*, Paris, France. European Language Resources Association (ELRA).

Kimmo Koskenniemi. 1983. *Two-level morphology*. Ph.D. thesis, University of Helsinki.

T. Lehmann. 1993. *A grammar of modern Tamil*. Pondicherry Institute of Linguistics and Culture, India.

Krister Lindén, Miikka Silfverberg, and Tommi Pirinen. 2009. HFST tools for morphology–an efficient open-source package for construction of morphological analyzers. In *International Workshop on Systems and Frameworks for Computational Morphology*, pages 28–47. Springer.

Leigh Lisker. 1951. Tamil verb classification. *Journal of the American Oriental Society*, 71(2):111–114.

Sivaneasharajah Lushanthan, AR Weerasinghe, and DL Herath. 2014. Morphological analyzer and generator for Tamil language. In *Advances in ICT for Emerging Regions (ICTer), 2014 International Conference on*, pages 190–196. IEEE.

S Menaka, Vijay Sundar Ram, and Sobha Lalitha Devi. 2010. Morphological generator for Tamil. *Proceedings of the Knowledge Sharing event on Morphological Analysers and Generators (March 22-23, 2010)*, pages 82–96.

M Nuhman. 1999. *Basic Tamil Grammar (In Tamil)*. Readers' Association, Sri Lanka.

K Paramasivam. 2011. *Contemporary Tamil Grammar*. Adaiyaalam.

K Parameshwari. 2011. An implementation of APERTIUM morphological analyzer and generator for Tamil. *Parsing in Indian Languages*, page 41.

Balaram Prasain. 2011. *Computational Analysis of Nepali Morphology: A Model for Natural Language Processing*. Ph.D. thesis, Faculty of Humanities and Social Sciences of Tribhuvan University, Nepal.

Mutee U Rahman. 2016. *Developing a Sindhi Computational Resource Grammar in Lexical Functional Grammar framework*. Ph.D. thesis, Faculty of Engineering Science and Technology, Isra University, Hyderabad.

S Rajaram. 1986. English-Tamil Pedagogical Dictionary. *Thanjavur: Tamil University*.

S Rajendran. 2012. Preliminaries To The Preparation Of A Spell And Grammar Checker For Tamil. *Upoaded in academia. edu and Reseach Gate.*

S Ramakrishnana, editor. 2014. *Cre-A: Dictionary of Contemporary Tamil.* Cre-A publishers, Chennai, India.

M Dolores Ruiz, Juan Gómez-Romero, Miguel Molina-Solana, Jesús R Campaña, and Maria J Martín-Bautista. 2016. Meta-association rules for mining interesting associations in multiple datasets. *Applied Soft Computing*, 49:212–223.

K Sarveswaran, Gihan Dias, and Miriam Butt. 2018. ThamizhiFST: A Morphological Analyser and Generator for Tamil Verbs. In *2018 3rd International Conference on Information Technology Research (ICITR)*, pages 1–6. IEEE.

Melanie Seiss. 2012. A rule-based morphological analyzer for murrinh-patha. In *Proceedings of the 8th International Conference on Language Resources and Evaluation (LREC 2012)*, pages 751–758. Istanbul,Turkey: EuropeanLanguage Resources Association (ELRA).

H Sithiraputhiran. 2004. *Vinaittiripu viḷakkamum moḻiyiyal kōṭpāṭum.* International Institute of Tamil Studies.

Distilling weighted finite automata from arbitrary probabilistic models

Ananda Theertha Suresh, Brian Roark, Michael Riley, Vlad Schogol
{ theertha, roark, riley, vlads }@google.com
Google Research

Abstract

Weighted finite automata (WFA) are often used to represent probabilistic models, such as n-gram language models, since they are efficient for recognition tasks in time and space. The probabilistic source to be represented as a WFA, however, may come in many forms. Given a generic probabilistic model over sequences, we propose an algorithm to approximate it as a weighted finite automaton such that the Kullback-Leibler divergence between the source model and the WFA target model is minimized. The proposed algorithm involves a counting step and a difference of convex optimization, both of which can be performed efficiently. We demonstrate the usefulness of our approach on some tasks including distilling n-gram models from neural models.

1 Introduction

Given a sequence of symbols $x_1, x_2, \ldots, x_{n-1}$, where symbols are drawn from the alphabet Σ, a probabilistic model S assigns to the next symbol $x_n \in \Sigma$ the conditional probability

$$p_s[x_n \mid x_{n-1} \ldots x_1].$$

Such a model might be Markovian, where

$$p_s[x_n \mid x_{n-1} \ldots x_1] = p_s[x_n \mid x_{n-1} \ldots x_{n-k+1}],$$

such as a k-gram language model (LM) (Chen and Goodman, 1998) or it might be non-Markovian such as a long short-term memory (LSTM) neural network language model (Sundermeyer et al., 2012). Our goal is to approximate a probabilistic model as a *weighted finite automaton* (WFA) such that the weight assigned by the WFA is close to the probability assigned by the source model. Specifically, we will seek to minimize the Kullback-Leibler (KL) divergence between the source S and the target WFA model.

Representing the target model as a WFA has many advantages including efficient use, compact representation, interpretability, and composability. WFA models have been used in many applications including speech recognition (Mohri et al., 2008), speech synthesis (Ebden and Sproat, 2015), optical character recognition (Breuel, 2008), machine translation (Iglesias et al., 2011), computational biology (Durbin et al., 1998), and image processing (Albert and Kari, 2009). One particular problem of interest is language models for on-device (virtual) keyboard decoding (Ouyang et al., 2017), where WFA models are used due to space and time constraints. However, storing the training data in a centralized server and training k-gram or other WFA models directly may not be feasible due to privacy constraints (Hard et al., 2018). Alternatively, an LSTM model can be trained by federated learning (Konečný et al., 2016; Hard et al., 2018), then converted to a WFA at the server for fast on-device inference. This not only may improve performance, but also provide additional privacy.

We allow *failure transitions* (Aho and Corasick, 1975; Mohri, 1997) in the target WFA, which are taken only when no immediate match is possible at a given state, for compactness. For example, in the WFA representation of a backoff k-gram model, failure transitions can compactly implement the backoff (Katz, 1987; Chen and Goodman, 1998; Allauzen et al., 2003; Novak et al., 2013; Hellsten et al., 2017). The inclusion of failure transitions will complicate our analysis and algorithms but is highly desirable in applications such as keyboard decoding. Further, to avoid redundancy that leads to inefficiency, we assume the target model is *deterministic*, which requires at each state there is at most one transition labeled with a given symbol.

The approximation problem can be divided into two steps: (1) select an unweighted automaton A that will serve as the *topology* of the target automaton and (2) weight the automaton A to form our weighted approximation $\hat{A}$. The main goal of this paper is the latter determination of the automaton's

87

Proceedings of the 14th International Conference on Finite-State Methods and Natural Language Processing, pages 87–97
Dresden, Germany, September 23-25, 2019. ©2019 Association for Computational Linguistics

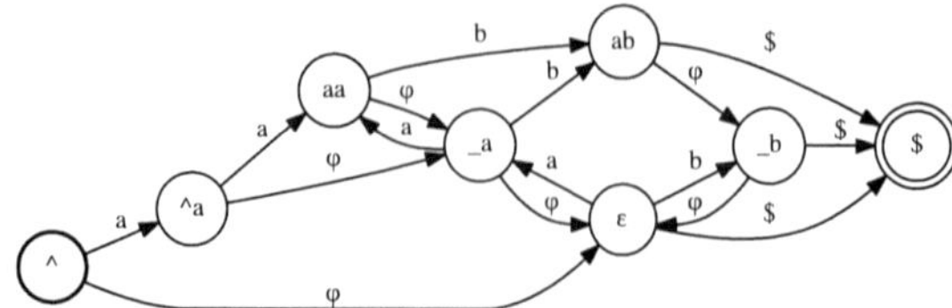

Figure 1: 3-gram topology example derived from the corpus aab. States are labeled with the context that is remembered, $\wedge$ denotes the initial context, ϵ the empty context, $\$$ the final context (and terminates accepted strings), and _ matches any symbol in a context. Failure transitions, labeled with φ, implement backoff from histories xy to $\_y$ to ϵ.

weighting in the approximation.

In some applications, the topology may be unknown. In such cases, one choice is to build a k-gram deterministic finite automaton (DFA) topology from a corpus drawn from S (Allauzen et al., 2003). This could be from an existing corpus or from random samples drawn from S. Figure 1 shows a trigram topology for the very simple corpus aab. This representation makes use of failure transitions. These allow modeling strings unseen in the corpus (e.g., $abab$) in a compact way by failing or *backing-off* to states that correspond to lower-order histories. Such models can be made more elaborate if some transitions represent classes, such as names or numbers, that are themselves represented by sub-automata. As mentioned previously, we will mostly assume we have a topology either pre-specified or inferred by some means and focus on how to weight that topology to best approximate the source distribution.

In previous work, there have been various approaches for estimating weighted automata. Methods include state merging and weight estimation from a prefix tree data representation (Carrasco and Oncina, 1994, 1999), the EM algorithm (Dempster et al., 1977) applied to fully connected HMMs or specific topologies (Eisner, 2001) and spectral methods applied to automata (Balle and Mohri, 2012; Balle et al., 2014). For approximating neural network (NN) models as WFAs, methods have been proposed to build n-gram models from RNN samples (Deoras et al., 2011), from DNNs trained at different orders (Arisoy et al., 2014; Adel et al., 2014), and from RNNs with quantized hidden states (Tiño and Vojtek, 1997; Lecorvé and Motlicek, 2012).

Our paper is distinguished in several respects from previous work. First, our general approach does not depend on the form the source distribution. Second, our targets are a wide class of deterministic automata with failure transitions. Third, we search for the minimal KL divergence between the source and target distributions, given a fixed target topology.

We remark that if the source probabilistic model is represented as a WFA, our approximation will in general give a different solution than forming the finite-state intersection with the topology and *weight-pushing* to normalize the result (Mohri, 2009; Mohri et al., 2008). Our approximation has the same states as the topology whereas a weight-pushed intersection could have many more states and and is not an approximation, but an exact representation, of the source distribution.

Before presenting and validating algorithms for a minimum KL divergence approximation when either the source itself is finite-state or not (in which case sampling is involved), we next present the theoretical formulation of the problem and the minimum KL divergence approximation.

2 Theoretical analysis

2.1 Probabilistic models

Let Σ be a finite alphabet. Let $x_i^n \in \Sigma^*$ denote the string $x_i x_{i+1} \ldots x_n$ and $x^n \triangleq x_1^n$. A probabilistic model p over Σ is a probabilistic distribution over the next symbol x_n, given the previous symbols x^{n-1}, such that[1]

$$\sum_{x \in \Sigma} p(x_n = x | x^{n-1}) = 1 \quad \wedge$$

$$\forall x \in \Sigma, \ p(x_n = x | x^{n-1}) \geq 0.$$

Without loss of generality, we assume that the model maintains an internal state q and updates it after observing the next symbol.[2] Furthermore, the probability of the subsequent state just depends on the state q

$$p(x_{i+1}^n | x^i) = p(x_{i+1}^n | q(x^i)),$$

for all i, n, x^i, x_{i+1}^n, where $q(x^i)$ is the state the model has reached after observing sequence x^i. Let $Q(p)$ be the set of possible states. Let the language $\mathcal{L}(p) \subseteq \Sigma^*$ defined by the distribution p be

---

[1] We define $x^0 \triangleq \epsilon$, the empty string, and adopt $p(\epsilon) = 0$.
[2] In the most general case, $q(x^n) = x^n$.

$$\mathcal{L}(p) \triangleq \{x^n \in \Sigma^* : p(x^n) > 0,$$
$$x_n = \$ \ \wedge \ x_i \neq \$ \, , i < n\}. \quad (1)$$

The symbol $\$$ is used as a stopping criterion. Further for all $x^n \in \Sigma^*, p(x_n | x^{n-1} : x_{n-1} = \$) = 0$.

The KL divergence between two models p_s and p_a is given by

$$D(p_s||p_a) = \sum_{x^n} p_s(x^n) \log \frac{p_s(x^n)}{p_a(x^n)}, \quad (2)$$

where for notational simplicity, we adopt the notion $0/0 = 1$ and $0 \log(0/0) = 0$ throughout the paper. Note that for the KL divergence to be finite, we need $\mathcal{L}(p_s) \subseteq \mathcal{L}(p_a)$. We first reduce the KL divergence between two models as follows (cf. Carrasco, 1997; Cortes et al., 2008). In the following, let q_* denote the states of the probability distribution p_*.

Lemma 1. *If* $\mathcal{L}(p_s) \subseteq \mathcal{L}(p_a)$, *then*

$$D(p_s||p_a) = \sum_{q_a \in Q_a} \sum_{x \in \Sigma} c(x, q_a) \log \frac{p_s(x|q_s)}{p_a(x|q_a)} \quad (3)$$

where $c(x, q_a)$ *is given by*

$$\sum_{q_s \in Q_s} \sum_{i=0}^{\infty} \sum_{x^i : q_s(x^i) = q_s, q_a(x^i) = q_a} p_s(x^i) \, p_s(x|q_s) \quad (4)$$

and does not depend on p_a.

Proof is omitted due to space limitations.

2.2 Weighted finite automata

A weighted finite automaton $A = (\Sigma, Q, E, i, f)$ over $\mathbb{R}_+$ is given by a finite alphabet Σ, a finite set of states Q, a finite set of transitions $E \subseteq Q \times \Sigma \times \mathbb{R}_+ \times Q$, an initial state $i \in Q$ and a final state $f \in Q$. A transition $e = (p[e], \ell[e], w[e], n[e]) \in E$ represents a move from the *source* or *previous* state $p[e]$ to the *destination* or *next* state $n[e]$ with the *label* $\ell[e]$ and *weight* $w[e]$. The transitions with source state q are denoted by $E[q]$ and the labels of those transitions as $L[q]$.

A deterministic WFA has at most one transition with a given label leaving each state. An *unweighted (finite) automaton* is a WFA that satisfies $w[e] = 1, \forall e \in E$. A *probabilistic (or stochastic) WFA* satisfies

$$\sum_{e \in E[q]} w[e] = 1 \text{ and } w[e] \geq 0, \quad \forall q \in Q - \{f\}.$$

Transitions e_1 and e_2 are *consecutive* if $n[e_i] = p[e_{i+1}]$. A path $\pi = e_1 \cdots e_n \in E^*$ is a finite sequence of consecutive transitions, the source and destination states of which we denote by $p[\pi]$ and $n[\pi]$, respectively. The label of a path is the concatenation of its transition labels $\ell[\pi] = \ell[e_1] \cdots \ell[e_n]$. The weight of a path is obtained by multiplying its transition weights $w[\pi] = w[e_1] \times \cdots \times w[e_n]$. For a non-empty path, the i-th transition is denoted by π_i.

$P(q, q')$ denotes the set of all paths in A from state q to q'. We extend this to sets in the obvious way: $P(q, R)$ denotes the set of all paths from state q to $q' \in R$ and so forth. A path π is successful if it is in $P(i, f)$ and in that case the automaton is said to accept the input string $\alpha = \ell[\pi]$.

The language accepted by an automaton A is the regular set $\mathcal{L}(A) = \{\alpha \in \Sigma^* : \alpha = \ell[\pi], \pi \in P(i, f)\}$. The weight of $\alpha \in \mathcal{L}(A)$ assigned by the automaton is $A(\alpha) = \Sigma_{\pi \in P(i,f) : \ell[\pi] = \alpha} w[\pi]$. Similar to Equation 1, we assume a symbol $\$ \in \Sigma$ such that

$$\mathcal{L}(A) \subseteq \{x^n \in \Sigma^* : x_n = \$ \text{ and } x_i \neq \$ \, , i < n\}.$$

Thus all successful paths are terminated by the symbol $\$$.

For a symbol $x \in \Sigma$ and a state $q \in Q$ of a deterministic, probabilistic WFA A, define a distribution $p_a(x|q) \triangleq w$ if $(q, x, w, q') \in E$ and $p_a(x|q) \triangleq 0$ otherwise. Then p_a is a probabilistic model over Σ as defined in the previous section. If $A = (\Sigma, Q, E, i, f)$ is an unweighted deterministic automaton, we denote by $\mathscr{P}(A)$ the set of all probabilistic models p_a representable as a weighted WFA $\hat{A} = (\Sigma, Q, \hat{E}, i, f)$ with the same topology as A where $\hat{E} = \{(q, x, p_a(x|q), q') : (q, x, 1, q') \in E\}$.

2.3 Weighted finite automata with failure transitions

A *weighted finite automaton with failure transitions* (φ-WFA) $A = (\Sigma, Q, E, i, f)$ is a WFA extended to allow a transition to have a special *failure* label denoted by φ. Then $E \subseteq Q \times (\Sigma \cup \{\varphi\}) \times \mathbb{R}_+ \times Q$.

A φ transition does not add to a path label; it consumes no input. However it is followed only when the input can not be read immediately. Specifically, a path $e_1 \cdots e_n$ in a φ-WFA is *disallowed* if it contains a subpath $e_i \cdots e_j$ such that $\ell[e_k] = \varphi$ for all $k, i \leq k < j$, and there is another transition $e \in E$ such that $p[e_i] = p[e]$ and

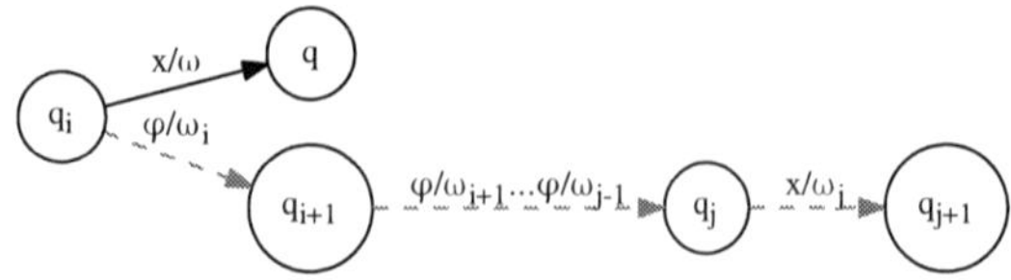

Figure 2: The (dashed red) path $e_i = (q_i, \varphi, \omega_i, q_{i+1})$ to $e_j = (q_j, x, \omega_j, q_{j+1})$ is disallowed since x can be read already on $e = (q_i, x, \omega, q)$.

$\ell[e_j] = \ell[e] \in \Sigma$ (see Figure 2). Since the label $x = l[e_j]$ can be read on e, we do not follow the failure transitions to read it on e_j as well.

We use $P^*(q, q') \subseteq P(q, q')$ to denote the set of (not dis-) allowed paths from state q to q' in a φ-WFA. This again extends to sets in the obvious way. A path π is successful in a φ-WFA if $\pi \in P^*(i, F)$ and only in that case is the input string $\alpha = \ell[\pi]$ accepted.

The language accepted by the φ-automaton A is the regular set $\mathcal{L}(A) = \{\alpha \in \Sigma^* : \alpha = \ell[\pi], \pi \in P^*(i, f)\}$. The weight of $\alpha \in \Sigma^*$ assigned by the automaton is $A(\alpha) = \Sigma_{\pi \in P^*(i,f): \ell[\pi]=\alpha} w[\pi]$. We assume each string in $\mathcal{L}(A)$ is terminated by the symbol \$ as before. We also assume there are no φ-labeled cycles and there is at most one exiting failure transition per state.

We express the φ-extended transitions leaving q as

$$E^*[q] = \Big\{ (q, x, \omega, q') : \ \pi \in P^*(q, Q), \ \omega = w[\pi],$$
$$x = \ell[\pi] = \ell[\pi_{|\pi|}] \in \Sigma, \ q' = n[\pi] \Big\}.$$

This is a set of (possibly new) transitions (q, x, ω, q'), one for each allowed path from source state q to destination state q' with optional leading failure transitions and a final x-labeled transition. Denote the labels of $E^*[q]$ by $L^*[q]$.

A *probabilistic (or stochastic) φ-WFA* satisfies

$$\sum_{e \in E^*[q]} w[e] = 1 \text{ and } w[e] \geq 0, \quad \forall q \in Q - \{f\}.$$

A deterministic φ-WFA is *backoff-complete* if a failure transition from state q to q' implies $L[q] \cap \Sigma \subseteq L[q'] \cap \Sigma$. Further, if $\varphi \notin L[q']$, then the containment is strict: $L[q] \cap \Sigma \subset L[q'] \cap \Sigma$. In other words, if a symbol can be read immediately from a state q it can also be read from a state failing (*backing-off*) from q and if q' does not have a backoff arc, then at least one additional label can be read from q' that cannot be read from q. For example, the topology depicted in Figure 1 has this

property. We restrict our target automata to have a topology with the backoff-complete property since it will simplify our analysis, make our algorithms efficient and is commonly found in applications.

For a symbol $x \in \Sigma$ and a state $q \in Q$ of a deterministic, probabilistic φ-WFA A, define $p_a^*(x|q) \triangleq w$ if $(q, x, w, q') \in E^*[q]$ and $p_a^*(x|q) \triangleq 0$ otherwise. Then p_a^* is a probabilistic model over Σ as defined in Section 2.1. Note the distribution p_a^* at a state q is defined over the φ-extended transitions $E^*[q]$ where p_a in the previous section is defined over the transitions $E[q]$. It is convenient to define a companion distribution $p_a \in P(A)$ to p_a^* as follows:[3] given a symbol $x \in \Sigma \cup \{\varphi\}$ and state $q \in Q$, define $p_a(x|q) \triangleq p_a^*(x|q)$ when $x \in L[q] \cap \Sigma$, $p_a(\varphi|q) \triangleq 1 - \sum_{x \in L[q] \cap \Sigma} p_a^*(x|q)$, and $p_a(x|q) \triangleq 0$ otherwise. The companion distribution is thus defined solely over the transitions $E[q]$.

When $A = (\Sigma, Q, E, i, f)$ is an unweighted deterministic, backoff-complete φ-WFA, we denote by $\mathscr{P}^*(A)$ the set of all probabilistic models p_a^* representable as a weighted φ-WFA $\hat{A} = (\Sigma, Q, \hat{E}, i, f)$ of same topology as A with

$$\hat{E} = \{(q, x, p_a(x|q), q') : (q, x, 1, q') \in E, x \in \Sigma\}$$
$$\cup \{(q, \varphi, \alpha(q, q'), q') : (q, \varphi, 1, q') \in E\}$$

where $p_a \in P(A)$ is the companion distribution to p_a^* and $\alpha(q, q') = p_a(\varphi|q)/d(q, q')$ is the weight of the failure transition from state q to q' with

$$d(q, q') = 1 - \sum_{x \in L[q] \cap \Sigma} p_a(x|q'). \qquad (5)$$

Note we have specified the weights on the automaton that represents $p_a^* \in P^*(A)$ entirely in terms of the companion distribution $p_a \in P(A)$, thanks to the backoff-complete property.

Conversely, each distribution $p_a \in \mathscr{P}(A)$ can be associated to a distribution $p_a^* \in \mathscr{P}^*(A)$ given a deterministic, backoff-complete φ-WFA A. First extend $\alpha(q, q')$ to any failure path as follows. Denote a failure path from state q to q' by $\pi_\varphi(q, q')$. Then define

$$\alpha(q, q') = \prod_{e \in \pi_\varphi(q,q')} \frac{p_a(\varphi|p[e])}{d(p[e], n[e])} \qquad (6)$$

where this quantity is taken to be 1 when the fail-

---

[3]The meaning of $P(A)$ when A is a φ-WFA is to interpret it as a WFA with the failure labels as regular symbols.

ure path is empty ($q = q'$). Finally define

$$p_a^*(x|q) = \begin{cases} \alpha(q, q^x)p_a(x|q^x), & x \in L^*[q] \\ 0, & \text{otherwise} \end{cases}$$
(7)

where for $x \in L^*[q]$, q^x signifies the first state q' on a φ-labeled path in A from state q for which $x \in L[q']$.

For (6) to be well-defined, we need $d(p[e], n[e]) > 0$. To ensure this condition, we restrict $\mathscr{P}(A)$ to contain distributions such that $p_a(x|q) \geq \epsilon$ for each $x \in L[q]$.[4]

Given an unweighted deterministic, backoff-complete, automaton A, our goal is to find the target distribution $p_a^* \in \mathscr{P}^*(A)$ that has the minimum KL divergence from our source probability model p_s. We can restate our goal in terms of the companion distribution $p_a \in \mathscr{P}(A)$. Let $B_n(q)$ be the set of states in A that back-off to state q in n failure transitions and let $B(q) = \bigcup_{n=0}^{|Q_a|} B_n(q)$.

Lemma 2. *If $\mathcal{L}(p_s) \subseteq \mathcal{L}(A)$ then*

$$\underset{p_a^* \in \mathscr{P}^*(A)}{\arg\min}\ D(p_s||p_a^*) =$$
(8)

$$\underset{p_a \in \mathscr{P}(A)}{\arg\max} \sum_{q \in Q_a} \left\{ \sum_{x \in L[q]} C(x, q) \log p_a(x|q) \right.$$

$$\left. - \sum_{q_0 \in B_1(q)} C(\varphi, q_0) \log d(q_0, q) \right\},$$

where

$$C(x, q) = \sum_{q_a \in B(q)} c(x, q_a)\mathbf{1}_{q=q_a^x}, \quad x \in \Sigma \quad (9)$$

$$C(\varphi, q) = \sum_{q_a \in B(q)} \sum_{x \in \Sigma} c(x, q_a)\mathbf{1}_{x \notin L[q]} \quad (10)$$

and do not depend on p_a.

Proof is omitted due to space limitations.

The quantity in braces in the statement of Lemma 2 depends on the distribution p_a only at state q so the minimum KL divergence $D(p_s||p_a^*)$ can be found by maximizing that quantity independently for each state.

3 Algorithms

Approximating a probabilistic source algorithmically as a weighted finite automaton requires two steps: (1) compute the quantity $C(x, q)$ in Lemma 2 and (2) use this quantity to find the minimum KL divergence solution. The first step, which we will refer to as *counting*, is covered in the next section and the KL divergence minimization step is covered afterwards.

3.1 Counting

How the counts are computed will depend on the source model form. We divide this into two cases.

3.1.1 φ-WFA source and target

When the source and target models are represented as φ-WFAs we compute $C(x, q_a)$ from Lemma 2. From Equation 9 this can be written as

$$C(x, q) = \sum_{q_a \in B(q)} \sum_{q_s \in Q_s} \gamma(q_s, q_a)p_s(x|q_s)\mathbf{1}_{q=q_a^x}$$
(11)

with $x \in \Sigma$ and

$$\gamma(q_s, q_a) = \sum_{i=0}^{\infty} \sum_{x^i} p_s(x^i : q_s(x^i) = q_s, q_a(x^i) = q_a).$$

The quantity $\gamma(q_s, q_a)$ can be computed as

$$\gamma(q_s, q_a) = \sum_{\pi \in P^*_{S \cap A}((i_s, i_a), (q_s, q_a))} w[\pi]$$

where $S \cap A$ is the weighted intersection of automata S and A formed using an efficient φ-WFA intersection that compactly retains failure transitions in the result, as described in Allauzen and Riley (2018). The quantity $\gamma(q_s, q_a)$ is the (generalized) *shortest distance* from the initial state to a specified state computed over the *positive real semiring* (Mohri, 2002; Allauzen and Riley, 2018). Equation 11 is the weighted count of the paths in $S \cap A$ allowed by the failure transitions that begin at the initial state and end in any transition leaving a state (q_s, q) labeled with x.

This computation can be simplified by the following transformation. First we convert $S \cap A$ to an equivalent WFA by replacing each failure transition with an epsilon transition and introducing a negatively-weighted transition to compensate for formerly disallowed paths (Allauzen and Riley, 2018). The result is then promoted to a transducer T with the output label used to keep track of the source state in A of the compensated positive transition (see Figure 3).[5]

---

[4]For brevity, we do not include ϵ in the notation of $\mathscr{P}(A)$.

[5]The construction illustrated in Figure 3 is sufficient when $S \cap A$ is acyclic. In the cyclic case a slightly modified construction is needed to ensure convergence in the shortest distance calculation (Allauzen and Riley, 2018).

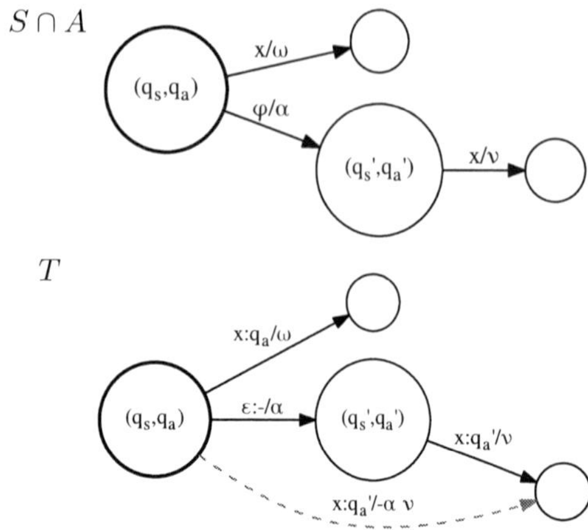

Figure 3: A φ-WFA is transformed into an equivalent WFA by replacing each failure transition by an ϵ-transition. To compensate for the formerly disallowed paths, new (dashed red) negatively-weighted transitions are added. The result is promoted to a transducer T with the output label used to keep track of the source state in A of the compensated positive transition.

Then, for $x \in \Sigma$,

$$C(x, q) = \sum_{((q_s,q_a),x,q,w,(q_s',q_a')) \in E_T} \gamma_T(q_s, q_a) w \tag{12}$$

where $e = (p[e], il[e], ol[e], w[e], n[e])$ is a transition in T and $\gamma_T(q_s, q)$ is the shortest distance from the initial state to (q_s, q_a) in T computed over the *real semiring* as described in Allauzen and Riley (2018). Equation 12 is the weighted count of all paths in $S \cap A$ that begin at the initial state and end in any transition leaving a state (q_s, q) labeled with x minus the weighted count of those paths that are disallowed by the failure transitions.

Finally, we compute $C(\varphi, q)$ as follows. The count mass entering a state must equal the count mass leaving a state

$$\sum_{(q_a,x,1,q) \in A} C(x, q) = \sum_{(q,x',1,q_a) \in A} C(x', q).$$

Thus

$$C(\varphi, q) = \sum_{(q_a,x,1,q) \in A} C(x, q) - \sum_{\substack{(q,x',1,q_a) \in A, \\ x' \in \Sigma}} C(x', q).$$

This quantity can be computed iteratively in the topological order of states with respect to the φ-labeled transitions.

3.1.2 Arbitrary source and φ-WFA target

In some cases, the source is a distribution with possibly infinite states, e.g., LSTMs. For these sources, computing $C(x, q)$ can be computationally intractable as (11) requires a summation over all possible states in the source machine, Q_s. We propose to use a sampling approach to approximate $C(x, q)$ for these cases. Let $x(1), x(2), \ldots, x(m)$ be independent random samples from p_s. Instead of $C(x, q)$, we propose to use

$$\hat{C}(x, q) = \sum_{q_a \in B(q)} \sum_{q_s \in Q_s} \hat{\gamma}(q_s, q_a) p_s(x|q_s) \mathbf{1}_{q=q_a^x}$$

with $x \in \Sigma$ and where

$$\hat{\gamma}(q_s, q_a) = \frac{1}{m} \sum_{j=1}^{m} \sum_{i \geq 0} \mathbf{1}_{q_s(x^i(j))=q_s, q_a(x^i(j))=q_a}.$$

Observe that the expectation $\mathbb{E}[\hat{\gamma}(q_s, q_a)]$ is given by

$$\frac{1}{m} \sum_{j=1}^{m} \sum_{i \geq 0} \mathbb{E}[\mathbf{1}_{q_s(x^i(j))=q_s, q_a(x^i(j))=q_a}]$$
$$= \sum_{i \geq 0} p_s(x^i : q_s(x^i) = q_s, q_a(x^i) = q_a),$$

hence $\hat{\gamma}(q_s, q_a)$ is an unbiased, asymptotically consistent estimator of $\gamma(q_s, q_a)$. Given $\hat{C}(x, q)$, we compute $C(\varphi, q)$ similarly to the previous section.

3.2 KL divergence minimization

As noted before, the quantity in braces in the statement of Lemma 2 depends on the distribution p_a only at state q so the minimum KL divergence $D(p_s||p_a^*)$ can be found by maximizing that quantity independently for each state.

Fix a state q and let $y_x \triangleq p_a(x|q)$ for $x \in L[q]$ and let $\mathbf{y} \triangleq [y_x]_{x \in L[q]}$[6]. Then our goal reduces to

$$\operatorname*{argmax}_{\mathbf{y}} \sum_{x \in L[q]} C(x, q) \log y_x - \tag{13}$$
$$\sum_{q_0 \in B_1(q)} C(\varphi, q_0) \log \left(1 - \sum_{x \in L[q_0] \cap \Sigma} y_x\right)$$

subject to the constraints $y_x \geq \epsilon$ for $x \in L[q]$ and $\sum_{x \in L[q]} y_x = 1$.

---

[6] We fix some total order on $\Sigma \cup \{\varphi\}$ so that $\mathbf{y}$ is well-defined.

$$
\boxed{
\begin{array}{l}
\hspace{4.5cm}\text{Algorithm KL-M\scriptsize INIMIZATION}\\[4pt]
\textbf{Notation:}\\
\quad\bullet\quad y_x = p_a(x|q) \text{ for } x \in L(q) \hspace{1.5cm} \bullet\quad \text{lb} = \max_{x\in L[q]} f(x,q,\mathbf{y}^n) + C(x,q)\\
\quad\bullet\quad C(x,q) \text{ from Equations 9 and 10} \hspace{0.7cm} \bullet\quad \text{ub} = \max_{x\in L[q]} f(x,q,\mathbf{y}^n) + C(q)\\
\quad\bullet\quad C(q) = \sum_{x'\in L[q]} C(x',q) \hspace{1.7cm} \bullet\quad k = |L[q]|\\
\quad\bullet\quad f(x,q,\mathbf{y}^n) \text{ from Equation 15} \hspace{1.0cm} \bullet\quad \epsilon = \text{lower bound on } y_x\\[6pt]
\textbf{Trivial case: } \text{If } C(q) = 0, \text{ output } \mathbf{y} \text{ given by } y_x = 1/k \text{ for all } x.\\
\textbf{Initialization: } \text{Initialize:}\\[4pt]
\hspace{4cm} y_x^0 = \frac{C(x,q)}{C(q)}\,(1 - k\epsilon) + \epsilon.\\[10pt]
\textbf{Iteration: } \text{Until convergence do:}\\[4pt]
\hspace{3.5cm} y_x^{n+1} = \max\left(\frac{C(x,q)}{\lambda - f(x,q,\mathbf{y}^n)}, \epsilon\right),\\[8pt]
\text{where } \lambda \in [\text{lb}, \text{ub}] \text{ is chosen (in a binary search) to ensure } \sum_{x\in L(q)} y_x = 1.
\end{array}
}
$$

Figure 4: KL-M\scriptsize INIMIZATION \normalsize Algorithm

This is a difference of two concave functions in $\mathbf{y}$ since $\log(f(\mathbf{y}))$ is concave for any linear function $f(\mathbf{y})$, the $C(x,q)$ are always non-negative and the sum of concave functions is also concave. We give a *DC programming* solution to this optimization (Horst and Thoai, 1999). Let

$$
\Omega = \{\mathbf{y} : \forall x, y_x \geq \epsilon,\ \sum_{x\in L(q)} y_x \leq 1\},
$$

be the function domain. The DC programming solution for such a problem uses an iterative procedure that linearizes the subtrahend in the concave difference about the current estimate and then solves the resulting concave objective for the next estimate. Using this procedure on Equation 13 gives $\mathbf{y}^{n+1}$ as

$$
\underset{\mathbf{y}\in\Omega}{\operatorname{argmax}} \sum_{x\in L[q]} \left\{ C(x,q)\log y_x + y_x f(x,q,\mathbf{y}^n) \right\}
\tag{14}
$$

where

$$
f(x,q,\mathbf{y}^n) = \sum_{q_0\in B_1(q)} \frac{C(\varphi,q_0)\mathbf{1}_{x\in L[q_0]\cap\Sigma}}{1 - \sum_{x'\in L[q_0]\cap\Sigma} y_{x'}^n}.
\tag{15}
$$

Observe that $1 - \sum_{x'\in L[q_0]\cap\Sigma} y_{x'}^n \geq \epsilon$ as the automaton is backoff-complete and $\mathbf{y}^n \in \Omega$.

Let $C(q)$ be defined as:

$$
C(q) = \sum_{x'\in L[q]} C(x',q)
$$

The following lemma provides the solution to the optimization problem in (14) which leads to a stationary point of the objective.

Lemma 3. *Solution to* (14) *given by*

$$
y_x^{n+1} = \max\left(\frac{C(x,q)}{\lambda - f(x,q,\mathbf{y}^n)}, \epsilon\right),
\tag{16}
$$

where λ is chosen so that $\sum_x y_x^n = 1$ and lies in

$$
\left[\max_{x\in L[q]} f(x,q,\mathbf{y}^n) + C(x,q),\ \max_{x\in L[q]} f(x,q,\mathbf{y}^n) + C(q)\right].
$$

Proof is omitted due to space limitations.

From this, we form the KL-M\scriptsize INIMIZATION \normalsize algorithm in Figure 4. Observe that if all the counts are zero, then any solution is an optimal solution and the algorithm returns a uniform distribution over labels. In other cases, we initialize the model based on counts such that $\mathbf{y}^0 \in \Omega$. We then repeat the DC programming algorithm iteratively until convergence. Since Ω is a convex compact set and both the functions are continuous and differentiable in Ω, the KL-M\scriptsize INIMIZATION \normalsize converges to a stationary point (Sriperumbudur and Lanckriet, 2009, Theorem 4).

4   Experiments

We now provide experimental evidence of the theory's validity and show its usefulness in various applications. For the ease of notation, we use WFA-A\scriptsize PPROX \normalsize to denote the exact counting algorithm described in Section 3.1.1 followed by the KL-M\scriptsize INIMIZATION \normalsize algorithm of Section 3.2. Similarly, we use WFA-S\scriptsize AMPLE\normalsize A\scriptsize PPROX\normalsize(N) to denote the sampled counting described in Section 3.1.2 with N sampled sentences followed by KL-M\scriptsize INIMIZATION\normalsize.

We first give experimental evidence that supports the theory in Section 4.1. We then show how to approximate neural models as WFAs in Section 4.2. We also use the proposed method to provide lower bounds on the perplexity given a target topology in Section 4.3.

For all the experiments we use the 1996 CSR Hub4 Language Model data, LDC98T31 from the Broadcast News (BN) task. We use the processed form of the corpus and further process it to downcase all the words and remove punctuation. The resulting dataset has 132M words in the training set, 20M words in the test set, and has 240K unique words. From this, we create a vocabulary of approximately 32K words consisting of all words that appeared more than 50 times in the training corpus. Using this vocabulary, we create a trigram Katz model and prune it to contain 2M n-grams using entropy pruning (Stolcke, 2000), which we use as a baseline in all our experiments. We use Katz smoothing since it is amenable to pruning (Chelba et al., 2010). The perplexity of this model on the test set is 144.4.[7] All algorithms were implemented using the open-source `OpenFst` and `OpenGrm` n-gram and stochastic automata (`SFst`) libraries[8] with the last library including these implementations (Allauzen et al., 2007; Roark et al., 2012; Allauzen and Riley, 2018).

4.1 Empirical evidence of theory

Recall that our goal is to find the distribution on a target DFA topology that minimizes the KL divergence to the source distribution. However, as shown in Section 3.2, when the target topology has failure transitions, the optimization objective is not convex so the stationary point solution may not be the global optimum. We now show that the model indeed converges to a good solution in various cases empirically.

Idempotency: When the target topology is the same as the source topology, we show that the performance of the approximated model matches the source model. Let p_s be the pruned Katz word model described above. We approximate

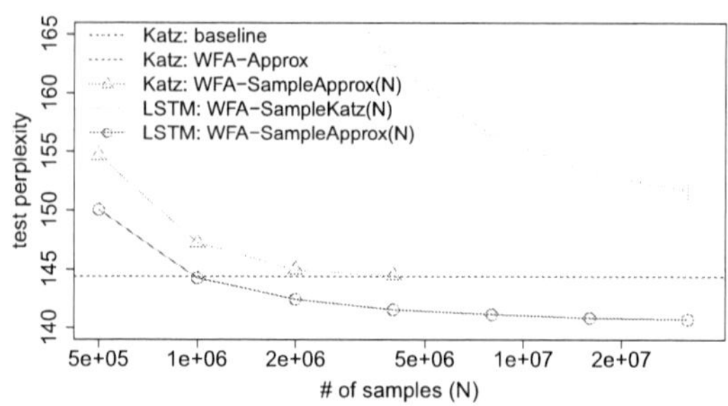

Figure 5: Test set perplexity for Katz baseline and various approximations of that baseline and of an LSTM model trained on the same data. Note that the Katz baseline and Katz WFA-Approx plots are identical.

p_s onto the same topology using WFA-APPROX and WFA-SAMPLEAPPROX($\cdot$) and then compute perplexity on the test corpus. The results are presented in Figure 5. The test perplexity of the WFA-APPROX model matches that of the source model and the performance of the WFA-SAMPLEAPPROX(N) model approaches that of the source model as the number of samples N increases.

Comparison to greedy pruning: Recall that entropy pruning (Stolcke, 2000) greedily removes n-grams such that the KL divergence to the original model p_s is small. Let p_{greedy} be the resulting model and A_{greedy} be the topology of p_{greedy}. If the KL-MINIMIZATION converges to a good solution, then approximating p_s onto A_{greedy} would give a model that is at least as good as p_{greedy}. We show that this is indeed the case; in fact, approximating p_s onto A_{greedy} performs better than p_{greedy}. In particular, let p_s again be the $2M$ n-gram Katz model described above. We prune it to have 1M n-grams and obtain p_{greedy}, which has a test perplexity of 157.4. We then approximate p_s on A_{greedy} and the resulting model has test perplexity of 155.6, which is smaller than the test perplexity of p_{greedy}. This shows that the approximation algorithm indeed finds a good solution.

4.2 Neural models to WFA conversion

Since neural models such as LSTMs give improved performance over n-gram models, we investigated if an LSTM distilled onto a WFA model can obtain better performance than the baseline WFA trained directly from Katz smoothing. As stated in the introduction, this could then be used together with federated learning for fast and pri-

---

[7] For all perplexity measurements we treat the unknown word as a single token instead of a class. To compute the perplexity with the unknown token being treated as class, multiply the perplexity by $k^{0.0115}$, where k is the number of tokens in the unknown class and 0.0115 is the out of vocabulary rate in the test dataset.

[8] These libraries are available at `www.openfst.org` and `www.opengrm.org`

vate on-device inference.

To explore this, we trained an LSTM language model on the training data. The model has 2 LSTM layers with 1024 states and embedding size of 1024. The resulting model has a test perplexity of 60.5. We approximate this model as an WFA in two ways from samples drawn from the LSTM.

The first way is to construct a Katz n-gram model on N LSTM samples and entropy-prune to 2M n-grams, which we denote by WFA-SAMPLEKATZ(N). The second way is is to approximate onto the baseline Katz 2M n-gram topology described above using WFA-SAMPLEAPPROX(N). The results are included in Figure 5. It shows that the WFA-SAMPLEKATZ(N) model performs significantly worse than the baseline Katz model even at 32M samples, while the WFA-SAMPLEAPPROX(N) models have better perplexity than the baseline Katz model with as little as 1M samples. With 32M samples this way of approximating the LSTM model as a WFA is 3.6 better in perplexity than the baseline Katz.

4.3 Lower bounds on perplexity

The neural model in Section 4.2 has a perplexity of 60.5, but the best perplexity for the approximated model is 140.8. Is there a better approximation algorithm for the given target topology? We place bounds on that next, in our final experiment.

Let T be the set of test sentences. The test-set log-perplexity of a model p can be written as

$$\frac{1}{|T|} \sum_{x^* \in T} \log \frac{1}{p(x^*)} = \sum_{x^*} \hat{p}_t(x^*) \log \frac{1}{p(x^*)},$$

where $\hat{p}_t$ is the empirical distribution of test sentences. Observe that the best model with topology A can be computed as

$$p'_a = \operatorname*{argmin}_{p_a \in \mathcal{P}(A)} \sum_{x^*} \hat{p}_t(x^*) \log \frac{1}{p_a(x^*)},$$

which is the model with topology A that has minimal KL divergence from the test distribution $\hat{p}_t$. This can be computed using WFA-APPROX . If we use this approach on the BN test set with the 2M n-gram Katz model, the result has a perplexity of 121.1. This demonstrates that, under the assumption that the algorithm finds the global KL divergence minimum, the test perplexity with this topology cannot be improved beyond 121.1, irrespective of the method.

What if we approximate the LSTM onto the best trigram topology? To test this, we build a trigram model from the test data and approximate the LSTM on the trigram topology. This approximated model has 11M n-grams and a perplexity of 81. This shows that for large datasets, the shortfall of n-gram models in the approximation is in the n-gram topology.

5   Summary

In this paper, we have presented an algorithm for minimizing the KL-divergence between a probabilistic source model over sequences and a WFA target model. Our algorithm is general enough to permit source models of arbitrary form (e.g., RNNs) and a wide class of target WFA models, importantly including those with failure transitions, such as n-gram models. We provide some experimental validation of our algorithm, including demonstrating that it is well-behaved in common scenarios and that it yields improved performance over baseline n-gram models using the same WFA topology. Additionally, we use our methods to provide lower bounds on how well a given WFA topology can model a given test set. All of the algorithms reported here are available in the open-source OpenGrm libraries at `http://www.opengrm.org`.

In addition to the above-mentioned results, we also demonstrated that optimizing the WFA topology for the given test set yields far better perplexities than were obtained using WFA topologies derived from training data alone, suggesting that the problem of deriving an appropriate WFA topology – something we do not really touch on in this paper – is particularly important.

References

Heike Adel, Katrin Kirchhoff, Ngoc Thang Vu, Dominic Telaar, and Tanja Schultz. 2014. Comparing approaches to convert recurrent neural networks into backoff language models for efficient decoding. In *Fifteenth Annual Conference of the International Speech Communication Association*.

Alfred V. Aho and Margaret J. Corasick. 1975. Efficient string matching: an aid to bibliographic search. *Communications of the ACM*, 18(6):333–340

Jürgen Albert and Jarkko Kari. 2009. Digital image compression. In *Handbook of weighted automata*. Springer.

Cyril Allauzen, Mehryar Mohri, and Brian Roark. 2003. Generalized algorithms for constructing language models. In *Proceedings of ACL*, pages 40–47.

Cyril Allauzen, Michael Riley, Johan Schalkwyk, Wojciech Skut, and Mehryar Mohri. 2007. OpenFst Library. *http://www.openfst.org*.

Cyril Allauzen and Michael D. Riley. 2018. Algorithms for weighted finite automata with failure transitions. In *International Conference on Implementation and Application of Automata*, pages 46–58. Springer.

Ebru Arisoy, Stanley F. Chen, Bhuvana Ramabhadran, and Abhinav Sethy. 2014. Converting neural network language models into back-off language models for efficient decoding in automatic speech recognition. *IEEE/ACM Transactions on Audio, Speech and Language Processing (TASLP)*, 22(1):184–192.

Borja Balle, Xavier Carreras, Franco M. Luque, and Ariadna Quattoni. 2014. Spectral learning of weighted automata. *Machine learning*, 96(1-2):33–63.

Borja Balle and Mehryar Mohri. 2012. Spectral learning of general weighted automata via constrained matrix completion. In *Advances in neural information processing systems*, pages 2159–2167.

Thomas M. Breuel. 2008. The OCRopus open source OCR system. In *Proceedings of IS&T/SPIE 20th Annual Symposium*.

Rafael C. Carrasco. 1997. Accurate computation of the relative entropy between stochastic regular grammars. *RAIRO-Theoretical Informatics and Applications*, 31(5):437–444.

Rafael C. Carrasco and José Oncina. 1994. Learning stochastic regular grammars by means of a state merging method. In *International Colloquium on Grammatical Inference*, pages 139–152. Springer.

Rafael C. Carrasco and Jose Oncina. 1999. Learning deterministic regular grammars from stochastic samples in polynomial time. *RAIRO-Theoretical Informatics and Applications*, 33(1):1–19.

Ciprian Chelba, Thorsten Brants, Will Neveitt, and Peng Xu. 2010. Study on interaction between entropy pruning and Kneser-Ney smoothing. In *Eleventh Annual Conference of the International Speech Communication Association*.

Stanley Chen and Joshua Goodman. 1998. An empirical study of smoothing techniques for language modeling. Technical report, TR-10-98, Harvard University.

Corinna Cortes, Mehryar Mohri, Ashish Rastogi, and Michael Riley. 2008. On the computation of the relative entropy of probabilistic automata. *International Journal of Foundations of Computer Science*, 19(01):219–242.

Arthur P. Dempster, Nan M. Laird, and Donald B. Rubin. 1977. Maximum likelihood from incomplete data via the EM algorithm. *Journal of the royal statistical society. Series B (methodological)*, pages 1–38.

Anoop Deoras, Tomáš Mikolov, Stefan Kombrink, Martin Karafiát, and Sanjeev Khudanpur. 2011. Variational approximation of long-span language models for LVCSR. In *Acoustics, Speech and Signal Processing (ICASSP), 2011 IEEE International Conference on*, pages 5532–5535. IEEE.

Richard Durbin, Sean R. Eddy, Anders Krogh, and Graeme J. Mitchison. 1998. *Biological Sequence Analysis: Probabilistic Models of Proteins and Nucleic Acids*. Camb. Univ. Press.

Peter Ebden and Richard Sproat. 2015. The Kestrel TTS text normalization system. *Natural Language Engineering*, 21(3):333–353.

Jason Eisner. 2001. Expectation semirings: Flexible EM for learning finite-state transducers. In *Proceedings of the ESSLLI workshop on finite-state methods in NLP*, pages 1–5.

Andrew Hard, Kanishka Rao, Rajiv Mathews, Françoise Beaufays, Sean Augenstein, Hubert Eichner, Chloé Kiddon, and Daniel Ramage. 2018. Federated learning for mobile keyboard prediction. *arXiv preprint arXiv:1811.03604*.

Lars Hellsten, Brian Roark, Prasoon Goyal, Cyril Allauzen, Françoise Beaufays, Tom Ouyang, Michael Riley, and David Rybach. 2017. Transliterated mobile keyboard input via weighted finite-state transducers. In *FSMNLP 2017*, pages 10–19.

Reiner Horst and Nguyen V. Thoai. 1999. DC programming: overview. *Journal of Optimization Theory and Applications*, 103(1):1–43.

Gonzalo Iglesias, Cyril Allauzen, William Byrne, Adrià de Gispert, and Michael Riley. 2011. Hierarchical phrase-based translation representations. In *EMNLP 2011*, pages 1373–1383.

Slava M. Katz. 1987. Estimation of probabilities from sparse data for the language model component of a speech recogniser. *IEEE Transactions on Acoustic, Speech, and Signal Processing*, 35(3):400–401.

Jakub Konečný, H. Brendan McMahan, Felix X. Yu, Peter Richtárik, Ananda Theertha Suresh, and Dave Bacon. 2016. Federated learning: Strategies for improving communication efficiency. *arXiv preprint arXiv:1610.05492*.

Gwénolé Lecorvé and Petr Motlicek. 2012. Conversion of recurrent neural network language models to weighted finite state transducers for automatic speech recognition. In *Thirteenth Annual Conference of the International Speech Communication Association*.

Mehryar Mohri. 1997. String-matching with automata. *Nord. J. Comput.*, 4(2):217–231.

Mehryar Mohri. 2002. Semiring frameworks and algorithms for shortest-distance problems. *Journal of Automata, Languages and Combinatorics*, 7(3):321–350.

Mehryar Mohri. 2009. Weighted automata algorithms. In *Handbook of Weighted Automata*, pages 213–254. Springer.

Mehryar Mohri, Fernando C. N. Pereira, and Michael Riley. 2008. Speech recognition with weighted finite-state transducers. In *Handbook on speech proc. and speech comm.* Springer.

Josef R. Novak, Nobuaki Minematsu, and Keikichi Hirose. 2013. Failure transitions for joint n-gram models and g2p conversion. In *INTERSPEECH*, pages 1821–1825.

Tom Ouyang, David Rybach, Françoise Beaufays, and Michael Riley. 2017. Mobile keyboard input decoding with finite-state transducers. *arXiv preprint arXiv:1704.03987*.

Brian Roark, Richard Sproat, Cyril Allauzen, Michael Riley, Jeffrey Sorensen, and Terry Tai. 2012. The OpenGrm open-source finite-state grammar software libraries. *Proceedings of the ACL 2012 System Demonstrations*, pages 61–66.

Bharath K. Sriperumbudur and Gert R.G. Lanckriet. 2009. On the convergence of the concave-convex procedure. In *Proceedings of the 22nd International Conference on Neural Information Processing Systems*, pages 1759–1767. Curran Associates Inc.

Andreas Stolcke. 2000. Entropy-based pruning of backoff language models. *arXiv preprint cs/0006025*.

Martin Sundermeyer, Ralf Schlüter, and Hermann Ney. 2012. LSTM neural networks for language modeling. In *Thirteenth annual conference of the international speech communication association*.

Peter Tiño and Vladimir Vojtek. 1997. Extracting stochastic machines from recurrent neural networks trained on complex symbolic sequences. In *Knowledge-Based Intelligent Electronic Systems, 1997. KES'97. Proceedings., 1997 First International Conference on*, volume 2, pages 551–558. IEEE.

Silent HMMs: Generalized Representation of Hidden Semi-Markov Models and Hierarchical HMMs

Kei Wakabayashi
1-2 Kasuga, Tsukuba, Ibaraki, Japan
University of Tsukuba
kwakaba@slis.tsukuba.ac.jp

Abstract

Modeling sequence data using probabilistic finite state machines (PFSMs) is a technique that analyzes the underlying dynamics in sequences of symbols. Hidden semi-Markov models (HSMMs) and hierarchical hidden Markov models (HHMMs) are PFSMs that have been successfully applied to a wide variety of applications by extending HMMs to make the extracted patterns easier to interpret. However, these models are independently developed with their own training algorithm, so that we cannot combine multiple kinds of structures to build a PFSM for a specific application. In this paper, we prove that silent hidden Markov models (silent HMMs) are flexible models that have more expressive power than HSMMs and HHMMs. Silent HMMs are HMMs that contain silent states, which do not emit any observations. We show that we can obtain silent HMM equivalent to given HSMMs and HHMMs. We believe that these results form a firm foundation to use silent HMMs as a unified representation for PFSM modeling.

1 Introduction

Probabilistic finite state machines (PFSMs) are widely used for modeling non-deterministic behaviors in languages (Wang and Manning, 2012). One of the powerful applications of PFSMs is automatic (unsupervised) induction of language patterns (Stratos et al., 2016). The automatic induction of finite state models can potentially impact the direction that research takes on finite state machines, which have been applied to natural language processing such as morphological modeling (Ehsani et al., 2017), word transduction between different languages (Sharma and Singh, 2017), dialog action (Torres, 2013), etc.

Hidden Markov models (HMMs) are the simplest and most well-known probabilistic finite

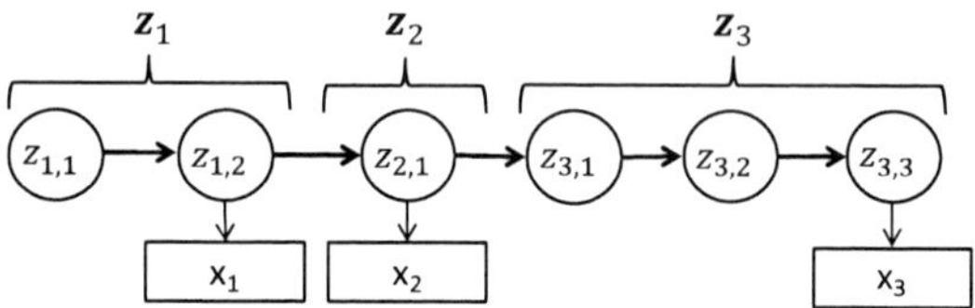

Figure 1: A hidden state sequence of silent HMM. $\mathbf{z}_t$ corresponds to multiple hidden states that constitute a silent Markov chain.

state machines. However, the unsupervised training of HMMs usually does not produce good finite state machines like the ones crafted by human experts because of the complexity of reconstructing language patterns from a finite number of observations. Human experts can build finite state machines that are comprehensible because they have intuition about the latent structure of languages.

This discussion suggests that we need to incorporate prior knowledge into the model structure of HMMs, which is a basic idea that pervades the recent methods of automatic induction of language patterns (Stratos et al., 2016; Jin et al., 2018). Several kinds of PFSMs, such as hidden semi-Markov models (HSMMs) (Moore and Savic, 2004; Yu, 2010) and hierarchical hidden Markov models (Fine et al., 1998; Wakabayashi and Miura, 2012), reflect several different additional structural assumptions. Each model comes with a specialized training algorithm that has to be implemented separately. This requirement prevents us from trying several models; more importantly, we cannot easily combine multiple assumptions that are implemented in different PFSMs. To move the research of automatic finite state machine induction forward, we need to develop a more flexible way to incorporate our prior knowledge into the PFSMs.

Proceedings of the 14th International Conference on Finite-State Methods and Natural Language Processing, pages 98–107
Dresden, Germany, September 23-25, 2019. ©2019 Association for Computational Linguistics

In this paper, we propose silent hidden Markov models (silent HMMs) as a generalized representation of other PFSMs that at least can express the structure that is assumed in HSMMs and HHMMs. A silent HMM is an HMM that contains silent states, which do not emit any observations. We prove that the expressive power of silent HMMs is better than HSMMs and HHMMs, and we propose a method that obtains a silent HMM that is equivalent to an HSMM and an HHMM. This result indicates that we can combine and/or customize the structural assumptions of HSMMs and HHMMs in the unified framework of silent HMMs, potentially leading us to more precise and flexible automatic induction of finite state machines.

The rest of the paper is organized as follows. In Section 2, we dfine silent HMMs. In Sections 3 and 4, we detail the HSMMs and HHMMs respectively and prove the expressivity of silent HMMs is better than these models. In Section 5, we discuss an inference algorithm of silent HMMs. In Section 6, we conclude the discussion and mention future work.

2 Silent HMMs

The concept of the silent states, also known as "null emission" in HMMs, has been used in speech recognition (Bahl et al., 1983; Rabiner, 1989) and DNA modeling in bioinformatics (Krogh et al., 1994; Eddy, 1998) to express optional sounds or letters in sequences that are implicitly dropped from observations. Recently, Wakabayashi (2018) applied a silent HMM to natural language sentences to extract phrase structures in an unsupervised manner. However, surprisingly few descriptions exist in literature that define silent HMMs in a formal way. In this section, we formally define silent HMMs.

Let $\mathbf{x}_{1:T} = x_1, \ldots, x_T$ be the sequence of observations and $\mathcal{X}$ be the domain of each observation ($x_t \in \mathcal{X}$). We denote the states that correspond to each observation x_t by $\mathbf{z}_t = z_{t,1}, \ldots, z_{t,|\mathbf{z}_t|}$. In silent HMMs, $\mathbf{z}_t$ can be a series of states that contain multiple silent states that precede a normal state producing x_t. Figure 1 illustrates the relationship between x_t and $\mathbf{z}_t$. $z_{t,1}, \ldots, z_{t,|\mathbf{z}_t|-1}$ are all silent states and $z_{t,|\mathbf{z}_t|}$ is a normal state.

A silent HMM is defined by a tuple $(\mathcal{X}, Q, C, R, \boldsymbol{\pi}, A, \Theta)$. Q is a finite set of states. Silence assignment $C : Q \rightarrow \{0, 1\}$ is a mapping that designates silent states. Each state is either a silent state or a normal state. $C(q) = 1$ indicates that the state $q \in Q$ is a silent state and $C(q) = 0$ means q is a normal state. The set of normal states is denoted by $Q_n = \{q \in Q | C(q) = 1\}$ and the set of silent states is denoted by $Q_s = \{q \in Q | C(q) = 0\}$.

R is a predicate that defines a transition topology. The domain of R is $Q \times Q$. If $R(q_1, q_2)$ is true, the transition from q_1 to q_2 is allowed. In the rest of the paper, we also use $q_1 \xrightarrow{R} q_2$ to indicate $R(q_1, q_2)$ is true.

The joint likelihood of $\mathbf{x}_{1:T}$ and $\mathbf{z}_{1:T}$ is described as follows.

$$p(\mathbf{x}_{1:T}, \mathbf{z}_{1:T}) = \prod_{t=1}^{T} p(\mathbf{z}_t | \mathbf{z}_{t-1}) p(x_t | z_{t,|\mathbf{z}_t|}). \quad (1)$$

Since $\mathbf{z}_t = z_{t,1}, \ldots, z_{t,|\mathbf{z}_t|}$, $p(\mathbf{z}_t | \mathbf{z}_{t-1})$ is the joint probability given as below.

$$p(\mathbf{z}_t | \mathbf{z}_{t-1}) = p(z_{t,1} | z_{t-1,|\mathbf{z}_{t-1}|}) \prod_{\tau=1}^{|\mathbf{z}_t|} p(z_{t,\tau} | z_{t,\tau-1}). \quad (2)$$

When $t = 1$, the first term in Eq (2), $p(z_{1,1} | z_{0,|\mathbf{z}_0|})$, is defined as an initial state probability. $\boldsymbol{\pi}$ is a $|Q|$ dimensional vector that represents the initial state distribution. A is a $|Q| \times |Q|$ matrix of which A_{q_1, q_2} indicates the transition probability from q_1 to q_2; e.g., $p(z_{t,\tau} = q_2 | z_{t,\tau-1} = q_1) = A_{q_1, q_2}$. For q_1, q_2 such that $R(q_1, q_2)$ is false, A_{q_1, q_2} is restricted to being zero. $\Theta = \{\boldsymbol{\theta}_q\}_{q \in Q_n}$ is parameters of the emission distribution $p(x_t | z_{t,|\mathbf{z}_t|})$ for each normal state.

$\mathcal{X}, Q, C, R$ are meta-parameters of silent HMMs, which are not trainable from data. These meta-parameters reflect prior knowledge of a structure of sequence data. In the following sections, we show that there is a set of meta-parameters that makes the likelihood function of silent HMM identical to the likelihood function of HSMMs and HHMMs.

3 Hidden Semi-Markov Models

3.1 Model Definition

A hidden semi-Markov model (HSMM) is a probabilistic automaton that allows a state to emit multiple observations. Figure 2 illustrates a hidden state sequence of HSMMs. HSMMs explicitly consider a probabilistic distribution of the duration. For example, in Figure 2, the duration of the

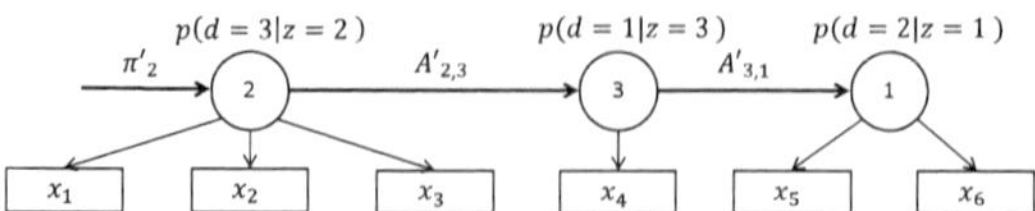

Figure 2: Example of a hidden state sequence of HSMM

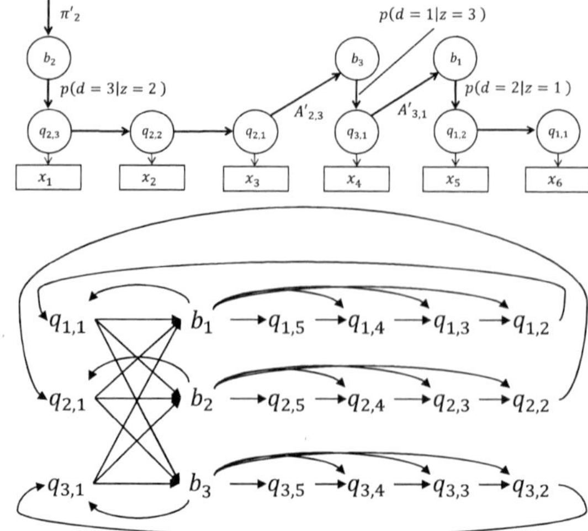

Figure 3: **(Top)** Hidden state sequence of the silent HMM that is equivalent to the state sequence of the HSMM in Figure 2 **(Bottom)** State transition diagram

first state $z_1 = 2$ is $d_1 = 3$, meaning the state keeps emitting three observations (x_1, x_2, and x_3) following the i.i.d. distribution of $p(x|z = 2)$. The duration of each state is stochastically determined depending on the state. While multiple ways to define the distribution of duration $p(d|z)$ have been proposed (Yu, 2010), we use categorical distributions with D possible classes to represent $p(d|z)$ where $D \in \mathbb{N}$ is the maximum duration.

An HSMM is defined by a tuple $(\mathcal{X}, Q', D, \pi', A', \Phi, \Theta')$. $\mathcal{X}$ is a domain of observations, Q' is a set of states, and $D \in \mathbb{N}$ is a maximum duration. A' is a transition probability matrix where the transition probability from the state i to j is $A'_{i,j}$. π' is an initial probability vector where the initialization probability of the state i is π'_i. $\Phi = \{\phi_i\}_{i \in Q'}$ is a set of parameters of duration distribution where $p(d|z) = \phi_{z,d}$. Θ' is a set of parameters for the emission distributions.

Let $\mathbf{x} = x_1, \ldots, x_T$ be a sequence of observations, $\mathbf{z} = z_1, \ldots, z_n$ be a sequence of hidden states, and $\mathbf{d} = d_1, \ldots, d_n$ be a sequence of duration variables. We use n to indicate the length of the hidden state sequence, which is not necessarily equal to T. Instead, $\sum_{\tau=1}^{n} d_\tau$ must be equal to T. The likelihood function of an HSMM is defined as follows;

$$p(\mathbf{x}_{1:T}, \mathbf{z}_{1:n}, \mathbf{d}_{1:n}) =$$

$$\pi'_{z_1} \prod_{\tau=2}^{n} A'_{z_{\tau-1}, z_\tau} \prod_{\tau=1}^{n} \phi_{z_\tau, d_\tau} \prod_{t=1}^{T} p(x_t | \boldsymbol{\theta}_{z_{c(t)}}), \quad (3)$$

where $c(t)$ is a function that returns the index of the hidden state that corresponds to the observation x_t.

$\mathcal{X}, Q', D$ are meta-parameters of HSMMs that are not trainable from data. In the next section, we demonstrate how an HSMM that has meta-parameters $\mathcal{X}, Q', D$ can be equivalently represented as a silent HMM.

3.2 Expressivity of HSMMs and Silent HMMs

Given an HSMM that has meta-parameters $\mathcal{X}, Q', D$, we can obtain an equivalent silent HMM that has meta-parameters $(\mathcal{X}, Q, C, R)$. Figure 3 depicts the representation of the transition dynamics of an HSMM by a silent HMM. The duration of each state is represented explicitly by a transition throughout "countdown states." A countdown state $q_{i,d}$ only changes to $q_{i,d-1}$. The state of the last count $q_{i,1}$ changes to b_j, which indicates a silent state that represents the beginning of the state j in HSMM. The transition probabilities from b_j correspond to the duration probability $p(d|z = j)$.

Here, we explain the proposed mapping from a tuple of meta-parameters (Q', D) of HSMMs to a tuple of meta-parameters (Q, C, R) of the equivalent silent HMMs. First, Q is constructed as a union of a set of countdown states Q_c and a set of beginning states Q_b. We define Q_c and Q_b as follows.

$$Q_c = \{q_{i,d}\}_{i \in Q', 1 \leq d \leq D}$$
$$Q_b = \{b_i\}_{i \in Q'}.$$

The whole set of states in the silent HMM is defined as $Q = Q_b \cup Q_c$. The elements in Q_c are normal states and the elements in Q_b are silent states.

$$C(q) = \begin{cases} 0 & q \in Q_c \\ 1 & q \in Q_b. \end{cases}$$

The transition topology R is defined as depicted in Figure 3 **(Bottom)**. More formally:

$$\forall i, d(b_i \xrightarrow{R} q_{i,d})$$
$$\forall i, j(q_{i,1} \xrightarrow{R} b_j)$$
$$\forall i, d > 1(q_{i,d} \xrightarrow{R} q_{i,d-1}).$$

To show the equivalency of the given HSMM and the obtained silent HMM, we also specify a surjective mapping from the distributions in the silent HMM parameterized by (π, A, Θ) to the distributions in the HSMM parameterized by $(\pi', A', \Phi, \Theta')$.

- The D-dimensional categorical distribution in the silent HMM for transition from the state $b_i \in Q_b$ parameterized by $\mathbf{A}_{b_i}$ is mapped into the categorical distribution in the HSMM for the duration of the state i parameterized by ϕ_i.

- The $|Q|$-dimensional categorical distribution in the silent HMM for transition from the state $q_{i,1}$ parameterized by $\mathbf{A}_{q_{i,1}}$ is mapped into the categorical distribution in the HSMM for the transition from the state i parameterized by $\mathbf{A}'_i$.

- The emission distribution of the state $q_{i,d}$ in the silent HMM is mapped into the emission distribution of the state i in the HSMM for any $d \in D$.

Note that the destination of the transition from $q_{i,d}$ is only $q_{i,d-1}$ for any $d > 1$; therefore, the transition probability from $q_{i,d}$ to $q_{i,d-1}$ is always one.

Lemma 1. *The likelihood function of the silent HMM constructed in the way described above is equivalent to the likelihood function of the given HSMM.*

This lemma can be proved straightforwardly by mapping random variables as shown in Figure 3 **(Top)** and putting mapped parameters in Eqs. (1) and (2).

Theorem 1. *The expressivity of silent HMMs is better than the expressivity of HSMMs. In other words, the mapping from an HSMM to a silent HMM that makes the likelihood function equivalent is injective and not surjective.*

Proof of being injective is easy: We can confirm that different HSMMs have different likelihood functions. If the mapping is not injective, two HSMMs with different likelihood functions are mapped into the same silent HMM. This contradicts the Lemma 1. Being not surjective is obvious; for silent HMMs, we can set different meta-parameters from ones explained above.

This result is useful in practice because we can use an implementation of the silent HMMs when we want to use HSMMs. We do not need to implement the training algorithm and the Viterbi algorithm just for HSMMs.

4 Hierarchical HMMs

4.1 Model Definition

A hierarchical HMM (HHMM) is a probabilistic automaton that simulates multiple Markov chains that have a hierarchical relationship. Figure 4 illustrates the dynamics of an HHMM that has three hierarchy levels. A hidden state sequence is in each level. Each state sequence can be terminated probabilistically when the sequence reaches a special End state. The state at level d is allowed to change to another state at time step t only when the state sequences at all the lower levels are terminated. If a state sequence at level d is terminated at time step t, a state sequence is initialized again at the next time step $t + 1$. Only the states at the bottom level emit the observation. The probabilistic distribution of state transitions and observation emissions depend on the combination of the states at all the upper levels[1]. For example, the state transition from the bottom state 2 to state 1 at time step $t = 1$ in Figure 4 depends on all the upper states, namely, state 2 at the top level $d = 1$ and state 1 at the middle level $d = 2$.

An HHMM is defined by a tuple $(\mathcal{X}, N, L, \pi'', A'', \Theta'')$ where N is the number of states in each Markov chain and L is the number of levels. The HHMM in Figure 4 has $N = 2$ and $L = 3$. When the states at level 1 to $d - 1$ are $\mathbf{k} = (k_1, \ldots, k_{d-1})$, the state transition probability from the state i to the state j at level d is denoted by $A''^{\mathbf{k}}_{i,j}$ and the state initialization probability of the state i at level d is represented by $\pi''^{\mathbf{k}}_i$. We consider a special symbol End as

---

[1] Another version of HHMMs shares the probabilistic distributions among the states that have different upper states (Bui et al., 2004). Although we could extend the discussion in this section to adapt to this version, we do not go into detail due to the length limitations.

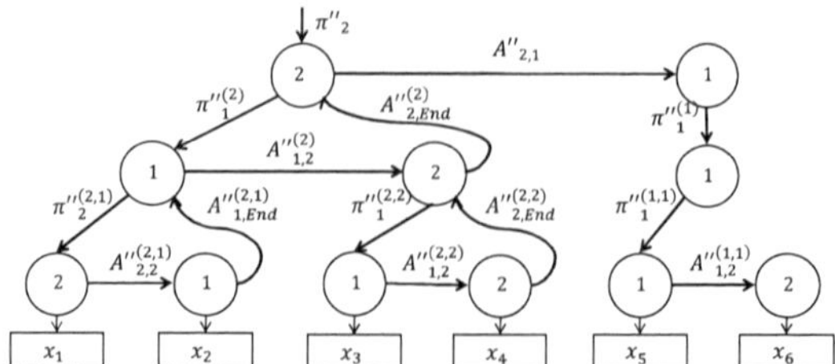

Figure 4: Example of a hidden state sequence of hierarchical HMM

another destination of state transition, which triggers the termination of the state sequence at that level. The transition parameters A'' satisfy the following condition for all i and $\mathbf{k}$.

$$\sum_{j \in \mathbb{N}_{\leq N} \cup \{End\}} A''^{\mathbf{k}}_{i,j} = 1,$$

where $\mathbb{N}_{\leq N}$ is a set of natural numbers that are less than or equal to N (representing the set of states on the Markov chain at that level).

The formulation of the likelihood function of HHMMs is complicated because the length of state sequence is different at each level. To simplify the situation, we apply a variable conversion proposed by (Murphy and Paskin, 2002) that explicitly considers random variables that represent the state at each time step for all levels. Formally, we define $\mathbf{z}^d = z^d_1, \ldots, z^d_T$ as a sequence of hidden states at level d. For example, the state sequences in Figure 4 are represented as $\mathbf{z}^1 = 2, 2, 2, 2, 1, 1$, $\mathbf{z}^2 = 1, 1, 2, 2, 1, 1$, and $\mathbf{z}^3 = 2, 1, 1, 2, 1, 2$. We also consider a set of binary auxiliary variables $\{f^d_t\}$ that indicate if the state sequence at level d is terminated at time step t. For example, $\mathbf{f}^{1:L}_1 = 0, 0, 0$, $\mathbf{f}^{1:L}_2 = 0, 0, 1$, $\mathbf{f}^{1:L}_3 = 0, 0, 0$, $\mathbf{f}^{1:L}_4 = 0, 1, 1$. f^d_t has to be 0 whenever $f^{d+1}_t = 0$ because the state does not change at level d if the state sequence at the lower level $d + 1$ is not terminated.

Using this representation, we can formulate the likelihood function of HHMMs as Eq. (4). For simplicity, we define $f^{L+1}_t = 1$. The first factor (a) corresponds to an initialization of the state sequences at time step $t = 1$. The second factor (b) indicates a product of termination probabilities, a transition probability, and initialization probabilities for each time step. For example, consider the case of $t = 4$ for the state sequences in Figure 4. Since $\mathbf{f}^{1:L}_4 = 0, 1, 1$, we calculate the product of two termination probabilities $A''^{(2,2)}_{2,End}, A''^{(2)}_{2,End}$ (for

$d = 3$ and $d = 2$), one transition probability $A''_{2,1}$ (for $d = 1$), and two initialization probabilities $\pi''^{(1)}_1, \pi''^{(1,1)}_1$ (for $d = 2, d = 3$). The third factor (c) is a product of emission probabilities for all observations.

Since the dynamics of HHMMs are complex, an inference algorithm needs to be reformulated as a specialized algorithm. Several inference methods have been proposed, such as a modified inside-outside algorithm (Fine et al., 1998), an inference based on dynamic Bayesian network (Murphy and Paskin, 2002), a method based on a variable conversion (Wakabayashi and Miura, 2012), etc. The unsupervised training of HHMMs produces finite state machines that reflect hierarchical sequential patterns on letter sequences in natural language text (Fine et al., 1998), musical pitch structure (Weiland et al., 2005), etc.

4.2 Expressivity of HHMMs and Silent HMMs

Given an HHMM that has meta-parameters $\mathcal{X}, N, L$, we show a method of obtaining a silent HMM that has the equivalent likelihood function. First, we represent the combination of the states in a tree structure as shown in Figure 6 because the probabilistic behaviors in HHMMs depend on the combination of states in all the upper levels. We denote the set of nodes in this tree, excluding the special $ROOT$ node by Ω. Let $parent : \Omega \rightarrow \Omega \cup \{ROOT\}$ be a function that maps a node to its parent node. We denote the children of the node $\omega \in \Omega$ by $child(\omega) = \{v | parent(v) = \omega\}$ and the siblings by $sib(\omega) = child(parent(\omega))$. We also denote the set of leaf nodes by $\Omega_l = \{v \in \Omega | child(v) = \phi\}$ and the set of non-leaf nodes by $\Omega_n = \Omega - \Omega_l$.

Figure 7 shows an equivalent representation of the hidden states of the HHMM in Figure 4, which illustrates the basic idea for obtaining a silent HMM that has an identical likelihood function. Each state in the silent HMMs corresponds to a node in Figure 6. A leaf node is represented as a normal state denoted by q, and a non-leaf node is represented as a silent state. Termination of a state sequence is represented by a state transition to a silent state denoted by e at an upper level. A state transition at an upper level is represented by a state transition from a silent state denoted by e to another silent state denoted by b. An initialization of a state at a lower level is represented by a state

$$
p(\mathbf{x}_{1:T}, \mathbf{z}_{1:T}^{1:L}, \mathbf{f}_{1:T}^{1:L}) =
$$

$$
\underbrace{\prod_{d=1}^{L} \pi''^{\mathbf{z}_{1}^{1:d-1}}_{z_{1}^{d}}}_{(a)}
\underbrace{\prod_{t=1}^{T-1} \prod_{d=1}^{L} \left(A''^{\mathbf{z}_{t}^{1:d-1}}_{z_{t}^{d}, End} \right)^{f_{t}^{d}} \left(A''^{\mathbf{z}_{t}^{1:d-1}}_{z_{t}^{d}, z_{t+1}^{d}} \right)^{f_{t}^{d+1}(1-f_{t}^{d})} \left(\pi''^{\mathbf{z}_{t+1}^{1:d-1}}_{z_{t+1}^{d}} \right)^{f_{t}^{d}}}_{(b)}
\underbrace{\prod_{t=1}^{T} p(x_{t}|\boldsymbol{\theta}''_{\mathbf{z}_{t}^{1:L}})}_{(c)} \quad (4)
$$

Figure 5: Likelihood function of HHMMs

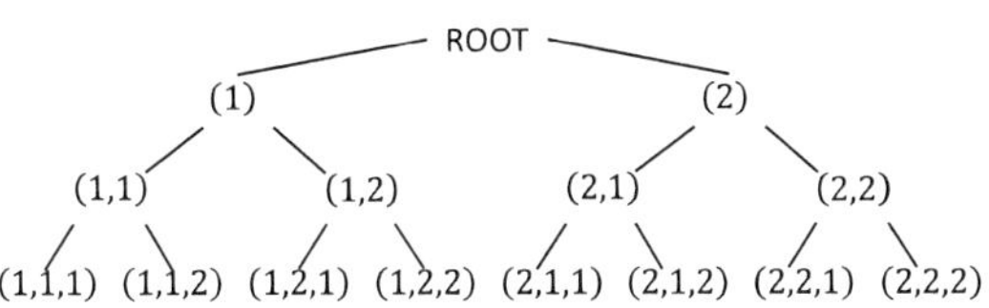

Figure 6: Tree structure that expresses the combination of states in the HHMM with $N = 2, L = 3$.

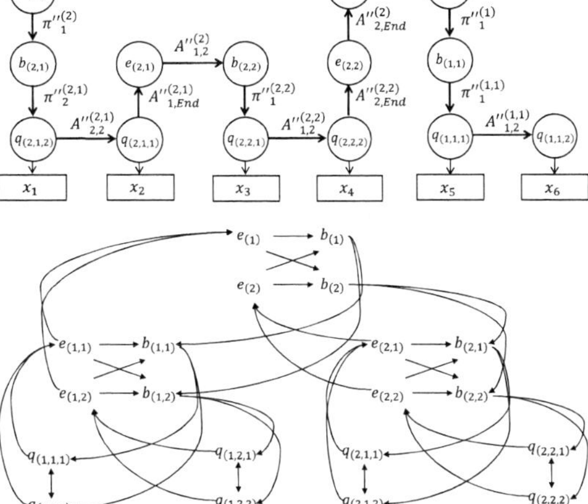

Figure 7: **(Top)** Hidden state sequence of the silent HMM that is equivalent to the state sequence of the hierarchical HMM in Figure 4. **(Bottom)** State transition diagram.

transition from a silent state denoted by b to a state at a lower level.

We propose a mapping from a tuple of meta-parameters (N, L) of HHMMs to a tuple of meta-parameters (Q, C, R) of silent HMMs to make equivalent likelihood functions. First, we construct the tree structure shown in Figure 6 from N and L and obtain the sets of nodes Ω, Ω_l, and Ω_n. We define a set of production states Q_q, a set of beginning states Q_b, and a set of ending states Q_e as follows:

$$
\begin{aligned}
Q_q &= \{q_\omega\}_{\omega \in \Omega_l} \\
Q_b &= \{b_\omega\}_{\omega \in \Omega_n} \\
Q_e &= \{e_\omega\}_{\omega \in \Omega_n}.
\end{aligned}
$$

The whole set of states in the silent HMM is $Q = Q_q \cup Q_b \cup Q_e$. The elements in Q_b and Q_e are silent states and elements in Q_p are normal states.

$$
C(q) = \begin{cases} 1 & q \in Q_b \cup Q_e \\ 0 & q \in Q_q \end{cases}
$$

The transition topology R is designed like in Fig-

ure 7 **(Bottom)**. More formally:

$$
\forall \omega \in \Omega_n, \forall \omega' \in child(\omega)(\omega' \in \Omega_n \implies b_\omega \xrightarrow{R} b_{\omega'})
$$

$$
\forall \omega \in \Omega_n, \forall \omega' \in child(\omega)(\omega' \in \Omega_l \implies b_\omega \xrightarrow{R} q_{\omega'})
$$

$$
\forall \omega \in \Omega_l, \forall \omega' \in sib(\omega)(q_\omega \xrightarrow{R} q_{\omega'})
$$

$$
\forall \omega \in \Omega_l(q_\omega \xrightarrow{R} e_{parent(\omega)})
$$

$$
\forall \omega \in \Omega_n, \forall \omega' \in sib(\omega)(e_\omega \xrightarrow{R} b_{\omega'})
$$

$$
\forall \omega \in \Omega_n(e_\omega \xrightarrow{R} e_{parent(\omega)}).
$$

The transition from b_ω corresponds to the initialization of the lower state sequence. The transition from q_ω or e_ω to $e_{parent(\omega)}$ indicates the termination of the state sequence at that level.

To show the equivalency of the likelihood function, we also specify a mapping from the distributions in the silent HMM parameterized by $\boldsymbol{\pi}, A, \Theta$

to the distributions in the given HHMM parameterized by π'', A'', Θ''.

- The N-dimensional categorical distribution in the silent HMM for transition from the state $b_{(i_1,\ldots,i_d)} \in Q_b$ is mapped into the categorical distribution in the HHMM for state initialization parameterized by $\pi''^{(i_1,\ldots,i_d)}$.

- The $(N+1)$-dimensional categorical distribution in the silent HMM for the transition from the state $q_{(i_1,\ldots,i_d)} \in Q_q$ and $e_{(i_1,\ldots,i_d)} \in Q_e$ is mapped into the categorical distribution in the HHMM for the state transition from i_d parameterized by $A''^{(i_1,\ldots,i_{d-1})}_{i_d}$. The state transition to $e_{(i_1,\ldots,i_{d-1})}$ is mapped into $A''^{(i_1,\ldots,i_{d-1})}_{i_d,End}$.

- The N-dimensional categorical distribution in the silent HMM for initialization probabilities parameterized by π is mapped into

Lemma 2. *The likelihood function of the silent HMM constructed in the way described above is equivalent to the likelihood function of the given HHMM.*

Proof. The proof of this lemma is based on a comparison between the likelihood function of the silent state sequence in Eq. (1) (2) and factors $(a), (b), (c)$ in Eq. (4).

Factor (a) For $t = 1$, the length of the silent state sequence is exactly L because the sequence starts from a state in Q_b at the top level and follows links to a state at the next lower level. As we defined above, the distribution in the silent HMM for the transition from the state in Q_b is mapped into the state initialization distribution in the HHMM parameterized by π. This product is identical to the first factor (a) in Eq. (4).

Factor (b) This factor depends on the values $\mathbf{f}_t$. We can say that $\mathbf{f}_t$ is a variable that indicates the level that holds a state transition. Let $l(\mathbf{f}_t)$ be the level that holds a state transition. For example, when $\mathbf{f}_t^{1:L} = 0,0,1$, the level 2 holds a state transition and $l(\mathbf{f}_t) = 2$. Given $\mathbf{f}_t$, the silent state sequence for the time step t is $e_{(z_t^1,\ldots,z_t^{L-1})}, \ldots, e_{(z_t^1,\ldots,z_t^{l(\mathbf{f}_t)})}, b_{(z_{t+1}^1,\ldots,z_{t+1}^{l(\mathbf{f}_t)})}, \ldots, b_{(z_{t+1}^1,\ldots,z_{t+1}^{L-1})}, q_{(z_{t+1}^1,\ldots,z_{t+1}^{L})}$. By putting the mapped parameters into the product of the transition probabilities in this trajectory, we can confirm that the probability is identical to the factor (b) in Eq. (4) for any $\mathbf{f}_t$.

Factor (c) Factor $\prod_{t=1}^{T} p(x_t|q_{(z_t^1,\ldots,z_t^L)})$ in Eq. (1) is identical to the factor (c). $\qquad\square$

Theorem 2. *The expressivity of silent HMMs is better than the expressivity of HHMMs.*

The theorem can be proved in the same way as Theorem 1. We emphasize again that this result is useful because we can use an implementation of the silent HMMs when we want to use HHMMs. This generalization also brings more flexibility to the modeling of PFSMs that will allow us to explore new useful classes of sequence models in future work.

5 Inference of silent HMMs

5.1 Silent Circuit Constraint

In this section, we discuss an inference algorithm used for EM training of silent HMMs. For inference of silent HMMs, we need to be careful of an infinite length of state sequence that possibly happen by an infinite loop of transitions between silent states. Explicit consideration of an infinite loop of state transitions obviously complicates an inference algorithm. In this paper, we impose a sufficient condition on meta-parameters (Q, C, R) that ensures the length of a state sequence is finite.

To derive the condition, we consider *silent transition topology*, a directed graph representing possible silent state transitions. The graph is obtained from the directed graph representation of R by omitting outlinks from all the normal states. More formally:

Definition 1 (Silent transition topology). *Let Q be a set of states, C be a mapping that indicates the silence assignment, and R be a transition topology. Let R_s be a set of edges defined as follows:*

$$R_s = \{(q_1, q_2) \in Q_s \times Q | q_1 \xrightarrow{R} q_2\}.$$

*A directed graph $G_s = (Q, R_s)$ is **silent transition topology** induced by (Q, C, R).*

Figure 8 shows an example of a silent transition topology. A silent transition topology represents all the possible transitions allowed in a state sequence at a single time step, $\mathbf{z}_t$. Based on the set of meta-parameters in Figure 8 **(Left)**, we can say a state sequence $\mathbf{z}_t = q_1, q_3, q_4$ never happens at a single time step because q_3 is a normal state that produces an observation. Therefore, the state sequence must split into $\mathbf{z}_t = q_1, q_3$ and $\mathbf{z}_{t+1} = q_4$. The state transition topology (Figure 8 **(Right)**) clearly expresses this property, since there is no link from q_3 to q_4.

We can use the definition of silent transition topology to derive a sufficient condition that ensures the length of state sequence at a single time step to be finite.

Definition 2 (Silent circuit constraint). *A set of meta-parameters (Q, C, R) satisfies **silent circuit constraint** if the silent transition topology induced by (Q, C, R) does not contain any circuits.*

Theorem 3. *If a silent HMM has meta-parameters satisfying the silent circuit constraint, $p(\mathbf{z}_t|\mathbf{z}_{t-1})$ is always zero whenever $|\mathbf{z}_t| > |Q_s| + 1$ for any t and $\mathbf{z}_{t-1}$.*

Proof. $p(\mathbf{z}_t|\mathbf{z}_{t-1})$ is greater than 0 only when $\mathbf{z}_t$ is a path in the silent transition topology because transition probabilities from q_1 to q_2 are restricted to being zero when $\neg q_1 \xrightarrow{R} q_2$. Since the silent transition topology contains no circuits and normal states have no outlinks, the length of a path in the silent transition topology is at most $|Q_s| + 1$. From these facts, $p(\mathbf{z}_t|\mathbf{z}_{t-1}) = 0$ when $|\mathbf{z}_t| > |Q_s| + 1$. $\square$

Silent HMMs that satisfy the silent circuit constraint form a subclass of general silent HMMs. The following theorems show that the constrained silent HMMs have more expressive power than HSMMs and HHMMs.

Theorem 4. *The silent HMM constructed from a given HSMM by using the method explained in Section 3.2 satisfies the silent circuit constraint.*

Theorem 5. *The silent HMM constructed from a given HHMM by using the method explained in Section 4.2 satisfies the silent circuit constraint.*

These theorems are easily proven by checking that the silent transition topologies contain no circuits. Based on these results, we can apply efficient inference algorithms (explained in the next section) to silent HMMs that are equivalent to HSMMs and HHMMs.

5.2 Inference Algorithms

The inference of silent HMMs indicates a calculation of the expectations of hidden states $\mathbf{z}$ given a sequence of observations $\mathbf{x}$. We describe a modified forward-backward algorithm for the inference of silent HMMs. The forward-backward algorithm is an inference algorithm for normal HMMs based on efficient computation of forward

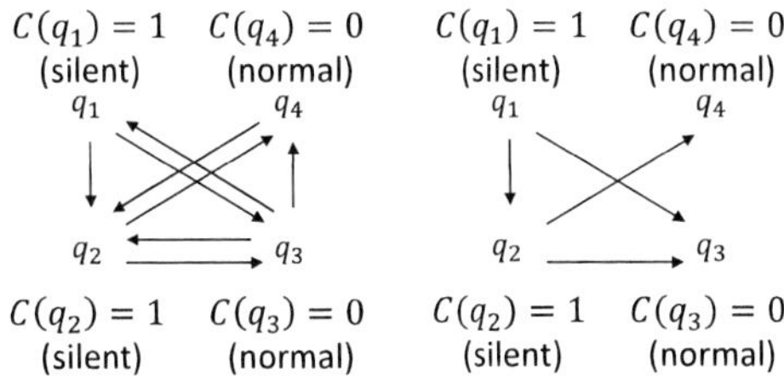

Figure 8: **(Left)** A set of meta-parameters (Q, C, R) that satisfies the silent circuit constraint. **(Right)** Silent transition topology obtained omitting the outlinks from the normal states.

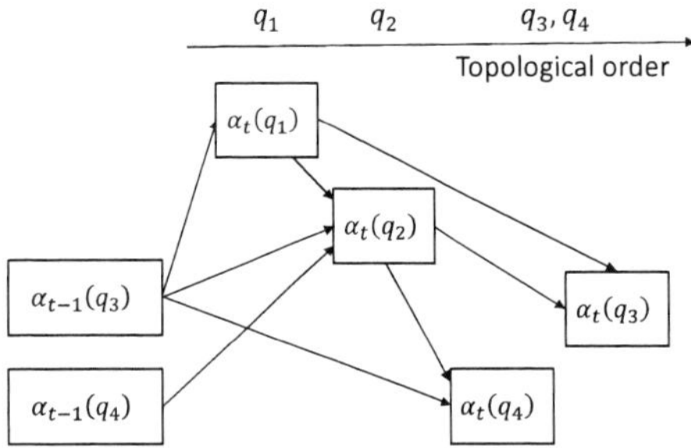

Figure 9: Propagation of the forward probabilities in the silent HMM that has a transition topology in Figure 8. We can calculate the forward probabilities in $O(T|Q|^2)$ with the same complexity as normal HMMs by processing in the topologically sorted order of the states.

and backward probabilities. In this paper, we explain the calculation of forward probabilities to handle the existence of silent states to apply the algorithm to silent HMMs. For details on the forward backward algorithm, please refer to (Rabiner, 1989).

The forward probability of state q_i at time step t is defined as the joint probability of the observations until the time step t. For silent HMMs, we divide cases for silent states and normal states as follows.

$$\alpha_t(q) = \begin{cases} p(z_t = q, x_{1:t-1}) & C(q) = 1\,(silent) \\ p(z_t = q, x_{1:t}) & C(q) = 0\,(normal). \end{cases}$$

While multiple transitions can be involved in a single time step t in silent HMMs, the forward probabilities can be efficiently calculated by following the topological order of states in the silent transition topology. Given a silent HMM with meta-parameters (Q, C, R), we obtain a silent transition topology and apply the topological sort algorithm to the directed graph of the silent transition topology. The obtained topological order reflects the possible order of transitions throughout the silent states at a single time step t. Figure 9 shows the flow of the computation of α_t for the silent HMM that has the transition topology expressed in Figure 8. By following the topological order we decided in this way, the computation of α_t for each state can be done with the computational complexity $O(|Q|^2)$, which has the same computational complexity as the normal HMMs. The recursive formula is derived as follows:

$$\alpha_t(q) = \sum_{q' \in Q_n} \alpha_{t-1}(q') A_{q',q}$$
$$+ \sum_{q' \in \mathcal{T}(q) \cap Q_s} \alpha_t(q') A_{q',q},$$

where $\mathcal{T}(q)$ is a set of states that are earlier than q in the topological order imposed on R.

While we are omitting the case for the backward probabilities due to length limitations, we can efficiently calculate the backward counterpart and apply the forward-backward algorithm to ensure the inference is the same computational complexity as normal HMMs. We are not detailing the algorithm that estimates the most likely hidden state sequence, but we can obtain the Viterbi algorithm straightforwardly by replacing the forward computation in the Viterbi algorithm for HMMs (Rabiner, 1989) with the method we explained above.

6 Conclusion

In this paper, we provided formal descriptions of silent HMMs and proposed methods to obtain silent HMMs that are equivalent to given HSMMs and HHMMs. We believe that our results establish a firm foundation to use silent HMMs as a unified framework for PFSM modeling.

Future work includes developing PFSMs for modeling structures in natural language (e.g., morphological structure) by combining the structural assumptions in HSMMs and HHMMs in the framework of silent HMMs. Other future work is more advanced Bayesian extensions of silent HMMs incorporating Dirichlet prior (Foti et al., 2014) and nonparametric Bayesian prior (Beal et al., 2002; Heller et al., 2009). These extensions coule enable us to estimate the number of states during the training process, offering more powerful PFSM modeling methods.

Acknowledgments

This work was supported by JSPS KAKENHI Grant Number 19K20333 and 16H02904.

References

Lalit R. Bahl, Frederick Jelinek, and Robert L. Mercer. 1983. A Maximum Likelihood Approach to Continuous Speech Recognition. *IEEE Transactions on Pattern Analysis and Machine Intelligence*, PAMI-5(2):179–190.

Matthew J. Beal, Zoubin Ghahramani, and Carl E. Rasmussen. 2002. The infinite hidden markov model. In *Advances in Neural Information Processing Systems 14*, pages 577–584.

Hung H. Bui, Dinh Q. Phung, and Svetha Venkatesh. 2004. Hierarchical hidden markov models with general state hierarchy. In *Proceedings of the 19th national conference on Artifical intelligence*, pages 324–329.

Sean R. Eddy. 1998. Profile hidden Markov models. *Bioinformatics*, 14(9):755–763.

Razieh Ehsani, Berke Ozenc, and Ercan Solak. 2017. A fst description of noun and verb morphology of azarbaijani turkish. In *Proceedings of the 13th International Conference on Finite State Methods and Natural Language Processing*, pages 62–68.

Shai Fine, Yoram Singer, and Naftali Tishby. 1998. The hierarchical hidden markov model: Analysis and applications. *Machine Learning*, 32(1):41–62.

Nick Foti, Jason Xu, Dillon Laird, and Emily Fox. 2014. Stochastic variational inference for hidden markov models. In *Advances in Neural Information Processing Systems 27*, pages 3599–3607.

Katherine Heller, Yee W. Teh, and Dilan Gorur. 2009. Infinite hierarchical hidden markov models. In *Proceedings of the Twelth International Conference on Artificial Intelligence and Statistics*, pages 224–231.

Lifeng Jin, Finale Doshi-Velez, Timothy Miller, William Schuler, and Lane Schwartz. 2018. Unsupervised grammar induction with depth-bounded pcfg. *Transactions of the Association for Computational Linguistics*, 6:211–224.

Anders Krogh, I. Saira Mian, and David Haussler. 1994. A hidden Markov model that finds genes in E.coli DNA. *Nucleic Acids Research*, 22(22):4768–4778.

Michael D. Moore and Michael I. Savic. 2004. Speech reconstruction using a generalized hsmm (ghsmm). *Digital Signal Processing*, 14(1):37–53.

Kevin P. Murphy and Mark A. Paskin. 2002. Linear Time Inference in Hierarchical HMMs. In *Advances in Neural Information Processing Systems 14*, pages 833–840.

Lawrence R. Rabiner. 1989. A tutorial on hidden Markov models and selected applications in speech recognition. *Proceedings of the IEEE*, 77(2):257–286.

Shashikant Sharma and Anil Kumar Singh. 2017. Word transduction for addressing the oov problem in machine translation for similar resource-scarce languages. In *Proceedings of the 13th International Conference on Finite State Methods and Natural Language Processing*, pages 56–63.

Karl Stratos, Michael Collins, and Daniel Hsu. 2016. Unsupervised part-of-speech tagging with anchor hidden markov models. *Transactions of the Association for Computational Linguistics*, 4:245–257.

M. Ines Torres. 2013. Stochastic bi-languages to model dialogs. In *Proceedings of the 11th International Conference on Finite State Methods and Natural Language Processing*, pages 9–17.

Kei Wakabayashi. 2018. Segmentation-based unsupervised phrase detection. In *Proceedings of the 20th International Conference on Information Integration and Web-based Applications & Services*, pages 138–142.

Kei Wakabayashi and Takao Miura. 2012. Forward-backward activation algorithm for hierarchical hidden markov models. In *Advances in Neural Information Processing Systems 25*, pages 1493–1501.

Mengqiu Wang and Christopher D. Manning. 2012. Probabilistic finite state machines for regression-based MT evaluation. In *Proceedings of the 2012 Joint Conference on Empirical Methods in Natural Language Processing and Computational Natural Language Learning*, pages 984–994.

Michèle Weiland, Alan Smaill, and Peter C. Nelson. 2005. Learning musical pitch structures with hierarchical hidden markov models. Technical report, University of Edinburgh.

Shun-Zheng Yu. 2010. Hidden semi-Markov models. *Artificial Intelligence*, 174(2):215–243.

Latin script keyboards for South Asian languages with finite-state normalization

Lawrence Wolf-Sonkin, Vlad Schogol, Brian Roark and Michael Riley
{wolfsonkin,vlads,roark,riley}@google.com
Google Research

Abstract

The use of the Latin script for text entry of South Asian languages is common, even though there is no standard orthography for these languages in the script. We explore several compact finite-state architectures that permit variable spellings of words during mobile text entry. We find that approaches making use of transliteration transducers provide large accuracy improvements over baselines, but that simpler approaches involving a compact representation of many attested alternatives yields much of the accuracy gain. This is particularly important when operating under constraints on model size (e.g., on inexpensive mobile devices with limited storage and memory for keyboard models), and on speed of inference, since people typing on mobile keyboards expect no perceptual delay in keyboard responsiveness.

1 Introduction

Many of the world's writing systems present challenges for machine readable text entry compared with alphabetic writing systems (such as the Latin script used for the English in this paper). For example, a very large character set, such as that used for Chinese, can be impractical to represent on a keyboard requiring direct selection of characters; hence specialized encoding methods are generally used based on smaller symbol sets. For example, the well-known pinyin system for text entry of Chinese relies on Latin alphabetic codes to input Chinese characters. South Asian languages, such as Tamil and Hindi, also use writing systems that, while lacking the thousands of characters as in Chinese, are nonetheless challenging for direct typing (particularly on mobile devices), and hence are frequently entered using the Latin alphabet. In those languages, however, unlike Chinese, there is

no single system that is used for *romanization*, rather individuals typically provide a rough phonetic transcription of the words in the Latin script.

The use of pinyin for Chinese is generally part of a system for converting the text into the native script, and this can also be achieved for keyboards in South Asian languages (Hellsten et al., 2017). However, for these languages, many individuals prefer to simply leave the text in the Latin script rather than converting to the native script. To provide full mobile keyboard functionality in such a scenario – including, e.g., word prediction and completion, and automatic correction of so-called fat finger errors in typing – language model support must be provided. Yet in the absence of a standard orthography, encoding word-to-word dependencies becomes more complicated, since there may be many possible versions of any given word.

In this paper, we examine a few practical alternatives to address the lack of a conventionalized Latin script orthography for use in a finite-state keyboard decoder. We use several different transducers that normalize input romanizations to either a native script word form or a "canonical" Latin script form[1] in order to combine with a word-based language model. To produce Latin script after this normalization, we must produce text from the input tape of these transducers. We also present an alternative method involving a compact representation of a large supplementary lexicon that covers highly likely romanizations of in-vocabulary words. All of these methods provide accuracy improvements over the baseline

---

[1] We use *canonical* in quotes here and elsewhere because there is no standard orthography hence no true canonical form; rather, for each native script word in our lexicon, we choose one romanization as "canonical".

Proceedings of the 14th International Conference on Finite-State Methods and Natural Language Processing, pages 108–117
Dresden, Germany, September 23-25, 2019. ©2019 Association for Computational Linguistics

(fixed vocabulary) method.

In the next section, we give some background on the problem before outlining our new methods. We then present experimental results of keyboard entry simulation for Hindi, in which we demonstrate over 50% relative reduction in error rate[2] over existing baselines.

2 Background and preliminaries

2.1 South Asian romanization

Romanized text entry is widely used in languages, such as Hindi and Arabic, for which there is no agreed-upon adherence to any particular conventionalized representation in the Latin script such as is found in Chinese. South Asian languages written natively in a Brahmic script, including Hindi, Bengali, Tamil and many others, are heavily romanized mainly due to the complexity of typing the scripts. These scripts are abugida (or alphasyllabary) writing systems that are based on consonant/vowel "syllables" (*akṣara*) that pair consonants with a default vowel. Alternative vowels (as well as the lack of a vowel) are designated through the use of various diacritic marks that can appear above, below, or on either side of the consonant (or consonant cluster). This, along with complex multi-consonant ligatures (known as conjuncts), makes direct use of native script keyboards relatively uncommon. An exemplar word in the Devanagari script containing such complex graphemes is given in Figure 1. Romanization is also used for Perso-Arabic scripts in South Asia, such as that used for Urdu, but not presumably due to complexities in representing such scripts on native keyboards, but rather due to historical reasons[3] and perhaps the influence of other regional languages.

As a result of having no conventionalized romanization system, text in, say, romanized Hindi has no standardized orthography, but rather words are usually represented via rough

$$\begin{array}{rcl} \text{ब} & \Rightarrow & \text{ब} \ /ba/ \\ \text{ब}+ \circ & \Rightarrow & \text{ब्} \ /b/ \\ \text{ब्}+ \text{र} & \Rightarrow & \text{ब्र} \ /bra/ \\ \text{ब्र}+ \circ\text{I} & \Rightarrow & \text{ब्रा} \ /br\bar{a}/ \\ \text{ह}+\circ+\text{म}+\circ\text{ी} & \Rightarrow & \text{ह्मी} \ /hm\bar{\imath}/ \\ \text{ब्रा}+\text{ह्मी} & \Rightarrow \text{ब्राह्मी} \ /br\bar{a}hm\bar{\imath}/ \end{array}$$

Figure 1: Demonstration of how the Hindi word ब्राह्मी /brāhmī/, meaning Brahmic, is decomposed into its unicode codepoints as written in Devanagari. Pronunciations are shown between slashes.

phonetic transcriptions in Latin script. For example, the Hindi words संस्कृत and संपूर्ण are commonly romanized as *sanskrit* and *sampuran*, respectively. Both words begin in Devanagari with the grapheme सं which is /sa/ with a diacritic indicating a nasal consonant (such as /n/) in the coda. Note that the nasal becomes either /n/ or /m/ depending on the following consonant,[4] demonstrating how these romanizations are driven by pronunciation rather than from the native orthography. Urdu has the same words, written سنسکرت and سمپورن respectively in the Perso-Arabic script, and they are romanized similarly to the Hindi words, also demonstrating the role of pronunciation rather than writing system in romanization for these languages.[5] In general, due to this lack of a standardized spelling in the Latin script, romanizations may vary due to dialectal variation, regional accent, or simply individual idiosyncrasies.

As a concrete example, a blog entry on the general topic of political corruption on a site run by the India Today Group from 2011 has comments in (1) English; (2) Hindi written in Devanagari (its native script and that is used in the blog post itself); and also extensively in (3) romanized Hindi.[6] One comment begins: "Bhrashtachar aam aadmi se chalu hota hai…", which presumably corresponds to the Devanagari: भ्रष्टाचार आम आदमी से चालू होता है and roughly translates to: "Corruption starts with the common man…" Given that corruption is the overall topic of the blog post, it is unsur-

---

[2]Word-error rate in this setting means recovery of the intended form typed by the user. We take the romanized strings in the validation set as the intended forms, despite spelling variation throughout.

[3]Languages using the Cyrillic script are also frequently romanized. There, and perhaps also for Perso-Arabic scripts, the issue is with historical lack of font and encoding support in certain scenarios.

[4]This is a process known as assimilation.

[5]Note that unlike in Devanagari, Perso-Arabic script Urdu does in fact graphically differentiate these phonetically differentiated onsets, spelling them respectively as سن ⟨sn⟩ and سم ⟨sm⟩.

[6]http://blogs.intoday.in/index.php?option= com_myblog&contentid=62323&show=Removal-of-corruption-from-the-beginning-itself&blogs=2

prising that the Hindi word for this shows up in many comments. It is, however, variously romanized. By our count: 16 times it is romanized as "bhrastachar"; 7 times as "bhrashtachar"; and once each as "barashtachaar", "bharastachar", "bharstachar", "bhastachar" and "bhrstachar". Google Translate provides both a translation and a romanization of the word ("bhrashtaachaar"[7]), a form which interestingly is not found in our (admittedly small) example blog comment sample.

2.2 Transliteration and romanized text

The need to transliterate between writing systems comes up in many application scenarios, but early work on the topic was largely focused on the needs of machine translation and information retrieval due to loanwords and proper names (Knight and Graehl, 1998; Chen et al., 1998; Virga and Khudanpur, 2003; Li et al., 2004). These approaches either explicitly modeled pronunciation in the languages (Knight and Graehl, 1998) or more directly modeled correspondences in the writing systems (Li et al., 2004). Models for machine transliteration have continued to improve, through the use of improved modeling methods including many-to-many substring alignment-based modeling, discriminative decoding, and multilingual multitask learning (Sherif and Kondrak, 2007; Cherry and Suzuki, 2009; Kunchukuttan et al., 2018), or by mining likely transliterations in large corpora (Sajjad et al., 2017). Transliteration models are also being deployed in increasingly challenging use scenarios, such as mixed-script information retrieval (Gupta et al., 2014) or for mobile text entry (Hellsten et al., 2017).

The volume of romanized text in languages that use other writing systems is an acknowledged issue, one which has grown in importance with the advent of SMS messaging and social media, due to the prevalence of romanized input method editors (IMEs) for these languages (Ahmed et al., 2011). The lack of standard orthography and resulting spelling variation found in romanization is also found in other natural language scenarios, such as OCR of historical documents (Garrette and Alpert-Abrams, 2016) and writing of dialectal

Arabic (Habash et al., 2012).

For this study, we make use of Wikipedia data originally written in the native script that has been romanized, and our task is to permit accurate text entry on mobile keyboards, rather than transliteration to the native script or normalization for use in other downstream tasks. In this case "accurate text entry" means fidelity to the intended text, even if that intended text is written without consistent spelling. If the user noisily types "bgrashtachsr" while intending "bhrashtachar", the keyboard should produce "bhrashtachar" not another romanization such as "bhrastachar". Given annotator-romanized Wikipedia text, we evaluate our ability to correctly recognize the actual romanizations used.

2.3 Mobile keyboard decoding

Virtual keyboards of the sort typically used on mobile devices convert a temporal sequence of interactions with the touchscreen (taps or continuous gestures) into text. Like speech recognition or optical character recognition, the mapping of noisy, continuous input signals to discrete text strings involves stochastic inference; further, given the low required latency during typing, models must be compact enough to run on the local device and inference with them must be fast. For this reason, the kinds of finite-state methods that have been used for speech recognition and OCR have also been used for this task (Ouyang et al., 2017). The work we present here will be in the context of such an FST-based keyboard decoder.

For touch typing, where the input consists of a sequence of taps, we designate with the term *literal* the string corresponding to the actual keys touched. The intended string may differ, due to such phenomena as so-called "fat finger" errors, i.e., hitting a neighboring key, omitting a key or including an extra tap.

Analogous to the acoustic model in speech recognition, which assigns probabilities to the continuous waveform given a sequence of phones, such a decoder makes use of a *spatial* model, assigning probabilities to the sequence of taps (or gestures) given a sequence of letters. Taps, for example, are modeled in Ouyang et al. (2017) with Gaussians centered on the middle of each key. Costs are thus assigned to alternative possible intended character strings

---

[7]translate.google.com/#en/hi/Corruption

which may have substitutions, deletions and insertions relative to the literal string.

In speech recognition, phones are typically split in the acoustic model based on the surrounding context, in order to capture co-articulation effects and other influences on the acoustics associated with a particular intended phone. Similarly, in the spatial model, keys are typically split based on the previous touched key, which we will term *bikey* representation. So, at the start of a word, the letter 'b' will be represented as '_b', whereas after the letter 'a', it would be represented as 'ab'. Later we will have methods that must be aware of the input representation.

The spatial model cost and the language model cost are combined by the decoder to score competing output strings. Typically these scored string alternatives will be compared to the literal string and only selected if the difference in score is above some threshold, to avoid spurious changes to what the user typed (Ouyang et al., 2017). To accept any string (including any possible literal string), a loop transition for every character with some fixed cost can be included at the unigram state (the base of the smoothing recursion, see Roark et al., 2012), so that every string in Σ^* has non-zero probability.

In addition to decoding for auto-correction, the language model may also be used for word prediction and completion, i.e., showing suggestions in a small dynamic portion of the keyboard. In this paper, we do not have much to say about this part of the process, other than to point out when its demands make certain approaches more complicated than others.

Such an architecture has also been used for transliteration from Latin script input to native script output (Hellsten et al., 2017), by interposing a finite-state transducer (FST) between the spatial model (defined over the Latin script) and the language model (defined over native script words). Some of our methods are related to these, although the output of the keyboard does not change script.

3   Methods

3.1   Word transliteration models

For both off-line model training and on-line transliteration-based decoding methods, we make use of pair n-gram (also known as "joint multi-gram") modeling methods (Bisani and Ney, 2008), which Hellsten et al. (2017) also use to train their transliteration models. Given a lexicon with words in the native script and possible romanizations of those words (see §4.1 for specifics on our data), expectation maximization is used to derive pairwise symbol alignments. For example, भ्रष्टाचार and "bhrashtachar" may yield a pairwise symbol alignment of:

भ:b ◌्:h र:r ϵ:a ष:s ◌्:h ट:t ◌ा:a च:c ϵ:h ◌ा:a र:r

where each symbol is composed of an input (native script) unicode codepoint (or ϵ, denoting the empty string) and an output (Latin script) unicode codepoint (or ϵ). These symbol pairs then become tokens in an n-gram language model encoded as an automaton. Finally, the automaton is converted to a transducer with native script on one side and Latin script on the other.

This model provides a joint probability distribution over input:output sequence pairs, e.g., for a word भ्रष्टाचार and a romanization "bhrashtachar", i.e., $P($भ्रष्टाचार$, \mathrm{bhrashtachar})$. As Hellsten et al. (2017) note, within most decoding settings that combine with a language model on the native script side, a conditional probability is actually what is needed: $P(\mathrm{bhrashtachar} \mid$ भ्रष्टाचार$)$. We refer readers to that paper for details on how to incorporate the appropriate normalization into an FST-based decoder. We use similar methods, permitting the model to be used in both on-line and off-line scenerios.

Note that it is trivial to swap the input and output symbols for such a model, either by changing the ordering of the pair symbols in the training data or simply inverting the resulting WFST. The same model can thus be used for transliteration from input Latin script to native script forms; or from input native script to romanizations.

For example, suppose T is a transliteration transducer (Latin script on the input side and native script on the output side) and S is an automaton that accepts a single native script word w for which we wish to find likely romanizations. If we compose $T \circ S$, this yields a transducer encoding alternative Latin/native script string relations with w as the output string. We can convert this transducer into an automaton accepting alternative romanizations of w by *projecting* all transitions onto their input labels, i.e., preserving only the input label on every transition. Some transitions in this acceptor of alternative romanizations might be epsilons, so we can remove epsilon transitions (Mohri, 2002), then select the n most likely paths (Mohri and Riley, 2002). All of these operations are general operations supported by the OpenFst library (Allauzen et al., 2007). The n unique shortest paths in $\text{RMEPSILON}(\text{PROJECTINPUT}(T \circ S))$ are the n most likely romanizations of w.

3.2 Baseline fixed-vocabulary system

Our baseline system relies on automatic romanization of native script language model training data. Using a transliteration transducer, trained as described in §3.1, each word in our fixed vocabulary is assigned a "canonical" (i.e., best scoring) romanization as its Latin script representation. We then replace the native script words in our language model training corpus with their canonical romanizations and retrain the model, yielding a language model over strings in the Latin script.

If the distribution over romanized alternatives for भ्रष्टाचार in the blog comments that were mentioned in §2.1 represented the distribution provided by our model, then "bhrastachar" would become its canonical romanization. Alternative spellings (e.g., bhrash̲tachar) would only match that word via the character loop method (mentioned in §2.3) permitting the omitted letter, generally with a cost.

3.3 Compact supplemental unigram

Not every substituted, inserted or omitted tap is created equal when it comes to likely romanization variants. For example, as we have seen in our running example, the use of 'h' to indicate aspiration for consonants such as भ may or may not be used in romanizations. Similarly long vowels and geminates are sometimes represented by doubling of Latin symbols, but often not. These variants are not random in the way that a character loop model would score them. One method for adding likely alternative romanizations is to simply add them as alternative word forms to the language model. These romanizations can be computed using the method outlined in §3.1.

However, adding many alternative romanizations of the same word can become space prohibitive, particulary for on-device methods, where storage and active memory usage are both at a premium. It is possible, however, to provide a very compact encoding specifically of the words stored exclusively in the unigram, i.e., words that are neither prefixes nor suffixes of any higher order n-grams in the language model. We achieve this in two steps. First, we build two automata that accept all and only this set of words: a weighted automaton W, which weights the path for each word with the appropriate cost for that word within the language model; and an unweighted automaton A which encodes the same set of words as W and has been determinized and minimized. Next we create a weighted automaton W_m that has the same topology as A, but which is weighted to minimize the KL-divergence (Kullback and Leibler, 1951) between W and W_m, using methods from Suresh et al. (2019). This is an approximation of the distribution represented in W over a much more compact topology. The methods to perform this approximation are part of the open-source `OpenGrm` stochastic automata (`SFst`) library (available at `http://www.opengrm.org`). We then integrate W_m into the larger language model automaton, with the unigram state of the language model serving as both the start and final state for the paths corresponding to those in W_m. This can be straightforwardly accomplished by using the *Replace* operation in the OpenFst library (`http://www.openfst.org`).

3.4 Transducer to canonical form

As we noted in §3.1, we build pair n-gram transliteration models between native script and romanized forms. In a similar way, we can build a transducer between *canonical* romanized forms and alternative romanizations. To re-use our example, if "bhrastachar" is the canonical romanization, and "bhrash̲tachar" is another attested form, we can use expectation maximization to derive an alignment:

b:b h:h r:r a:a s:s ε:h t:t a:a c:c h:h a:a r:r

A pair n-gram model built from this would allow weighted transduction from input romanizations to the canonical form, which corresponds to tokens in the language model. We

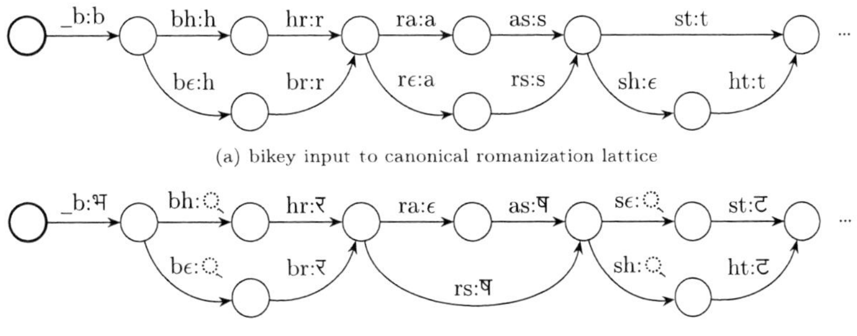

(a) bikey input to canonical romanization lattice

(b) bikey input to native script lattice

Figure 2: Lattices illustrating how reading from the input tape rather than the output tape can provide support for varied romanized input, for either native script or "canonical" romanized output.

can thus use a transducer much in the way described in Hellsten et al. (2017) to transliterate[8] between variant romanizations and the chosen canonical romanizations.

There is, however, a complication with using this method within the keyboard, in contrast to the earlier described methods. If the keyboard actually performed the transduction from input romanization to the canonical Latin script form, then it would enforce a normalization on the user's spelling of the word. If the user types "bhrashtachar", this system, as it has been described, will output "bhrastachar" (without the 'h'), since that is our chosen canonical form. However, there is no standard orthography in the Latin script for Hindi, i.e., there is no correct spelling. Our canonical form is chosen for convenience to be the highest scoring romanization from the model. Even if we were to choose some kind of generally common version as our canonical form, however, for any given individual we may end up coercing the output of a form that they disprefer. Instead, we would like to allow them to maintain their preferred form, i.e., they should be able to type their intended string.

Because the decoder is based on WFSTs, we have a particularly straightforward solution to this: output the string from the input tape rather than the output tape. That is, we use the transducer within the decoder just as is done in Hellsten et al. (2017), however we output the string on the input side corresponding to the best scoring solution. In this way, we derive the modeling benefit from the language

model without imposing a canonical romanization on the user. Note that it would be possible to perform this large composition and project onto input labels off-line rather than on-the-fly, but the size of the off-line composition is prohibitively large for on-device operation, for reasons similar to those discussed in Hellsten et al. (2017). The output labels are thus preserved in one of the transducers used during on-the-fly composition.

Figure 2a shows a WFST lattice representing alternative paths through the decoder, with bikey inputs and canonical romanization outputs.[9] For convenience, bikey representations of outputs with no corresponding input display the previous key followed by an epsilon, e.g., 'bε' signifies an omitted key following a 'b'. Note that every path through this lattice has an output string corresponding to "bhrast", the prefix of the canonical romanization of our running example. Different paths represent different input string variations corresponding to this word.

To read a string off of the input side of such a lattice, we take the last symbol of the bikey at each transition, with ε representing the empty string. In such a way, the presented lattice encodes the alternatives *bhrast*, *brast*, *bhrsht*, *bhrasht*, etc. Whichever path has the lowest cost during decoding would be the version that is produced by the keyboard.

3.5 Transducer to native script

If, as discussed in the previous section, we output from the input tape of our WFSTs, then

---

[8]Note this isn't quite transliteration in the usual sense since the strings stay in the same writing system, but we co-opt the term since Hellsten et al. (2017) used an identical architecture for transliteration.

[9]Note that, during decoding, partial results may be displayed to the user to improve responsiveness, so these figures should be taken as an illustration not a depiction of the decoding process.

there is no strong reason[10] to have Latin script on the output tape. Instead, we use a native script language model and the same sort of pair n-gram transducer as used in a transliterating keyboard, then simply read the result from the input tape.

Figure 2b has a set of paths, all of which produce the native script word prefix (भट) on the output side. As with the other lattice, the paths represent different input romanizations corresponding to this string, which can be recovered from the transition labels.

3.6 Native script OOV modeling

One question we have only briefly touched upon is how to deal with out-of-vocabulary (OOV) items when using a transliteration transducer, i.e., words not in the language model being used for decoding. The simple default method is to have a *character loop* at the unigram state of the language model that accepts each character. That loop then gets an approximated language model cost from the transliteration transducer, to the extent that that model provides a joint probability of input and output strings. Alternatively, we can build a character language model, or even more complicated data structures, to assign probabilities to OOV words.

We opt to follow an approach that provides flexibility to move between two extremes, the most permissive but least accurate being the character loop, and the most restrictive but most accurate being a weighted character trie. The trade-off is controlled by a single parameter N, which is the number of states we wish to use to represent the OOV model. We start with a large collection of native script words and their unigram probabilities. We first build a weighted character trie representing these words. The trie is weight-pushed so that the probability mass of a state is seen as early as possible by the decoder. Next we rank each state of the trie by the total probability mass of all words reachable from that state. Finally we remove any state beyond the first N

states in the ranking. All transitions from retained states to removed states are redirected to a state with the original character loop. In this way, we provide a mechanism to smoothly scale between a full trie representation (no states removed) down to a single-state character loop (all states removed), and everything in between. This approach, like the character loop baseline, permits arbitrary word-forms to be typed, but it does so in a way that better captures the distribution of word forms in the language. The pruned trie provides an approximation to the distribution in the full trie, which permits a graceful tradeoff between the size of the encoding and the quality of the approximation.

4 Experiments

4.1 Data

Transliteration models were trained from a proprietary lexicon of Hindi words and attested romanizations, consisting of approximately 110,000 native script words and on average 3.1 romanizations per word. These aligned Devanagari–Latin word pairs were used to build a WFST transliteration model using methods detailed in §3.1. We built pair 3-gram models, pruned to contain just 110,000 n-grams prior to conversion to a transducer.

Language models, both in Devanagari and canonical Latin forms, were trained on a large and diverse set of Devanagari Hindi text collected from the web, and were not trained for any specific domain. The 150,000 most frequent words in the training set were retained in the language model, and trigram word-based models were trained and then pruned to retain just 750,000 n-grams, so as to fit within on-device space limits.[11] For a single experiment, we additionally considered a language model containing 1,500,000 n-grams, double the n-gram count of the others.

For methods using a transducer to native script within decoding, the language model is in the native script; whereas in other conditions, the language model is in the Latin script. To train the Latin script language

---

[10]This is not strictly speaking true, since, as is pointed out in §2.3, the models may also be used for word prediction and completion. In order to seamlessly integrate with such processes, predicted and completed words would have to be presented in the Latin script, hence some additional information would need to be provided for each word in the vocabulary.

[11]Our work as targeted South Asian languages, where inexpensive smartphones are the norm, hence, as mentioned in Hellsten et al. (2017) we have generally targeted total model sizes around 10MB.

Method	Word error rate (%)	Tap avg ms	Avg active states	arcs	Model size (MB)
Literal	45.0	-	-	-	-
Fixed vocabulary (canonical only)	22.6	0.95	164.8	417.9	4.9
Fixed vocab + supplemental unigram	12.4	1.00	122.3	404.4	10.6
Fixed vocab + transducer to canonical	12.9	1.01	75.6	225.6	9.3
Transducer to native script	13.1	0.95	66.7	184.7	11.0
Transducer to native + OOV model	**10.5**	1.08	67.5	181.8	11.2

(a) An operating point of approximately 1.0ms per tap

Method	Word error rate (%)	Tap avg ms	Avg active states	arcs	Model size (MB)
Literal	45.0	-	-	-	-
Fixed vocabulary (canonical only)	22.5	0.59	71.8	202.5	4.9
Fixed vocab + supplemental unigram	**12.1**	0.53	38.1	132.0	10.6
Fixed vocab + transducer to canonical	14.1	0.54	24.4	80.9	9.3
Transducer to native script	14.0	0.60	31.8	91.6	11.0
Transducer to native + OOV model	12.3	0.54	19.7	54.9	11.2

(b) An operating point of approximately 0.55ms per tap

Table 1: The word error rate for the decoding of noisy touchpoints into Latin script strings at two operating points along the speed–accuracy tradeoff. The average number of milliseconds required per character as well as the average number of states and transitions active during decoding and the model size in megabytes are listed. The best performing (lowest) word error rate method for each operating point is bolded.

model for Hindi, each word in the vocabulary (each of which is in Devanagari), is replaced with its "canonical" romanization, i.e., the highest probability romanization according to the trained transliteration model.

Devanagari script sentences from Hindi Wikipedia were manually romanized by native speakers, and 4,000 of these (for a total of 36,027 word tokens) were used as our development set for validation of the methods presented above.

4.2 Evaluation

To evaluate our methods, we simulate touch points of a tapping keyboard as follows. For each symbol in the (Latin script) input strings, we sample a touch point from Gaussian distributions in two dimensions, with mean value at the center of the key. To establish how much noise is introduced by this method, we evaluate the error rate of simply emitting the literal sequence, i.e., the symbols associated with the keys that our noisy touch points actually fall within. Improvements over the literal baseline are due to decoder auto-correction.

The resulting touchpoints are then fed into the decoder under each of our conditions, and the strings output from the decoder are then compared with the original text strings, which are taken to be the intended strings. As mentioned elsewhere in the paper, the goal is to allow users to type their intended strings, without normalizing away their versions of the romanized words. Thus we measure word-error

rate versus the reference version in the romanized string. Note that the keyboard decoder has various meta-parameters that can impact, e.g., the speed–accuracy trade-off. In addition to sweeping over such parameters for a given method, as shown in Figure 3, we compare performance across the methods at comparable operating points (in terms of average milliseconds per character) in Tables 1a and 1b.

Note that the absolute numerical values of the latencies are not meaningful, just the comparisons between the latencies. As discussed in Hellsten et al. (2017) and mentioned earlier, latencies must be low enough that no lag in keyboard responsiveness is perceived, and target values on device are often around 20ms per tap. However this must be the case also for inexpensive devices with low processing power, and the decision to deploy a model would depend on device trials. For the purposes of this paper, however, we just report values on a single device that can be used for comparison purposes. The operating points chosen for the Tables are two that are plausible candidates for use on such inexpensive devices.

4.3 Results

While analyzing the entire operating curve as shown in Figure 3 gives us an idea of the full potential of any particular model, in a resource-constrained scenario such as a mobile keyboard, we are ultimately restricted to working at a particular operating point on the speed–accuracy tradeoff. At a higher operat-

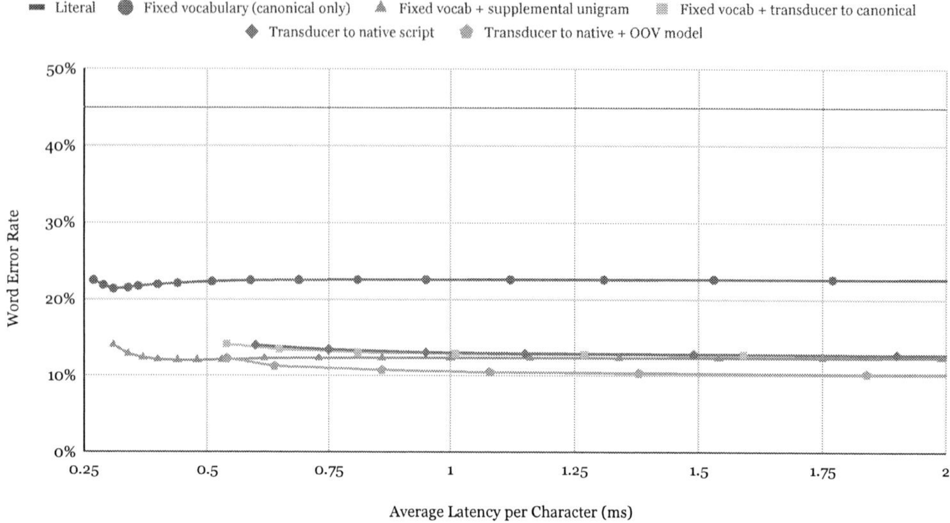

Figure 3: Word error rate versus latency for the models presented in §3 as evaluated on simulated touchpoints for Latin Hindi text. Various decoding-time parametrizations were explored to demonstrate the word error rate–latency tradeoff. The literal baseline shows how accurate the decoding procedure would be without a model at all on this data set.

ing point of 1.0ms per tap (as in Table 1a), the native script transducer with OOV model is the best option, bringing the WER down from 22.6% for the fixed vocabulary to 10.5%, a substantial 54% relative decrease. This does come at the cost of model size, with the model taking up 2.3x as much space. For the case where one chooses a lower operating point such as 0.55ms per tap (as in Table 1b), the supplemental unigram wins out providing a 46% relative decrease in word error rate compared to the fixed vocabulary baseline's WER of 22.5%; all in a relatively compact model taking up only 2.2x more space than the baseline. Additionally, we note that at all operating points, a doubly-sized fixed-vocabulary system (described in §4.1) in fact achieves a slightly worse WER compared with a commensurately sized, otherwise identical language model. We take this as evidence that this model's inability to capture the variant orthographic forms found in this domain is not corrected by simply increasing the model's n-gram count.

Looking at Figure 3, in the limit as latency increases, we find that while the supplemental unigram, fixed vocabulary with transducer to canonical, and transducer to native script converge to similar word error rates of about $12.4 \sim 12.8\%$, the transducer to native with OOV model can reach even 10.3% WER.

5 Summary

We have presented results for various approaches for handling romanized text entry for South Asian languages within an FST-based mobile keyboard decoder. Compared to baseline methods that naïvely rely upon a single canonical romanization for each word in the vocabulary, we can achieve 54% relative error rate reduction by making use of a transliteration transducer and reading the output from the input tape. Even at very constrained operating points, our best method cuts the error rate nearly in half.

Further, we have demonstrated that an alternative of compactly encoding a large supplemental lexicon in the language model, consisting of alternative romanizations of words, is competitive to the transducer-based normalization, at some space savings. This method has the further virtue of relatively straightforward support for other parts of the keyboard application – such as word prediction and completion, as well as personalization mechanisms – since the decoder outputs from its output tape as in typical operation. Deploying methods presented here that read from the input tape into a keyboard app requires additional integration with these other modules.

References

Umair Z Ahmed, Kalika Bali, Monojit Choudhury, and VB Sowmya. 2011. Challenges in designing input method editors for Indian languages: The role of word-origin and context. In *Proceedings of the Workshop on Advances in Text Input Methods (WTIM 2011)*, pages 1–9.

Cyril Allauzen, Michael Riley, Johan Schalkwyk, Wojciech Skut, and Mehryar Mohri. 2007. Openfst: A general and efficient weighted finite-state transducer library. In *International Conference on Implementation and Application of Automata*, pages 11–23. Springer.

Maximilian Bisani and Hermann Ney. 2008. Joint-sequence models for grapheme-to-phoneme conversion. *Speech Communication*, 50(5):434–451.

Hsin-Hsi Chen, Sheng-Jie Hueng, Yung-Wei Ding, and Shih-Chung Tsai. 1998. Proper name translation in cross-language information retrieval. In *Proceedings of the 17th international conference on Computational linguistics-Volume 1*, pages 232–236. Association for Computational Linguistics.

Colin Cherry and Hisami Suzuki. 2009. Discriminative substring decoding for transliteration. In *Proceedings of the 2009 Conference on Empirical Methods in Natural Language Processing: Volume 3-Volume 3*, pages 1066–1075. Association for Computational Linguistics.

Dan Garrette and Hannah Alpert-Abrams. 2016. An unsupervised model of orthographic variation for historical document transcription. In *Proceedings of the 2016 Conference of the North American Chapter of the Association for Computational Linguistics: Human Language Technologies*, pages 467–472.

Parth Gupta, Kalika Bali, Rafael E Banchs, Monojit Choudhury, and Paolo Rosso. 2014. Query expansion for mixed-script information retrieval. In *Proceedings of the 37th international ACM SIGIR conference on Research & development in information retrieval*, pages 677–686. ACM.

Nizar Habash, Mona T Diab, and Owen Rambow. 2012. Conventional orthography for dialectal Arabic. In *LREC*, pages 711–718.

Lars Hellsten, Brian Roark, Prasoon Goyal, Cyril Allauzen, Françoise Beaufays, Tom Ouyang, Michael Riley, and David Rybach. 2017. Transliterated mobile keyboard input via weighted finite-state transducers. In *Proceedings of the 13th International Conference on Finite State Methods and Natural Language Processing (FSMNLP 2017)*, pages 10–19.

Kevin Knight and Jonathan Graehl. 1998. Machine transliteration. *Computational Linguistics*, 24(4):599–612.

Solomon Kullback and Richard A Leibler. 1951. On information and sufficiency. *The annals of mathematical statistics*, 22(1):79–86.

Anoop Kunchukuttan, Mitesh Khapra, Gurneet Singh, and Pushpak Bhattacharyya. 2018. Leveraging orthographic similarity for multilingual neural transliteration. *Transactions of the Association of Computational Linguistics*, 6:303–316.

Haizhou Li, Min Zhang, and Jian Su. 2004. A joint source-channel model for machine transliteration. In *Proceedings of the 42nd Annual Meeting of the Association for Computational Linguistics (ACL-04)*, pages 159–166.

Mehryar Mohri. 2002. Generic ϵ-removal and input ϵ-normalization algorithms for weighted transducers. *International Journal of Foundations of Computer Science*, 13(01):129–143.

Mehryar Mohri and Michael Riley. 2002. An efficient algorithm for the n-best-strings problem. In *Seventh International Conference on Spoken Language Processing*.

Tom Ouyang, David Rybach, Françoise Beaufays, and Michael Riley. 2017. Mobile keyboard input decoding with finite-state transducers. *arXiv preprint arXiv:1704.03987*.

Brian Roark, Richard Sproat, Cyril Allauzen, Michael Riley, Jeffrey Sorensen, and Terry Tai. 2012. The OpenGrm open-source finite-state grammar software libraries. In *Proceedings of the ACL 2012 System Demonstrations*, pages 61–66.

Hassan Sajjad, Helmut Schmid, Alexander Fraser, and Hinrich Schütze. 2017. Statistical models for unsupervised, semi-supervised, and supervised transliteration mining. *Computational Linguistics*, 43(2):349–375.

Tarek Sherif and Grzegorz Kondrak. 2007. Substring-based transliteration. In *Proceedings of the 45th Annual Meeting of the Association of Computational Linguistics*, pages 944–951.

Ananda Theertha Suresh, Brian Roark, Michael Riley, and Vlad Schogol. 2019. Distilling weighted finite automata from arbitrary probabilistic models. In *Proceedings of the 14th International Conference on Finite State Methods and Natural Language Processing (FSMNLP 2019)*.

Paola Virga and Sanjeev Khudanpur. 2003. Transliteration of proper names in cross-lingual information retrieval. In *Proceedings of the ACL 2003 workshop on Multilingual and mixed-language named entity recognition-Volume 15*, pages 57–64. Association for Computational Linguistics.

Transition-Based Coding and Formal Language Theory for Ordered Digraphs

Anssi Yli-Jyrä

University of Helsinki, P.O. Box 4, FIN-00014, Finland

`anssi.yli-jyra@helsinki.fi`

Abstract

Transition-based parsing of natural language uses transition systems to build directed annotation graphs (digraphs) for sentences. In this paper, we define, for an arbitrary ordered digraph, a unique decomposition and a corresponding linear encoding that are associated bijectively with each other via a new transition system. These results give us an efficient and succinct representation for digraphs and sets of digraphs. Based on the system and our analysis of its syntactic properties, we give structural bounds under which the set of encoded digraphs is restricted and becomes a context-free or a regular string language. The context-free restriction is essentially a superset of the encodings used previously to characterize properties of noncrossing digraphs and to solve maximal subgraphs problems. The regular restriction with a tight bound is shown to capture the Universal Dependencies v2.4 treebanks in linguistics.

1 Introduction

Transition systems have been a widely used mechanism in language understanding, cognitive modelling of natural language processing and syntactic and semantic parsing of sentences. The combination of high parsing speed of transition systems with the accuracy of the attached statistical models have paved the way for practical applications of parsing and similar data transformations enabled by these systems (Yamada and Matsumoto, 2003; Nivre and Scholz, 2004; Zhang and Nivre, 2011; Chen and Manning, 2014; Dyer et al., 2015; Andor et al., 2016; Kiperwasser and Goldberg, 2016; Shi et al., 2017). Transition systems may also be used to encode dependency trees, DAGs and other ordered digraphs, and to connect these to the classical formal language theory and to the problems of *graph representation* (Turán, 1984; Farzan and Munro, 2013; Yli-Jyrä, 2019), *graph enumeration* (Pólya, 1937; Conte et al., 2018; Yli-Jyrä, 2019), *integer sequence discovery* (Hoppe and Petrone, 2016; Yli-Jyrä and Gómez-Rodríguez, 2017), *maximum subgraph inference* (Conte et al., 2019; Yli-Jyrä and Gómez-Rodríguez, 2017), *algebraic representations of graph queries* (Courcelle, 1990; Ogawa, 2004; Yli-Jyrä and Gómez-Rodríguez, 2017), *encoder-decoder parsing* (Vinyals et al., 2015; Strzyz et al., 2019) and *parsing as sequence labeling* (Gómez-Rodríguez and Vilares, 2018).

The study of transition systems in general ranges from Turing complete transition systems (Woods, 1970; Goldin et al., 2004; Thomas, 2002) to well-understood transition systems that build projective dependency structures, context-free parse trees and noncrossing graphs (Nivre, 2003, 2004; Goldberg and Elhadad, 2010; Kuhlmann et al., 2011; Sagae and Tsujii, 2008; Honnibal and Johnson, 2015). The need to model non-local dependencies and crossing edges in parses have motivated the study of transition systems that balance the computational complexity and the coverage of the possible outputs. Many of these systems are extensions of stack-based transition systems (Attardi, 2006; Nivre, 2009; Gómez-Rodríguez and Nivre, 2013; de Lhoneux et al., 2017; Qi and Manning, 2017; Gómez-Rodríguez et al., 2018) but there are also some proposals for transition systems that are based, solely or additionally, on some other memory model, such as a shack, a list, registers, a set, or a cache (Kornai and Tuza, 1992; Covington, 2000;

Proceedings of the 14th International Conference on Finite-State Methods and Natural Language Processing, pages 118–131
Dresden, Germany, September 23-25, 2019. ©2019 Association for Computational Linguistics

Choi and McCallum, 2013; Pitler and McDonald, 2015; Fernández-González and Gómez-Rodríguez, 2018; Gildea et al., 2018; Vilares and Gómez-Rodríguez, 2018; Coavoux and Cohen, 2019).

In this paper, we present a transition system that implements an efficient, invertible function between its action sequences and arbitrary ordered digraphs. The action sequences of the system can also viewed as strings of balanced brackets, constituting formal languages that have elegant Chomsky-Schützenberger representations and many desirable characteristics of input-driven languages. The transition-based transformation between the relational and sequential representations of digraphs opens a possibility to apply classical formal language theory of subsets of free monoids to the classes of digraphs.

Our transition system takes advantage of a new kind of decomposition of a digraph: the *rope decomposition* views the underlying graph as a union of subgraphs what we call *ropes*. The longest edge of a rope shares exactly one endpoint with each of the other edges in it.

The theoretical notions of rope decompositions and the new transition system are introduced in Sections 3-4. The action sequences of the transition system are related to formal languages in Sections 5-6. Sections 7-8 contain corpus-based empirical evaluation and a discussion that argues that the developed encoding for digraphs contributes to the work in some related and important research areas in graph theory and computer science.

2 Basic Definitions

Denote the empty string with ϵ. Denote transpose of a binary relation X as X^T. Define the composition of two binary relations X, Y as $X \circ Y = \{(x, z) \mid (x, y) \in X, (y, z) \in Y\}$. Abbreviate an assignment $S \leftarrow S \cup T$ as $S \overset{\cup}{\leftarrow} T$. Let V_n denote the finite set of integers $\{1, ..., n\}$. Let the parameter $d \in \{<, >, <>\}$ indicate the choice between leftward, rightward and bidirectional orientation of arcs in actions that produce these arcs.

A *(finite ordered) graph* is a pair (V_n, E) where V_n is a finite set of ordered vertices and $E \subseteq \{(u, v) \in V_n \times V_n \mid u < v\}$ is a set of edges. For each edge $(i, j) \in E$,

we call i the left index and j the right index of the edge. A *(finite ordered) digraph* is a pair (V_n, A) where V_n is a set of vertices and $A \subseteq \{(u, v) \in V_n \times V_n \mid u \neq v\}$ is a set of arcs. The underlying graph of a digraph (V_n, A) is the graph (V_n, E_A), where $E_A = \{(i, j) \mid (i, j) \in A \cup A^T, i < j\}$.

3 New Notions

3.1 Rope Cover

Definition 3.1. Let (V_n, E) be an ordered graph. In this graph, edge (h, k), where $h < k$, is a *(properly-longer shared-endpoint) covering edge* for a shorter edge (i, j) if either $h = i$ and $i < j < k$, or $j = k$ and $h < i < j$. Denote this situation by $(h, k) : (i, j)$.

Definition 3.2. A subset $R \subseteq E$ is a *rope cover* of the graph (V_n, E) if, for every edge $e \in E \backslash R$, there is an edge $c \in R$ such that $c : e$. Moreover, R is a *proper rope cover (PRC)* if is there is no edges $c_1, c_2 \in R$ s.t. $c_1 : c_2$.

Proposition 3.1. *Any element in a PRC can be identified by specifying either its left index or its right index.*

Proposition 3.2. *Every graph has a PRC.*

Theorem 3.3. *The PRC is unique.*

Proof. Let (V_n, E) be an arbitrary graph and let $R, R' \subseteq E$ be two PRCs of the graph. Assuming that $R \neq R'$ and that there is $(x_0, y_0) \in R \backslash R'$, we show, by induction, that there is an infinite sequence of distinct edges $(x_0, y_0), (x_2, y_2), (x_4, y_4), ... \in R \backslash R'$ and $(x_1, y_1), (x_3, y_3), (x_5, y_5), ... \in R' \backslash R$ where $(x_{i+1}, y_{i+1}) : (x_i, y_i)$ for every $i \geq 0$. To prove the required induction steps, there is, by the definition of a PRC, a covering edge (x_{i+1}, y_{i+1}) in $R' \backslash R$ for every edge $(x_i, y_i) \in R \backslash R'$, and there is a covering edge $(x_{i+1}, y_{i+1}) \in R \backslash R'$ for every edge $(x_i, y_i) \in R' \backslash R$. Such an infinite sequence of distinct edges requires E to be infinite. By contradiction, the PRC of the graph is unique. $\square$

Definition 3.3. For graph (V_n, E) with a PRC R, the *rope-thickness of a vertex* $i \in V_{n-1}$ is the number of edges $(h, j) \in R$ satisfying $h \leq i < j$. The *rope-thickness of the graph* is the maximum over the rope-thicknesses of all vertices $i \in V_{n-1}$ in the graph.

Lemma 3.4. *For any graph of n vertices, its PRC is constructed in $O(n^3)$.*

Proof. Let (V_n, E) be a graph. To construct the PRC, start with $R_0 = \emptyset$ and $E_0 = E$. Given R_i and E_i, $i \geq 0$, construct R_{i+1} as the set all edges in E_i that do not have a covering edge in E_i, and E_{i+1} as the set of all edges in E_i that do not have a covering edge in R_{i+1}. Each such iteration is computed in $O(n^2)$. Clearly, $E_{i+1} \subsetneq E_i$ unless $E_i = \emptyset$, and $E_{\lfloor n/2 \rfloor} = \emptyset$. The PRC of the graph is the set $R = R_1 \cup R_2 \cup ... \cup R_{\lfloor n/2 \rfloor}$, and it is constructed in $O(n^3)$ time. $\qquad\square$

Corollary 3.5. *The rope thickness of a graph can be computed in cubic time.*

Example (4) is a graph $([6], \{(1,6),(1,5),(2,5),(3,5),(4,5)\})$ for which we obtain sets

$$R_0 = \{\} \qquad E_0 = E \qquad (1)$$
$$R_1 = \{(1,6)\} \quad E_1 = \{(2,5),(3,5),(4,5)\} \quad (2)$$
$$R_2 = \{(2,5)\} \quad E_2 = \{\} \qquad (3)$$

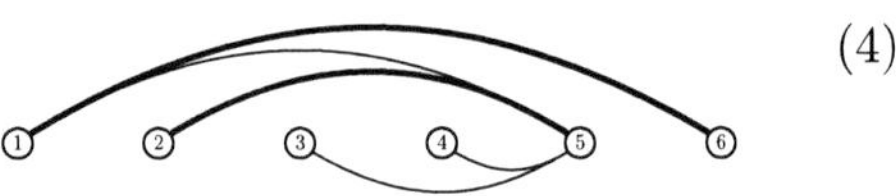

$$(4)$$

Convention 3.4 ("LEFT INDEX"). We will sometimes refer to the edges in a PRC by their left indices (see Proposition 3.1).

Convention 3.5 ("INDIRECT EDGES"). When an edge (i,j) has a covering edge (h,j), $h < i < j$, we refer to the edge (i,j) indirectly, via the pair (i,h) where h is the LEFT INDEX of the covering edge.

The PRC of the graph (4) comprises the edges $\{(1,6),(2,5)\}$, while the remaining edges are covered by these. Edge $(1,5)$ is a usual edge, and there are INDIRECT EDGES, $(3,2)$ and $(4,2)$, that we draw under the vertices. The rope thickness of vertices $2-4$ is two, which is also the maximum for the whole graph.

3.2 Ropes

Definition 3.6. An ordered graph (V_n, E) is called a *rope* if $n = 1$ or the PRC of the graph is $\{(1,n)\}$. This is *complete* if $E = \{(i,n) \mid 1 \leq i < n\} \cup \{(1,j) \mid 1 < j \leq n\}$.

Ropes can be used in algorithms that construct graphs while processing vertices. Example (5) shows a digraph whose underlying graph is a complete rope. Some of its edges would cross one another if the edges were drawn above a line containing the vertices.

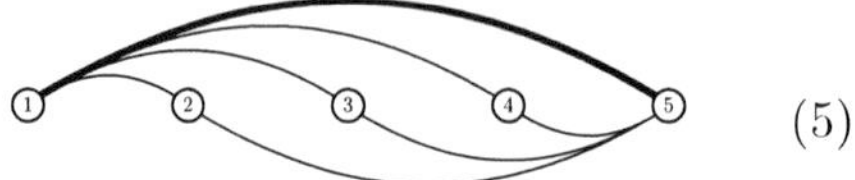

$$(5)$$

Two-way algorithms can build a complete rope in two passes with a vertex counter and one memory unit that contains a reference to one index of the covering edge. After memorizing the left index of the covering edge to variable x, such an algorithm processes vertices 2 to 5 in Example (5) and builds edges $(x,2)$, $(x,3)$, $(x,4)$ and $(x,5)$. During the backward pass over the vertices, the algorithm saves the right index of the covering edge to variable x and builds edges $(4,x)$, $(3,x)$, and $(2,x)$.

One-way algorithms process each vertex only once as their output can represent the edges (i,n), $2 \leq i \leq n-1$, in Example (5) indirectly, by a reference to the left index of the respective covering edge. In the output, the edge $(2,5)$ is represented as an INDIRECT EDGE $(2,1)$ where 1 identifies the LEFT INDEX of the covering edge $(1,5)$. After processing the vertices, the composition of $(2,1)$ and $(1,5)$ is computed to obtain the actual edge $(2,5)$.

3.3 Rope Assignment

Theorem 3.6. *There are graphs where an edge has two distinct covering edges in the PRC.*

Proof. The PRC of the graph of Example (6) is $\{(1,3),(2,4)\}$.

$$(6)$$

The edge $(2,3)$ is covered by the edge $(1,3)$ with which it shares the right index, and by the edge $(2,4)$ with which it shares the left index. $\qquad\square$

When an edge has two covering edges, we need a consistent policy for treating them. In (6), we can *assign* the edge $(2,3)$ to either of the covering edges $(1,3)$, $(2,4)$, or both.

Convention 3.7 ("Earliest"). We adopt a convention according to which the ambiguity between two possible covering edges is resolved by assigning the edge to the earliest available covering edge.

By Convention 3.7, the arc $(2,3)$ in Example (6) will be assigned to the Earliest covering edge $(1,3)$, which can be identified by its Left index 1, by Convention 3.4. The covered arc $(2,3)$ is thus represented as an Indirect edge $(2,1)$ by Convention 3.5.

3.4 Rope Decomposition

This section introduces a new representation for digraphs. The idea is to start from the PRC of the underlying graph, and then assign the remaining arcs to covering edges.

Definition 3.8. A *rope decomposition* of an (ordered) digraph (V_n, A) is a tuple $(V_n, R, A_{<}, A_{>}, I_{<}, I_{>})$ satisfying the following conditions:

1. edges $R \subseteq E_A$ constitute a PRC of the underlying graph (V_n, E_A),

2. $A_{<} \subseteq \{(i,j) \in A^T | (i,k) \in R, i<j\leq k\}$ and $A_{>} \subseteq \{(i,j) \in A | (i,k) \in R, i<j\leq k\}$ are, respectively, left and right arcs whose left index coincides with the left index of the covering edge,

3. $I_{<} \subseteq \{(i,h)|(i,j) \in A^T, (h,j) \in R, h<i<j\}$ and $I_{>} \subseteq \{(i,h)|(i,j) \in A, (h,j) \in R, h<i<j\}$ are, respectively, indirect representations for arcs whose right index coincides with the respective covering edge but is represented indirectly, via the left index of the respective covering edge.

4. The four sets of arcs represent together the original set of arcs: $A = A_{<}^T \cup (I_{<} \circ R)^T \cup A_{>} \cup (I_{>} \circ R)$.

Lemma 3.7. *Under the "Earliest" convention, the relation between digraphs and rope decompositions is a bijection.*

Proof. $(\rightarrow)$: Let $G = (V_n, A)$ be a digraph and $G' = (V_n, E_A)$ its underlying graph. By Theorem 3.3, G' has a unique PRC $R \subseteq E_A$. By the "Earliest" convention, we choose the earliest available covering edge for each edge and first construct the sets of indirect arcs $I_{<} = \{(i,h) \mid (i,j) \in A^T, (h,j) \in R, h<i<j\}$ and $I_{>} = \{(i,h) \mid (i,j) \in A, (h,j) \in R, h<i<j\}$. After this, we construct the sets of arcs whose left index coincides with the covering edges: $A_{<} = \{(i,j) \in A^T \backslash (I_{<} \circ R)|(i,k) \in R, i<j\leq k\}$ and $A_{>} \subseteq \{(i,j) \in (A \backslash (I_{>} \circ R) \mid (i,k) \in R, i<j\leq k\}$.

$(\Leftarrow)$: Let $(G = V_n, R, A_{<}, A_{>}, I_{<}, I_{>})$ be a rope decomposition. We obtain the corresponding graph as $(V_n, A^T_{<} \cup (I_{<} \circ R)^T \cup A_{>} \cup (I_{>} \circ R))$. $\square$

4 A New Transition System

By Lemma 3.7, there is a bijection between (a class of) rope decompositions and digraphs. We complement this result by relating each rope decomposition bijectively to a sequence of actions. The actions are controlled by a transition system.

Our transition system has a *buffer* $\beta \in \mathbb{N}$, a *main stack* $\sigma \in \mathbb{N}^*$ and an *auxiliary stack* $\tau \in \mathbb{N}^*$, each containing vertex indices. The tuple (σ, τ, β) of these three structures forms the core of the configurations between which the transition system moves. As an *input*, the system takes a sequence of actions that tell how to build a rope decomposition in an incremental manner. The possible types of actions of the transition system are listed in Table 1.

Initially, both the stacks are empty and the buffer β consists of the list of positive integers. The final configurations of the system consists of all those configurations $(\epsilon, \epsilon, \beta)$ where both stacks are empty, and β contains a suffix $[n, n+1, ...]$ of the list of positive integers. When the system reaches a final configuration, it has produced a relational structure $(V_n, R, A_{<}, A_{>}, I_{<}, I_{>})$ of a rope decomposition. By doing so, the transition system maps the input sequence of actions to a rope decomposition that represents a digraph. It is not too difficult to define the inverse of this function, but we suppress the details in the interest of space.

4.1 Main Actions

The most important actions of the transition system create the set of edges in the PRC R. By a *shift* (SH) action, the system removes a

Table 1: Transition system for rope decompositions.

action	transition between configurations		effect on the decomposition
SH	$\sigma, \epsilon, i\beta, [\_, \_, \_]$	$\Rightarrow \sigma i, \epsilon,\ \beta, [-\text{INS}, -\ \text{RE}, -\ \underset{0}{\text{PASS}}]$	
NX	$\sigma, \epsilon, i\beta, [\_, \_, \_]$	$\Rightarrow \sigma\ , \epsilon,\ \beta, [-\text{INS}, -\ \text{RE}, -\ \underset{0}{\text{PASS}}]$	
$\underset{d}{\text{RE}}$	$\sigma i, \epsilon, j\beta, [-\text{INS}, -\ \text{RE}, \_]$	$\Rightarrow \sigma\ , \epsilon, j\beta, [-\text{INS}, +\ \text{RE}, -\ \underset{0}{\text{PASS}}]$	$R \overset{\cup}{\leftarrow} \{(i,j)\}, \underset{d}{A} \overset{\cup}{\leftarrow} \{(i,j)\}$
$\underset{0}{\text{PASS}}$	$\sigma i, \tau, j\beta, [-\text{INS}, \alpha\ \text{RE}, \_]$	$\Rightarrow \sigma, i\tau, j\beta, [-\text{INS}, \alpha\ \text{RE}, +\ \underset{0}{\text{PASS}}]$	
$\underset{d}{\text{PASS}}$	$\sigma i, \tau, j\beta, [-\text{INS}, \_, \_]$	$\Rightarrow \sigma, i\tau, j\beta, [-\text{INS}, +\ \text{RE}, -\ \underset{0}{\text{PASS}}]$	$\underset{d}{A} \overset{\cup}{\leftarrow} \{(i,j)\}$
$\underset{0}{\text{INS}}$	$\sigma, i\tau, j\beta, [\_, \_, -\ \underset{0}{\text{PASS}}]$	$\Rightarrow \sigma i, \tau, j\beta, [+\text{INS}, +\ \text{RE}, -\ \underset{0}{\text{PASS}}]$	
$\underset{d}{\text{INS}}$	$\sigma, i\tau, j\beta, [\_, \_, \_]$	$\Rightarrow \sigma i, \tau, j\beta, [+\text{INS}, +\ \text{RE}, -\ \underset{0}{\text{PASS}}]$	$\underset{d}{I} \overset{\cup}{\leftarrow} \{(j,i)\}$

vertex index i from the front of the buffer and places it to the top of the stack in order to prepare for a future situation where the index i is the left index of an edge in the PRC, i.e., $\exists j.R(i,j)$. When the index j becomes available in the front of the buffer, the system creates the edge $(i,j) \in R$ by a *reduce* (RE) action and removes the index i from the stack. The specifier $d \in \{<, >, <>\}$ of the action tells whether the corresponding arc (i,j) is to be added to $\underset{<}{A}$, $\underset{>}{A}$ or both. Only one *reduce* action is allowed in a row. By a *next* (NX) action, the system removes an index i from the front of the buffer to secure the situation where no covering edge has vertex i as its left index, i.e., $\neg \exists j.R(i,j)$.

Example (7) is a digraph whose underlying graph is a complete graph with an edge between every pair of vertices. The PRC of this graph is $\{(1,7), (2,6), (3,5)\}$.

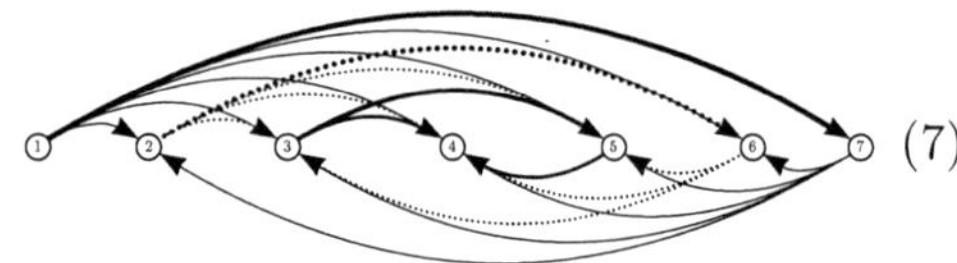

$$(7)$$

The PRC R, and the corresponding arcs in $\underset{<}{A}$ and $\underset{>}{A}$ of the rope decomposition of this digraph are created by the action sequence:

$$(\epsilon, \epsilon, [1..]) \overset{\text{SH}}{\Rightarrow} ([1], \epsilon, [2..]) \overset{\text{SH}}{\Rightarrow} ([1,2], \epsilon, [3..]) \overset{\text{SH}}{\Rightarrow}$$
$$([1..3], \epsilon, [4..]) \overset{\text{NX}}{\Rightarrow} ([1..3], \epsilon, [5..]) \overset{\underset{>}{\text{RE}}}{\Rightarrow} ([1,2], \epsilon, [5..]) \overset{\text{NX}}{\Rightarrow} \quad (8)$$
$$([1,2], \epsilon, [6..]) \overset{\underset{>}{\text{RE}}}{\Rightarrow} ([1], \epsilon, [6..]) \overset{\text{NX}}{\Rightarrow} ([1], \epsilon, [7..]) \overset{\underset{>}{\text{RE}}}{\Rightarrow} (\epsilon, \epsilon, [7..])$$

The main actions involved in this example do not use the auxiliary stack. The edges in R and the corresponding arcs are created by the reduce actions as follows:

configuration	action	effect
$([1..3], \epsilon, [5..])$	$\underset{>}{\text{RE}}$	$R \overset{\cup}{\leftarrow} \{(3,5)\}, \underset{>}{A} \overset{\cup}{\leftarrow} \{(3,5)\}$
$([1,2], \epsilon, [6..])$	$\underset{>}{\text{RE}}$	$R \overset{\cup}{\leftarrow} \{(2,6)\}, \underset{>}{A} \overset{\cup}{\leftarrow} \{(2,6)\}$
$([1], \epsilon, [7..])$	$\underset{>}{\text{RE}}$	$R \overset{\cup}{\leftarrow} \{(1,7)\}, \underset{>}{A} \overset{\cup}{\leftarrow} \{(1,7)\}$

$$(9)$$

4.2 Intermediate Actions

In order to create arcs whose underlying edges do not belong to the PRC, some additional, intermediate actions are needed. Such intermediate actions allow the front of the buffer to form arcs with non-top elements of the main stack.

For instance, the first visit to configuration $([1..3], \epsilon, [4..])$ allows actions that move the elements of the main stack temporarily to the auxiliary stack before restoring the original configuration:

$$... \Rightarrow ([1..3], \epsilon, [4..]) \overset{\underset{>}{\text{PASS}}}{\Rightarrow} ([1,2], [3], [4..]) \overset{\underset{>}{\text{PASS}}}{\Rightarrow} ([1], [2,3], [4..])$$
$$\overset{\underset{>}{\text{PASS}}}{\Rightarrow} (\epsilon, [1..3], [4..]) \overset{\underset{>}{\text{INS}}}{\Rightarrow} ([1], [2,3], [4..]) \overset{\underset{>}{\text{INS}}}{\Rightarrow} ([1,2], [3], [4..])$$
$$\overset{\underset{>}{\text{INS}}}{\Rightarrow} ([1..3], \epsilon, [4..]) \Rightarrow ... \quad (10)$$

The *pass* (PASS) and *insert* (INS) actions create arcs whose underlying edges do not belong to the PRC:

configuration	action	effect
$([1..3], \epsilon, [4..])$	$\underset{>}{\text{PASS}}$	$\underset{>}{A} \overset{\cup}{\leftarrow} \{(3,4)\}$
$([1,2], [3], [4..])$	$\underset{>}{\text{PASS}}$	$\underset{>}{A} \overset{\cup}{\leftarrow} \{(2,4)\}$
$([1], [2,3], [4..])$	$\underset{>}{\text{PASS}}$	$\underset{>}{A} \overset{\cup}{\leftarrow} \{(1,4)\}$
$(\epsilon, [1..3], [4..])$	$\underset{>}{\text{INS}}$	$\underset{>}{I} \overset{\cup}{\leftarrow} \{(4,1)\}$
$([1], [2,3], [4..])$	$\underset{>}{\text{INS}}$	$\underset{>}{I} \overset{\cup}{\leftarrow} \{(4,2)\}$
$([1,2], [3], [4..])$	$\underset{>}{\text{INS}}$	$\underset{>}{I} \overset{\cup}{\leftarrow} \{(4,3)\}$

$$(11)$$

To prevent multiple re-entry to the same configuration and repeating the intermediate actions, the detailed configurations of the transition system include control variables that restrict the available actions in different phases of the transition system. As the *insert* actions set +INS, the *reduce* and *pass* astions become blocked until the next *shift/next* action.

Some intermediate actions do not create arcs. These intermediate actions have an important role in allowing other actions to access the non-top elements of the main stack. Yet the sequence $\text{PASS}_0\ \text{INS}_0$ is blocked by the control variable PASS_0 as a useless sequence.

A *reduce* action can be immediately preceded by several PASS_0 actions. Example (6) has a PRC $\{(1,3),(2,4)\}$ that is created through a sequence that involves intermediate actions. The preceding *pass* and the following *insert* actions allow the first *reduce* action to get access to a non-top element of the main stack and to remove it from the stack:

$$(\epsilon, \epsilon, [1..]) \overset{\text{SH}}{\Rightarrow} ([1], \epsilon, [2..]) \overset{\text{SH}}{\Rightarrow} ([1,2], \epsilon, [3..]) \overset{\text{PASS}_0}{\Rightarrow}$$
$$([1],[2],[3..]) \overset{\text{RE}_{>}}{\Rightarrow} (\epsilon, [2], [3..]) \overset{\text{INS}_0}{\Rightarrow} ([2], \epsilon, [3..]) \overset{\text{NX}}{\Rightarrow} \quad (12)$$
$$([2], \epsilon, [4..]) \overset{\text{RE}_{>}}{\Rightarrow} (\epsilon, \epsilon, [4..])$$

The configuration $([1], \epsilon, [2..])$ allows a combination of a *pass* and *insert* actions. The *insert* action puts, to $I_{<}$, the pair $(2,1)$ representing the arc $(3,2)$ in Example (6).

$$... \overset{\text{SH}}{\Rightarrow} ([1], \epsilon, [2..]) \overset{\text{PASS}_0}{\Rightarrow} (\epsilon, [1], [2..]) \overset{\text{INS}_{<}}{\Rightarrow} ([1], \epsilon, [2..]) \overset{\text{SH}}{\Rightarrow} ... \quad (13)$$

4.3 Correctness

Lemma 4.1. *For every digraph, there is a unique action sequence that creates the edges of its PRC.*

Proof sketch. By Proposition 3.1, no vertex needs to start or finish more than one edge in the PRC. The transition system allows to start one covering edge per vertex with a *shift* action and finish any previously started cover edge with a *reduce* action. A crossing cover edge can be finished by accessing the non-topmost stack elements with PASS_0 and INS_0 actions in their appropriate time.

Theorem 4.2. *The transition system is able to produce every possible rope decomposition, capturing every digraph.*

Proof sketch. By Lemma 4.1, we have a way to create the PRC and the corresponding arcs. The set of arcs is extended to represent the rest of the arcs via *pass* and *insert* actions that create the arcs that are properly covered by the edges in the PRC.

5 Linear Encoding

The action sequences of the transition system can be seen as linearisations for the digraphs.

In particular, the undirected graph in Example (6) is encoded as the action sequence in (14). To make the linearisation more convenient for eyes, we replace actions with brackets and other symbols in (15).

$$\text{SH}\ \text{PASS}_0\ \text{INS}_{<>}\ \text{SH}\ \text{PASS}_0\ \text{RE}_{<>}\ \text{INS}_0\ \text{NX}\ \text{RE}_{<>} \quad (14)$$

$$\llbracket\ \bullet\ ]_0\ [_{<>}\ \llbracket\ \bullet\ ]_0\ \rrbracket_{<>}\ [_0\ \bullet\ \rrbracket_{<>} \quad (15)$$

Convention 5.1. By convention, the bracketing scheme renames the actions of the transition system as follows:

$$\frac{\text{NX}\qquad \text{SH}\qquad \text{PASS}_0\quad \text{PASS}_d\quad \text{INS}_0\quad \text{INS}_d\quad \text{RE}_d}{\bullet \qquad \llbracket \bullet \qquad]_0 \qquad]_d \qquad [_0 \qquad [_d \qquad \rrbracket_d} \quad (16)$$

The convention improves the readability of action sequence and gives compact action sequences: especially, the digraph in Example (7) is encoded as string
$$\llbracket \bullet]\underset{><}{[\llbracket \bullet]]}\underset{>><<}{[[\llbracket \bullet]]]}\underset{>>><<<}{[[[\bullet \rrbracket]]}\underset{>>><<}{[[\bullet \rrbracket]}\underset{><}{[\bullet \rrbracket}_{>}.$$
Example (17) demonstrates how the bracket(s) now correspond almost iconically to the represented arcs.

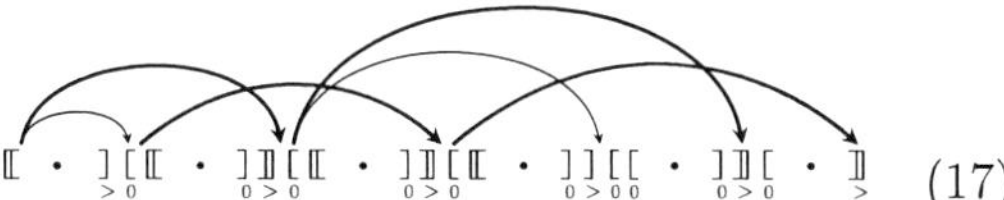

$$\llbracket\ \bullet\ ]\underset{>0}{[\llbracket\ \bullet\ ]\rrbracket}\underset{0>0}{[\llbracket\ \bullet\ ]\rrbracket}\underset{0>0}{[\llbracket\ \bullet\ ]]}\underset{0>00}{[[\ \bullet\ ]\rrbracket}\underset{0>0}{[\ \bullet\ \rrbracket}_{>} \quad (17)$$

Convention 5.1 benefits us when we analyse the formal, language theoretic properties of such action sequences although the encoding is not otherwise meant for human inspection and its direct manipulation by hand is prone to errors. The convention borrows ideas from Yli-Jyrä (2017) but differs from it in four important aspects:

1. The vertices are separated with a bullet symbol ($\bullet$) instead of curly brackets ($\{\}$).

2. The left brackets $\{\llbracket, [, [_0\}$ match the right brackets $\{\rrbracket,],]_0\}$.

3. Weak brackets may be stacked (like in $]]][[[$) in order to deal with stacked pass and insert actions.

4. A strong closing bracket may occur inside a stack of weak brackets (like in $]]_0\rrbracket[[_0[$).

These changes are necessary to deal with crossing arcs and the actions that operate on two stacks.

5.1 Syntactic Properties

In order to analyse the formal properties of the transition system, we need to understand how the actions, or the corresponding brackets, form strings that correspond to ordered graphs in a bijective manner. We induce the following principles:

1. Each vertex corresponds to a sequence of closing brackets followed by a sequence of opening brackets.

2. Between "$\rrbracket$" and the closest preceding "$\bullet$", there can be only "$]_0$"-brackets. This corresponds to the convention 3.7 that always chooses the "EARLIEST" covering edge in the PRC of the underlying graph. We do not need "$]$"-brackets to produce arcs as we have an opportunity to produce same arcs with "$[$"-brackets earlier.

3. The unnecessary pair of pass and insert actions, marked with bracket substring "$]_0\,[_0$" do not occur in the strings.

4. The strong opening bracket "$\llbracket$" always occurs right before the vertex boundary "$\bullet$".

5. The maximum number of brackets per vertex is $n - 1$.

6. Left brackets $B_L = \{\llbracket, [_0, [_d\}$ match right brackets $B_R = \{\rrbracket_d,]_0,]_d\}$.

7. The rope thickness of the (di)graph is the maximum number of momentarily open brackets in its encoding.

According to the principles 1-4, the bracket substrings that correspond to different vertices constitute a context-free language W that is generated by the grammar G_W:

$$
\begin{aligned}
S &\to T^? \mid T^? \llbracket \qquad & T^? &\to T \mid \epsilon \\
R' &\to \rrbracket_< \mid \rrbracket_> \mid \rrbracket_{<>} & L' &\to L \mid [_0 \\
R &\to]_< \mid]_> \mid]_{<>} & L &\to [_< \mid [_> \mid [_{<>} \\
T &\to R'\, T^? \mid R\, T^?\, L' \mid]_0\, T^?\, L \mid]_0\, T\, [_0
\end{aligned}
\tag{18}
$$

Lemma 5.1. *The action sequences that conform to the seven principles allow only one way to represent each ordered digraph.*

Proof. The strong brackets are crucial for encoding all arcs of the digraph and the PRC of its underlying graph in particular. Every digraph (V_n, A) has a unique PRC, and, due to the principles 1-4, it is not possible to build the same PRC with the correct arc orientations in two different ways. By the second principle, all non-PRC arcs are assigned to a unique covering edge. There is thus only one moment when the right combination of indices is available in the configuration for constructing each arc, and there is only one action sequence that can construct any given digraph. $\square$

We also observe that string concatenation of two action sequences gives an action sequence that produces a digraph concatenation of two ordered digraphs with one shared vertex.

Proposition 5.2. *The encoding from digraphs to strings is a mapping that preserves the structure of the digraph concatenation monoid and sends it the structure of a string concatenation monoid.*

6 Formal Language Theory

Chomsky-Schützenberger (CS) parsing (Yli-Jyrä, 2005, 2012; Hulden, 2009; Yli-Jyrä and Gómez-Rodríguez, 2017; Ruprecht and Denkinger, 2019) combines a particular kind of language representations with weighted automata techniques. A prototypical CS style language representation $h(\mathcal{L} \cap \mathcal{D})$ involves a homomorphic mapping (h) applied to an intersection of a a regular language component $\mathcal{L}$ and a Dyck language $\mathcal{D}$. Yli-Jyrä and Gómez-Rodríguez (2017) used this kind of language representations to show that their encoding for the noncrossing digraphs ($L_{\text{NC-DIGRAPH}}$) is a context-free language and admits an efficient algorithm for finding maximal constrained subdigraphs in a weighted complete digraph.

This section gives a CS style representation for the language of all encoded digraphs (L_{DIGRAPH}) by relaxing the requirement that the $\mathcal{L}$ component of the language representation is a regular language. The represented language is then not context-free, but the representation is *loosely speaking* of "the CS style". The similarity becomes more obvious when we derive a context-free approximation of it.

Lemma 6.1. *There is a CS style representation for the language* L_{DIGRAPH}.

Proof. We start by defining a Dyck language $\mathcal{D}$ that checks for balanced bracketing. Let the internal alphabet of the representation be $\Sigma = \{\langle, \rangle\} \cup \{[_{(l,r)},]_{(l,r)} \mid l \in B_L, r \in B_R\}$. Let $\mathcal{D}$ be the language generated by the grammar

$$S \to \epsilon \mid SS \mid \langle S \rangle \mid [_{(l,r)} S]_{(l,r)} \qquad (19)$$

where $l \in B_L$ and $r \in B_R$. Let $h : \Sigma^* \to (\{\bullet\} \cup B_L \cup B_R)^*$ be a homomorphism defined in such a way that, for all $l \in B_L, r \in B_R$,

$$
\begin{aligned}
h(ab) &= h(a)h(b) & h(\epsilon) &= \epsilon \\
h([_{(l,r)}) &= l & h(\langle) &= \epsilon \\
h(]_{(l,r)}) &= r & h(\rangle) &= \bullet .
\end{aligned}
\qquad (20)
$$

Instead of the usual regular component of CS representations, we use a marked concatenation closure of a context-free language: let $\mathcal{L}$ be the context-free language $W(\bullet W)^{n-1}$, whose inverse homomorphims $h^{-1}(\mathcal{L})$ is also a marked concatenation closure of a context-free language.

The set of encoded digraphs is now given as $L_{\mathrm{DIGRAPH}} = h(h^{-1}(\mathcal{L}) \cap \mathcal{D}) = \mathcal{L} \cap h(\mathcal{D})$. $\qquad \square$

Lemma 6.2. *The subset of the encoded digraphs* L_{DIGRAPH}, *where the number of brackets per vertex is bounded by k, is context-free.*

Proof. We start from the CS style representation (the proof of lemma 6.1) for L_{DIGRAPH} and replace the context-free language $\mathcal{L}$, with a regular approximation $\mathcal{L}_{<k} = W_{<k}(\bullet W_{<k})^*$ where $W_{<k}$ is a finite subset of W restricted to contain at most k nested brackets in the strings. This gives a more prototypical CS representation $L_{\mathrm{DIGRAPH},k} = h(h^{-1}(\mathcal{L}_{<k}) \cap D) = \mathcal{L}_{<k} \cap h(\mathcal{D})$, which yields a context-free subset of L_{DIGRAPH}. $\qquad \square$

Lemma 6.3. *The subset of encoded graphs* L_{DIGRAPH}, *where the rope thickness of the encoded digraphs is bounded by t, is regular.*

Proof. As the rope thickness is bounded by t, the number of brackets per vertex is bounded by $2t$. Thus, we start from the CS style representation (the proof of Lemma 6.2) for encoded graphs where the number of brackets per vertex is bounded. By the bound t for the rope thickness, we replace the context-free language $\mathcal{D}$ with a regular subset $\mathcal{D}_t \subset \mathcal{D}$ that can contain t levels of nested brackets. The $2t, t$-bounded set of encoded graphs is given by $L_{\mathrm{DIGRAPH},2t,t} = h(h^{-1}(\mathcal{L}_{<2t}) \cap \mathcal{D}_t) = \mathcal{L}_{<2t} \cap h(\mathcal{D}_t)$. By the closure properties of regular languages, $L_{\mathrm{DIGRAPH},2t,t}$ is regular. $\qquad \square$

7 Evidence for Linguistic Relevance

To assess the linguistic relevance of the currently presented encoding, we carried out a small experiment where we computed the rope-thickness of dependency trees in the Universal Dependencies v 2.4 treebanks (Nivre et al., 2019). The compacted results are presented in Table 2. The results indicate that a very high proportion of the observations is captured when rope-thickness is 4 or higher.

According to our preliminary experiments on graph banks, a very similar distribution of rope-thickness is observed in more general annotation graphs.

8 Discussion

Among the earliest encoding schemes for graphs are the Prüfer sequences for labeled trees (Prüfer, 1918) that have been extened to DAGs (Steinsky, 2003). More recently, Turán (1984) introduced the problem of *graph representation* given an adjacency matrix. There are now some efficient representations for unlabled and labeled graphs (Turán, 1984; Naor, 1990; Farzan and Munro, 2013). Our representation for digraphs is also *efficient*: it has a cubic-time encoder and a linear-time decoder.

The currently presented encoding for digraphs is a generalisation of an earlier representation (Yli-Jyrä, 2017, 2019) that is itself an optimized alternative for the balanced bracketing proposed for weighted dependency parsing in (Yli-Jyrä, 2012). Several edge-weighted parsing algorithms have been presented earlier (Dixon et al., 1992; Charniak et al., 1998; Sasano et al., 2000; Kuhlmann and Jonsson, 2015), but these newer methods apply to up to 50 families of dependency graphs and the currently presented encoding is expected to help in their generalization. It would be also interesting to study how rope graphs relate to 1-endpoint crossing graphs (Pitler et al., 2013; Kurtz and Kuhlmann, 2017).

language	trees	rope-thickness 1	2	3	4	5	6	7	8
Arabic	28,402	4.9%	20.5%	63.5%	94.0%	99.64%	99.986%	100.000%	100.000%
Czech	127,507	13.3%	48.3%	89.3%	98.8%	99.91%	99.992%	100.000%	100.000%
Dutch	20,735	21.3%	63.4%	92.9%	98.9%	99.92%	99.986%	100.000%	100.000%
English	34,601	15.6%	54.9%	92.3%	99.3%	99.98%	99.997%	100.000%	100.000%
Finnish	34,641	37.0%	78.7%	96.8%	99.6%	99.97%	99.994%	100.000%	100.000%
German	191,757	10.1%	49.2%	90.5%	99.2%	99.96%	99.997%	100.000%	100.000%
Hindi	19,545	2.9%	44.4%	85.3%	98.3%	99.87%	99.980%	100.000%	100.000%
Italian	34,057	5.6%	49.9%	90.3%	98.8%	99.89%	99.997%	100.000%	100.000%
Korean	34,702	15.5%	65.6%	94.7%	99.5%	99.95%	99.994%	100.000%	100.000%
Latvian	12,558	12.7%	50.0%	89.8%	98.8%	99.90%	99.992%	99.992%	100.000%
Russian	87,377	15.0%	55.5%	90.7%	98.9%	99.91%	99.994%	99.999%	100.000%
Chinese	18,628	46.1%	73.7%	91.9%	98.6%	99.89%	99.989%	100.000%	100.000%
all 83 languages	1,232,262	15.1%	54.8%	90.5%	99.0%	99.93%	99.995%	100.000%	100.000%

Table 2: The cumulative coverage of bounded rope-thickness in the UD v2.4 dataset from which we purged the trees containing ellipsis.

The languages of encoded graphs have applications to constrained graph enumeration problems. Hoppe and Petrone (Hoppe and Petrone, 2016) have exhaustively enumerated all simple, connected graphs of a finite order and computed a selection of invariants over the sets in order to discover and add 141 new integer sequences to the Online Encyclopedia of Integer Sequences (OEIS). Our previous encoding scheme (Yli-Jyrä and Gómez-Rodríguez, 2017) gave context-free characterisations for some graph properties. This led to the discovery of dozens of known and new integer sequences by graph enumeration. These new computational methods complement the research that spans from the "Abzählsatz" of (Pólya, 1937) to more recent work on graph enumeration (Wormald, 1979; Mckay, 1983; Kapoor and Ramesh, 2000; Acuña et al., 2012; Conte et al., 2018; Equi et al., 2019).

The language L_{DIGRAPH} is not only context-sensitive but even an indexed language (Aho, 1968): it is possible to construct an indexed grammar that generates the same set of strings. However, the existence of a simple transition system, a finite representation, and a finite indexed grammar for the encoded digraphs should not be confused with condition under which digraphs themselves become finitely generated. Ogawa (2004) has presented a complete, infinite set of generators for the graphs. We also need an infinite set of generators for the language L_{DIGRAPH}, because the the paths that take the transition system from one final configuration to another final configuration constitute an infinite set of code words over which the encoded digraphs are generated. This set remains infinite even for digraphs with bounded rope thickness, but the context-free and regular subsets of L_{DIGRAPH}

may have some other ways to motivate finite algebraic axiomatisations.

9 Conclusion

This paper contributes to the research on graph representations (Turán, 1984) by developing a linear-time decodable encoding for arbitrary labeled digraphs that we preferred to call ordered digraphs. The particular design of our linear encoding is motivated by the success of similar representations (Yli-Jyrä, 2005, 2012; Yli-Jyrä and Gómez-Rodríguez, 2017) in the characterisations of several families of noncrossing digraphs and by the effectiveness of the recently improved representation (Yli-Jyrä, 2017, 2019). Evidently, both kinds of graph representations have potential applications in graph enumeration (Yli-Jyrä and Gómez-Rodríguez, 2017) and weighted Chomsky-Schützenberger parsing (Yli-Jyrä, 2005, 2012; Hulden, 2009; Yli-Jyrä and Gómez-Rodríguez, 2017; Ruprecht and Denkinger, 2019).

More specifically, the paper contributes a general transition system that decodes arbitrary digraphs from linear action sequences. Crucial notions – the proper rope cover (PRC) and the related rope decomposition – are defined and used in this transition system. The first PRC-based measure for the complexity of the graphs is introduced. Context-free and regular approximations of the encoded graphs are defined and shown to contain the dependency annotations of the UD 2.4 treebanks.

References

Vicente Acuña, Etienne Birmelé, Ludovic Cottret, Pierluigi Crescenzi, Fabien Jourdan, Vincent Lacroix, Alberto Marchetti-Spaccamela, Andrea Marino, Paulo Vieira Milreu, Marie-France Sagot, and Leen Stougie. 2012. Telling stories: Enumerating maximal directed acyclic graphs with a constrained set of sources and targets. *Theoretical Computer Science*, 457:1 – 9.

Alfred V. Aho. 1968. Indexed grammars – an extension of context-free grammars. *Journal of the ACM*, 15(4):647–671.

Daniel Andor, Chris Alberti, David Weiss, Aliaksei Severyn, Alessandro Presta, Kuzman Ganchev, Slav Petrov, and Michael Collins. 2016. Globally normalized transition-based neural networks. In *Proceedings of the 54th Annual Meeting of the Association for Computational Linguistics (Volume 1: Long Papers)*, pages 2442–2452, Berlin, Germany. Association for Computational Linguistics.

Giuseppe Attardi. 2006. Experiments with a multilanguage non-projective dependency parser. In *Proceedings of the Tenth Conference on Computational Natural Language Learning*, CoNLL-X '06, pages 166–170. Association for Computational Linguistics.

Jill Burstein, Christy Doran, and Thamar Solorio, editors. 2019. *Proceedings of the 2019 Conference of the North American Chapter of the Association for Computational Linguistics: Human Language Technologies, NAACL-HLT 2019, Minneapolis, MN, USA, June 2-7, 2019, Volume 1 (Long and Short Papers)*. Association for Computational Linguistics.

Eugene Charniak, Sharon Goldwater, and Mark Johnson. 1998. Edge-based best-first chart parsing. In *Sixth Workshop on Very Large Corpora, VLC@COLING/ACL 1998, Montreal, Quebec, Canada, August 15-16, 1998*.

Danqi Chen and Christopher Manning. 2014. A fast and accurate dependency parser using neural networks. In *Proceedings of the 2014 Conference on Empirical Methods in Natural Language Processing (EMNLP)*, pages 740–750, Doha, Qatar. Association for Computational Linguistics.

Jinho D. Choi and Andrew McCallum. 2013. Transition-based dependency parsing with selectional branching. In *Proceedings of the 51st Annual Meeting of the Association for Computational Linguistics (Volume 1: Long Papers)*, pages 1052–1062, Sofia, Bulgaria. Association for Computational Linguistics.

Maximin Coavoux and Shay B. Cohen. 2019. Discontinuous constituency parsing with a stack-free transition system and a dynamic oracle. *CoRR*, abs/1904.00615.

Alessio Conte, Roberto Grossi, Andrea Marino, and Romeo Rizzi. 2018. Efficient enumeration of graph orientations with sources. *Discrete Applied Mathematics*, 246:22 – 37.

Alessio Conte, Roberto Grossi, Andrea Marino, and Luca Versari. 2019. Listing maximal subgraphs satisfying strongly accessible properties. *SIAM Journal on Discrete Mathematics*, 33(2):587–613.

Bruno Courcelle. 1990. The monadic second-order logic of graphs. I. recognizable sets of finite graphs. *Information and Computation*, 85(1):12–75.

Michael A. Covington. 2000. A fundamental algorithm for dependency parsing. In *In Proceedings of the 39th Annual ACM Southeast Conference*, pages 95–102, Athens, GA. Association for Computing Machinery.

Brandon Dixon, Monika Rauch, and Robert Endre Tarjan. 1992. Verification and sensitivity analysis of minimum spanning trees in linear time. *SIAM Journal on Computing*, 21(6):1184–1192.

Chris Dyer, Miguel Ballesteros, Wang Ling, Austin Matthews, and Noah A. Smith. 2015. Transition-based dependency parsing with stack long short-term memory. In *Proceedings of the 53rd Annual Meeting of the Association for Computational Linguistics and the 7th International Joint Conference on Natural Language Processing (Volume 1: Long Papers)*, pages 334–343, Beijing, China. Association for Computational Linguistics.

Massimo Equi, Roberto Grossi, Veli Mäkinen, and Alexandru I. Tomescu. 2019. On the complexity of string matching for graphs. In *46th International Colloquium on Automata, Languages, and Programming, ICALP 2019, July 9 12, 2019, Patras, Greece.*, volume 132 of *LIPIcs*, pages 55:1–55:15. Schloss Dagstuhl - Leibniz-Zentrum fuer Informatik.

Arash Farzan and J. Ian Munro. 2013. Succinct encoding of arbitrary graphs. *Theoretical Computer Science*, 513:38 – 52.

Daniel Fernández-González and Carlos Gómez-Rodríguez. 2018. Non-projective dependency parsing with non-local transitions. In *Proceedings of the 2018 Conference of the North American Chapter of the Association for Computational Linguistics: Human Language Technologies, Volume 2 (Short Papers)*, pages 693–700, New Orleans, Louisiana. Association for Computational Linguistics.

Daniel Gildea, Giorgio Satta, and Xiaochang Peng. 2018. Cache transition systems for graph parsing. *Computational Linguistics*, 44(1):85–118.

Yoav Goldberg and Michael Elhadad. 2010. An efficient algorithm for easy-first non-directional dependency parsing. In *Human Language Technologies: The 2010 Annual Conference of the North American Chapter of the Association for Computational Linguistics*, HLT '10, pages 742–750. Association for Computational Linguistics.

Dina Q. Goldin, Scott A. Smolka, Paul C. Attie, and Elaine L. Sonderegger. 2004. Turing machines, transition systems, and interaction. *Information and Computation*, 194(2):101 – 128. Special Issue Commemorating the 50th Birthday Anniversary of Paris C. Kanellakis.

Carlos Gómez-Rodríguez and Joakim Nivre. 2013. Divisible transition systems and multiplanar dependency parsing. *Computational Linguistics*, 39(4):799–845.

Carlos Gómez-Rodríguez, Tianze Shi, and Lillian Lee. 2018. Global transition-based non-projective dependency parsing. In *Proceedings of the 56th Annual Meeting of the Association for Computational Linguistics (Volume 1: Long Papers)*, pages 2664–2675, Melbourne, Australia. Association for Computational Linguistics.

Carlos Gómez-Rodríguez and David Vilares. 2018. Constituent parsing as sequence labeling. In *Proceedings of the 2018 Conference on Empirical Methods in Natural Language Processing, Brussels, Belgium, October 31 - November 4, 2018*, pages 1314–1324. Association for Computational Linguistics.

Matthew Honnibal and Mark Johnson. 2015. An improved non-monotonic transition system for dependency parsing. In *Proceedings of the 2015 Conference on Empirical Methods in Natural Language Processing*, pages 1373–1378, Lisbon, Portugal. Association for Computational Linguistics.

Travis Hoppe and Anna Petrone. 2016. Integer sequence discovery from small graphs. *Discrete Appl. Math.*, 201(C):172–181.

Mans Hulden. 2009. Parsing CFGs and PCFGs with a Chomsky-Schützenberger representation. In *Human Language Technology. Challenges for Computer Science and Linguistics - 4th Language and Technology Conference, LTC 2009, Poznan, Poland, November 6-8, 2009, Revised Selected Papers*, volume 6562 of *Lecture Notes in Computer Science*, pages 151–160. Springer.

S. Kapoor and H. Ramesh. 2000. An algorithm for enumerating all spanning trees of a directed graph. *Algorithmica*, 27(2):120–130.

Eliyahu Kiperwasser and Yoav Goldberg. 2016. Simple and accurate dependency parsing using bidirectional LSTM feature representations.

Transactions of the Association for Computational Linguistics, 4:313–327.

András Kornai and Zsolt Tuza. 1992. Narrowness, pathwidth, and their application in natural language processing. *Discrete Applied Mathematics*, 36(1):87–92.

Marco Kuhlmann, Carlos Gómez-Rodríguez, and Giorgio Satta. 2011. Dynamic programming algorithms for transition-based dependency parsers. In *Proceedings of the 49th Annual Meeting of the Association for Computational Linguistics: Human Language Technologies - Volume 1*, HLT '11, pages 673–682. Association for Computational Linguistics.

Marco Kuhlmann and Peter Jonsson. 2015. Parsing to noncrossing dependency graphs. *TACL*, 3:559–570.

Robin Kurtz and Marco Kuhlmann. 2017. Exploiting structure in parsing to 1-endpoint-crossing graphs. In *Proceedings of the 15th International Conference on Parsing Technologies*, pages 78–87, Pisa, Italy. Association for Computational Linguistics.

Miryam de Lhoneux, Sara Stymne, and Joakim Nivre. 2017. Arc-hybrid non-projective dependency parsing with a static-dynamic oracle. In *Proceedings of the 15th International Conference on Parsing Technologies, IWPT 2017, Pisa, Italy, September 20-22, 2017*, pages 99–104. Association for Computational Linguistics.

Brendan D. Mckay. 1983. Applications of a technique for labelled enumeration. *Congressus Numerantium*, 40:207–221.

Moni Naor. 1990. Succinct representation of general unlabeled graphs. *Discrete Applied Mathematics*, 28(3):303 – 307.

Joakim Nivre. 2003. An efficient algorithm for projective dependency parsing. In *Proceedings of the Eighth International Workshop on Parsing Technologies (IWPT)*, pages 149–160.

Joakim Nivre. 2004. Incrementality in deterministic dependency parsing. In *Proceedings of the Workshop on Incremental Parsing: Bringing Engineering and Cognition Together*, IncrementParsing '04, pages 50–57. Association for Computational Linguistics.

Joakim Nivre. 2009. Non-projective dependency parsing in expected linear time. In *Proceedings of the Joint Conference of the 47th Annual Meeting of the ACL and the 4th International Joint Conference on Natural Language Processing of the AFNLP: Volume 1 - Volume 1*, ACL '09, pages 351–359. Association for Computational Linguistics.

Joakim Nivre, Mitchell Abrams, Željko Agić, Lars Ahrenberg, Gabrielė Aleksandravičiūtė, Lene Antonsen, Katya Aplonova, Maria Jesus Aranzabe, Gashaw Arutie, Masayuki Asahara, Luma Ateyah, Mohammed Attia, Aitziber Atutxa, Liesbeth Augustinus, Elena Badmaeva, Miguel Ballesteros, Esha Banerjee, Sebastian Bank, Verginica Barbu Mititelu, Victoria Basmov, John Bauer, Sandra Bellato, Kepa Bengoetxea, Yevgeni Berzak, Irshad Ahmad Bhat, Riyaz Ahmad Bhat, Erica Biagetti, Eckhard Bick, Agnė Bielinskienė, Rogier Blokland, Victoria Bobicev, Loïc Boizou, Emanuel Borges Völker, Carl Börstell, Cristina Bosco, Gosse Bouma, Sam Bowman, Adriane Boyd, Kristina Brokaitė, Aljoscha Burchardt, Marie Candito, Bernard Caron, Gauthier Caron, Gülşen Cebiroğlu Eryiğit, Flavio Massimiliano Cecchini, Giuseppe G. A. Celano, Slavomír Čéplö, Savas Cetin, Fabricio Chalub, Jinho Choi, Yongseok Cho, Jayeol Chun, Silvie Cinková, Aurélie Collomb, Çağrı Çöltekin, Miriam Connor, Marine Courtin, Elizabeth Davidson, Marie-Catherine de Marneffe, Valeria de Paiva, Arantza Diaz de Ilarraza, Carly Dickerson, Bamba Dione, Peter Dirix, Kaja Dobrovoljc, Timothy Dozat, Kira Droganova, Puneet Dwivedi, Hanne Eckhoff, Marhaba Eli, Ali Elkahky, Binyam Ephrem, Tomaž Erjavec, Aline Etienne, Richárd Farkas, Hector Fernandez Alcalde, Jennifer Foster, Cláudia Freitas, Kazunori Fujita, Katarína Gajdošová, Daniel Galbraith, Marcos Garcia, Moa Gärdenfors, Sebastian Garza, Kim Gerdes, Filip Ginter, Iakes Goenaga, Koldo Gojenola, Memduh Gökırmak, Yoav Goldberg, Xavier Gómez Guinovart, Berta González Saavedra, Matias Grioni, Normunds Grūzītis, Bruno Guillaume, Céline Guillot-Barbance, Nizar Habash, Jan Hajič, Jan Hajič jr., Linh Hà Mỹ, Na-Rae Han, Kim Harris, Dag Haug, Johannes Heinecke, Felix Hennig, Barbora Hladká, Jaroslava Hlaváčová, Florinel Hociung, Petter Hohle, Jena Hwang, Takumi Ikeda, Radu Ion, Elena Irimia, Ọlájídé Ishola, Tomáš Jelínek, Anders Johannsen, Fredrik Jørgensen, Hüner Kaşıkara, Andre Kaasen, Sylvain Kahane, Hiroshi Kanayama, Jenna Kanerva, Boris Katz, Tolga Kayadelen, Jessica Kenney, Václava Kettnerová, Jesse Kirchner, Arne Köhn, Kamil Kopacewicz, Natalia Kotsyba, Jolanta Kovalevskaitė, Simon Krek, Sookyoung Kwak, Veronika Laippala, Lorenzo Lambertino, Lucia Lam, Tatiana Lando, Septina Dian Larasati, Alexei Lavrentiev, John Lee, Phương Lê Hồng, Alessandro Lenci, Saran Lertpradit, Herman Leung, Cheuk Ying Li, Josie Li, Keying Li, KyungTae Lim, Yuan Li, Nikola Ljubešić, Olga Loginova, Olga Lyashevskaya, Teresa Lynn, Vivien Macketanz, Aibek Makazhanov, Michael Mandl, Christopher Manning, Ruli Manurung, Cătălina Mărănduc, David Mareček, Katrin Marheinecke, Héctor Martínez Alonso, André Martins, Jan Mašek, Yuji Matsumoto, Ryan McDonald, Sarah McGuinness, Gustavo Mendonça, Niko Miekka, Margarita Misirpashayeva, Anna Missilä, Cătălin Mititelu, Yusuke Miyao, Simonetta Montemagni, Amir More, Laura Moreno Romero, Keiko Sophie Mori, Tomohiko Morioka, Shinsuke Mori, Shigeki Moro, Bjartur Mortensen, Bohdan Moskalevskyi, Kadri Muischnek, Yugo Murawaki, Kaili Müürisep, Pinkey Nainwani, Juan Ignacio Navarro Horñiacek, Anna Nedoluzhko, Gunta Nešpore-Bērzkalne, Lương Nguyễn Thị, Huyền Nguyễn Thị Minh, Yoshihiro Nikaido, Vitaly Nikolaev, Rattima Nitisaroj, Hanna Nurmi, Stina Ojala, Adédayọ̀ Olúòkun, Mai Omura, Petya Osenova, Robert Östling, Lilja Øvrelid, Niko Partanen, Elena Pascual, Marco Passarotti, Agnieszka Patejuk, Guilherme Paulino-Passos, Angelika Peljak-Łapińska, Siyao Peng, Cenel-Augusto Perez, Guy Perrier, Daria Petrova, Slav Petrov, Jussi Piitulainen, Tommi A Pirinen, Emily Pitler, Barbara Plank, Thierry Poibeau, Martin Popel, Lauma Pretkalniņa, Sophie Prévost, Prokopis Prokopidis, Adam Przepiórkowski, Tiina Puolakainen, Sampo Pyysalo, Andriela Rääbis, Alexandre Rademaker, Loganathan Ramasamy, Taraka Rama, Carlos Ramisch, Vinit Ravishankar, Livy Real, Siva Reddy, Georg Rehm, Michael Rießler, Erika Rimkutė, Larissa Rinaldi, Laura Rituma, Luisa Rocha, Mykhailo Romanenko, Rudolf Rosa, Davide Rovati, Valentin Roșca, Olga Rudina, Jack Rueter, Shoval Sadde, Benoît Sagot, Shadi Saleh, Alessio Salomoni, Tanja Samardžić, Stephanie Samson, Manuela Sanguinetti, Dage Särg, Baiba Saulīte, Yanin Sawanakunanon, Nathan Schneider, Sebastian Schuster, Djamé Seddah, Wolfgang Seeker, Mojgan Seraji, Mo Shen, Atsuko Shimada, Hiroyuki Shirasu, Muh Shohibussirri, Dmitry Sichinava, Natalia Silveira, Maria Simi, Radu Simionescu, Katalin Simkó, Mária Šimková, Kiril Simov, Aaron Smith, Isabela Soares-Bastos, Carolyn Spadine, Antonio Stella, Milan Straka, Jana Strnadová, Alane Suhr, Umut Sulubacak, Shingo Suzuki, Zsolt Szántó, Dima Taji, Yuta Takahashi, Fabio Tamburini, Takaaki Tanaka, Isabelle Tellier, Guillaume Thomas, Liisi Torga, Trond Trosterud, Anna Trukhina, Reut Tsarfaty, Francis Tyers, Sumire Uematsu, Zdeňka Urešová, Larraitz Uria, Hans Uszkoreit, Sowmya Vajjala, Daniel van Niekerk, Gertjan van Noord, Viktor Varga, Eric Villemonte de la Clergerie, Veronika Vincze, Lars Wallin, Abigail Walsh, Jing Xian Wang, Jonathan North Washington, Maximilan Wendt, Seyi Williams, Mats Wirén, Christian Wittern, Tsegay Woldemariam, Taksum Wong, Alina Wróblewska, Mary Yako, Naoki Yamazaki, Chunxiao Yan, Koichi Yasuoka, Marat M. Yavrumyan, Zhuoran Yu, Zdeněk Žabokrtský, Amir Zeldes, Daniel Zeman, Manying Zhang, and Hanzhi Zhu. 2019. Universal Dependencies 2.4. LINDAT/CLARIN digital library at the Institute of Formal and Applied Linguistics (ÚFAL), Faculty of Mathematics and Physics, Charles University.

Joakim Nivre and Mario Scholz. 2004. Deterministic dependency parsing of English text. In *COLING 2004, 20th International Conference on Computational Linguistics, Proceedings of the Conference, 23-27 August 2004, Geneva, Switzerland*.

Mizuhito Ogawa. 2004. Complete axiomatization of an algebraic construction of graphs. In *Functional and Logic Programming*, pages 163–179, Berlin, Heidelberg. Springer Berlin Heidelberg.

Emily Pitler, Sampath Kannan, and Mitchell Marcus. 2013. Finding optimal 1-endpoint-crossing trees. *TACL*, 1:13–24.

Emily Pitler and Ryan McDonald. 2015. A linear-time transition system for crossing interval trees. In *Proceedings of the 2015 Conference of the North American Chapter of the Association for Computational Linguistics: Human Language Technologies*, pages 662–671, Denver, Colorado. Association for Computational Linguistics.

Heinz Prüfer. 1918. Neuer Beweis eines Satzes über Permutationen (New proof of a theorem on permutations). *Archiv der Mathematik und Physik*, 27(3):142–144.

G. Pólya. 1937. Kombinatorische Anzahlbestimmungen für Gruppen, Graphen und chemische Verbindungen. *Acta Math.*, 68:145–254.

Peng Qi and Christopher D. Manning. 2017. Arc-swift: A novel transition system for dependency parsing. In *Proceedings of the 55th Annual Meeting of the Association for Computational Linguistics, ACL 2017, Vancouver, Canada, July 30 - August 4, Volume 2: Short Papers*, pages 110–117. Association for Computational Linguistics.

Thomas Ruprecht and Tobias Denkinger. 2019. Implementation of a Chomsky-Schützenberger *n*-best parser for weighted multiple context-free grammars. In (Burstein et al., 2019), pages 178–191.

Kenji Sagae and Jun'ichi Tsujii. 2008. Shift-reduce dependency DAG parsing. In *Proceedings of COLING 2008, the 22nd International Conference on Computational Linguistics*, pages 753–760, Manchester, UK. Coling 2008 Organizing Committee.

Isao Sasano, Zhenjiang Hu, Masato Takeichi, and Mizuhito Ogawa. 2000. Make it practical: a generic linear-time algorithm for solving maximum-weightsum problems. In *Proceedings of the Fifth ACM SIGPLAN International Conference on Functional Programming (ICFP '00), Montreal, Canada, September 18-21, 2000.*, pages 137–149. Association for Computing Machinery.

Tianze Shi, Liang Huang, and Lillian Lee. 2017. Fast(er) exact decoding and global training for transition-based dependency parsing via a minimal feature set. In *Proceedings of the 2017 Conference on Empirical Methods in Natural Language Processing*, pages 12–23, Copenhagen, Denmark. Association for Computational Linguistics.

B. Steinsky. 2003. Efficient coding of labeled directed acyclic graphs. *Soft Computing*, 7(5):350–356.

Michalina Strzyz, David Vilares, and Carlos Gómez-Rodríguez. 2019. Viable dependency parsing as sequence labeling. In (Burstein et al., 2019), pages 717–723.

Wolfgang Thomas. 2002. A short introduction to infinite automata. In *Developments in Language Theory*, pages 130–144, Berlin, Heidelberg. Springer Berlin Heidelberg.

György Turán. 1984. On the succinct representation of graphs. *Discrete Applied Mathematics*, 8(3):289 – 294.

David Vilares and Carlos Gómez-Rodríguez. 2018. A transition-based algorithm for unrestricted AMR parsing. In *Proceedings of the 2018 Conference of the North American Chapter of the Association for Computational Linguistics: Human Language Technologies, Volume 2 (Short Papers)*, pages 142–149, New Orleans, Louisiana. Association for Computational Linguistics.

Oriol Vinyals, Lukasz Kaiser, Terry Koo, Slav Petrov, Ilya Sutskever, and Geoffrey E. Hinton. 2015. Grammar as a foreign language. In *Advances in Neural Information Processing Systems 28: Annual Conference on Neural Information Processing Systems 2015, December 7-12, 2015, Montreal, Quebec, Canada*, pages 2773–2781.

W. A. Woods. 1970. Transition network grammars for natural language analysis. *Communications of the ACM*, 13(10):591–606.

Nicholas C. Wormald. 1979. Enumeration of labelled graphs II: Cubic graphs with a given connectivity. *Journal of the London Mathematical Society*, s2-20(1):1–7.

H. Yamada and Y. Matsumoto. 2003. Statistical Dependency Analysis with Support Vector machines. In *The 8th International Workshop of Parsing Technologies (IWPT2003)*.

Anssi Yli-Jyrä. 2005. Approximating dependency grammars through intersection of star-free regular languages. *International Journal of Foundations of Computer Science*, 16(3):565–579.

Anssi Yli-Jyrä. 2012. On dependency analysis via contractions and weighted FSTs. In *Shall We Play the Festschrift Game?, Essays on the Occasion of Lauri Carlson's 60th Birthday*, pages 133–158. Springer.

Anssi Yli-Jyrä. 2017. Bounded-depth high-coverage search space for noncrossing parses. In *Proceedings of the 13th International Conference on Finite State Methods and Natural Language Processing, FSMNLP 2017, Umeå, Sweden, September 2017*, pages 30–40. Association for Computational Linguistics.

Anssi Yli-Jyrä. 2019. How to embed noncrossing trees in Universal Dependencies treebanks in a low-complexity regular language. *Journal of Language Modelling*. Forthcoming.

Anssi Yli-Jyrä and Carlos Gómez-Rodríguez. 2017. Generic axiomatization of families of noncrossing graphs in dependency parsing. In *Proceedings of the 55th Annual Meeting of the Association for Computational Linguistics, ACL 2017, Vancouver, Canada, July 30 - August 4, Volume 1: Long Papers*, pages 1745–1755. Association for Computational Linguistics.

Yue Zhang and Joakim Nivre. 2011. Transition-based dependency parsing with rich non-local features. In *The 49th Annual Meeting of the Association for Computational Linguistics: Human Language Technologies, Proceedings of the Conference, 19-24 June, 2011, Portland, Oregon, USA - Short Papers*, pages 188–193. The Association for Computer Linguistics.

Author Index

Allauzen, Cyril, 18

Björklund, Johanna, 7
Butt, Miriam, 76

Cognetta, Marco, 18
Cohen, Shay B., 7

Demirsahin, Isin, 65
Dias, Gihan, 76
Drewes, Frank, 3, 7

Fernando, Tim, 27

Gebhardt, Kilian, 4

Janicki, Maciej, 37

Kayadelen, Tolga, 65

Mörbitz, Richard, 46

Nederhof, Mark-Jan, 56

Ozturel, Adnan, 65

Ranta, Aarne, 1
Riley, Michael, 18, 87, 108
Roark, Brian, 87, 108

Sarveswaran, Kengatharaiyer, 76
Satta, Giorgio, 7
Schogol, Vlad, 87, 108
Suresh, Ananda Theertha, 87

Vogel, Carl, 27
Vogler, Heiko, 46, 56

Wakabayashi, Kei, 98
Wolf-Sonkin, Lawrence, 108
Woods, David, 27

Yli-Jyrä, Anssi, 118

Association for Computational Linguistics
209 N. Eighth Street
Stroudsburg, Pennsylvania 18360

ISBN 978-1-5108-9440-2